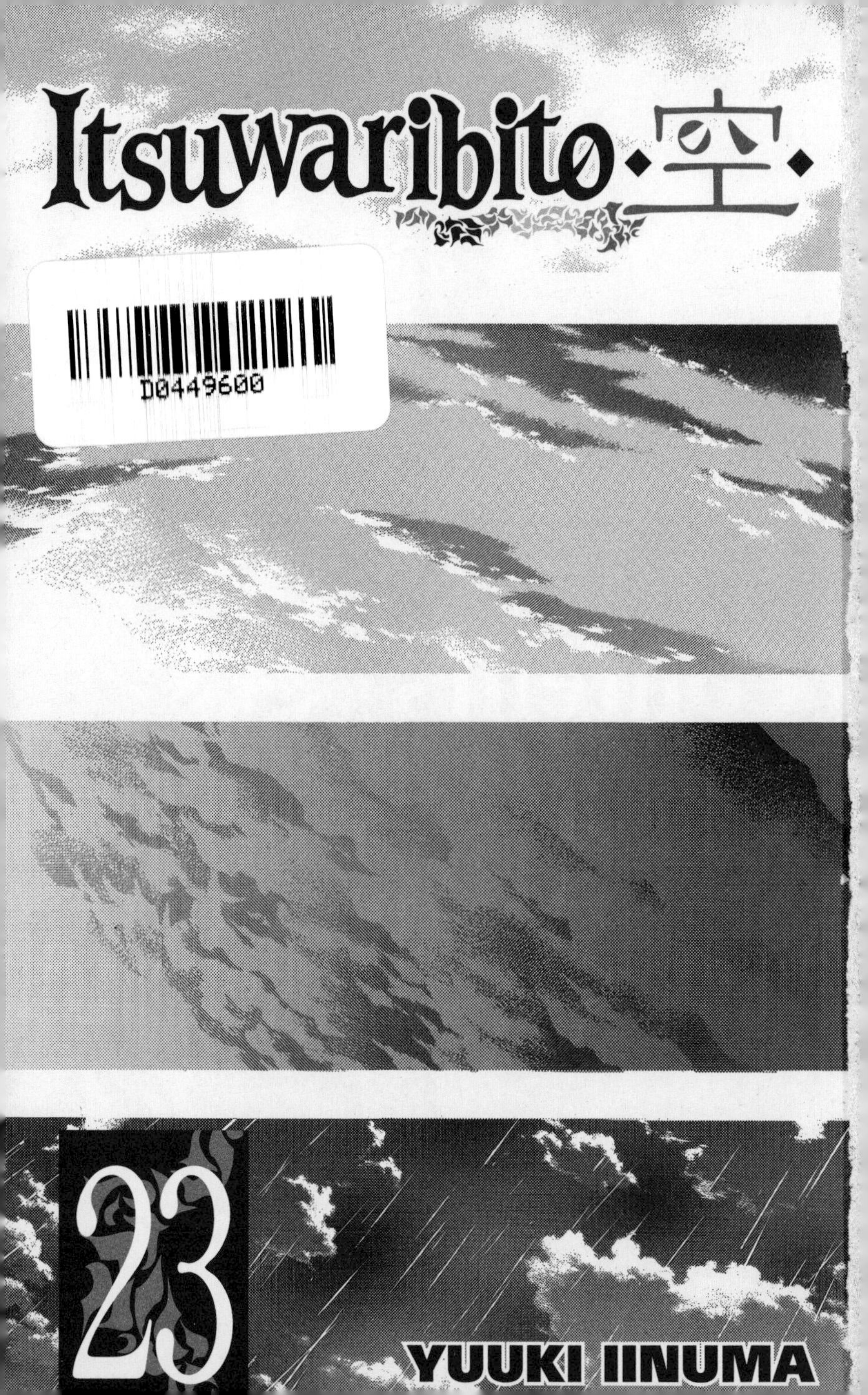
Itsuwaribito・空・
23
YUUKI IINUMA

Contents

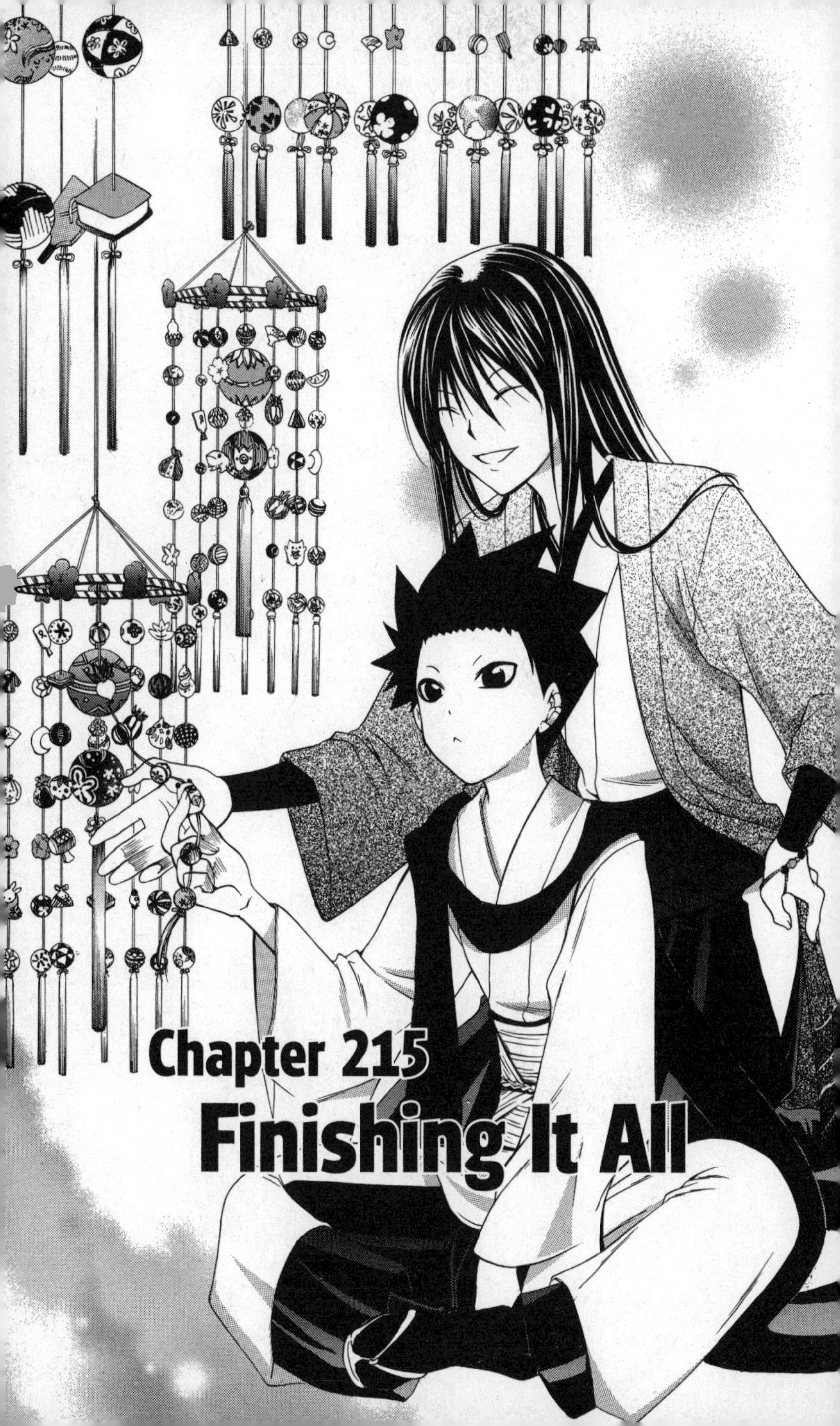
Chapter 215
Finishing It All

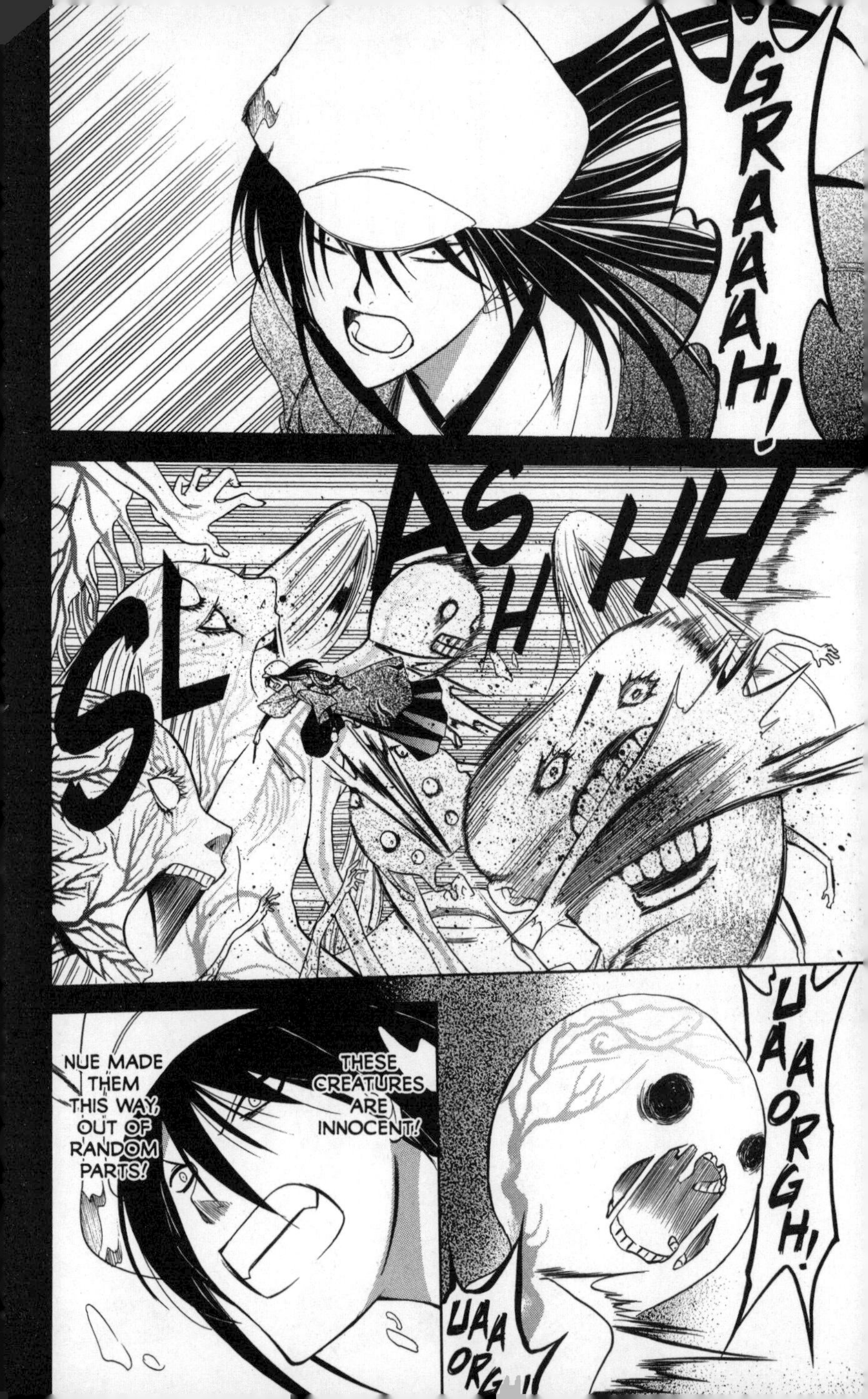
GRAAAH!
SLASHHH
UAAAORGH!
UAAAORG
THESE CREATURES ARE INNOCENT!
NUE MADE THEM THIS WAY, OUT OF RANDOM PARTS!

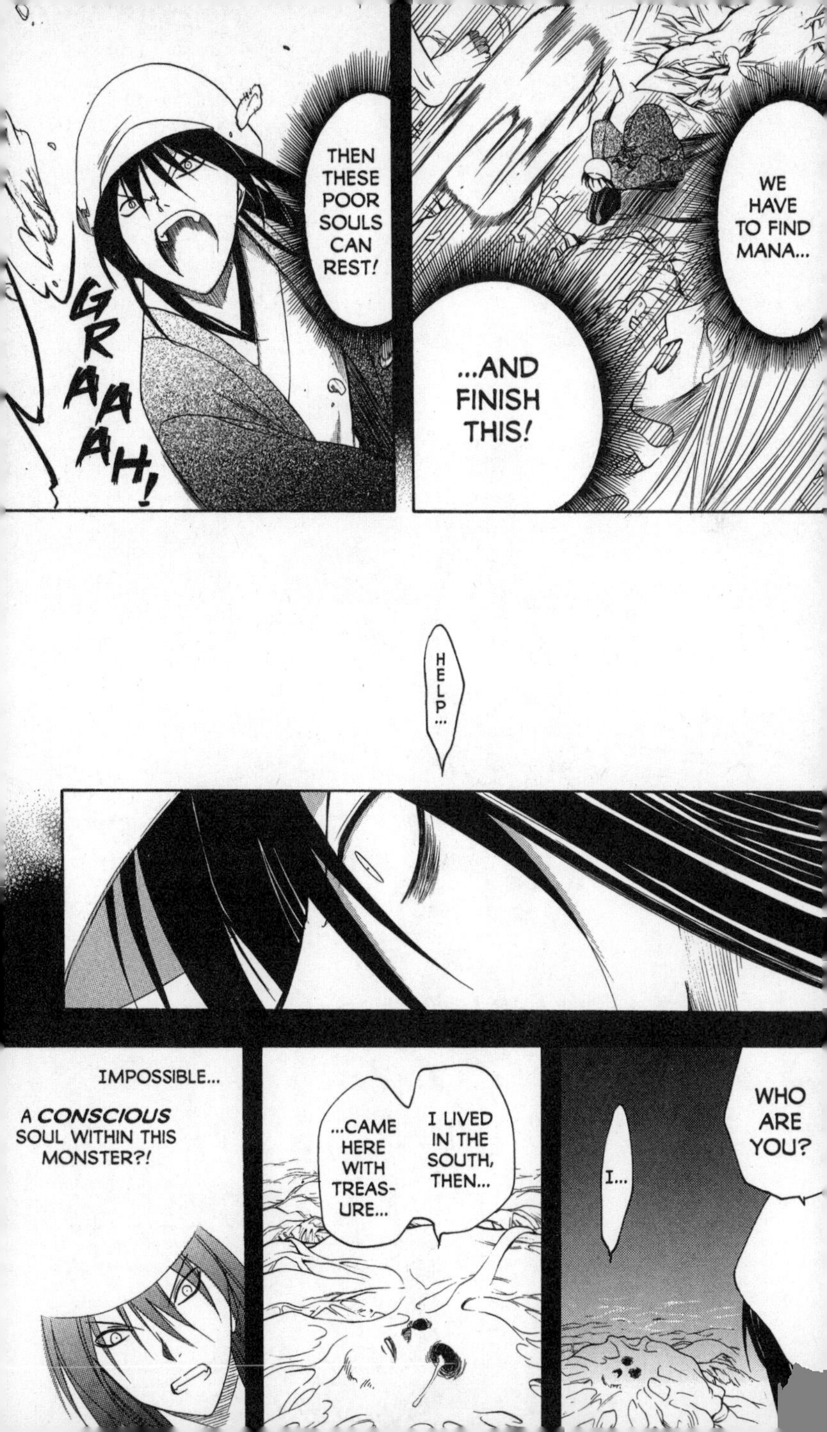
WE HAVE TO FIND MANA...
...AND FINISH THIS!
THEN THESE POOR SOULS CAN REST!
GRAAAH!
HELP...
WHO ARE YOU?
I...
I LIVED IN THE SOUTH, THEN...
...CAME HERE WITH TREASURE...
IMPOSSIBLE...
A *CONSCIOUS* SOUL WITHIN THIS MONSTER?!

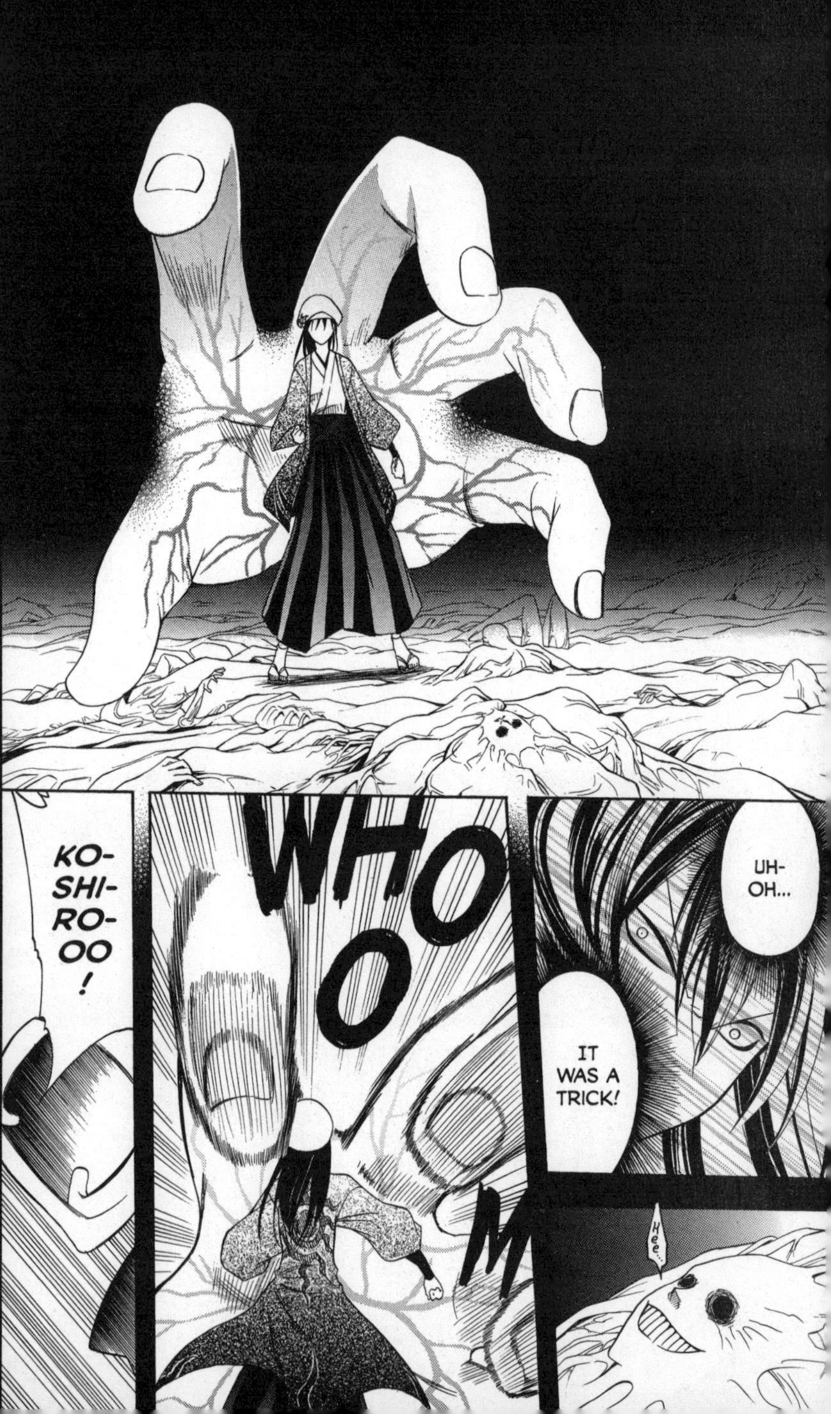
UH-OH...
IT WAS A TRICK!
Hee...
WHOOOM
KO-SHI-RO-OO!

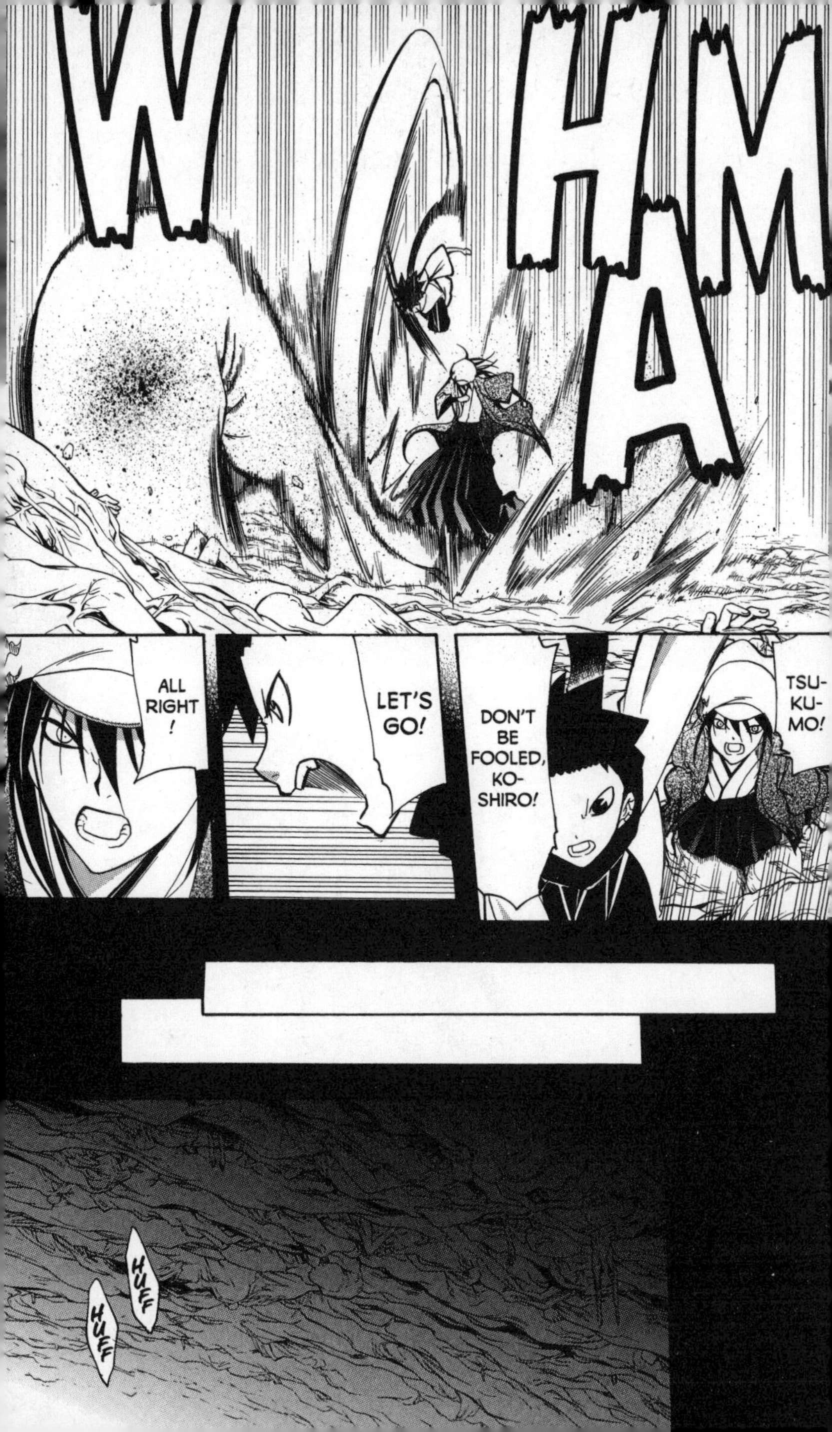
WHAM
TSU-KUMO!
DON'T BE FOOLED, KO-SHIRO!
LET'S GO!
ALL RIGHT!
HUFF
HUFF

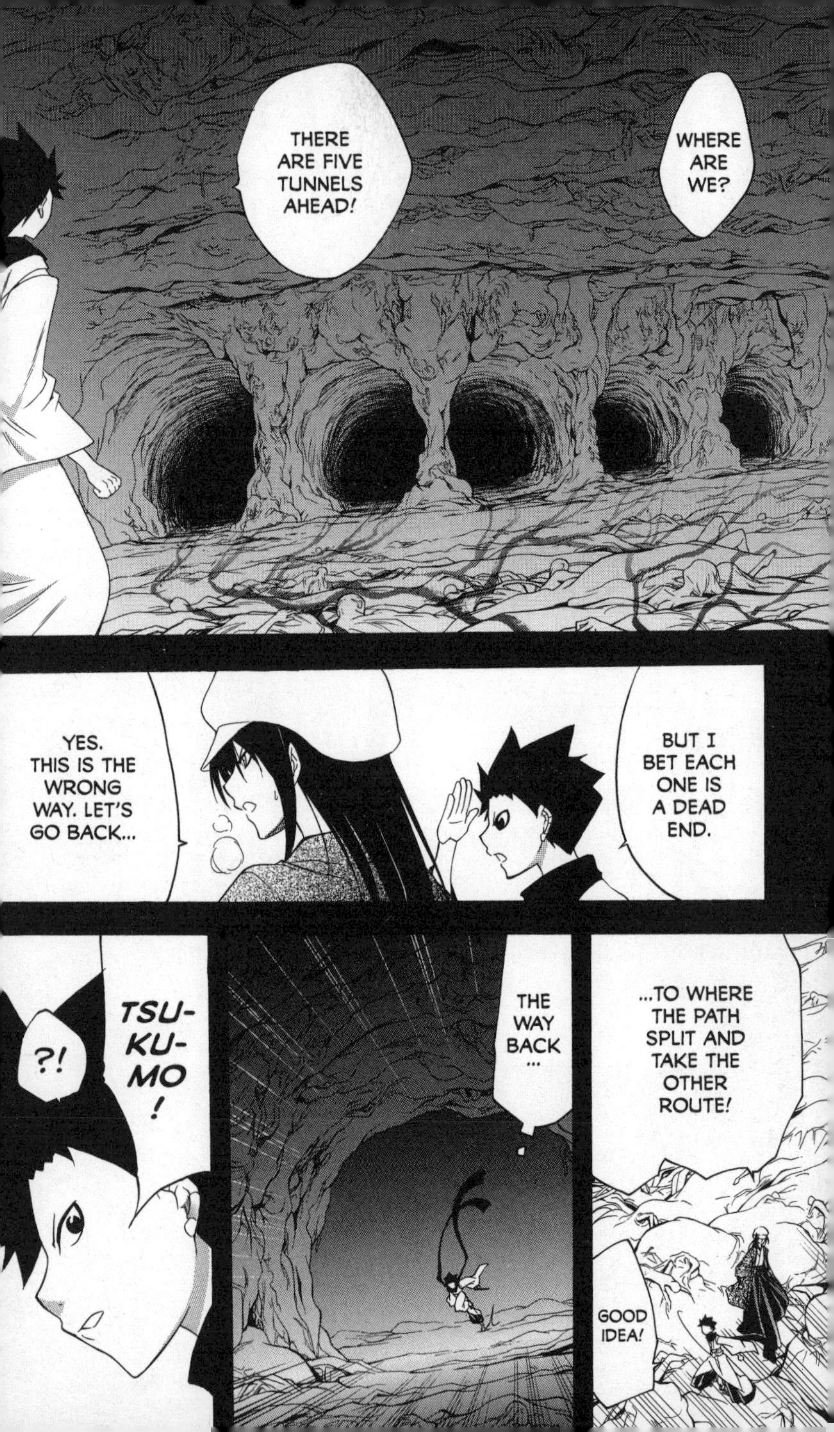
WHERE ARE WE?
THERE ARE FIVE TUNNELS AHEAD!
BUT I BET EACH ONE IS A DEAD END.
YES. THIS IS THE WRONG WAY. LET'S GO BACK...
...TO WHERE THE PATH SPLIT AND TAKE THE OTHER ROUTE!
GOOD IDEA!
THE WAY BACK...
TSU-KU-MO!
?!

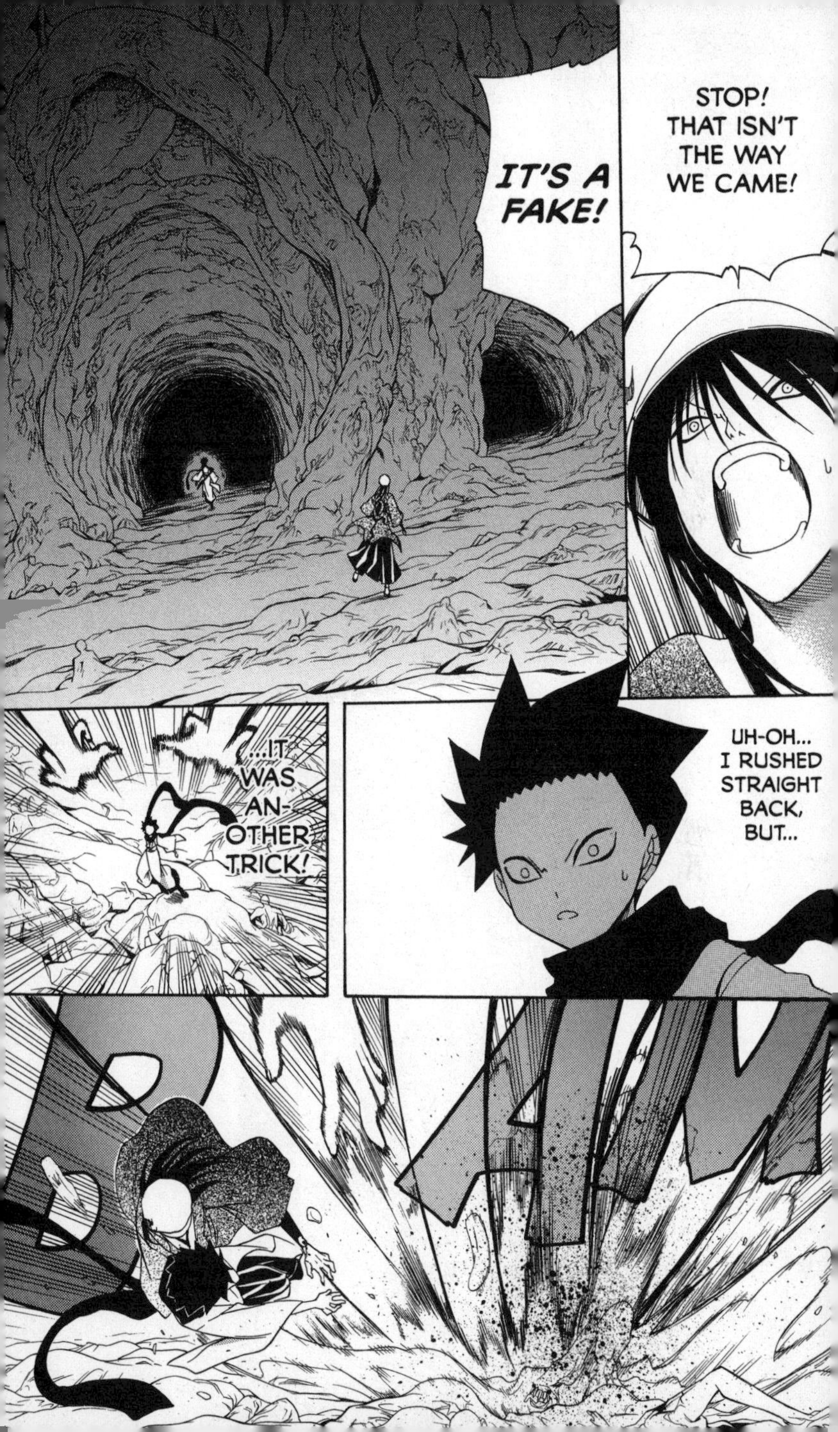
STOP! THAT ISN'T THE WAY WE CAME!
IT'S A FAKE!
UH-OH... I RUSHED STRAIGHT BACK, BUT...
...IT WAS ANOTHER TRICK!

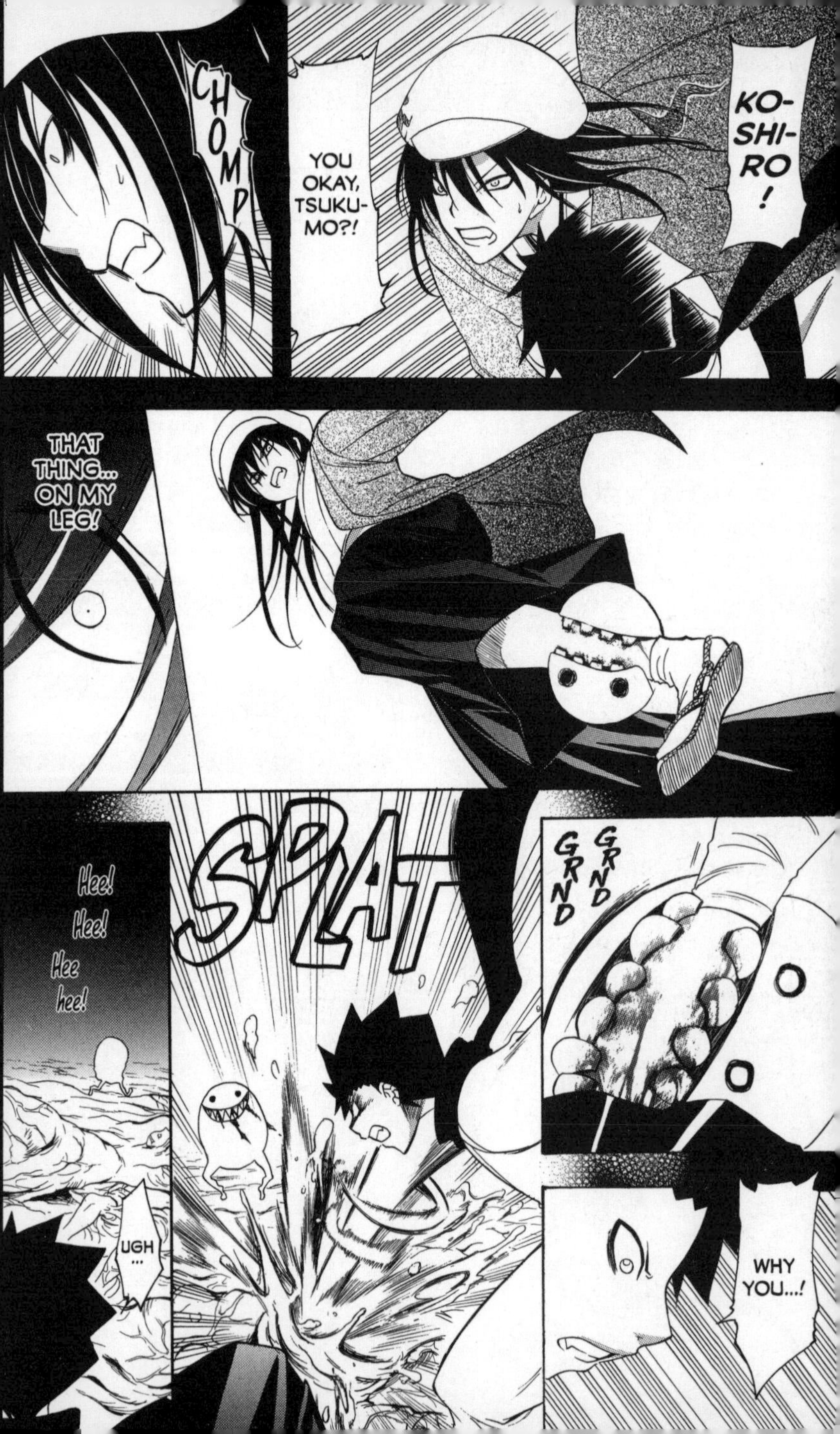
KO-SHI-RO!
YOU OKAY, TSUKUMO?!
CHOMP
THAT THING... ON MY LEG!
GRND GRND
WHY YOU...!
SPLAT
Hee! Hee! Hee hee!
UGH...

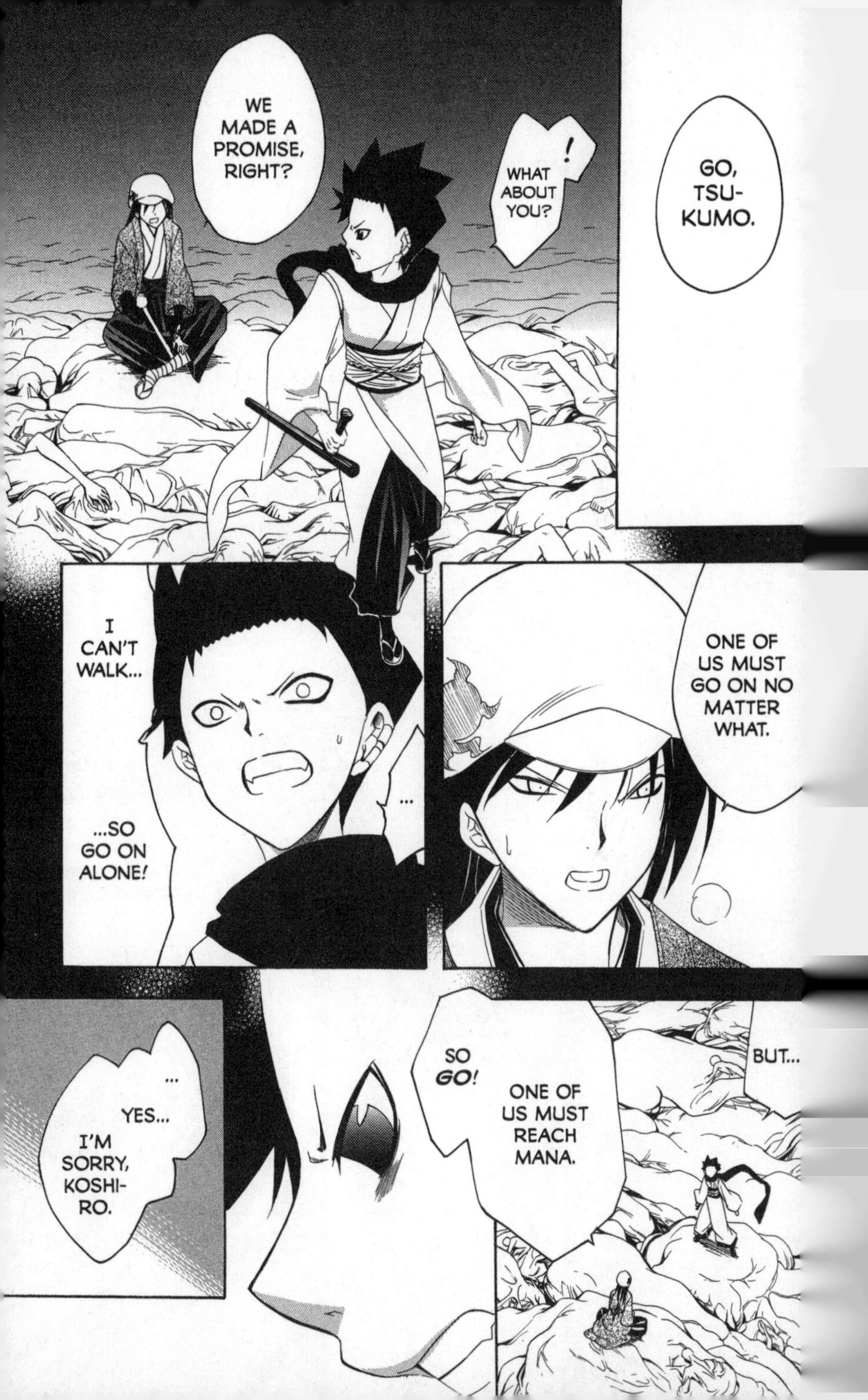
GO, TSU-KUMO.
!
WHAT ABOUT YOU?
WE MADE A PROMISE, RIGHT?
ONE OF US MUST GO ON NO MATTER WHAT.
...
I CAN'T WALK...
...SO GO ON ALONE!
BUT...
ONE OF US MUST REACH MANA.
SO *GO*!
...
YES...
I'M SORRY, KOSHI-RO.

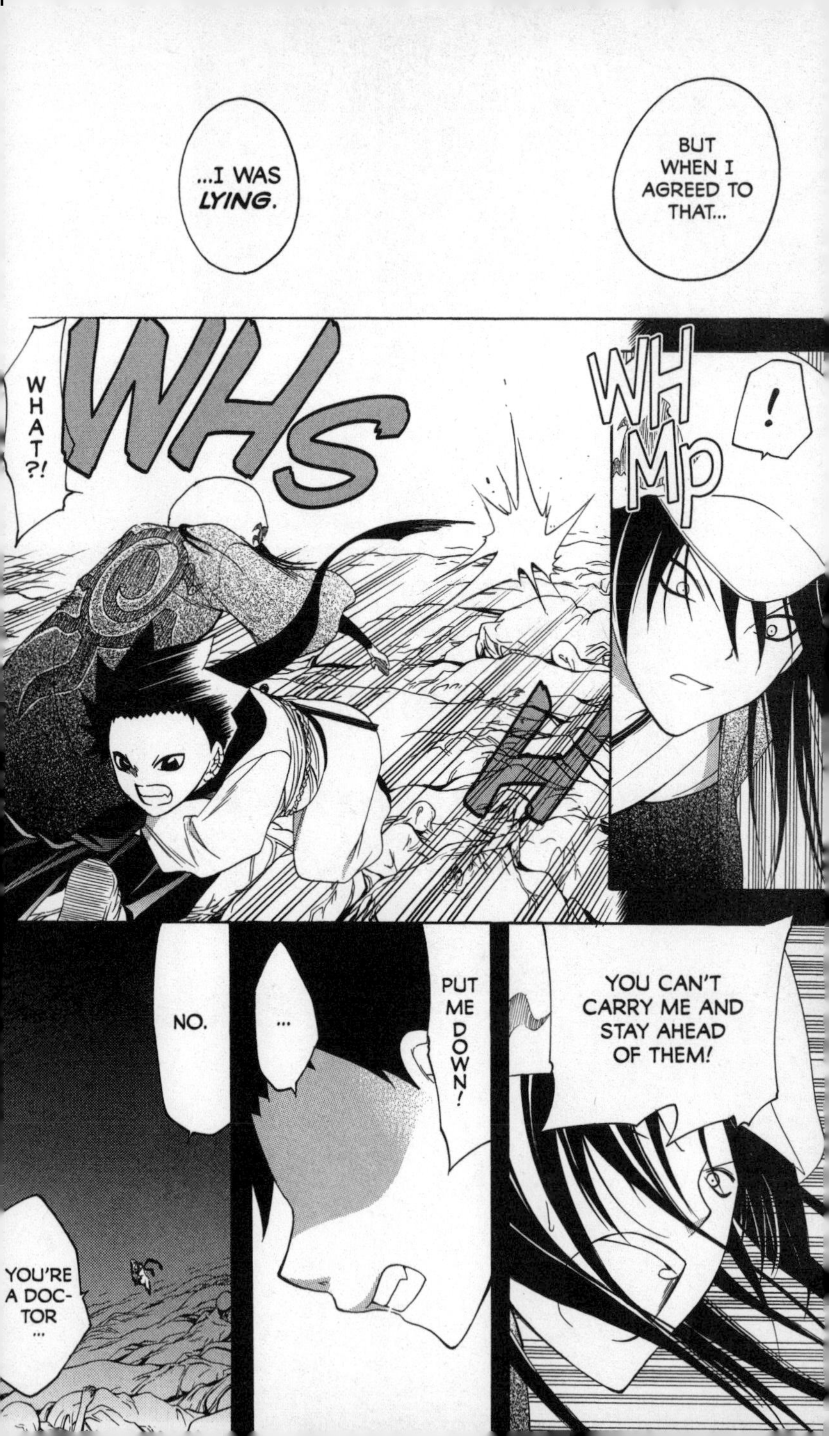

BUT WHEN I AGREED TO THAT...
...I WAS *LYING*.
WHMp
!
WHS
WHAT?!
YOU CAN'T CARRY ME AND STAY AHEAD OF THEM!
PUT ME DOWN!
...
NO.
YOU'RE A DOCTOR...

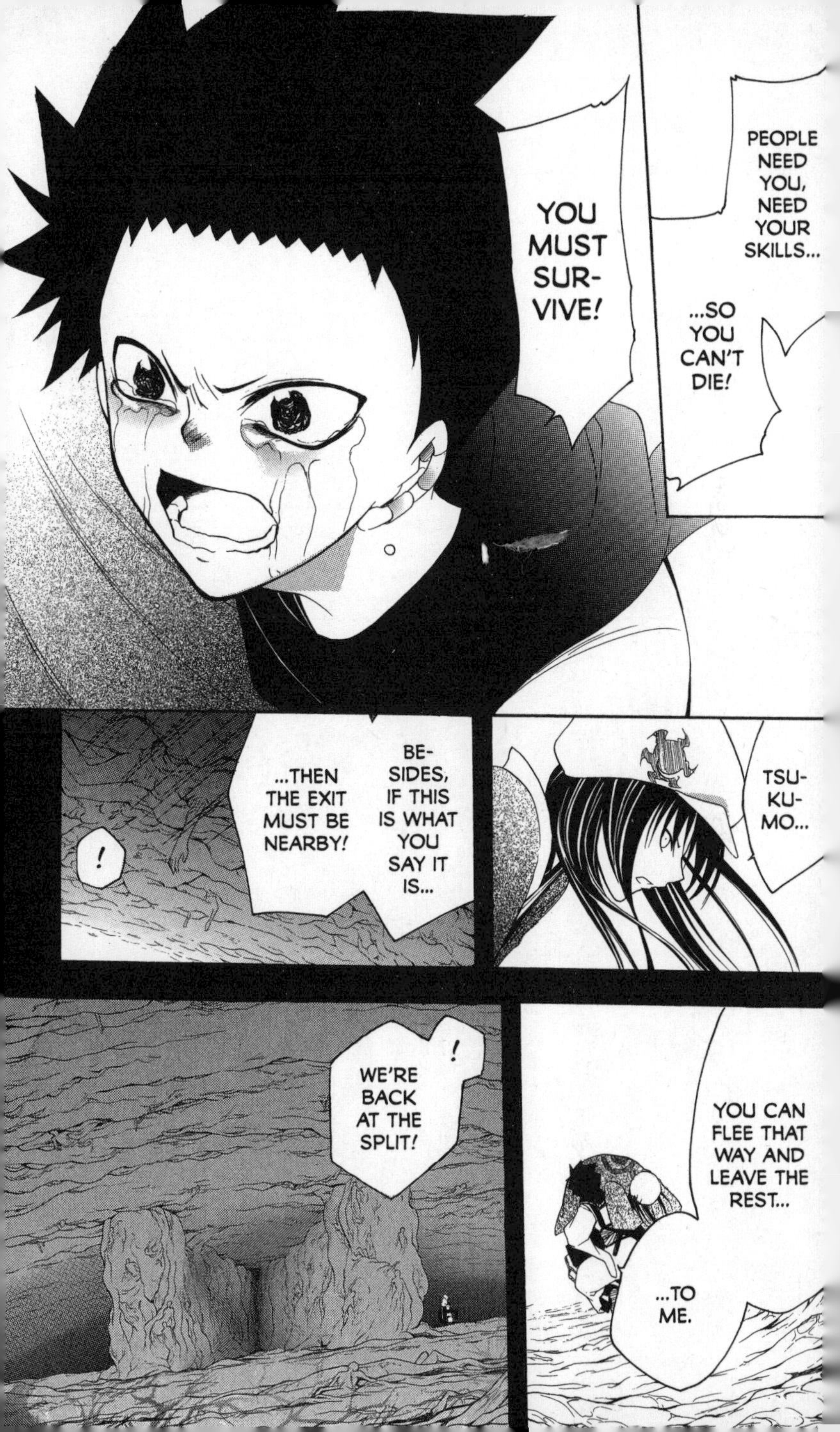
PEOPLE NEED YOU, NEED YOUR SKILLS...
...SO YOU CAN'T DIE!
YOU MUST SUR-VIVE!
TSU-KU-MO...
BE-SIDES, IF THIS IS WHAT YOU SAY IT IS...
...THEN THE EXIT MUST BE NEARBY!
!
YOU CAN FLEE THAT WAY AND LEAVE THE REST...
...TO ME.
!
WE'RE BACK AT THE SPLIT!

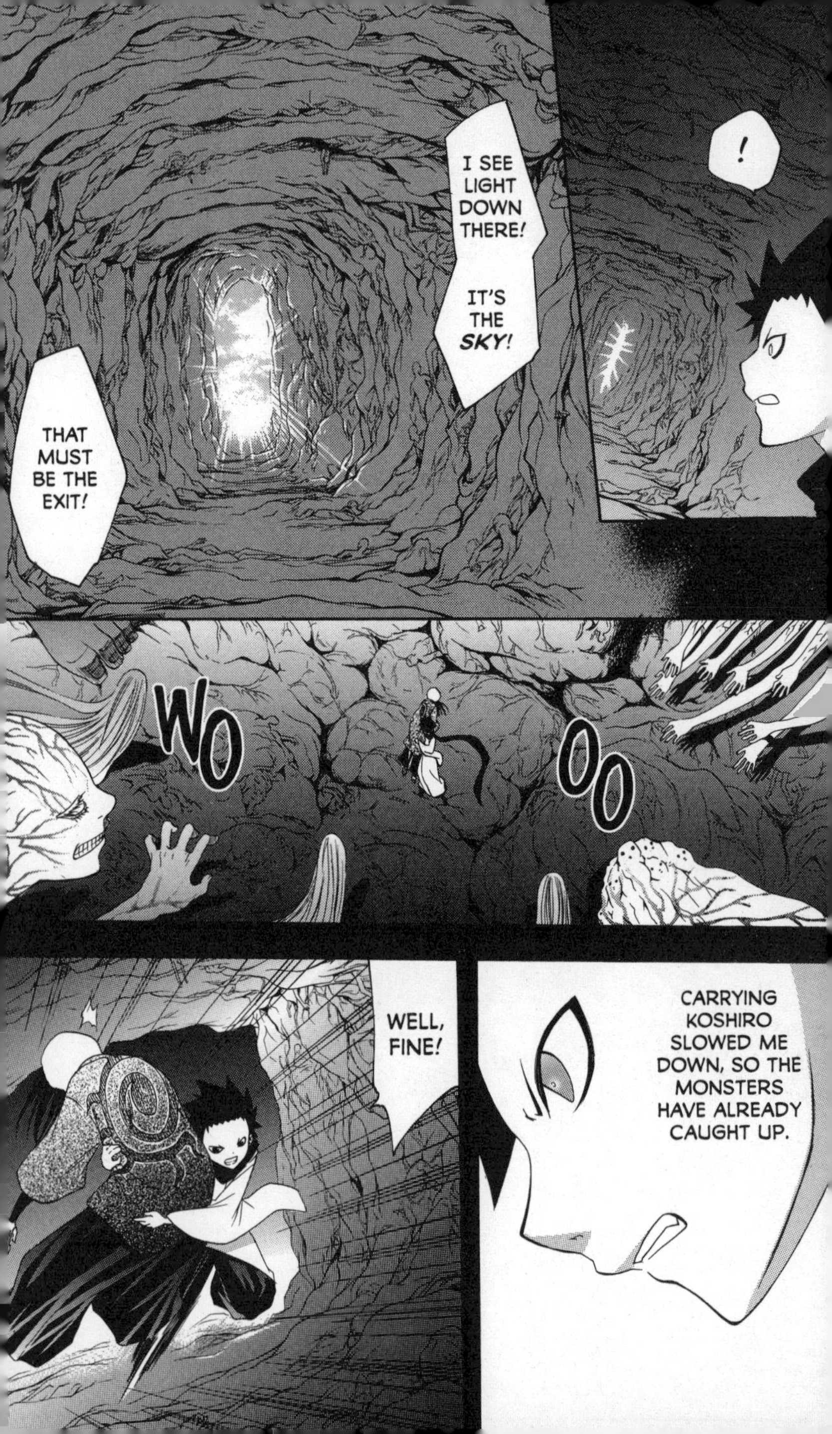
!
I SEE LIGHT DOWN THERE!
IT'S THE *SKY*!
THAT MUST BE THE EXIT!
WO OO
CARRYING KOSHIRO SLOWED ME DOWN, SO THE MONSTERS HAVE ALREADY CAUGHT UP.
WELL, FINE!

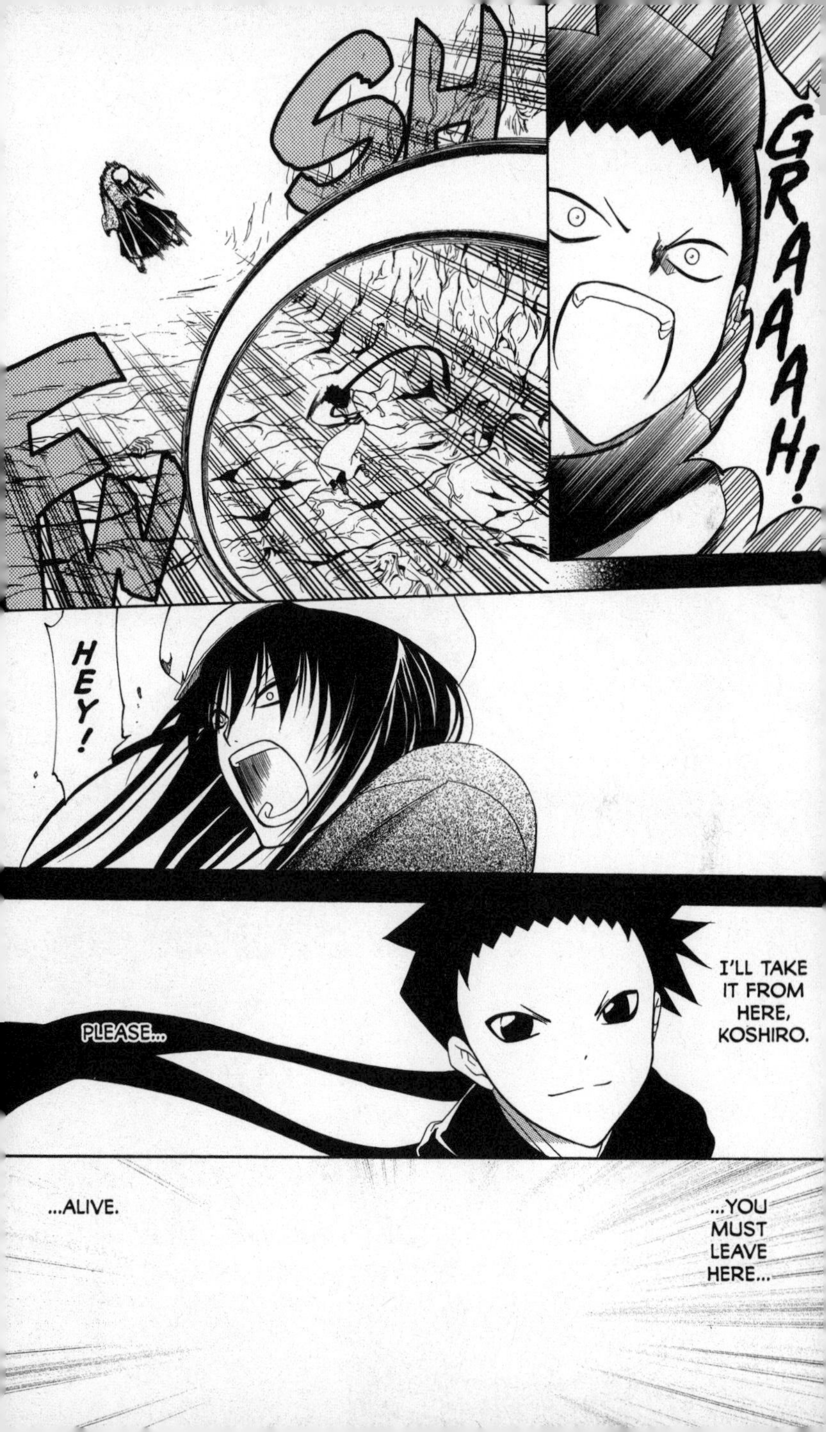
GRAAAH!
HEY!
I'LL TAKE IT FROM HERE, KOSHIRO.
PLEASE...
...YOU MUST LEAVE HERE...
...ALIVE.

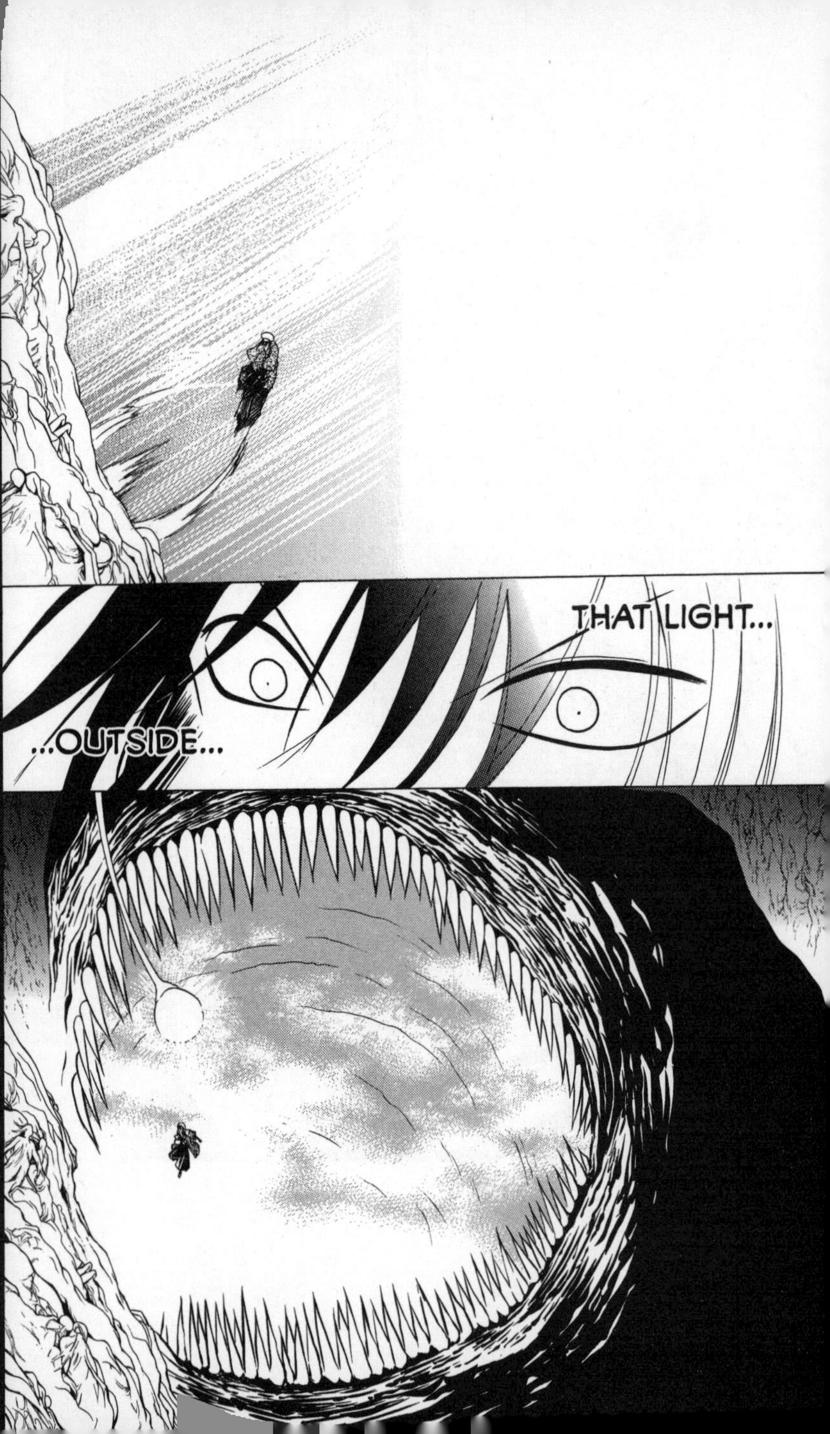
THAT LIGHT...
...OUTSIDE...

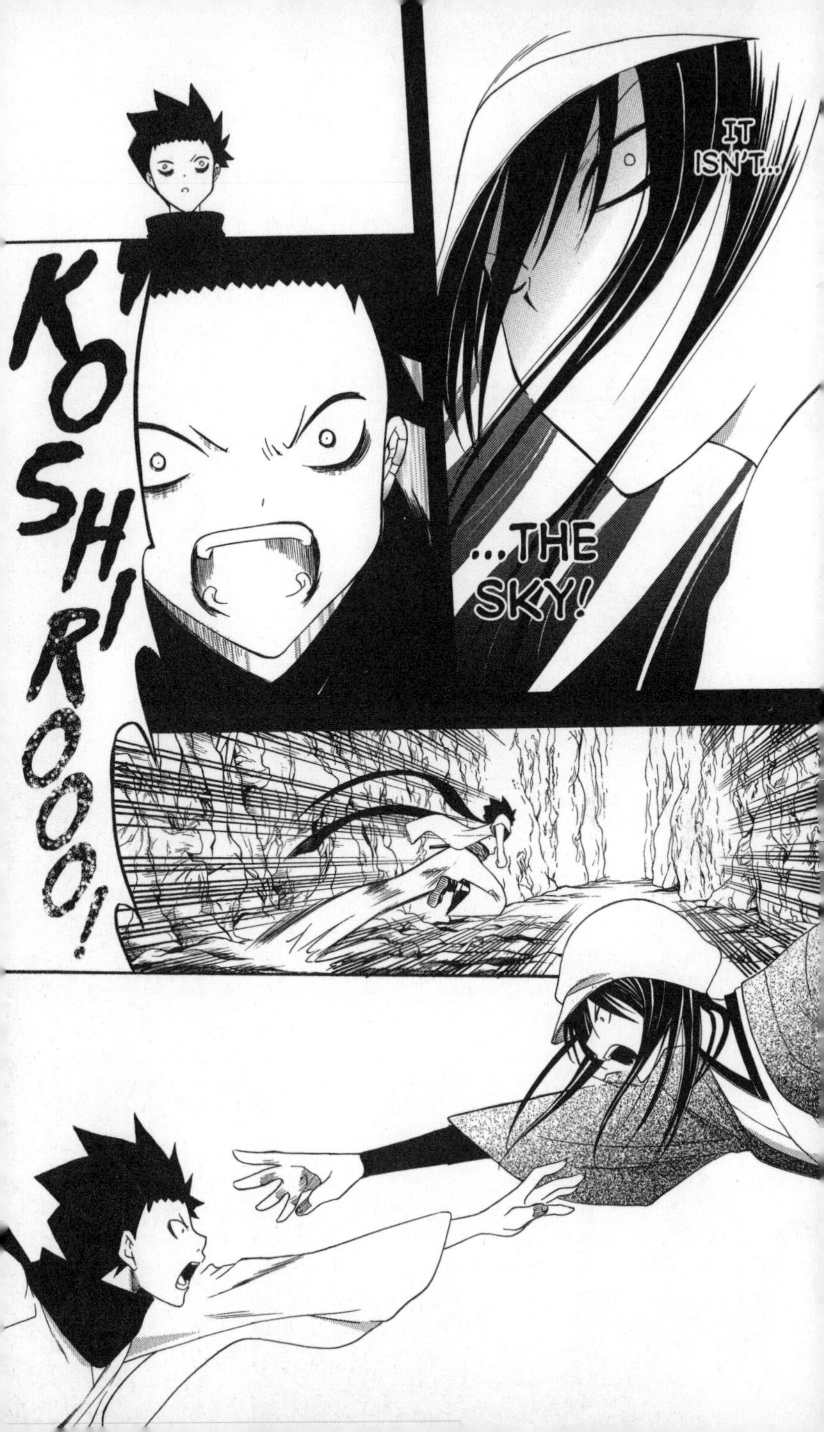
IT ISN'T...
...THE SKY!
KOSHIROOO!

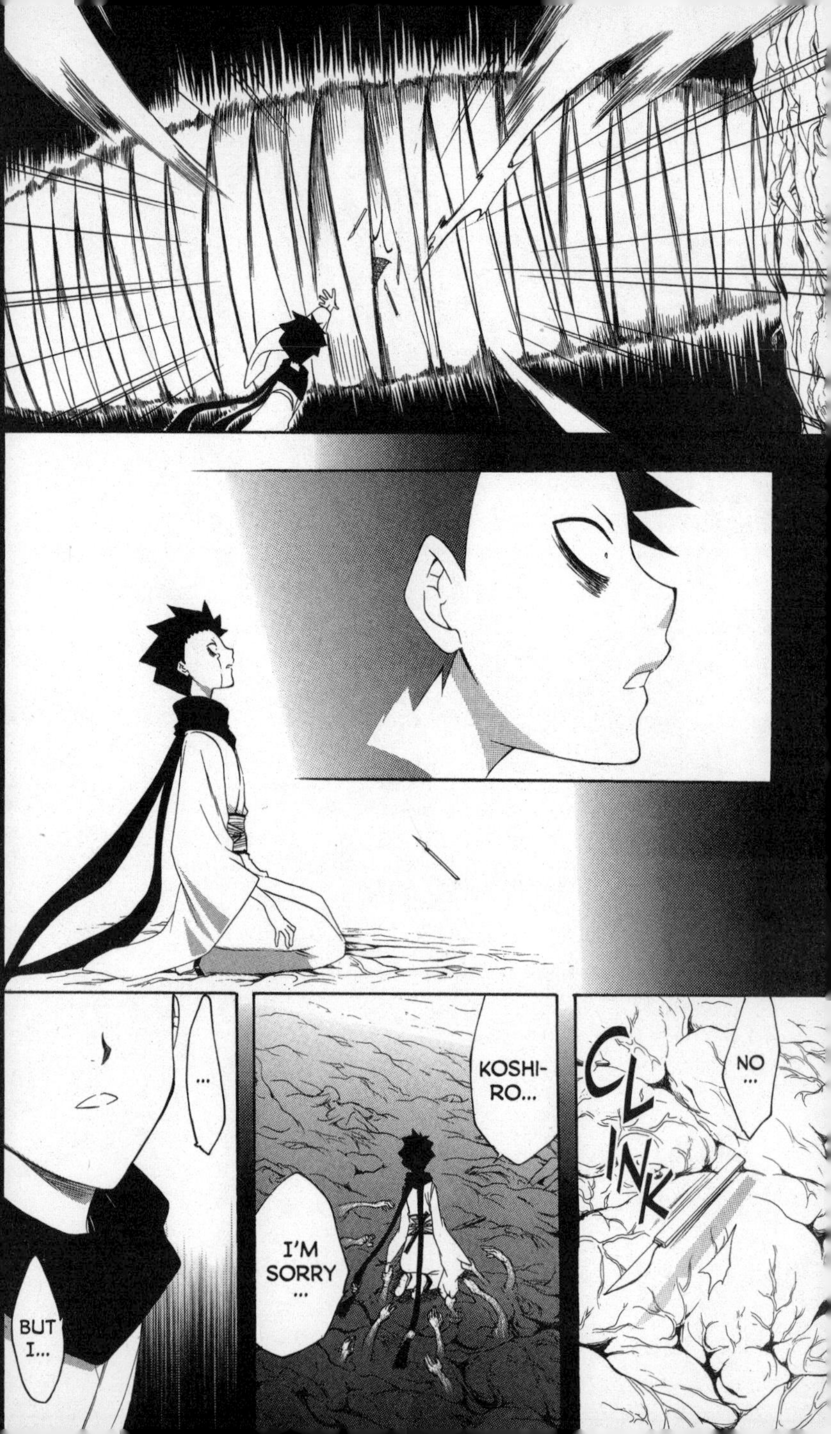
NO ...
CLINK
KOSHI-RO...
I'M SORRY ...
...
BUT I...

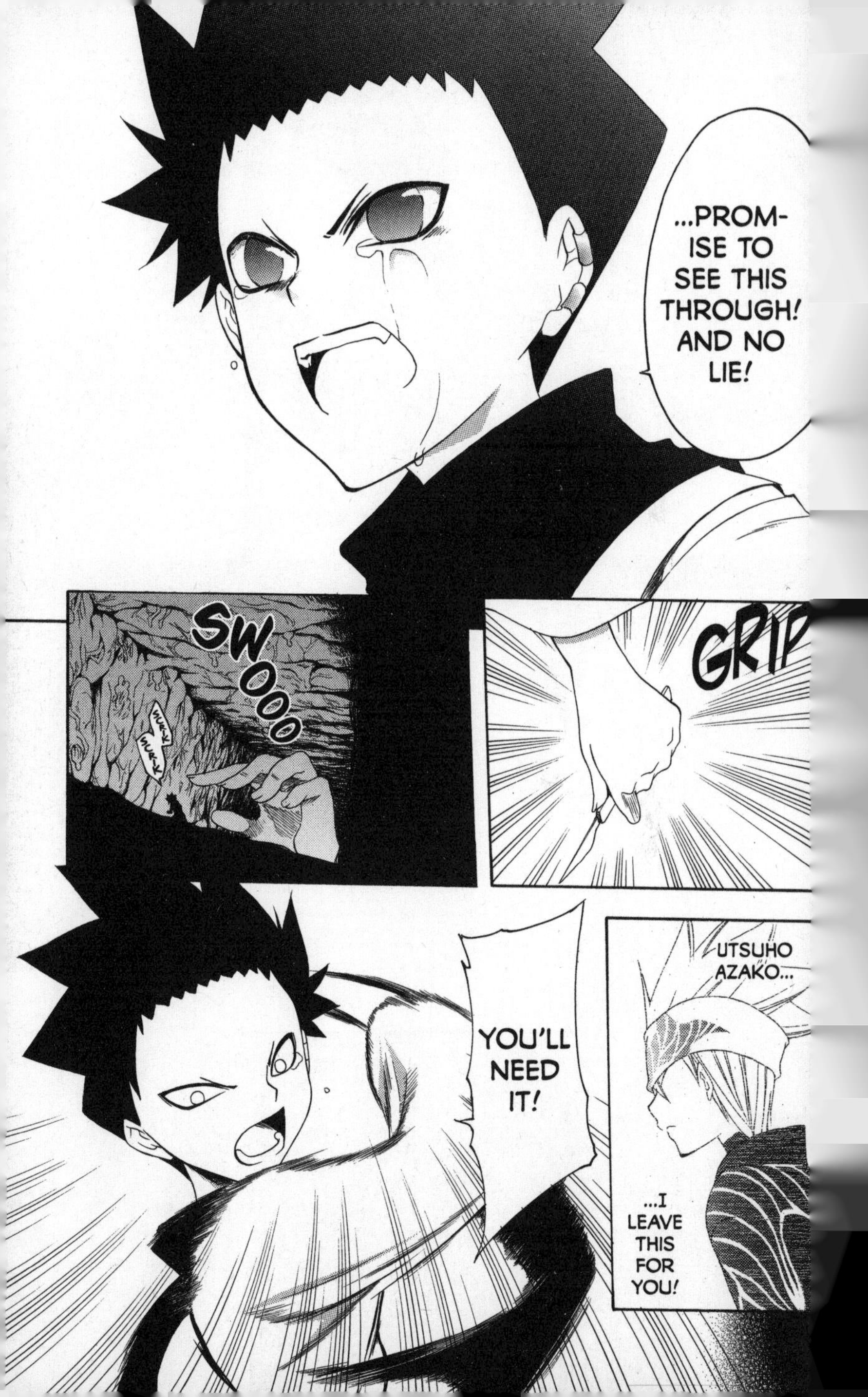
...PROM-ISE TO SEE THIS THROUGH! AND NO LIE!
GRIP
SWOOO
SCRIK
SCRIK
UTSUHO AZAKO...
...I LEAVE THIS FOR YOU!
YOU'LL NEED IT!

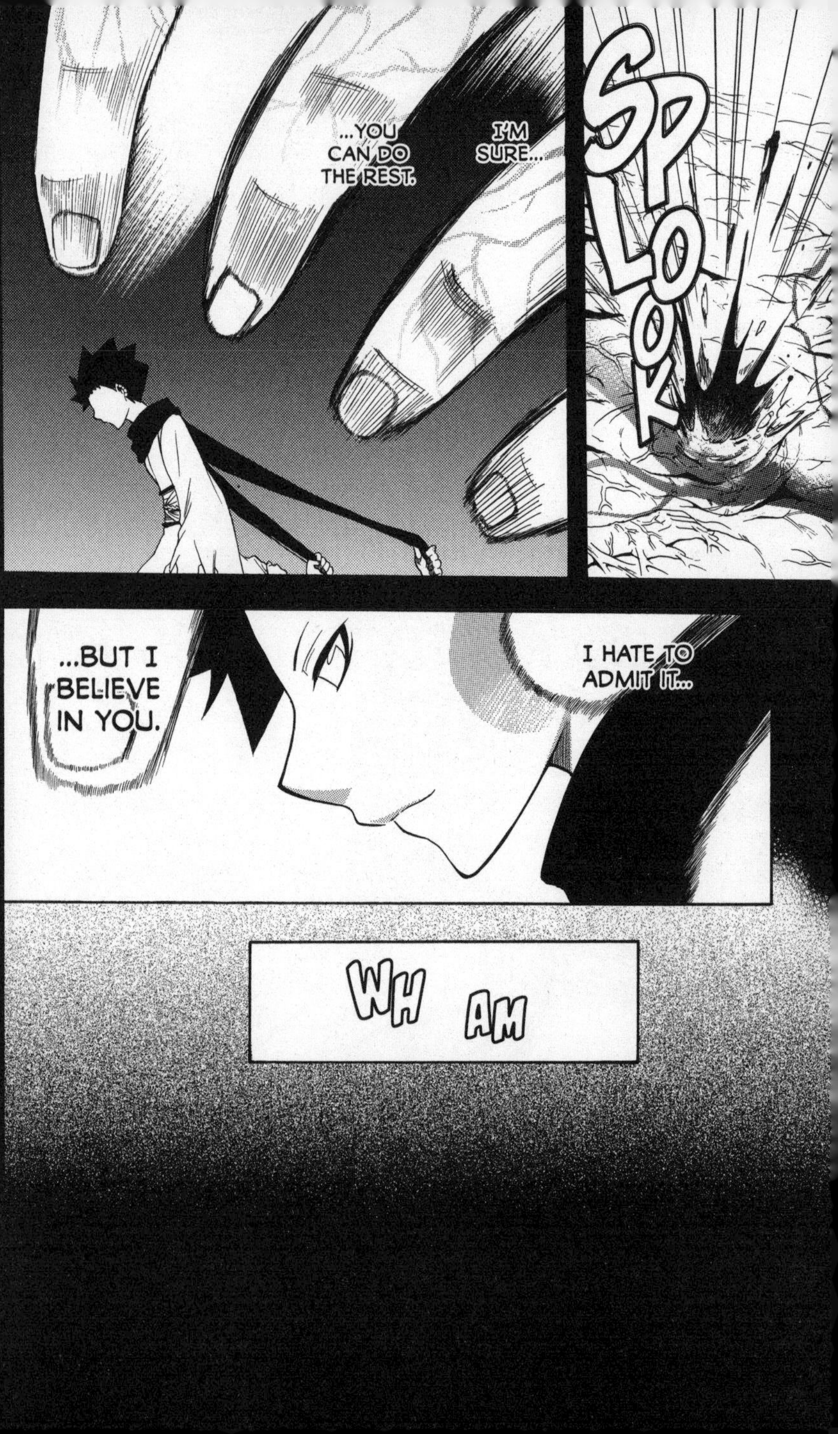
SPLOOK
I'M SURE...
...YOU CAN DO THE REST.
I HATE TO ADMIT IT...
...BUT I BELIEVE IN YOU.
WHAM

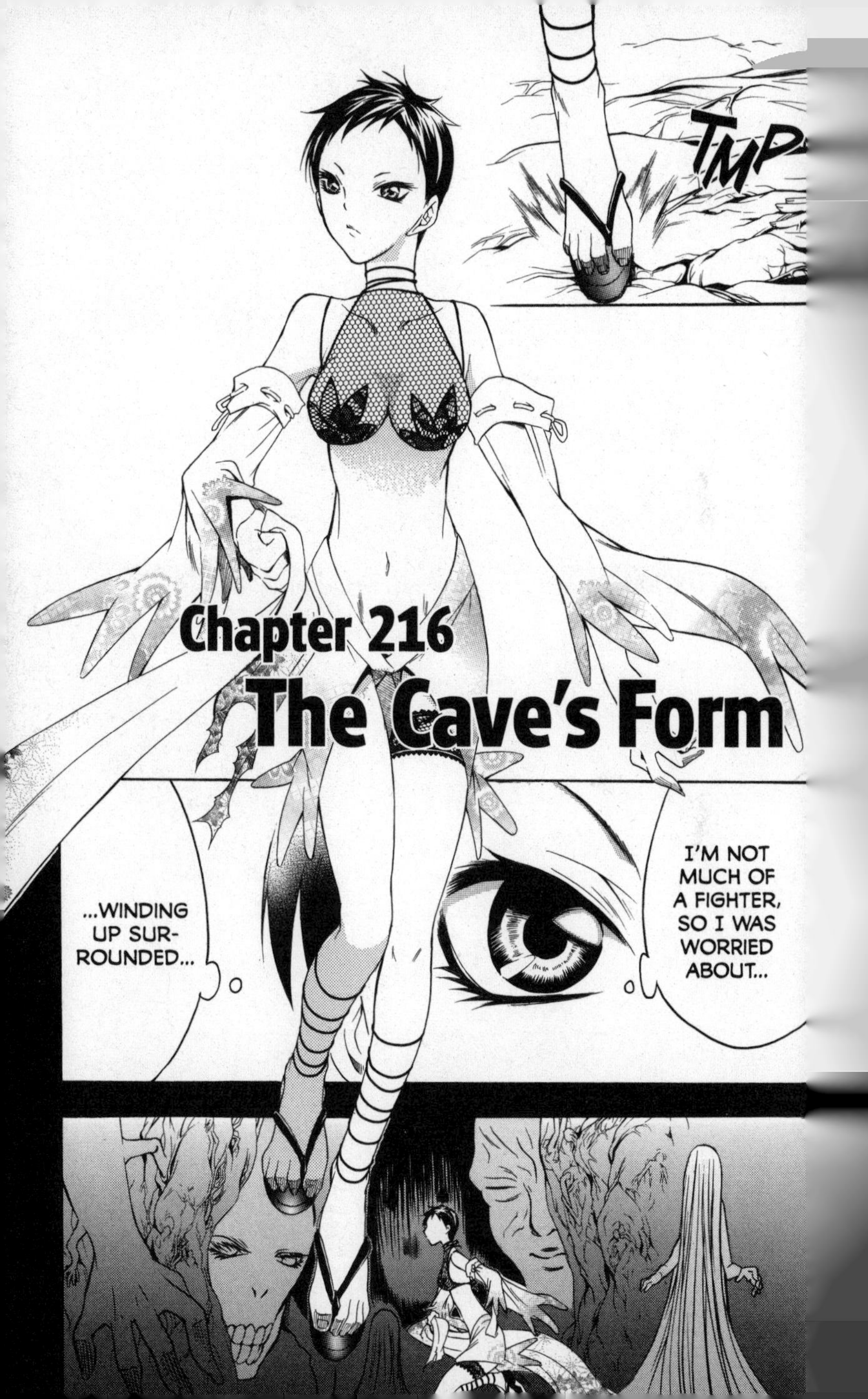
TMP
Chapter 216
The Cave's Form
I'M NOT MUCH OF A FIGHTER, SO I WAS WORRIED ABOUT...
...WINDING UP SURROUNDED...

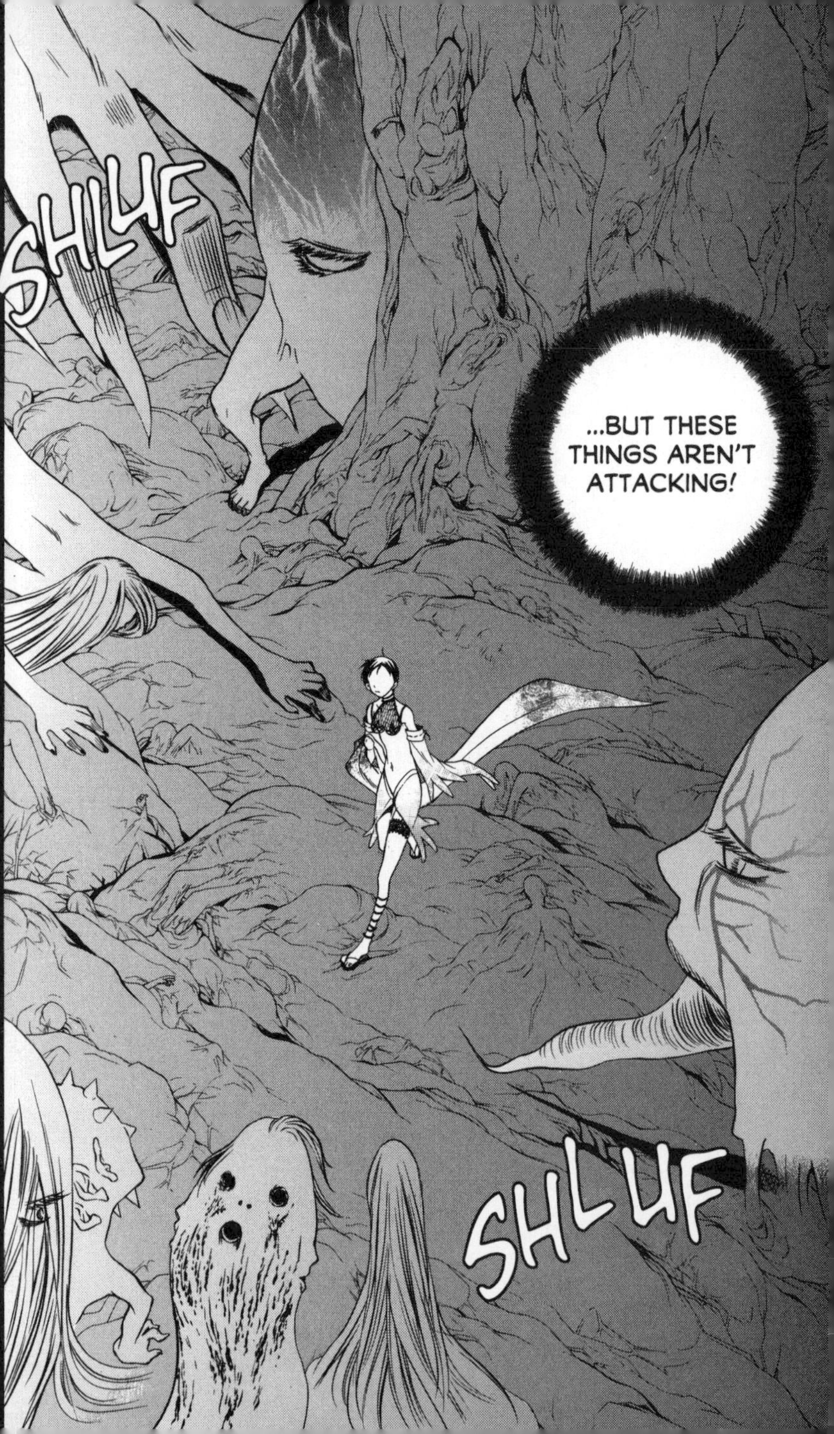
SHLUF
...BUT THESE THINGS AREN'T ATTACKING!
SHLUF

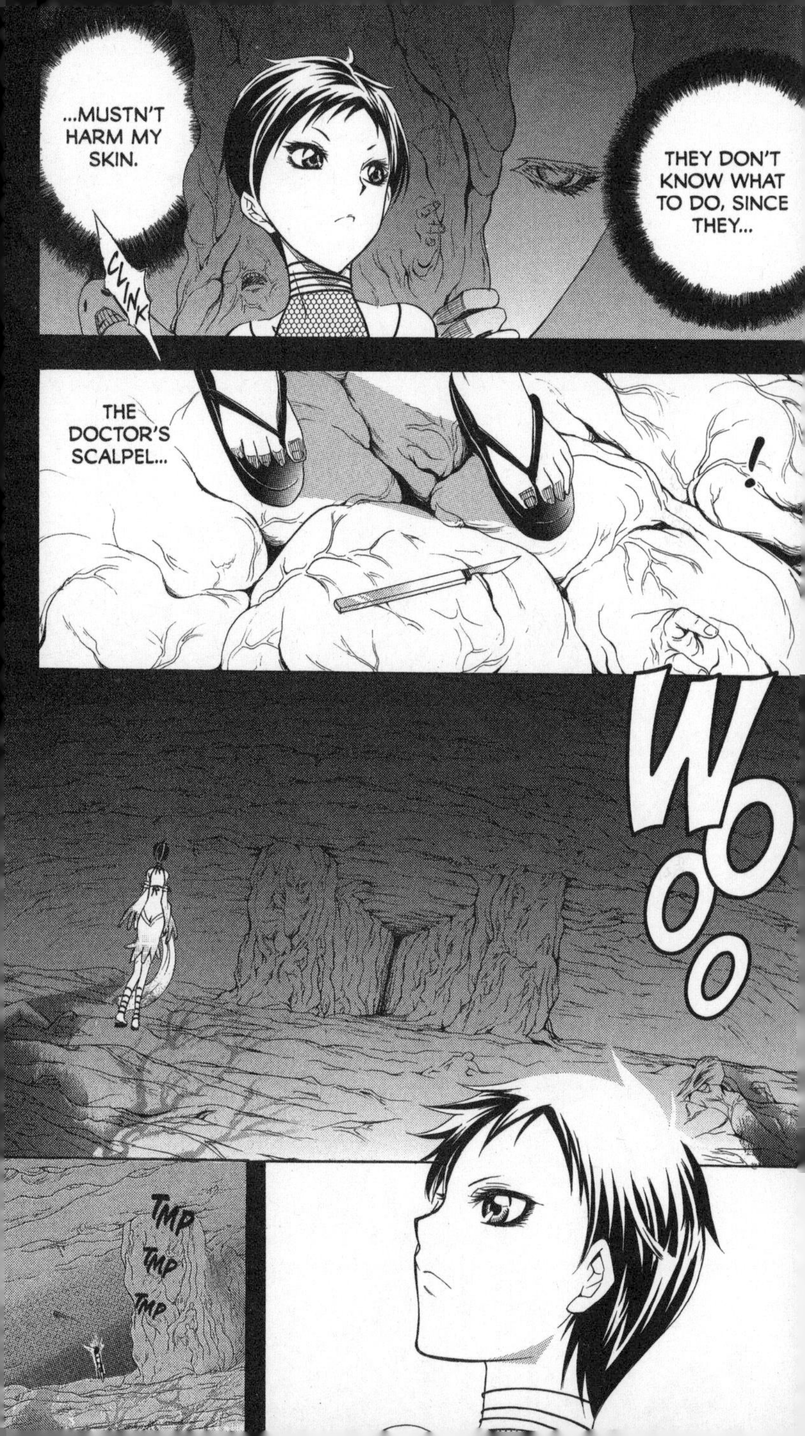
THEY DON'T KNOW WHAT TO DO, SINCE THEY...
...MUSTN'T HARM MY SKIN.
CLINK
!
THE DOCTOR'S SCALPEL...
WOOOO
TMP
TMP
TMP

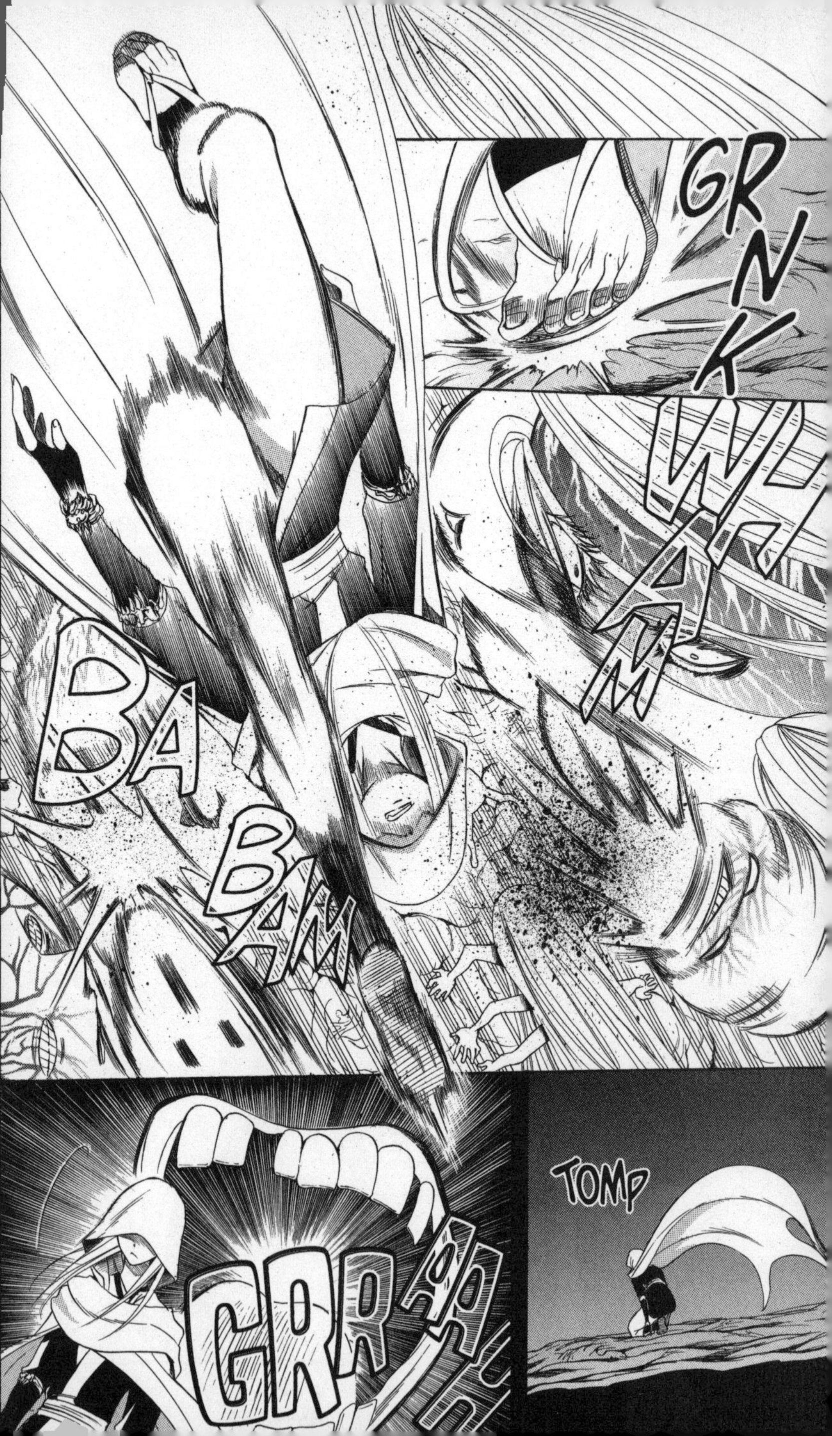
GRNK
WHAM
BABAM
TOMP
GRRAAA

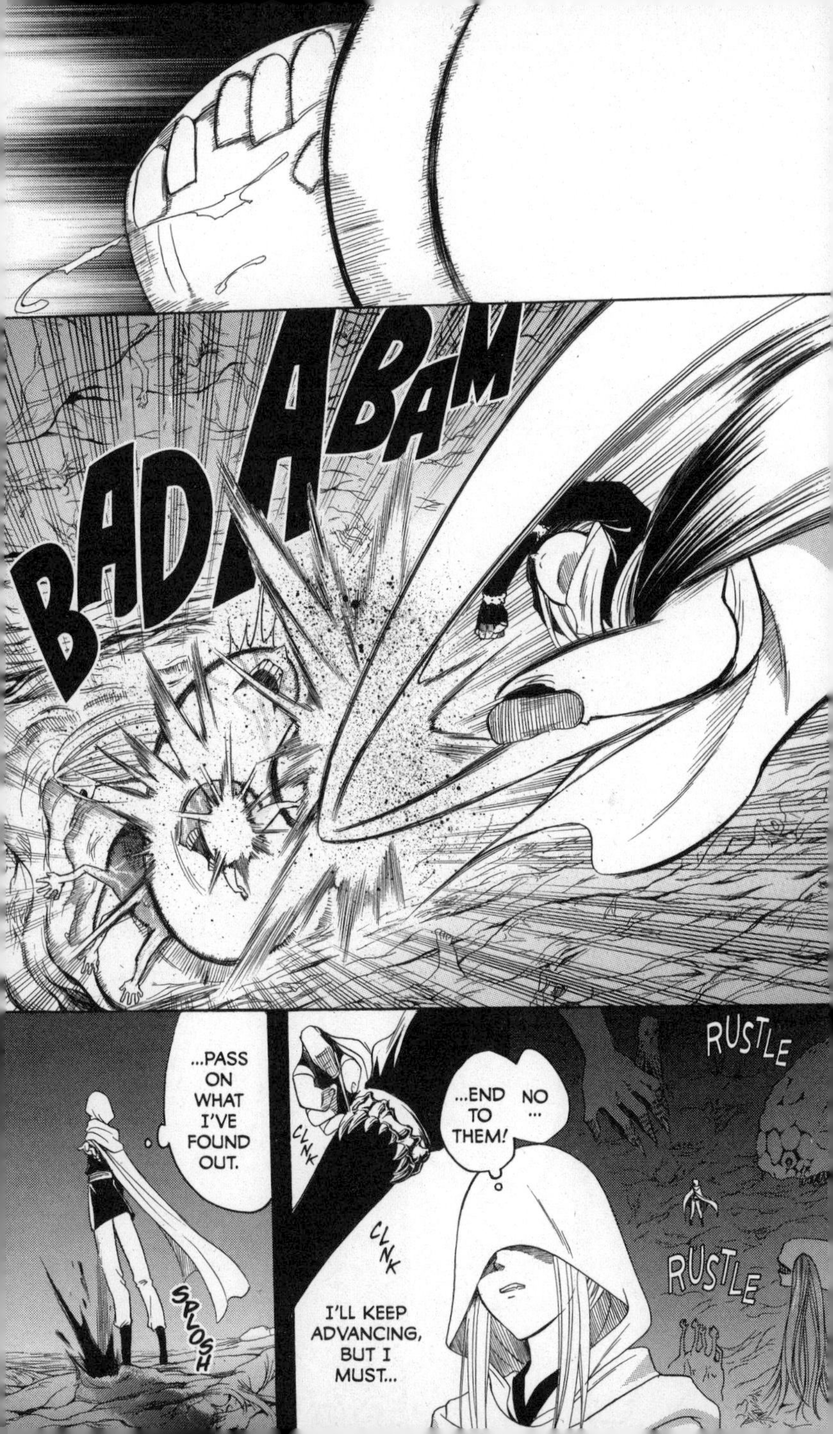
BADABAM
RUSTLE
NO...
...END TO THEM!
CLNK
RUSTLE
CLNK
I'LL KEEP ADVANCING, BUT I MUST...
...PASS ON WHAT I'VE FOUND OUT.
SPLOSH

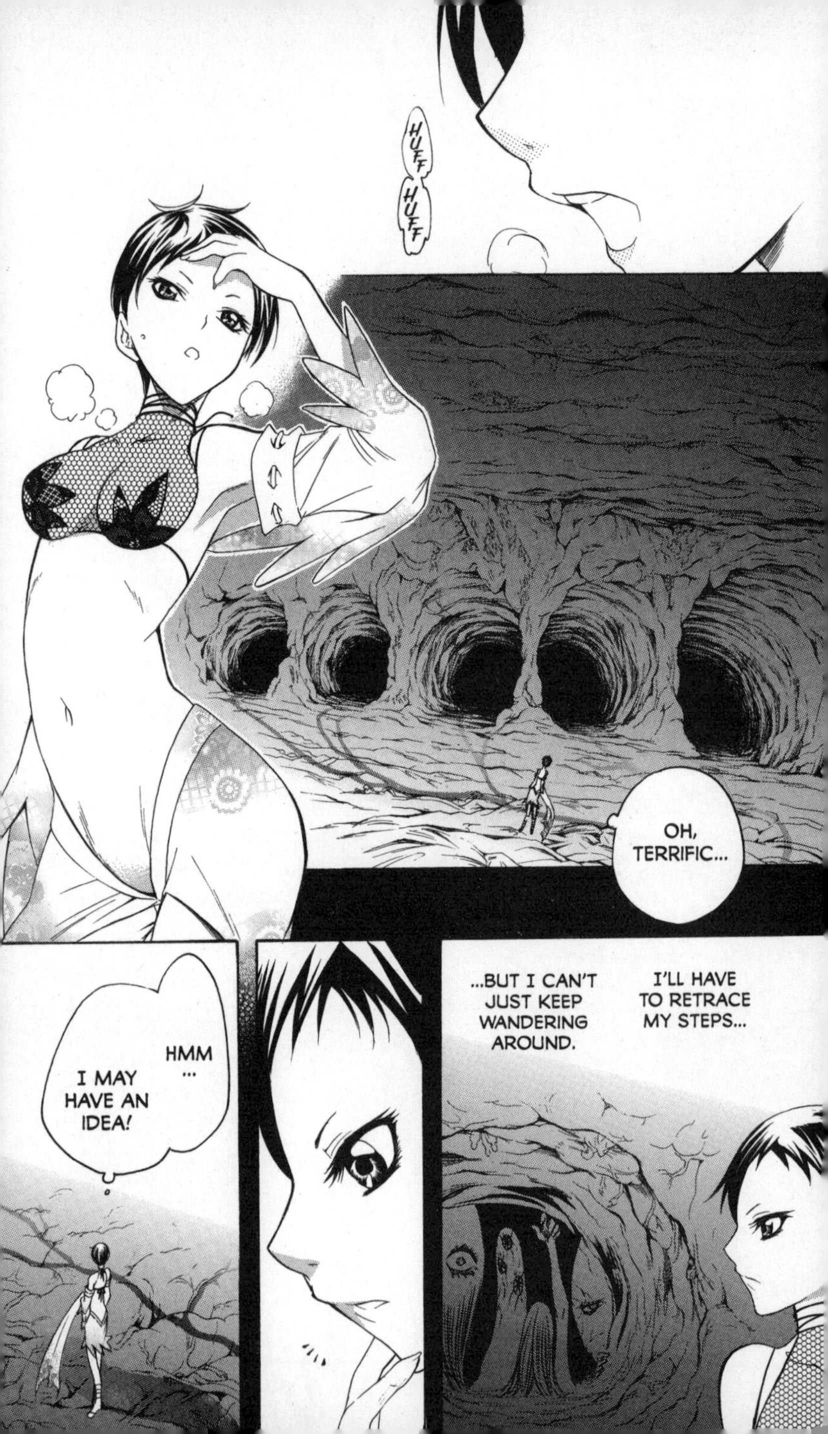
HUFF
HUFF
OH, TERRIFIC...
I'LL HAVE TO RETRACE MY STEPS...
...BUT I CAN'T JUST KEEP WANDERING AROUND.
...
HMM ...
I MAY HAVE AN IDEA!

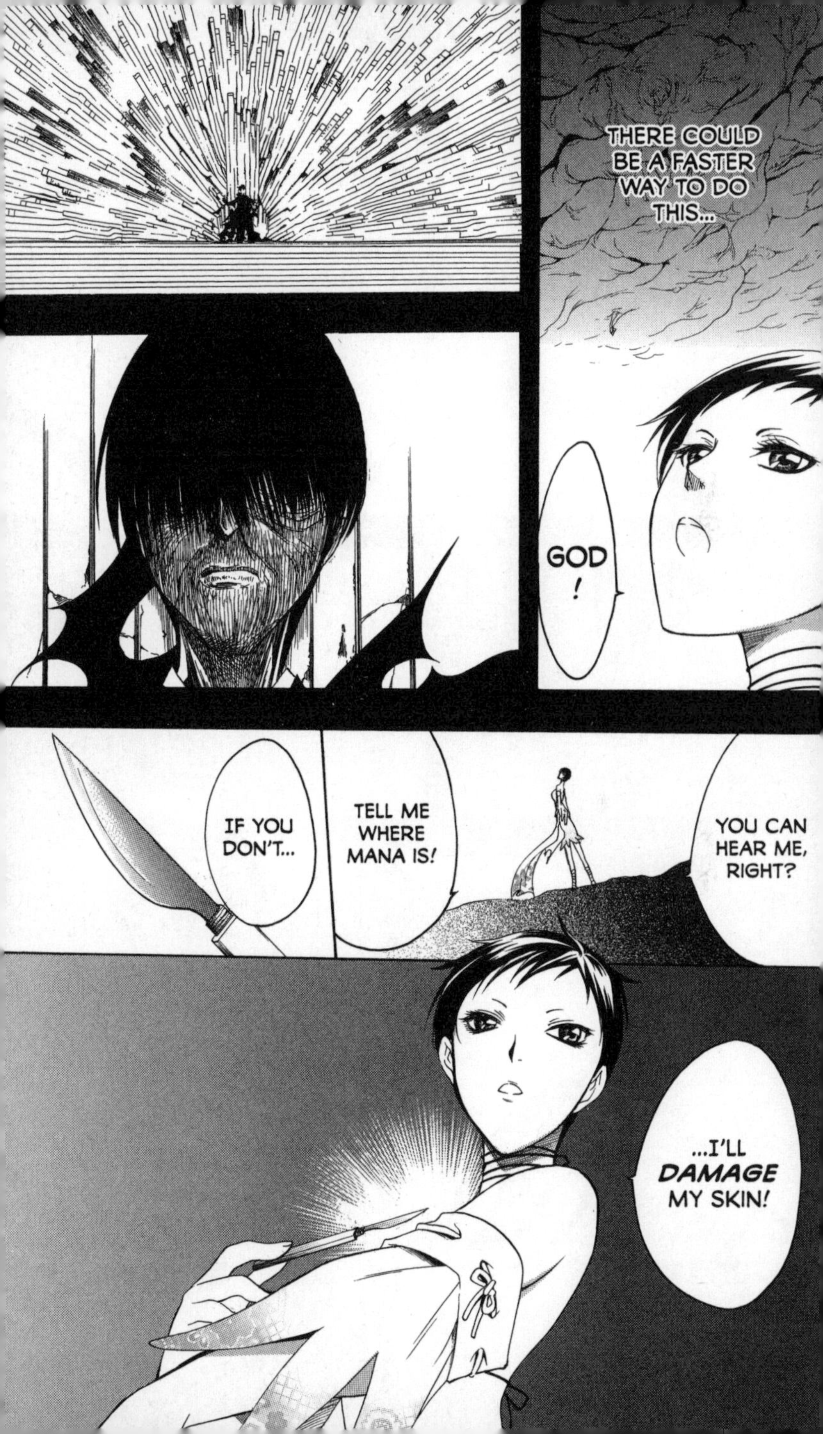
THERE COULD BE A FASTER WAY TO DO THIS...
GOD!
YOU CAN HEAR ME, RIGHT?
TELL ME WHERE MANA IS!
IF YOU DON'T...
...I'LL *DAMAGE* MY SKIN!

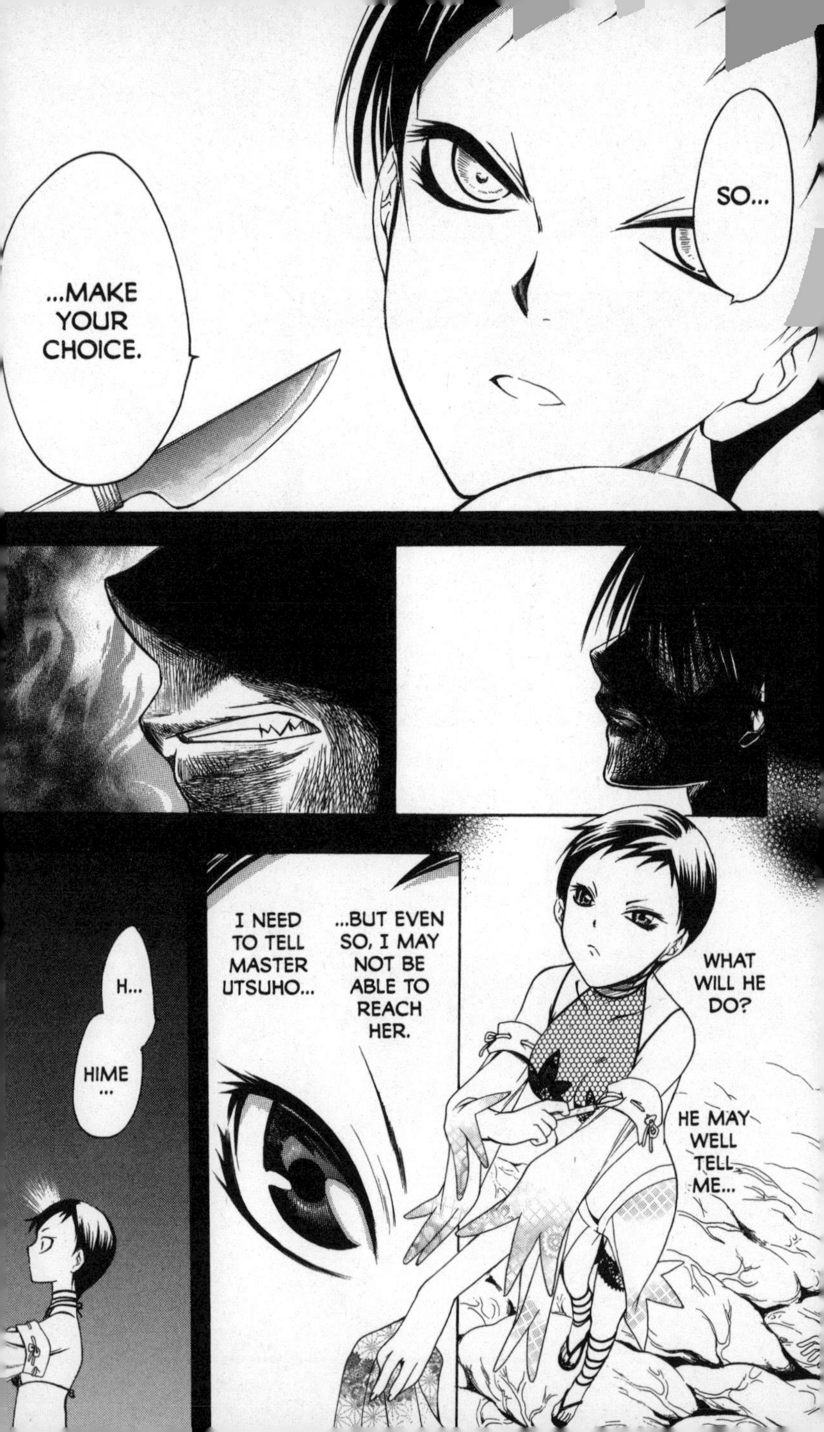
SO...
...MAKE YOUR CHOICE.
WHAT WILL HE DO?
HE MAY WELL TELL ME...
...BUT EVEN SO, I MAY NOT BE ABLE TO REACH HER.
I NEED TO TELL MASTER UTSUHO...
H...
HIME ...

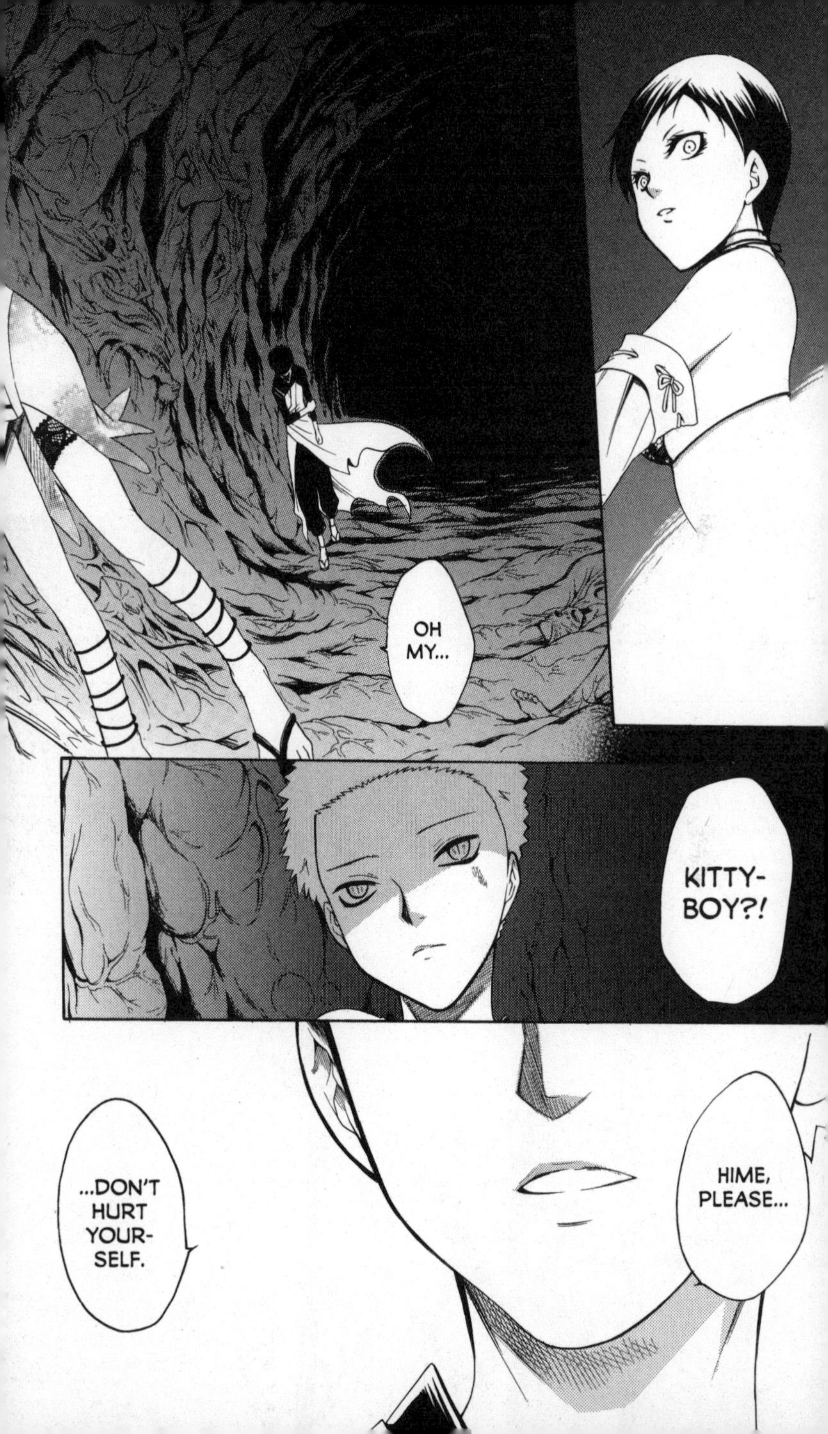
OH MY...
KITTY-BOY?!
HIME, PLEASE...
...DON'T HURT YOURSELF.

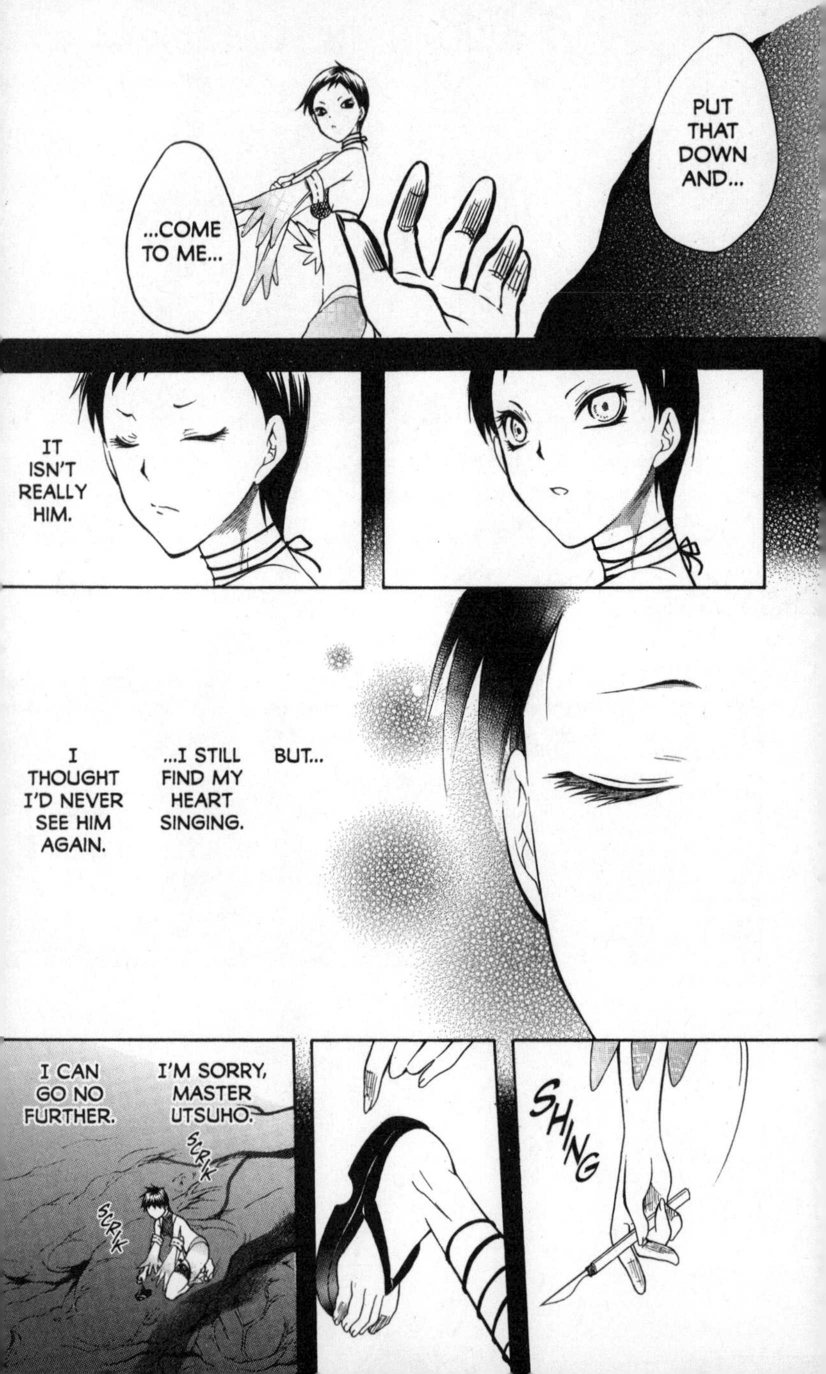
PUT THAT DOWN AND...
...COME TO ME...
IT ISN'T REALLY HIM.
BUT...
...I STILL FIND MY HEART SINGING.
I THOUGHT I'D NEVER SEE HIM AGAIN.
SHING
I'M SORRY, MASTER UTSUHO.
I CAN GO NO FURTHER.
SCRIK
SCRIK

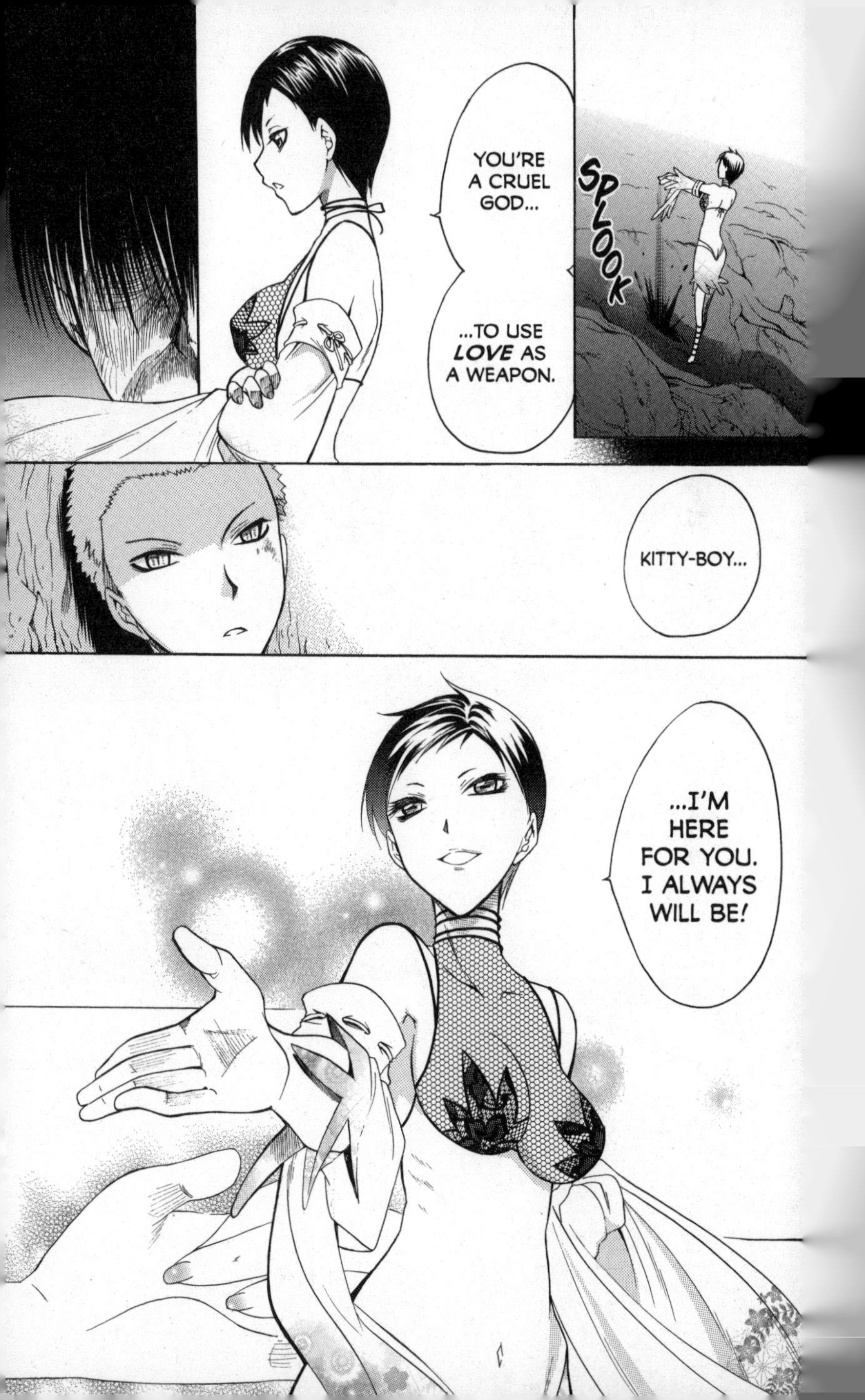
SPLOOK
YOU'RE A CRUEL GOD...
...TO USE *LOVE* AS A WEAPON.
KITTY-BOY...
...I'M HERE FOR YOU. I ALWAYS WILL BE!

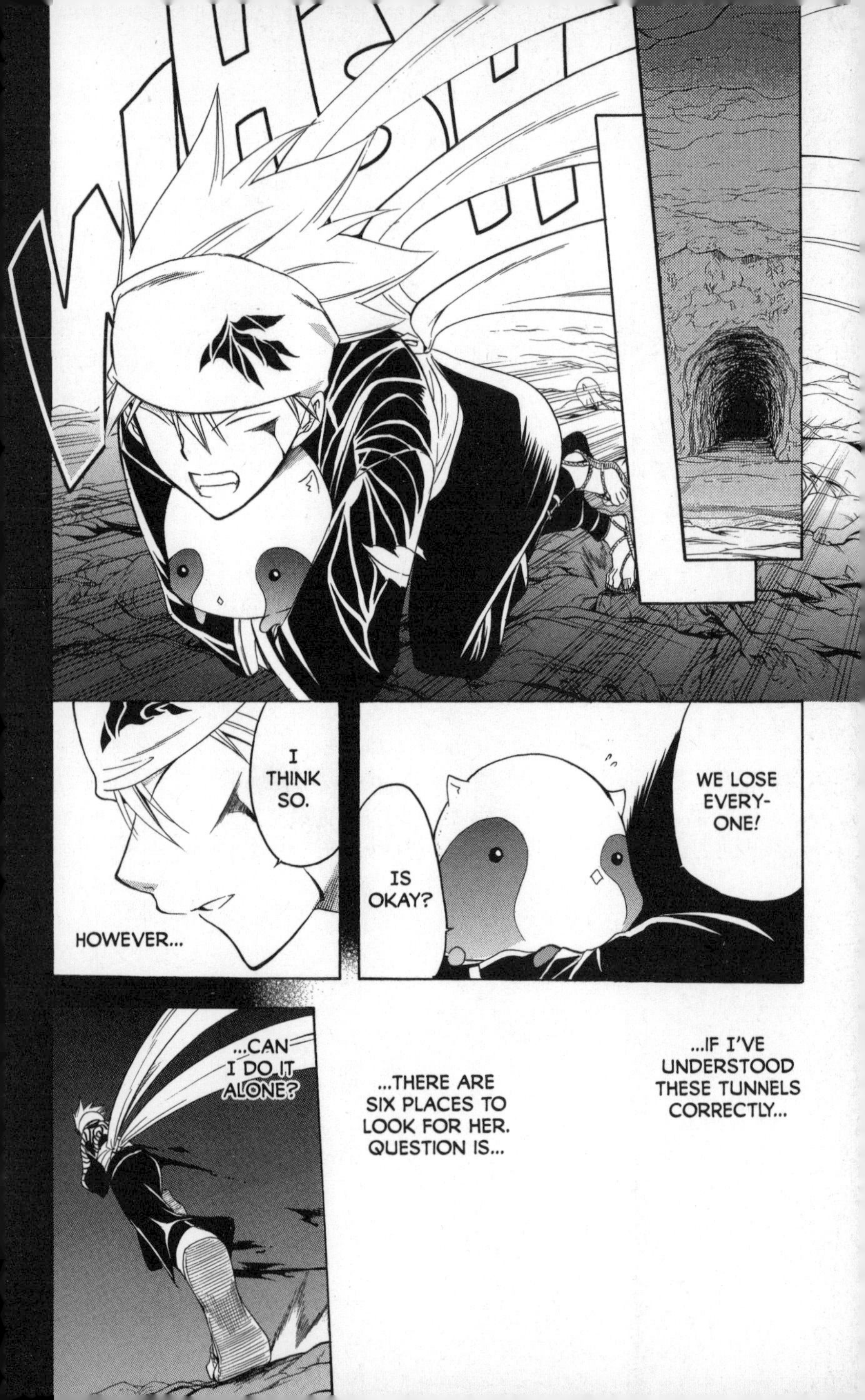
WE LOSE EVERY-ONE!
IS OKAY?
I THINK SO.
HOWEVER...
...IF I'VE UNDERSTOOD THESE TUNNELS CORRECTLY...
...THERE ARE SIX PLACES TO LOOK FOR HER. QUESTION IS...
...CAN I DO IT ALONE?

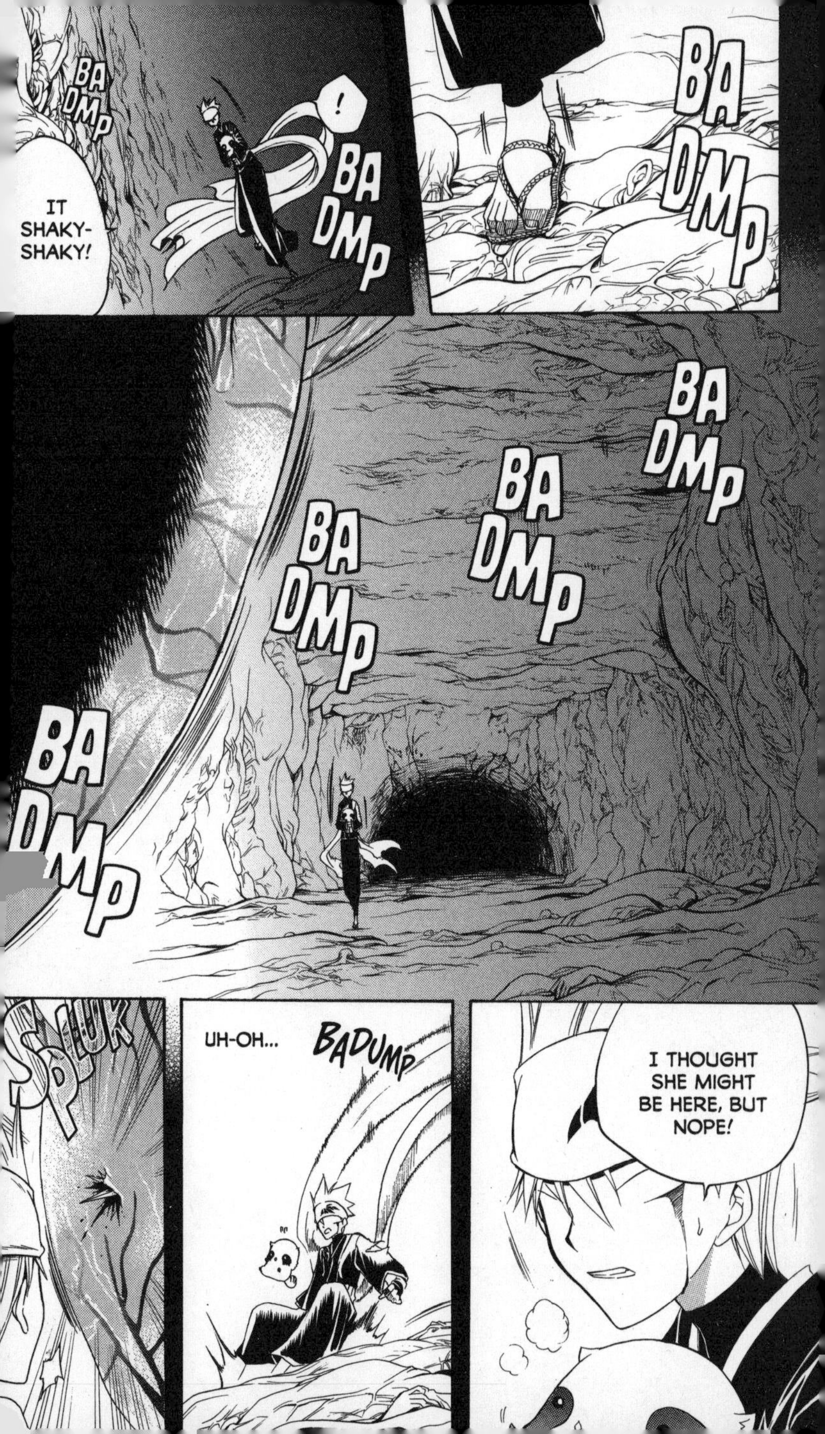
BA DMP
!
BA DMP
BA DMP
IT SHAKY-SHAKY!
BA DMP
BA DMP
BA DMP
BA DMP
I THOUGHT SHE MIGHT BE HERE, BUT NOPE!
BADUMP
UH-OH...
SPLUK

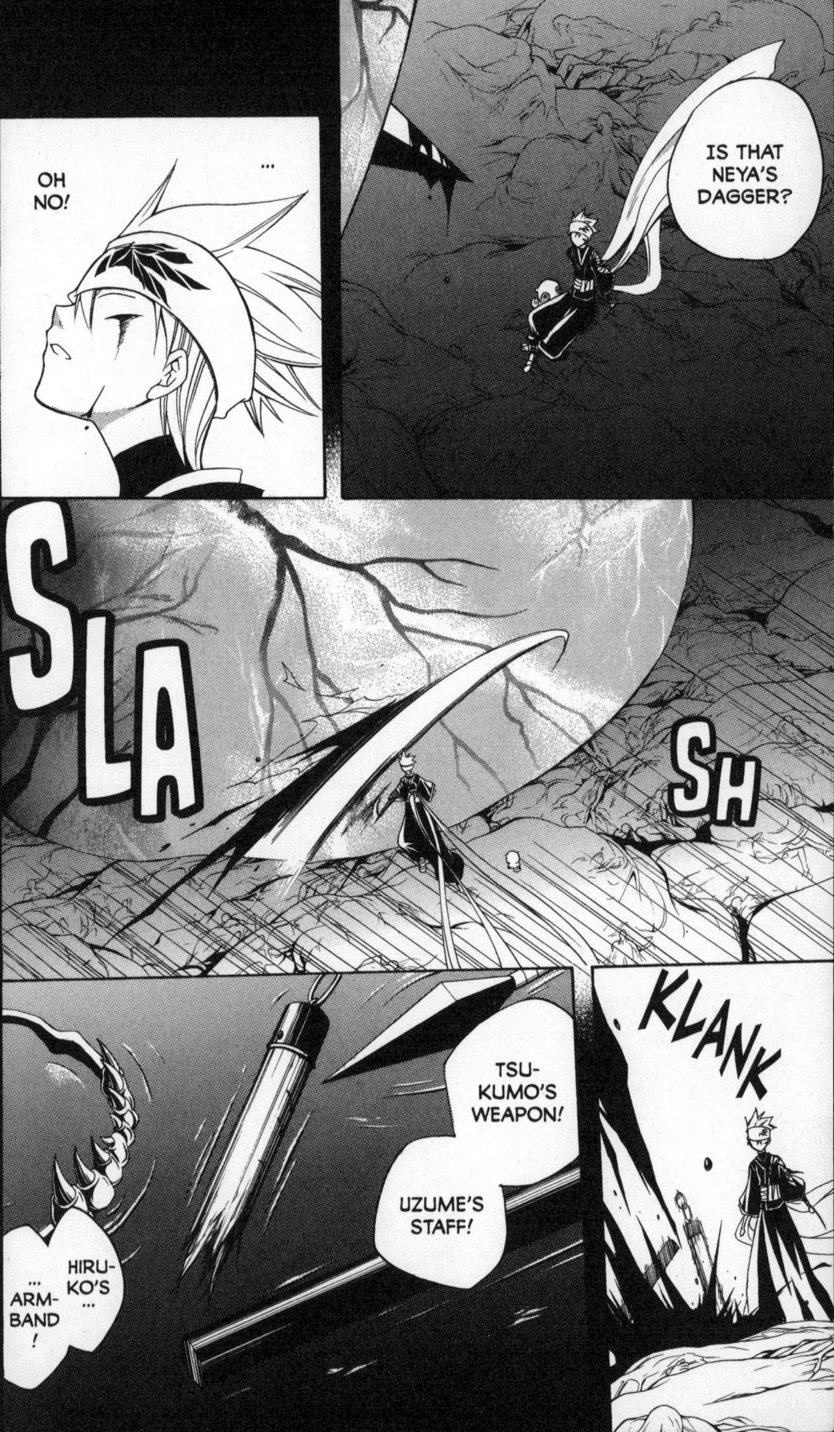
IS THAT NEYA'S DAGGER?
...
OH NO!
SLASH
KLANK
TSU-KUMO'S WEAPON!
UZUME'S STAFF!
HIRU-KO'S ...
... ARM-BAND!

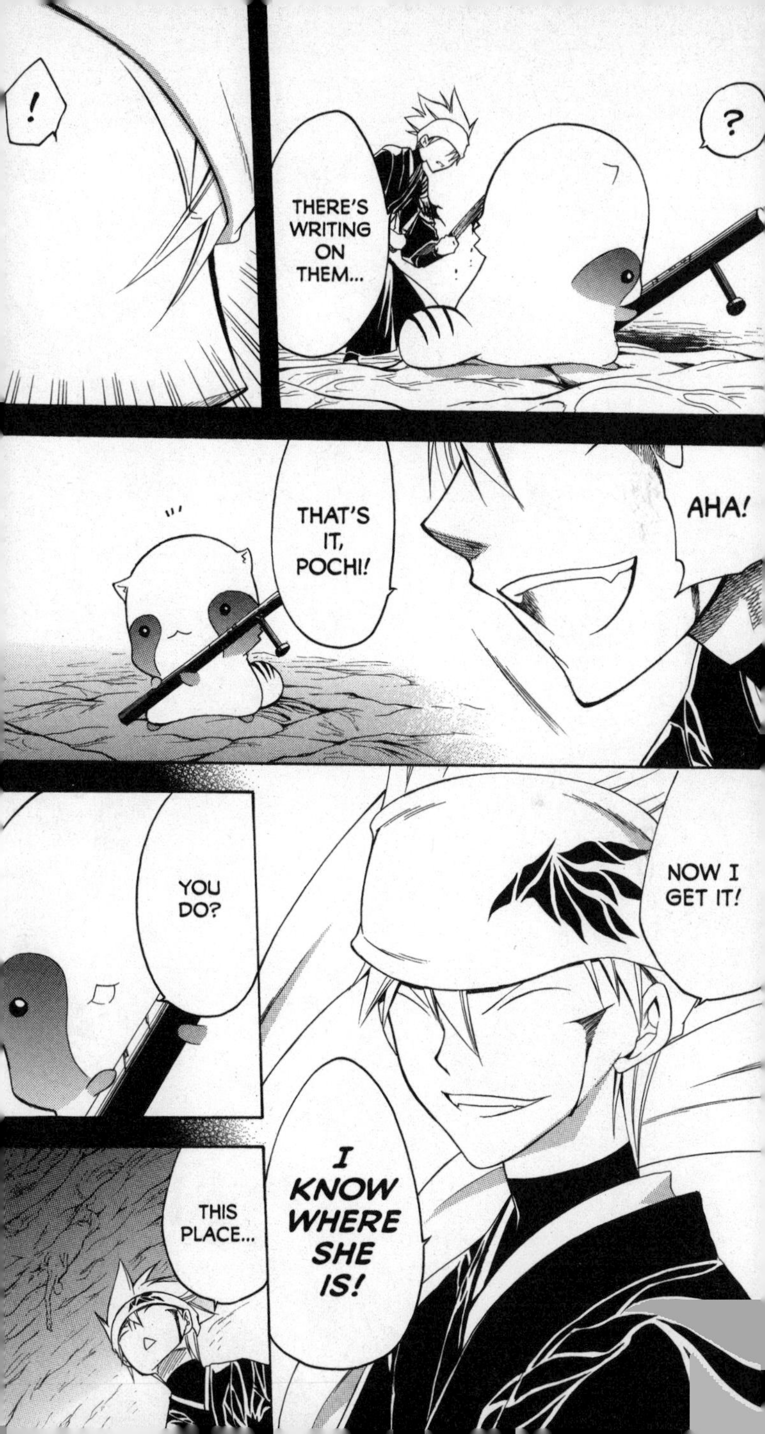
?
THERE'S WRITING ON THEM...
!
AHA!
THAT'S IT, POCHI!
NOW I GET IT!
I KNOW WHERE SHE IS!
YOU DO?
THIS PLACE...

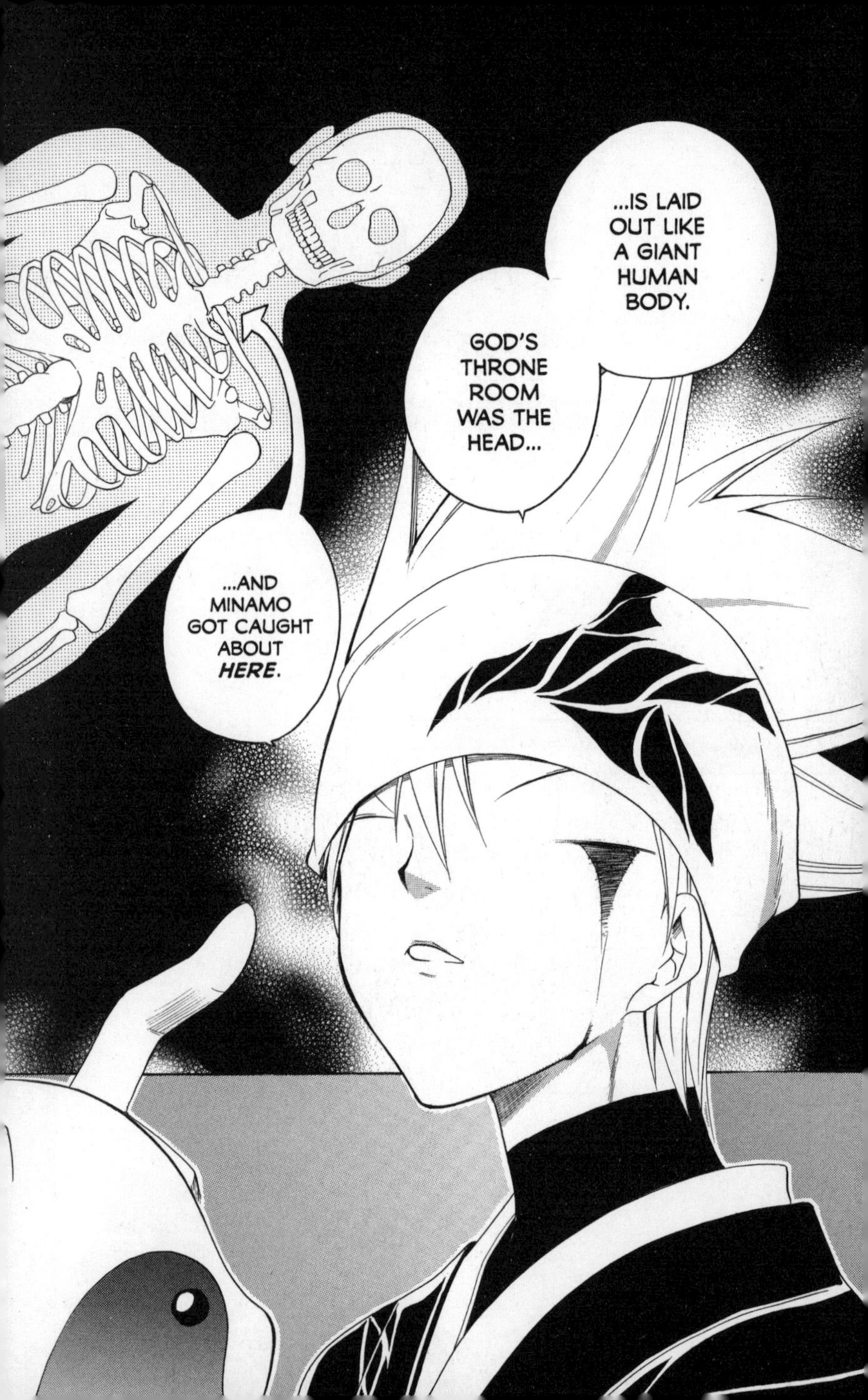
...IS LAID OUT LIKE A GIANT HUMAN BODY.
GOD'S THRONE ROOM WAS THE HEAD...
...AND MINAMO GOT CAUGHT ABOUT *HERE*.

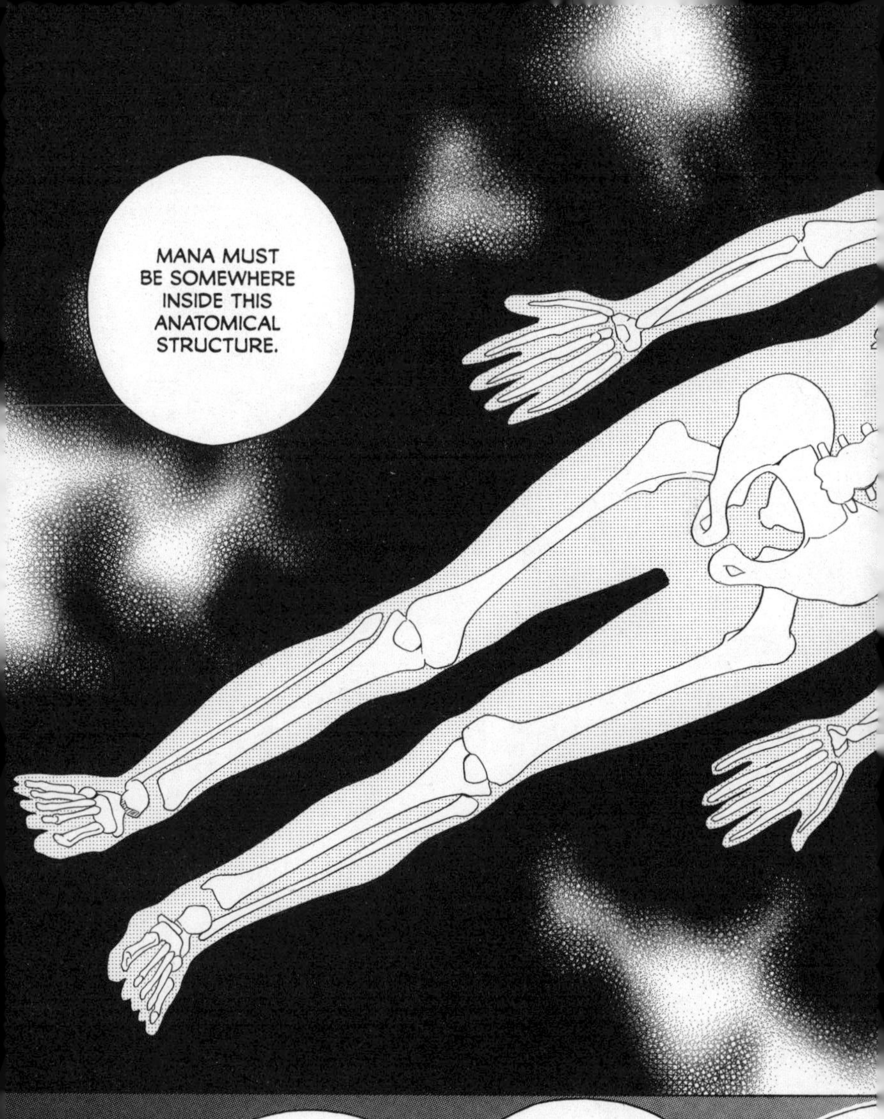
MANA MUST BE SOMEWHERE INSIDE THIS ANATOMICAL STRUCTURE.
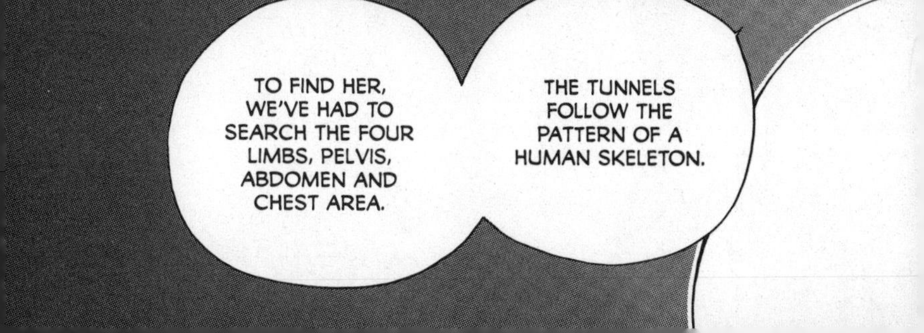
THE TUNNELS FOLLOW THE PATTERN OF A HUMAN SKELETON.
TO FIND HER, WE'VE HAD TO SEARCH THE FOUR LIMBS, PELVIS, ABDOMEN AND CHEST AREA.

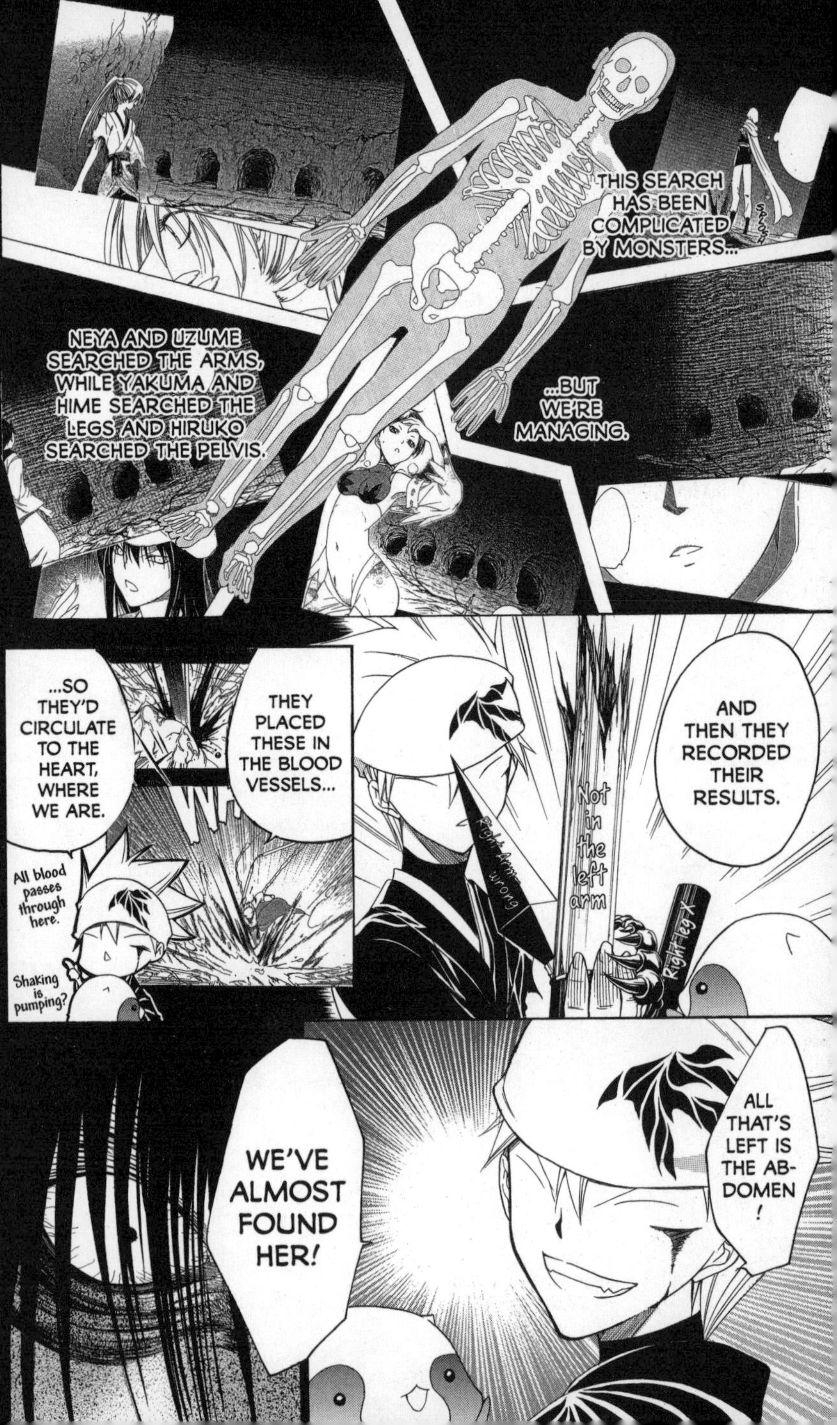
THIS SEARCH HAS BEEN COMPLICATED BY MONSTERS...
SPLOSH
...BUT WE'RE MANAGING.
NEYA AND UZUME SEARCHED THE ARMS, WHILE YAKUMA AND HIME SEARCHED THE LEGS AND HIRUKO SEARCHED THE PELVIS.
AND THEN THEY RECORDED THEIR RESULTS.
Not in the left arm
Right Arm wrong
Right leg X
THEY PLACED THESE IN THE BLOOD VESSELS...
...SO THEY'D CIRCULATE TO THE HEART, WHERE WE ARE.
All blood passes through here.
Shaking is pumping?
ALL THAT'S LEFT IS THE AB-DOMEN!
WE'VE ALMOST FOUND HER!

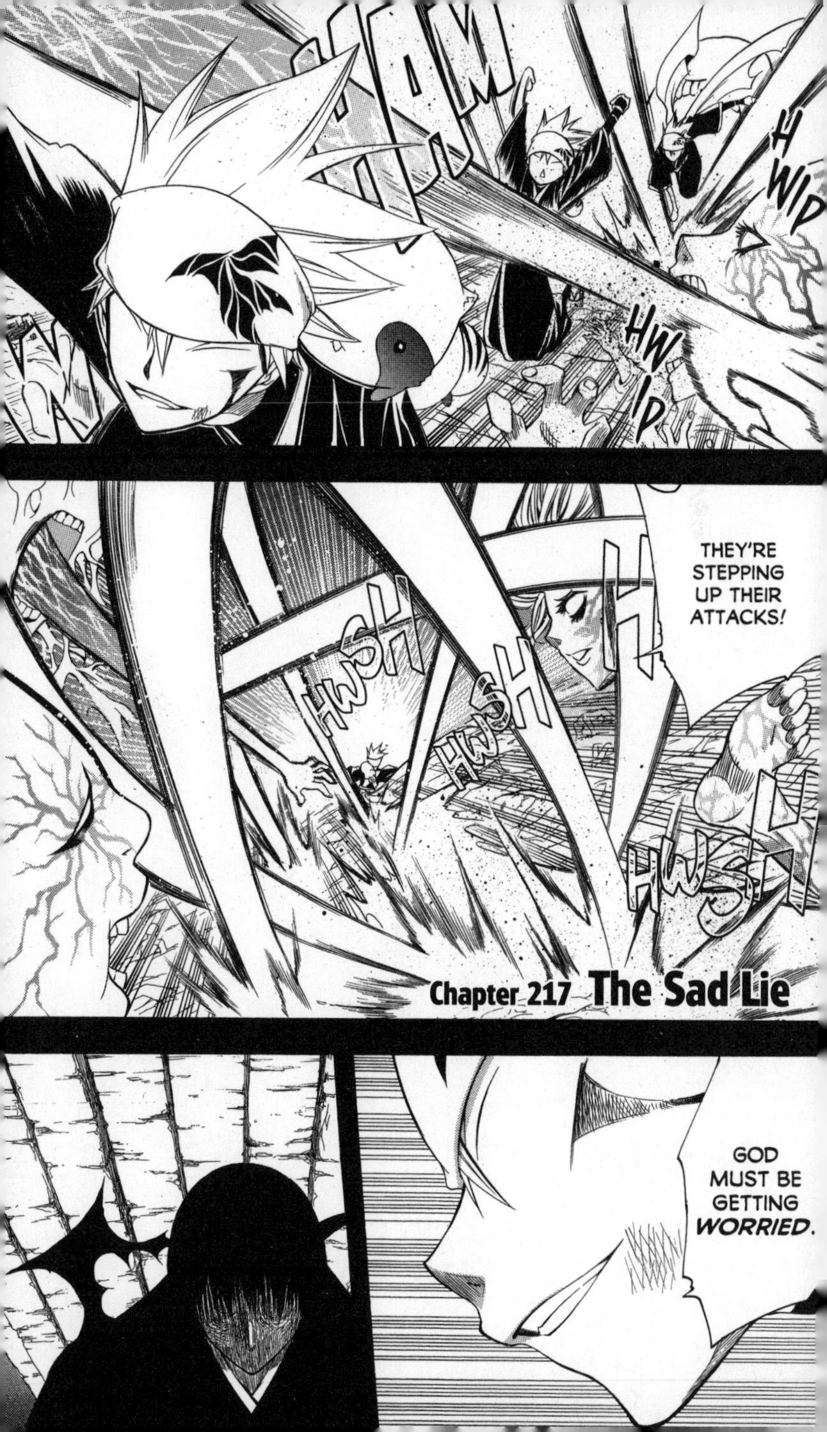
HWIP
HWIP
THEY'RE STEPPING UP THEIR ATTACKS!
HWSH
HWSH
HWSH
HWSH
Chapter 217 The Sad Lie
GOD MUST BE GETTING *WORRIED*.

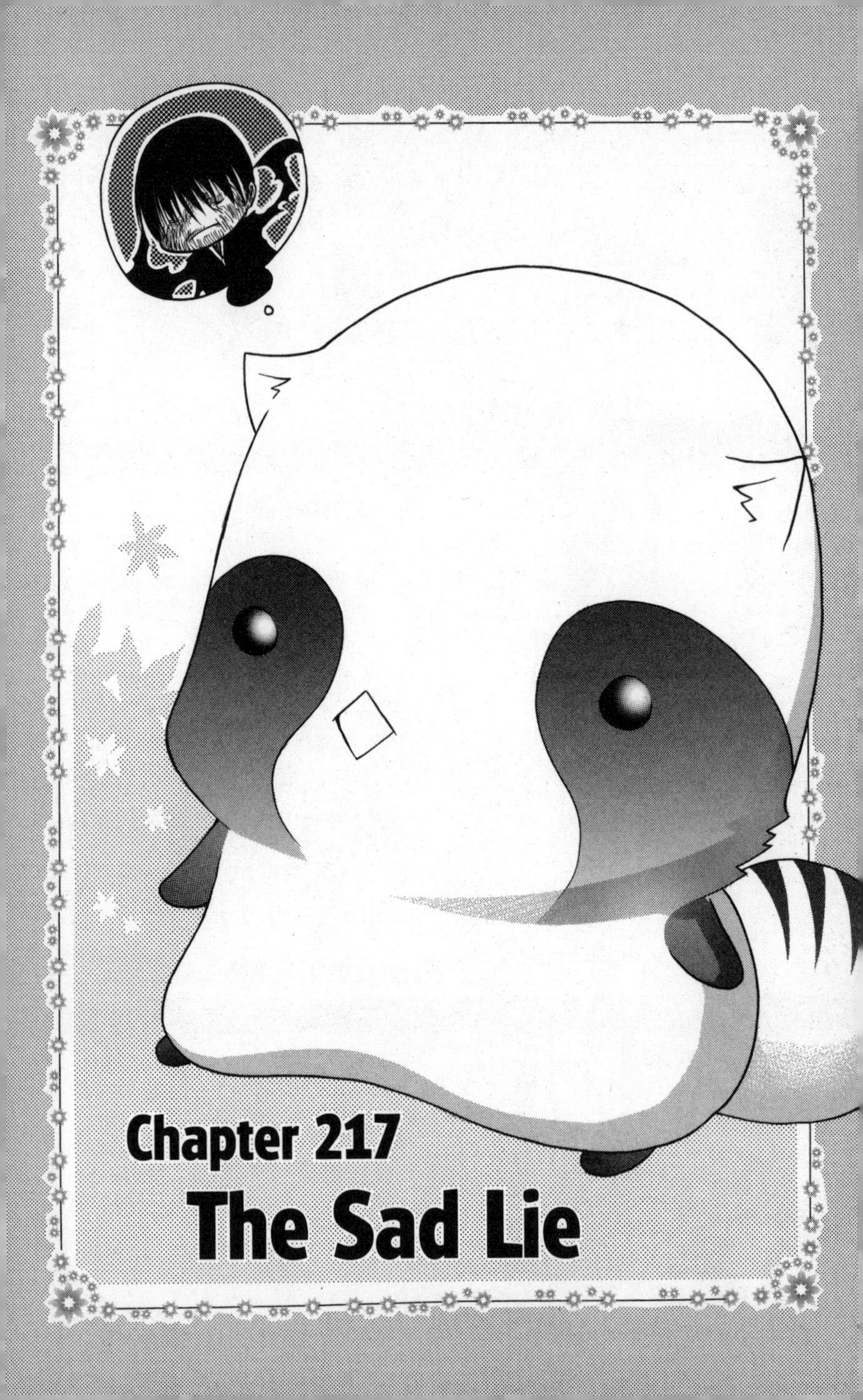

Chapter 217
The Sad Lie

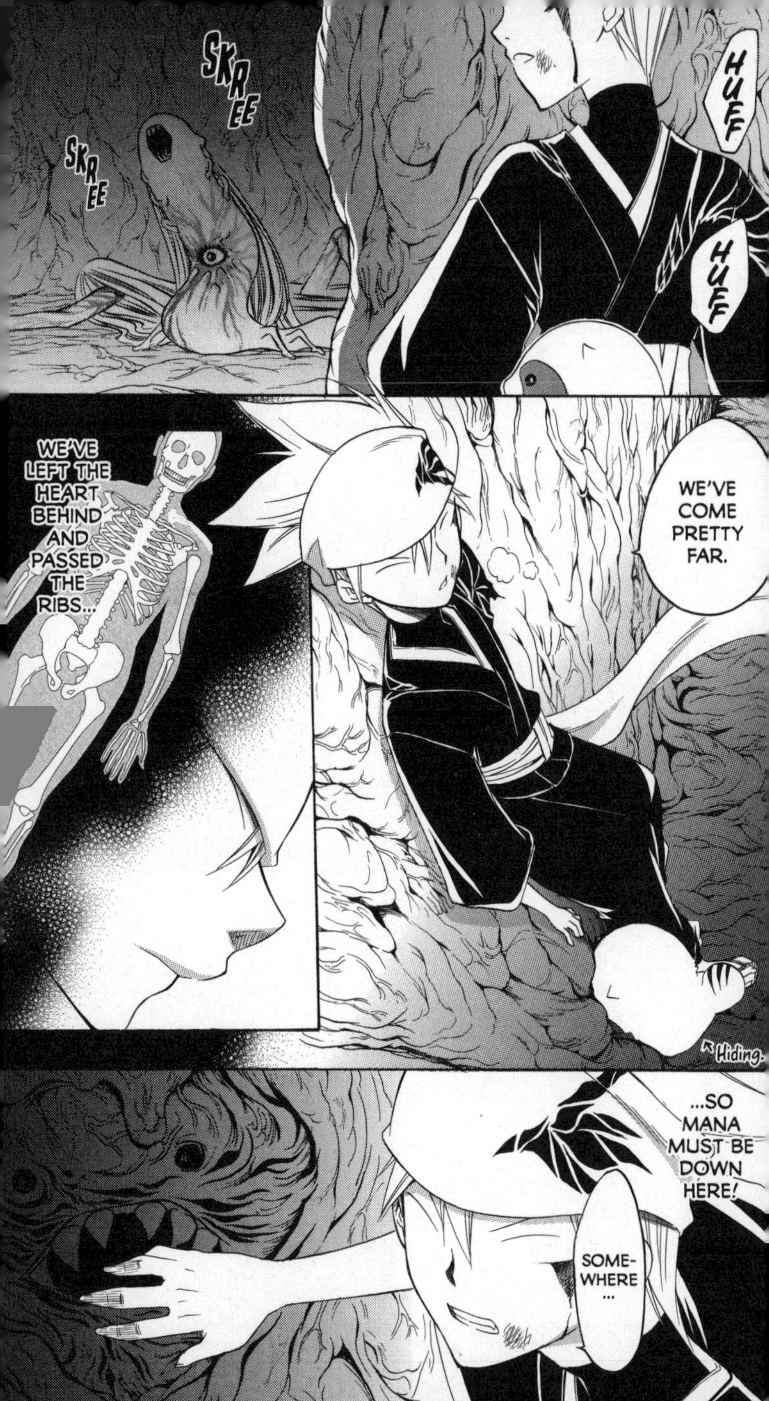
HUFF
HUFF
SKREE
SKREE
WE'VE COME PRETTY FAR.
Hiding.
WE'VE LEFT THE HEART BEHIND AND PASSED THE RIBS...
SOME-WHERE ...
...SO MANA MUST BE DOWN HERE!

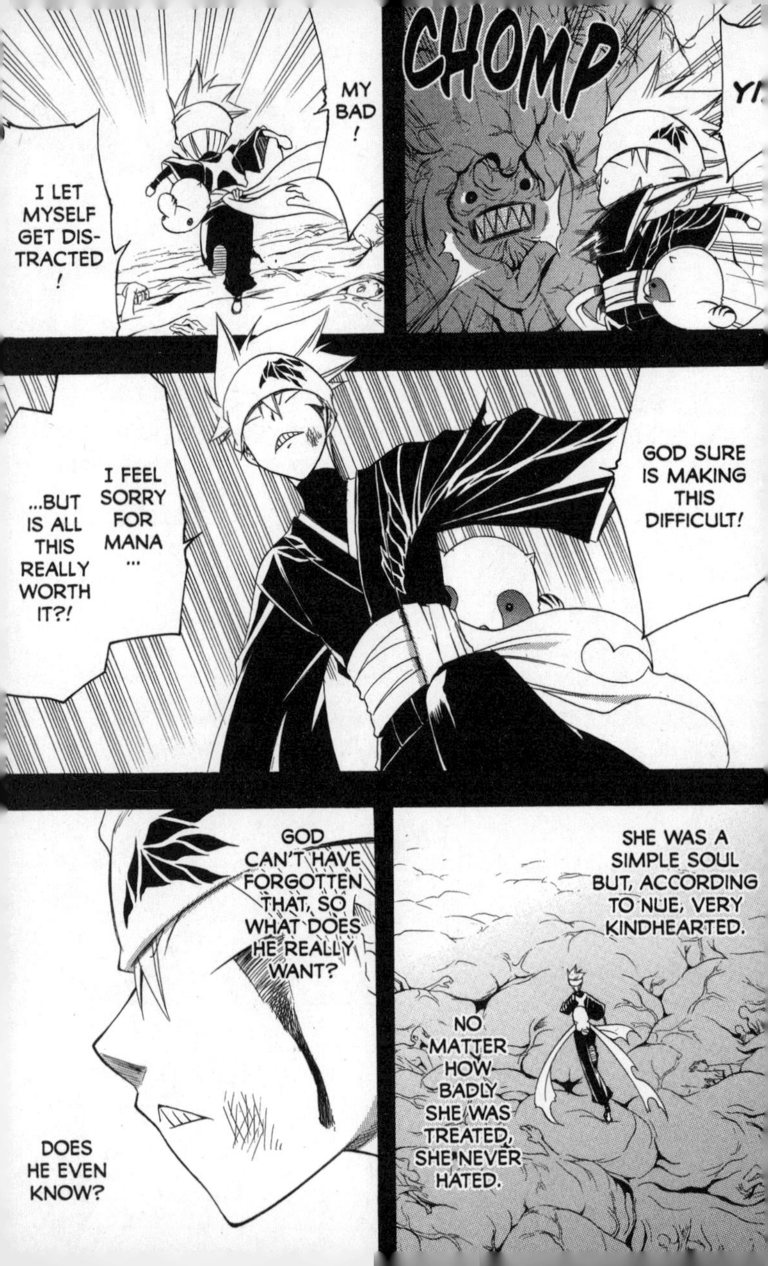
CHOMP
MY BAD!
I LET MYSELF GET DIS-TRACTED!
GOD SURE IS MAKING THIS DIFFICULT!
I FEEL SORRY FOR MANA...
...BUT IS ALL THIS REALLY WORTH IT?!
SHE WAS A SIMPLE SOUL BUT, ACCORDING TO NUE, VERY KINDHEARTED.
NO MATTER HOW BADLY SHE WAS TREATED, SHE NEVER HATED.
GOD CAN'T HAVE FORGOTTEN THAT, SO WHAT DOES HE REALLY WANT?
DOES HE EVEN KNOW?

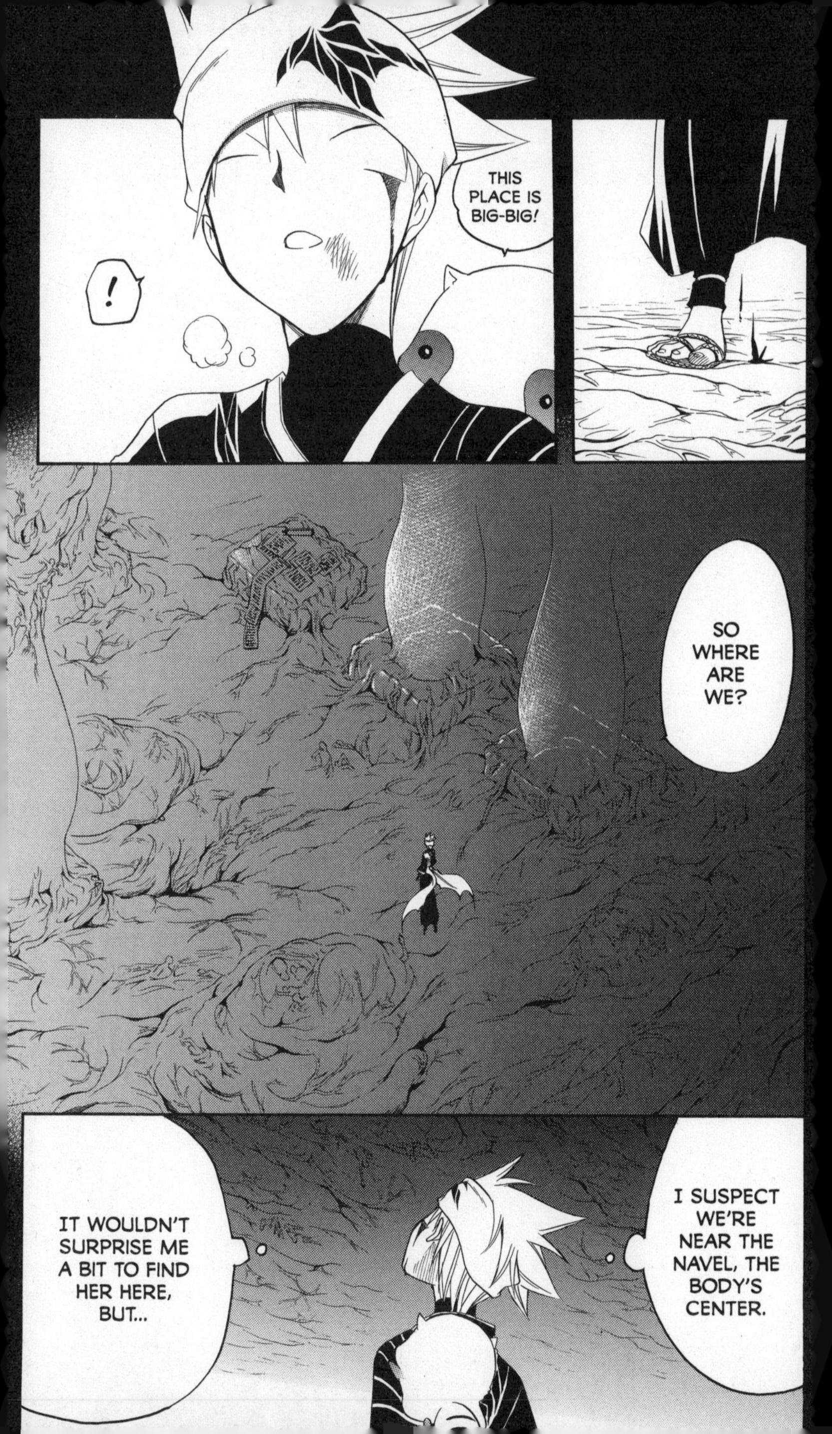
THIS PLACE IS BIG-BIG!
!
SO WHERE ARE WE?
I SUSPECT WE'RE NEAR THE NAVEL, THE BODY'S CENTER.
IT WOULDN'T SURPRISE ME A BIT TO FIND HER HERE, BUT...

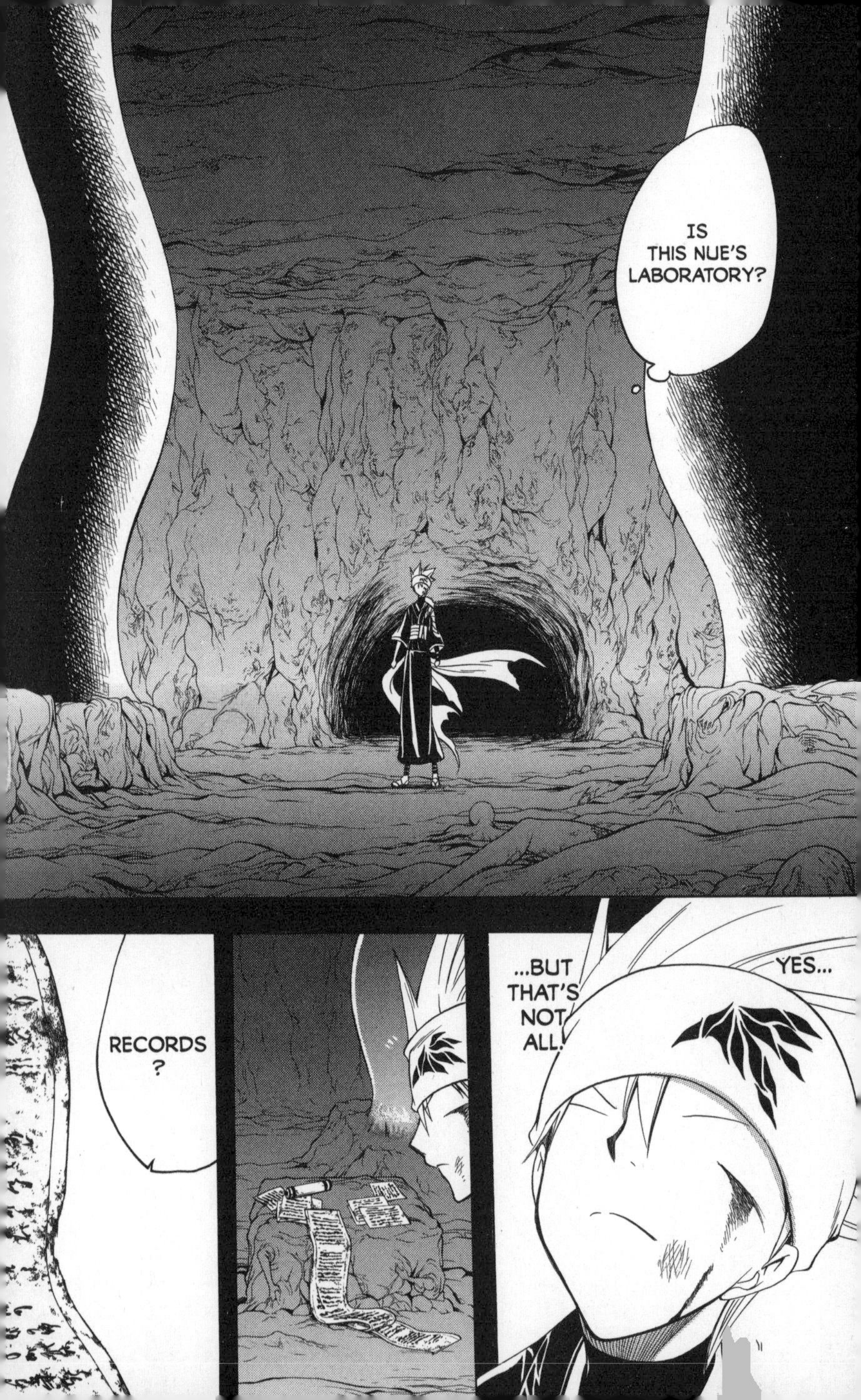
IS THIS NUE'S LABORATORY?
YES...
...BUT THAT'S NOT ALL!
RECORDS ?

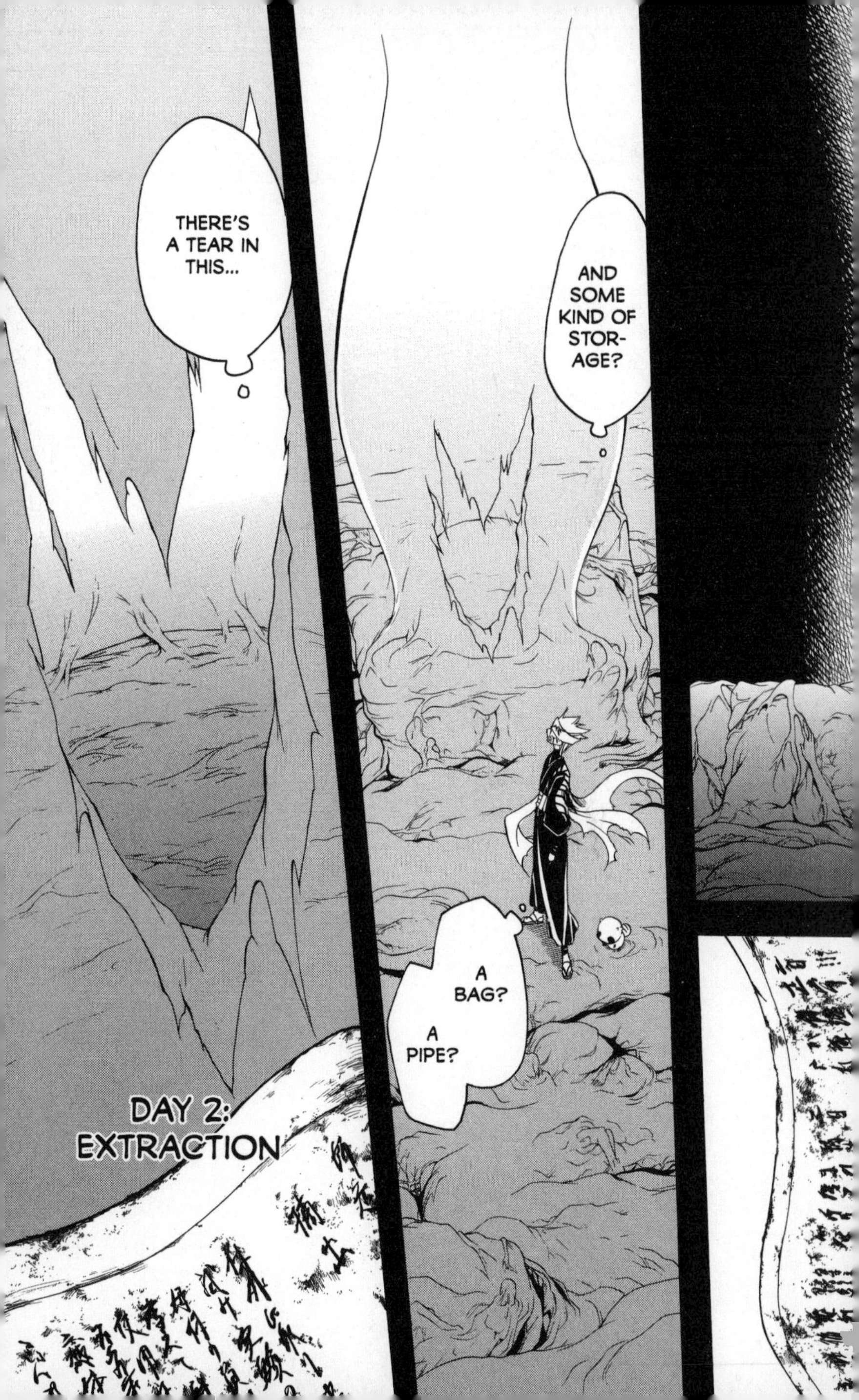
AND SOME KIND OF STOR-AGE?
A BAG? A PIPE?
THERE'S A TEAR IN THIS...
DAY 2: EXTRACTION

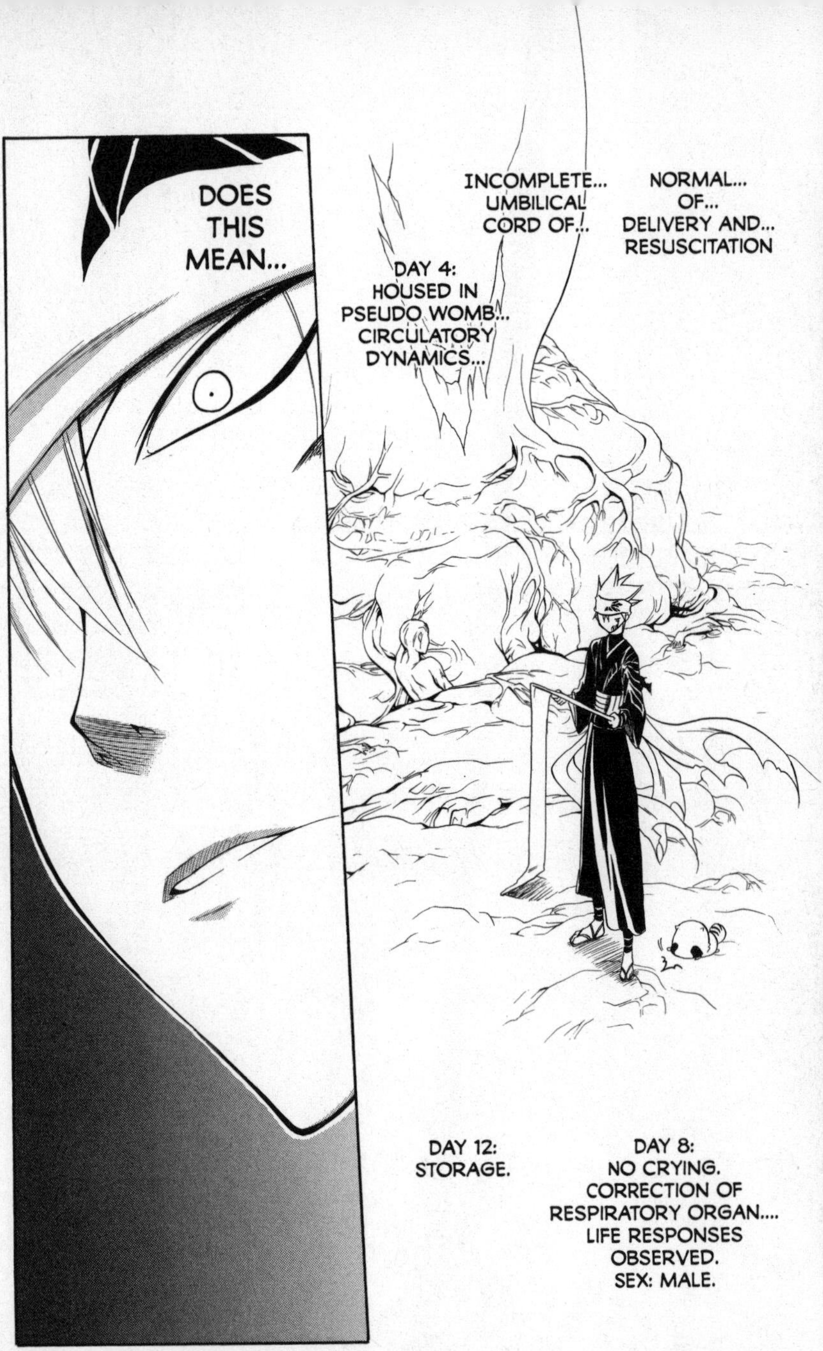
NORMAL... OF... DELIVERY AND... RESUSCITATION
INCOMPLETE... UMBILICAL CORD OF...
DAY 4: HOUSED IN PSEUDO WOMB... CIRCULATORY DYNAMICS...
DAY 8: NO CRYING. CORRECTION OF RESPIRATORY ORGAN.... LIFE RESPONSES OBSERVED. SEX: MALE.
DAY 12: STORAGE.
DOES THIS MEAN...

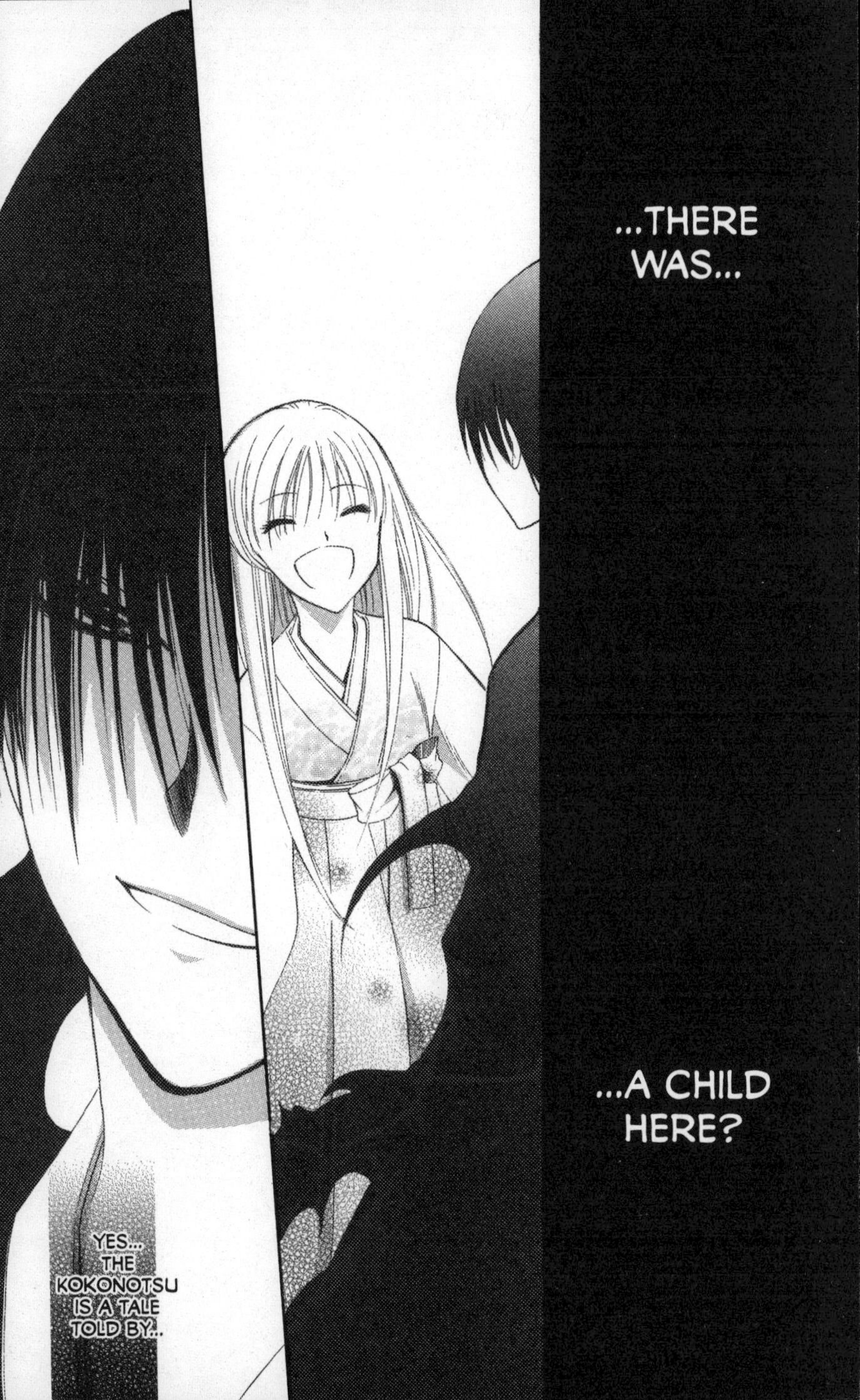
...THERE WAS...
...A CHILD HERE?
YES... THE KOKONOTSU IS A TALE TOLD BY...

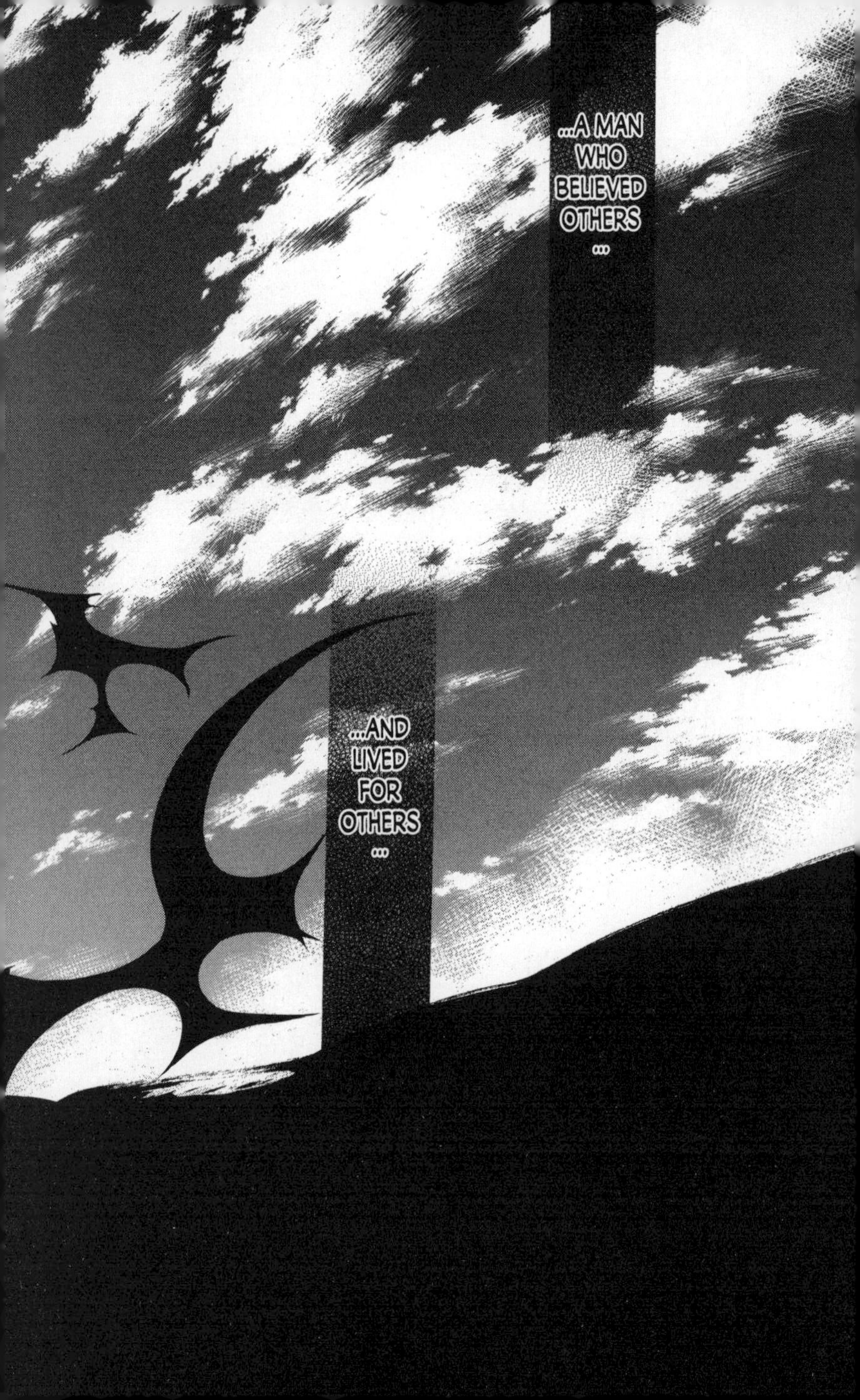
...A MAN WHO BELIEVED OTHERS ...
...AND LIVED FOR OTHERS ...

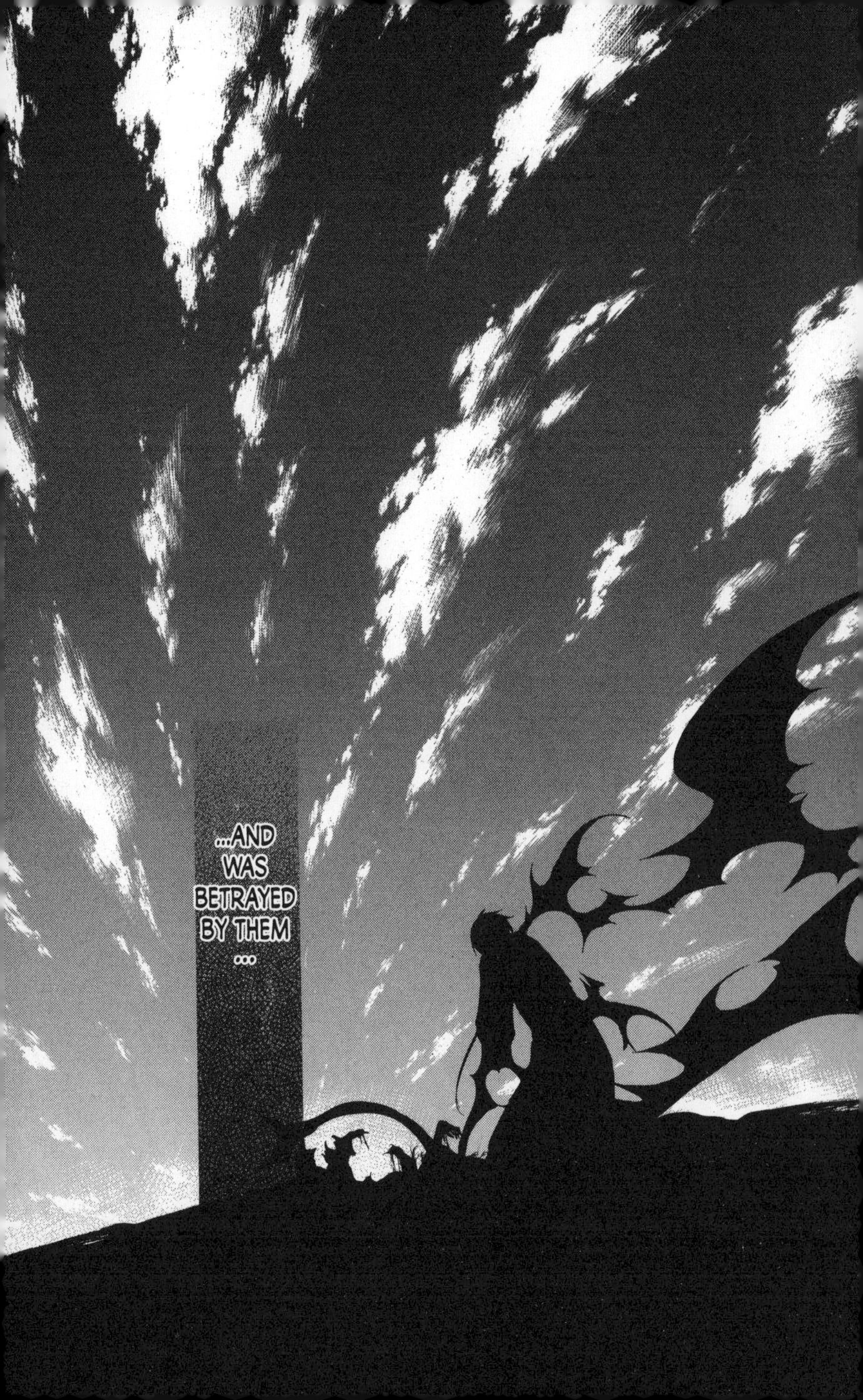
...AND WAS BETRAYED BY THEM ...

...AND IT'S A LIE HE CLINGS TO.

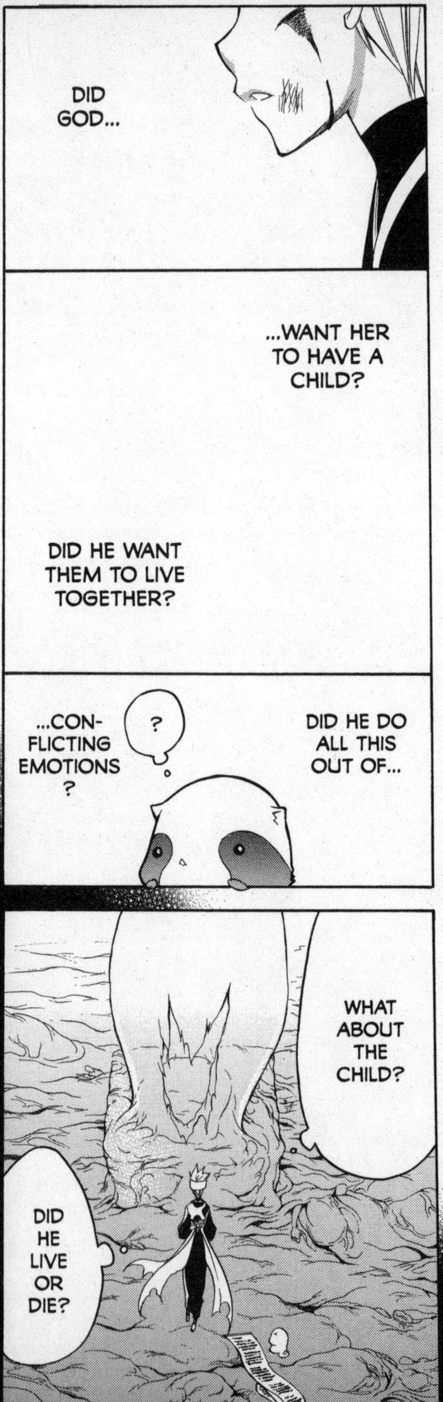
DID GOD...
...WANT HER TO HAVE A CHILD?
DID HE WANT THEM TO LIVE TOGETHER?
DID HE DO ALL THIS OUT OF...
?
...CON-FLICTING EMOTIONS?
WHAT ABOUT THE CHILD?
DID HE LIVE OR DIE?

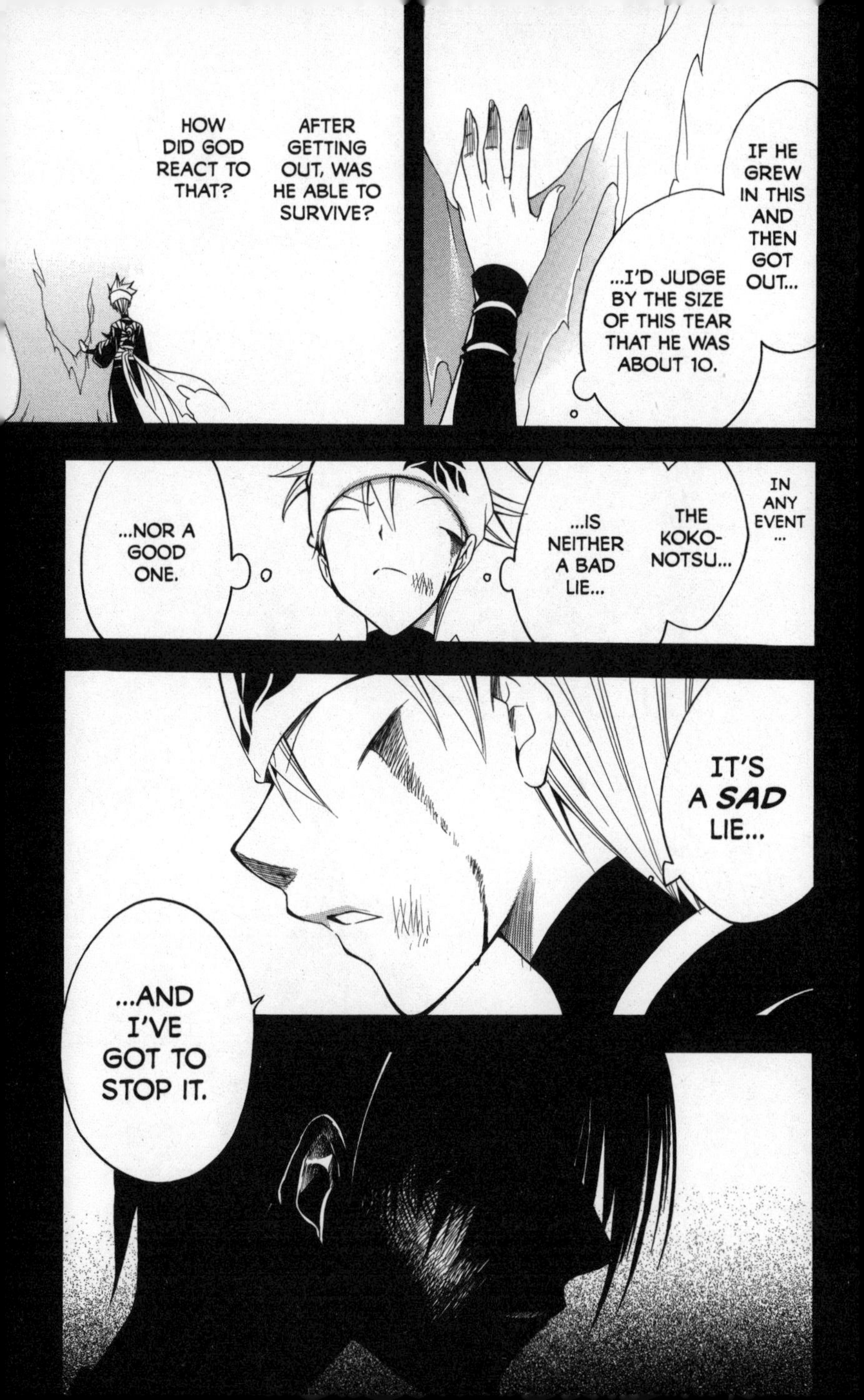
IF HE GREW IN THIS AND THEN GOT OUT...
...I'D JUDGE BY THE SIZE OF THIS TEAR THAT HE WAS ABOUT 10.
AFTER GETTING OUT, WAS HE ABLE TO SURVIVE?
HOW DID GOD REACT TO THAT?
IN ANY EVENT...
THE KOKO-NOTSU...
...IS NEITHER A BAD LIE...
...NOR A GOOD ONE.
IT'S A *SAD* LIE...
...AND I'VE GOT TO STOP IT.

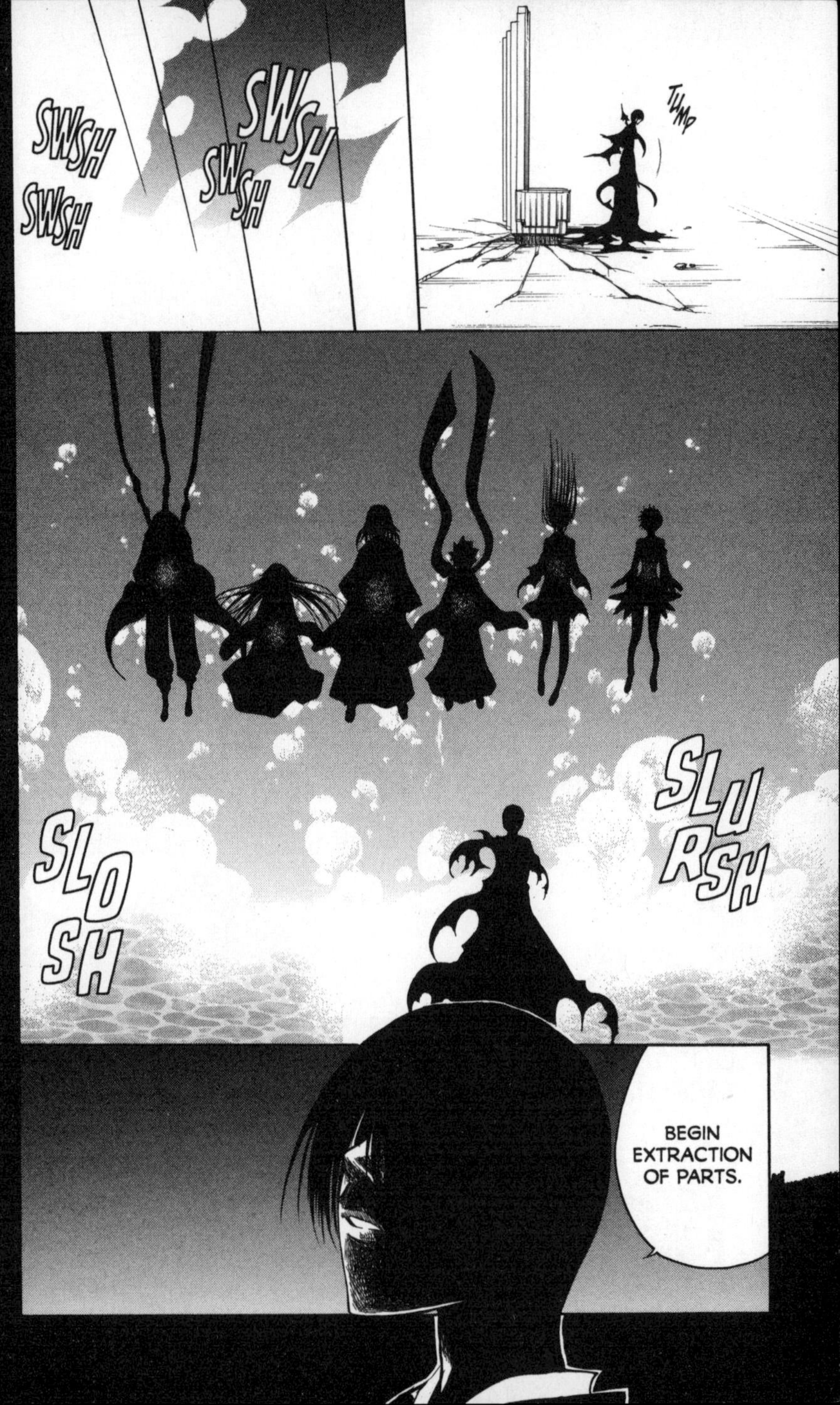

TUMP
SWSH
SWSH
SWSH
SWSH
SLURSH
SLOSH
BEGIN EXTRACTION OF PARTS.

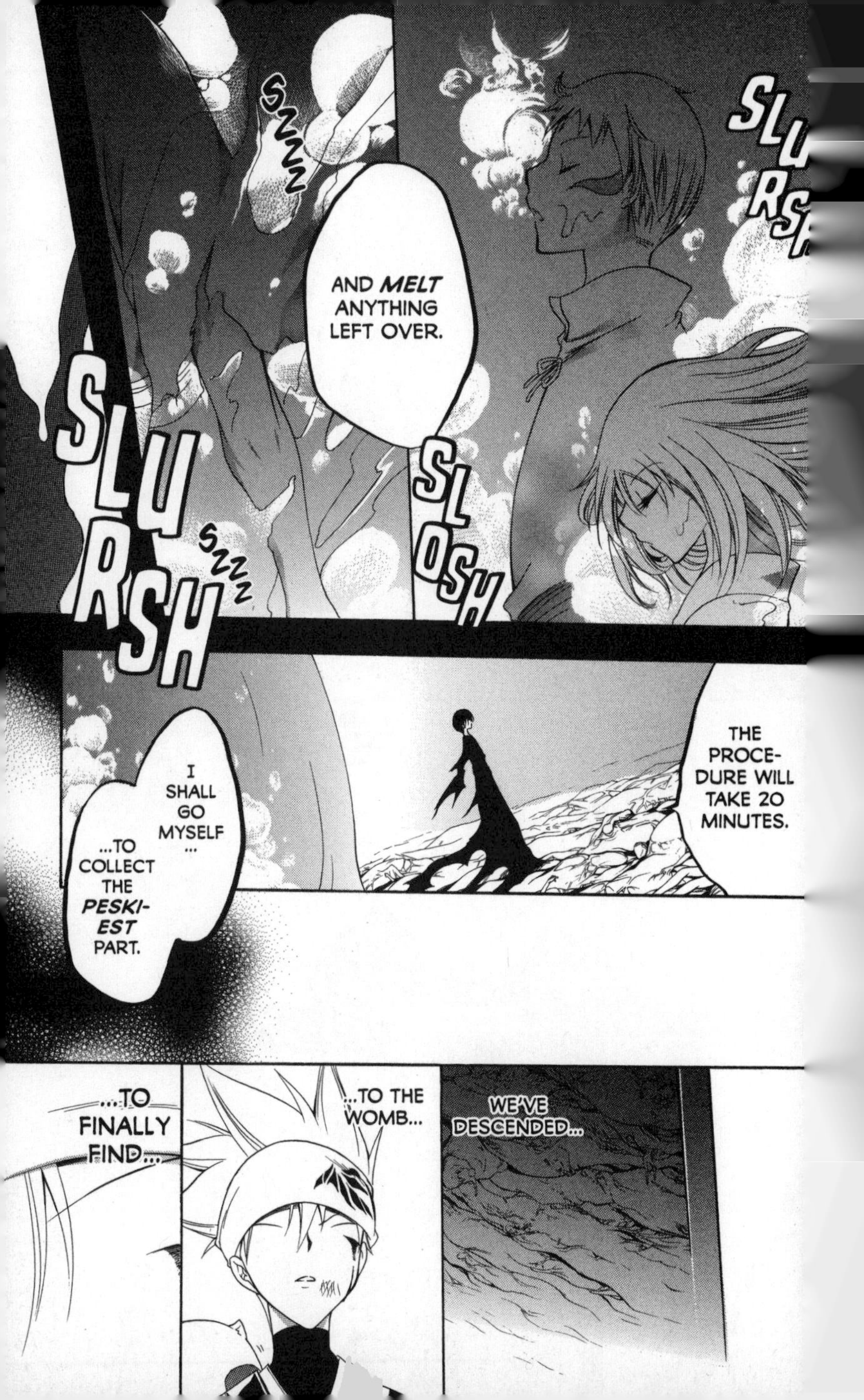
SLURS
AND *MELT* ANYTHING LEFT OVER.
SLOSH
SZZZ
SLURSH
SZZZ
THE PROCE-DURE WILL TAKE 20 MINUTES.
I SHALL GO MYSELF ...
...TO COLLECT THE *PESKI-EST* PART.
WE'VE DESCENDED...
...TO THE WOMB...
...TO FINALLY FIND...

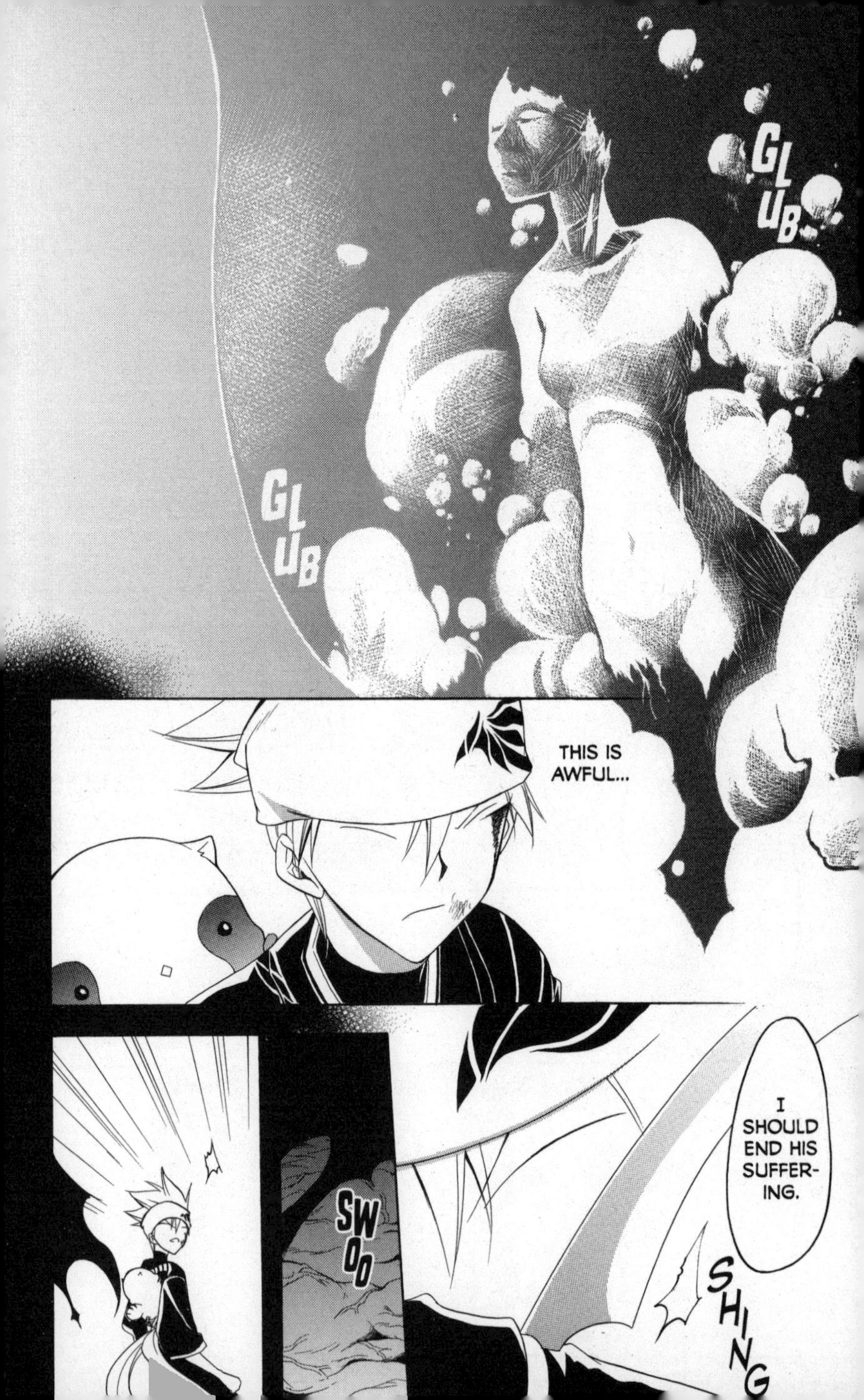
GLUB
GLUB
THIS IS AWFUL...
I SHOULD END HIS SUFFER-ING.
SHING
SWOO

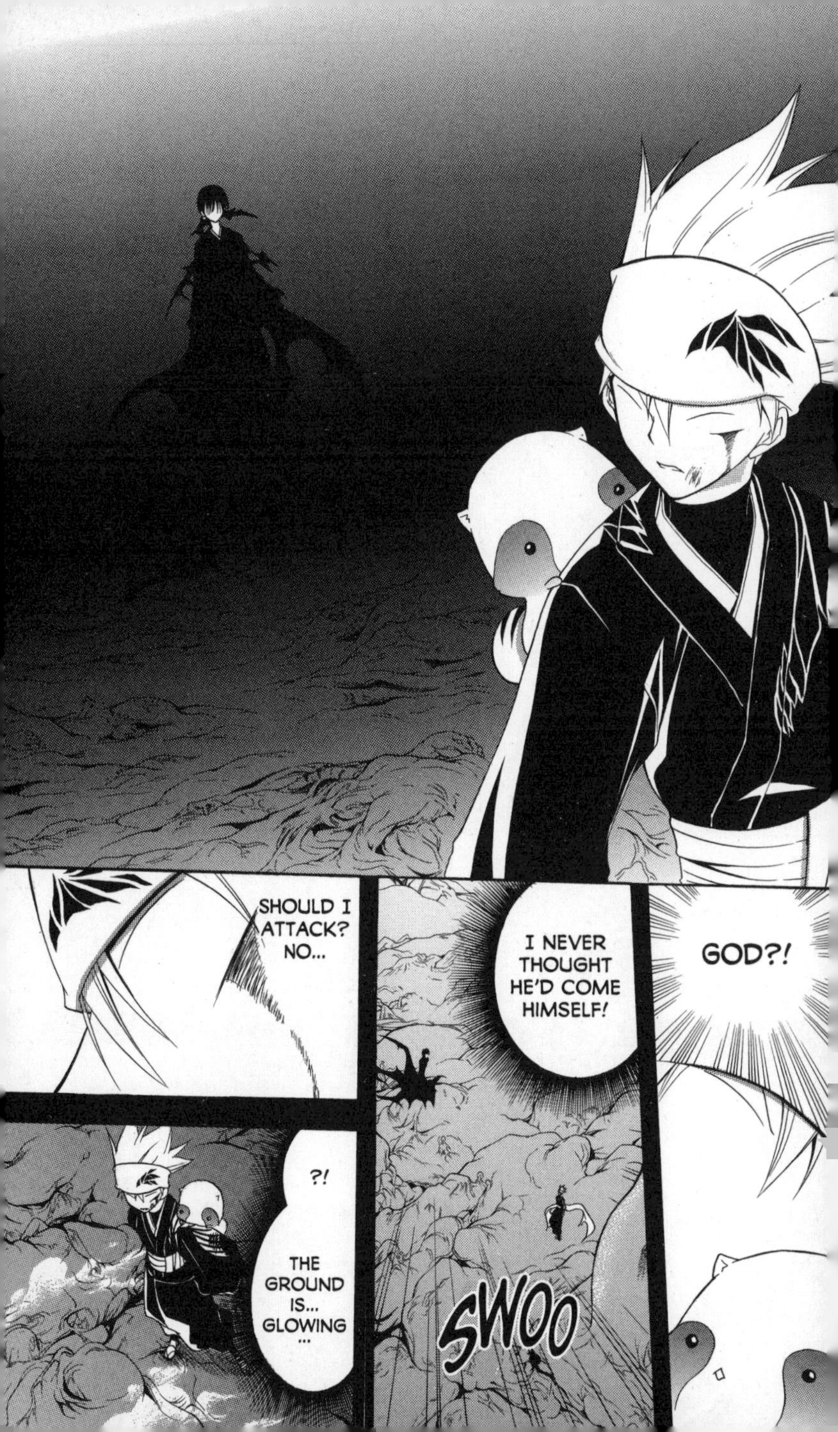
GOD?!
I NEVER THOUGHT HE'D COME HIMSELF!
SWOO
SHOULD I ATTACK? NO...
?!
THE GROUND IS... GLOWING...

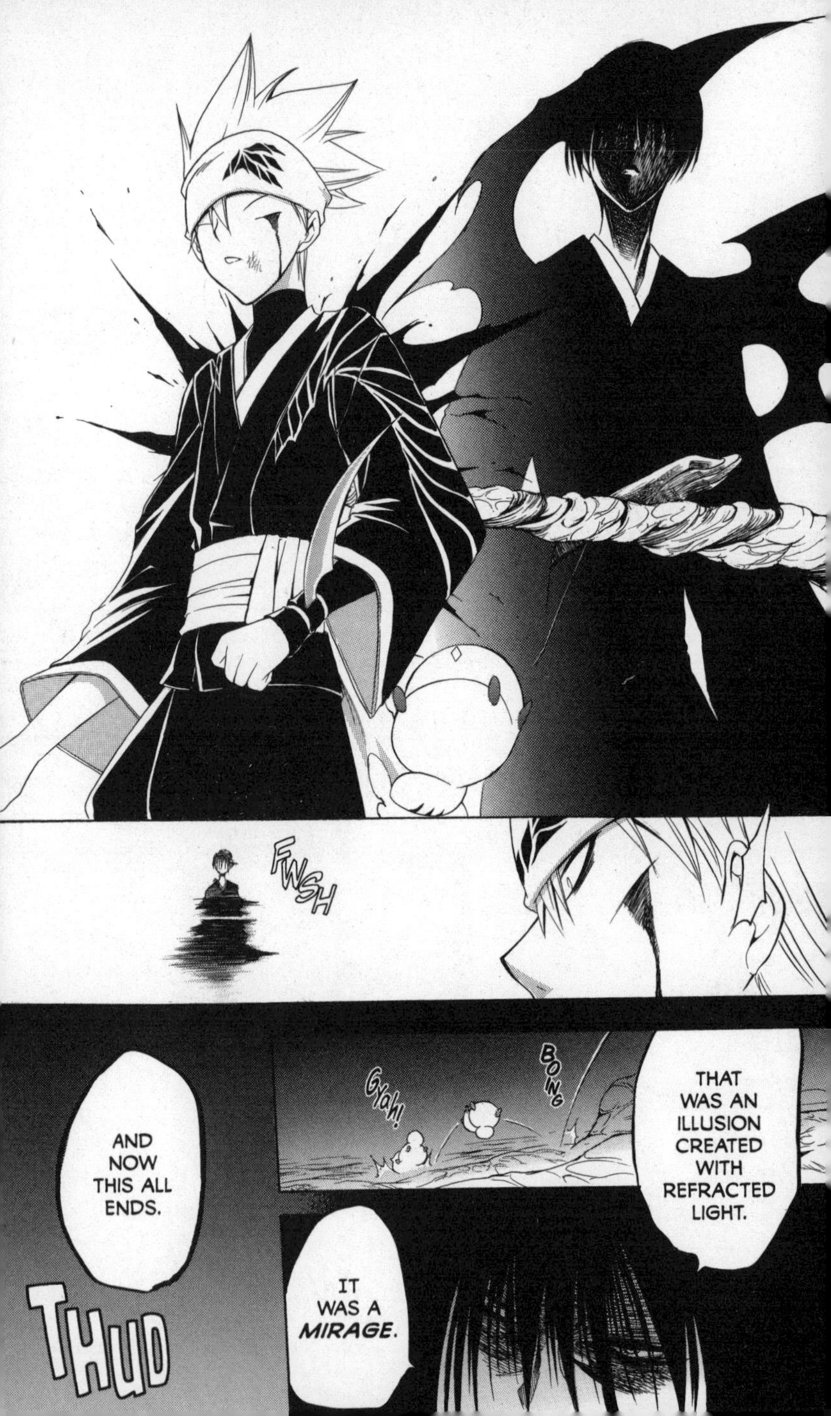
FWSH
THAT WAS AN ILLUSION CREATED WITH REFRACTED LIGHT.
BOING
Gyah!
IT WAS A MIRAGE.
AND NOW THIS ALL ENDS.
THUD

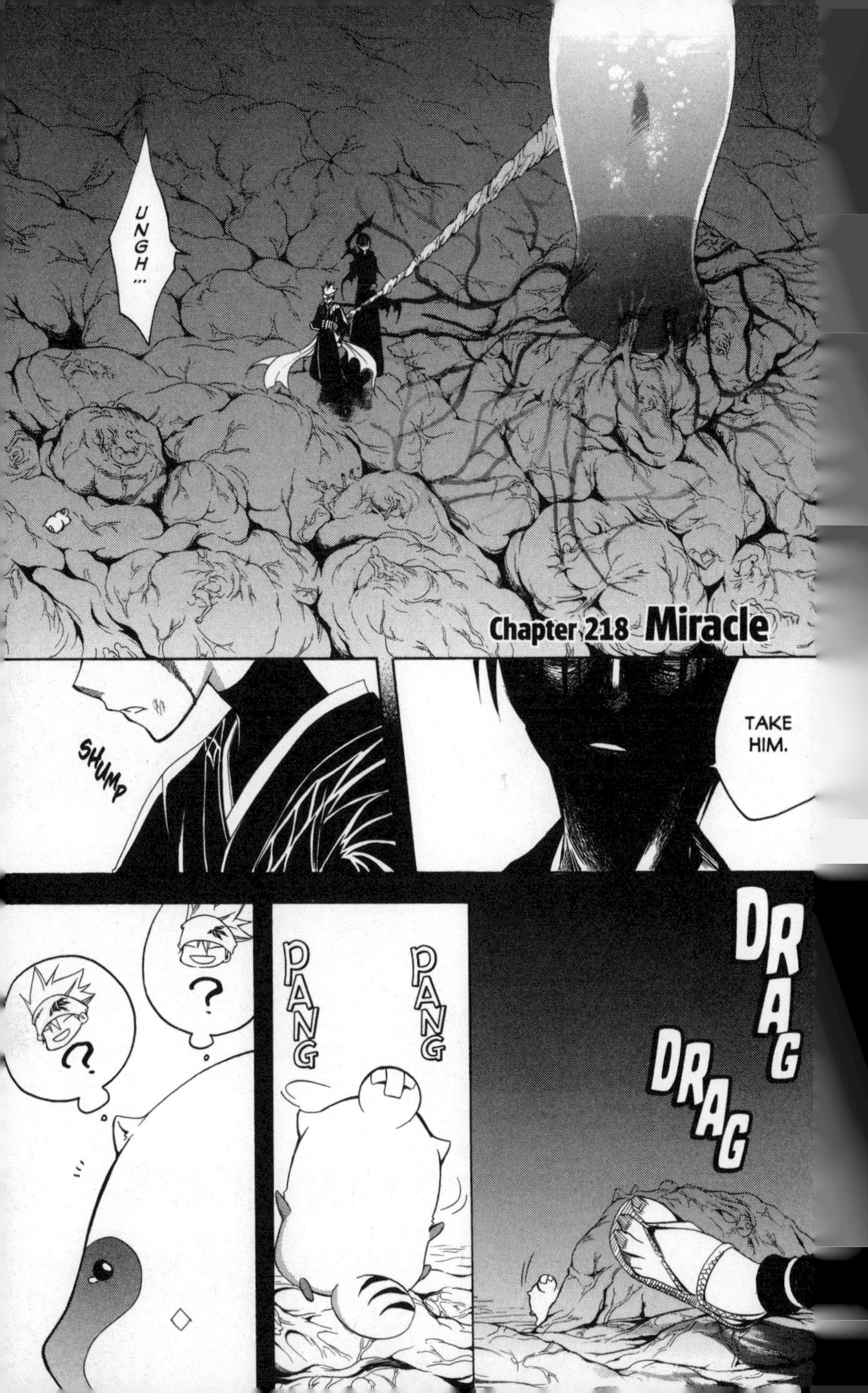
UNGH...
Chapter 218 Miracle
TAKE HIM.
SHUMP
DRAG
DRAG
PANG
PANG
?
?

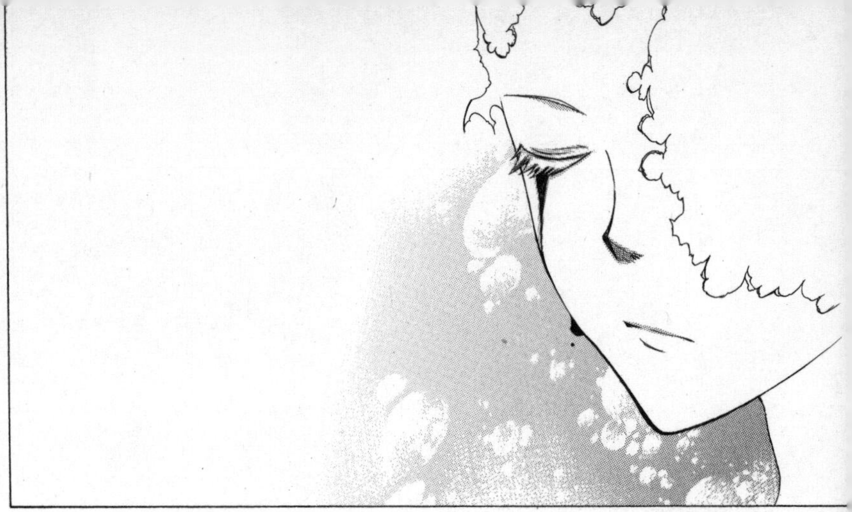

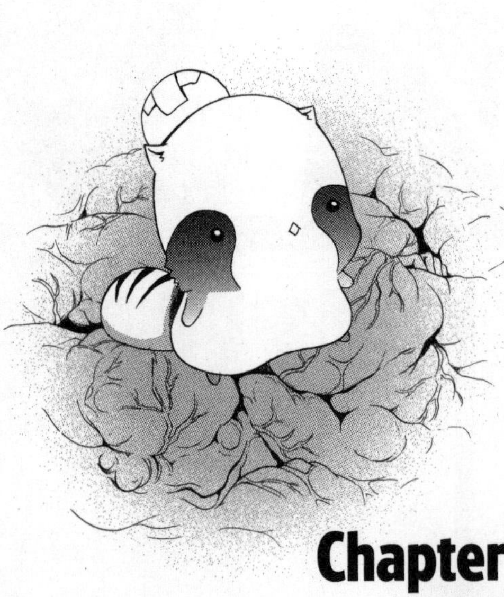

Chapter 218
Miracle

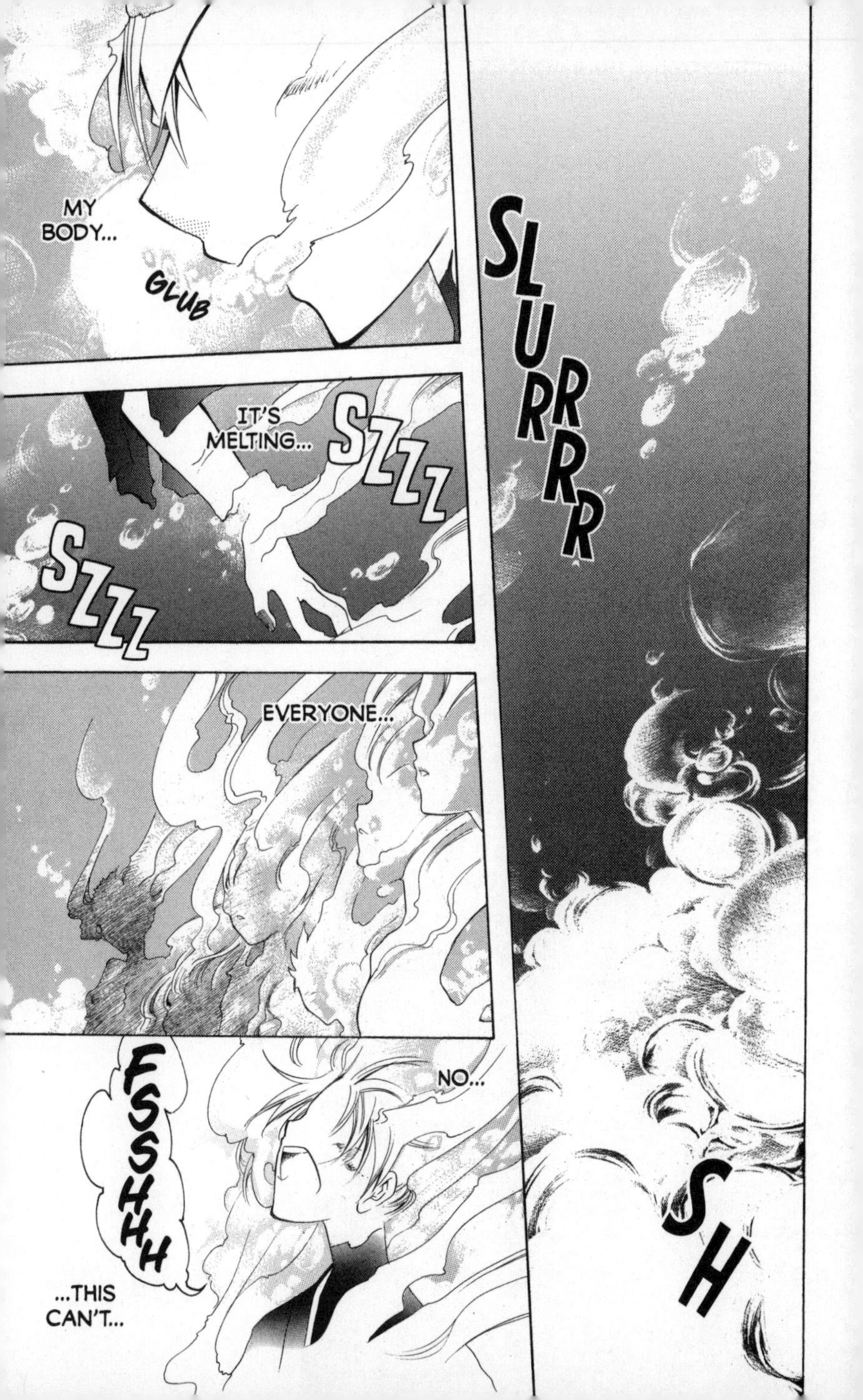
SLURRRR
MY BODY...
GLUB
IT'S MELTING...
SZZZ
SZZZ
EVERYONE...
NO...
FSSHHH
...THIS CAN'T...
SH

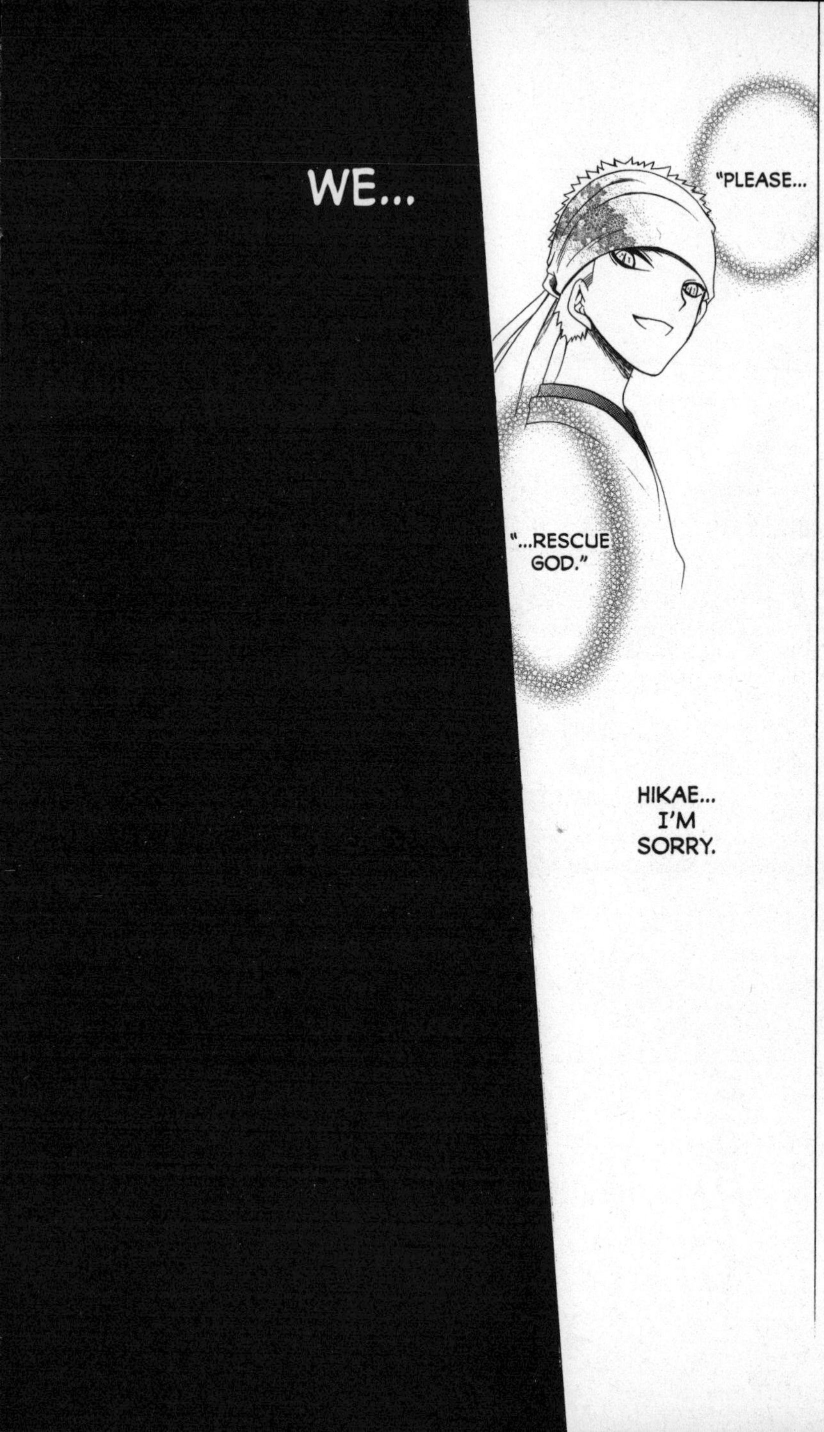
"PLEASE...
"...RESCUE GOD."
HIKAE... I'M SORRY.
WE...

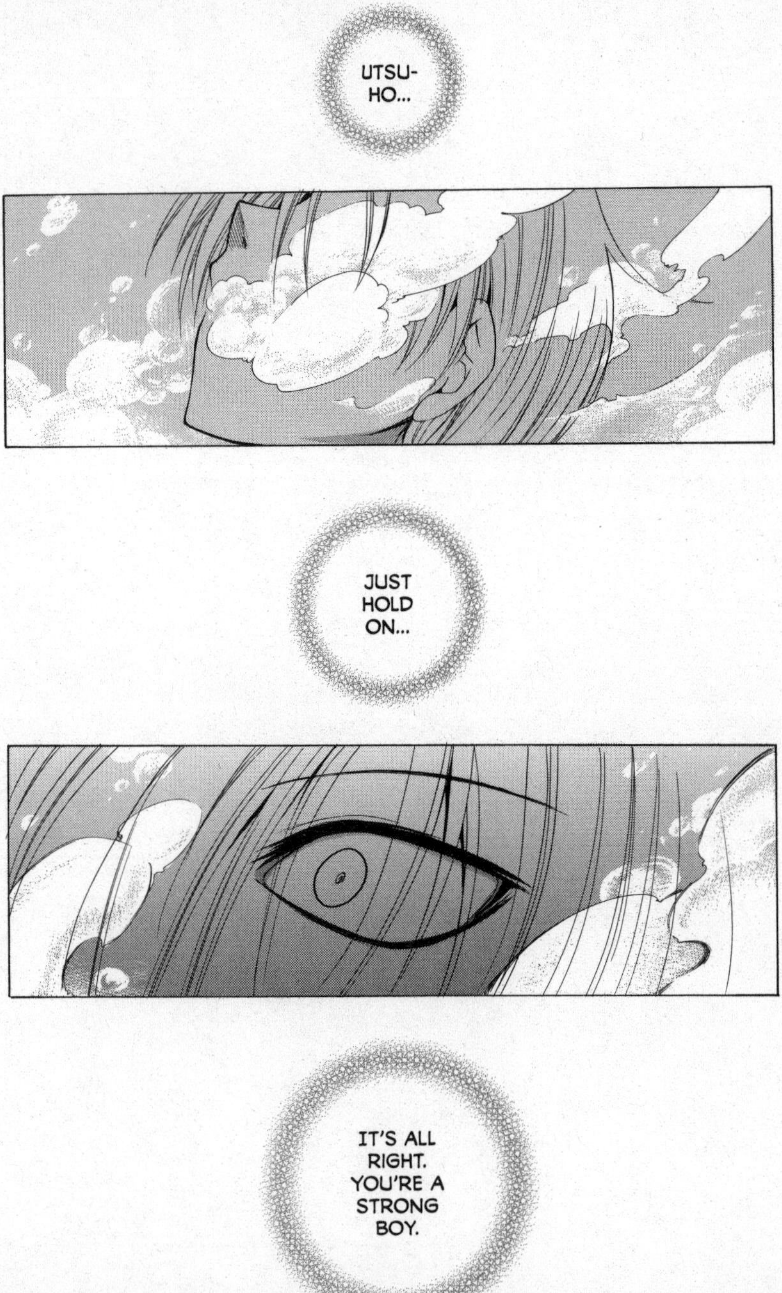
UTSU-HO...
JUST HOLD ON...
IT'S ALL RIGHT. YOU'RE A STRONG BOY.

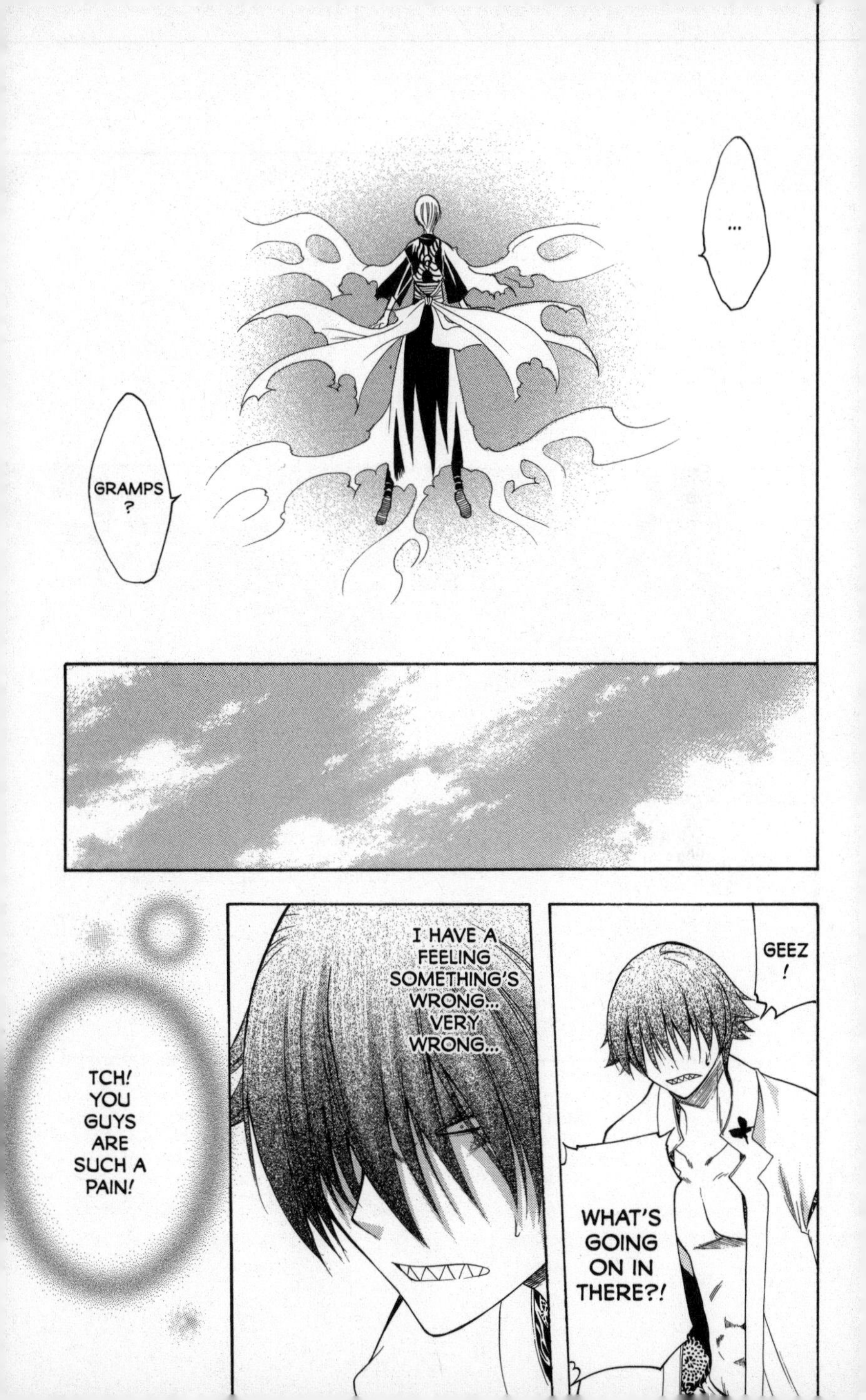
...
GRAMPS?
GEEZ!
WHAT'S GOING ON IN THERE?!
I HAVE A FEELING SOMETHING'S WRONG... VERY WRONG...
TCH! YOU GUYS ARE SUCH A PAIN!

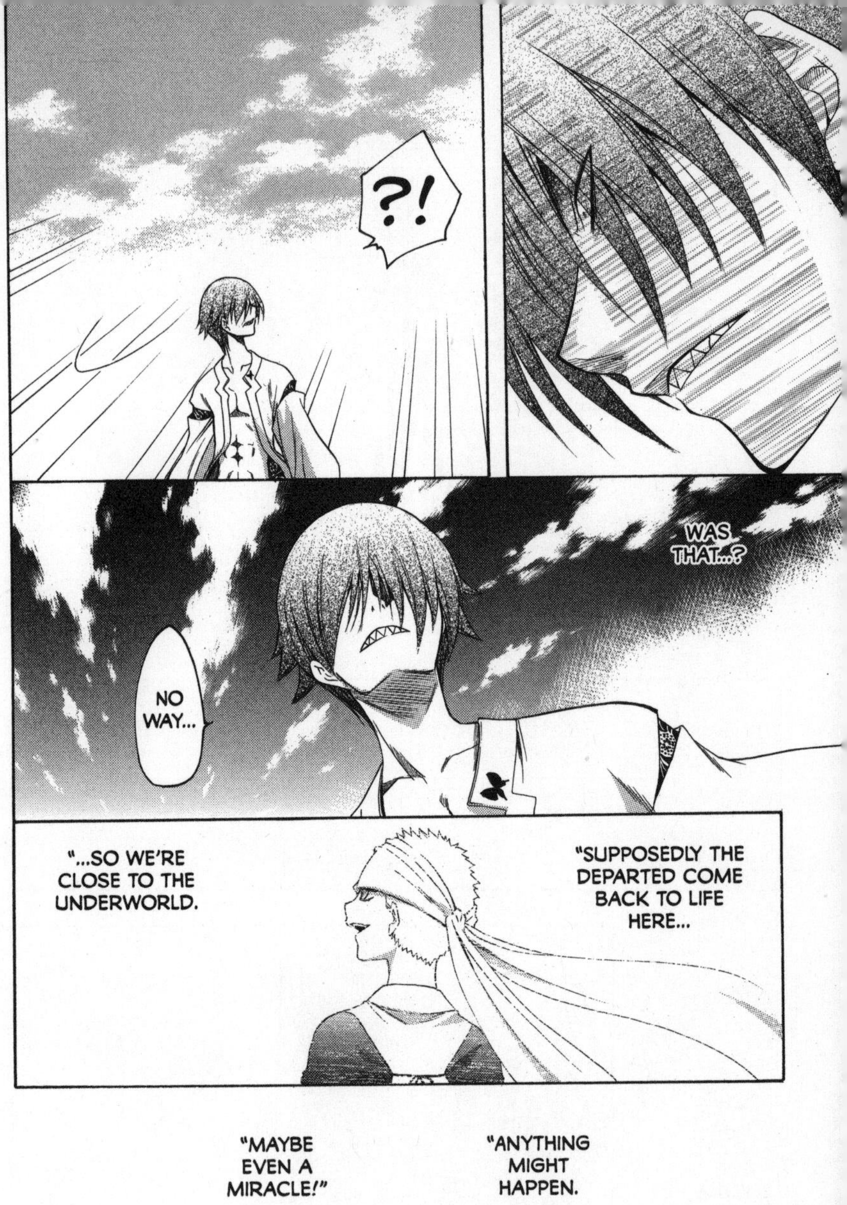
?!
WAS THAT...?
NO WAY...
"SUPPOSEDLY THE DEPARTED COME BACK TO LIFE HERE...
"...SO WE'RE CLOSE TO THE UNDERWORLD.
"ANYTHING MIGHT HAPPEN.
"MAYBE EVEN A MIRACLE!"

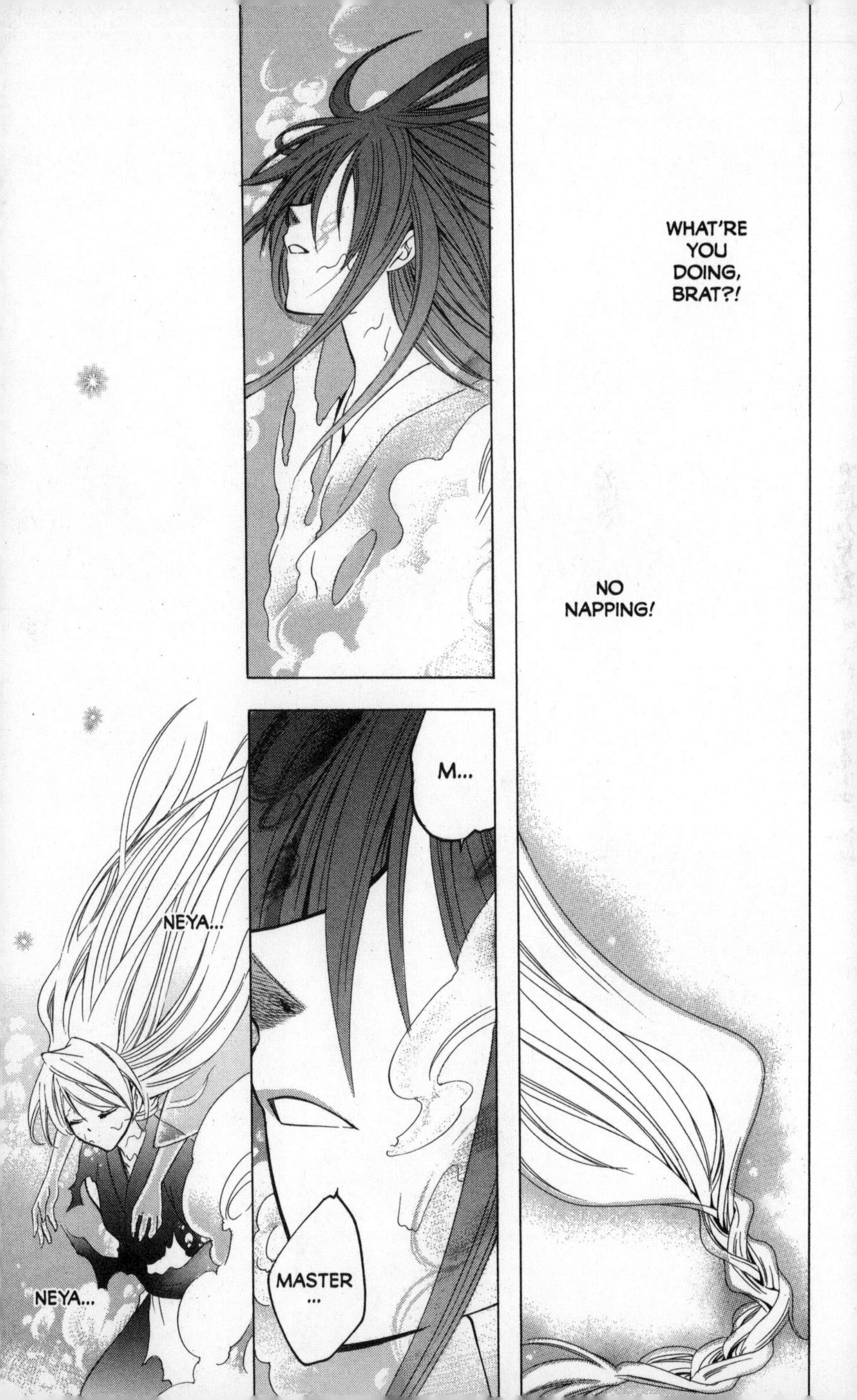
WHAT'RE YOU DOING, BRAT?!
NO NAPPING!
M...
MASTER ...
NEYA...
NEYA...

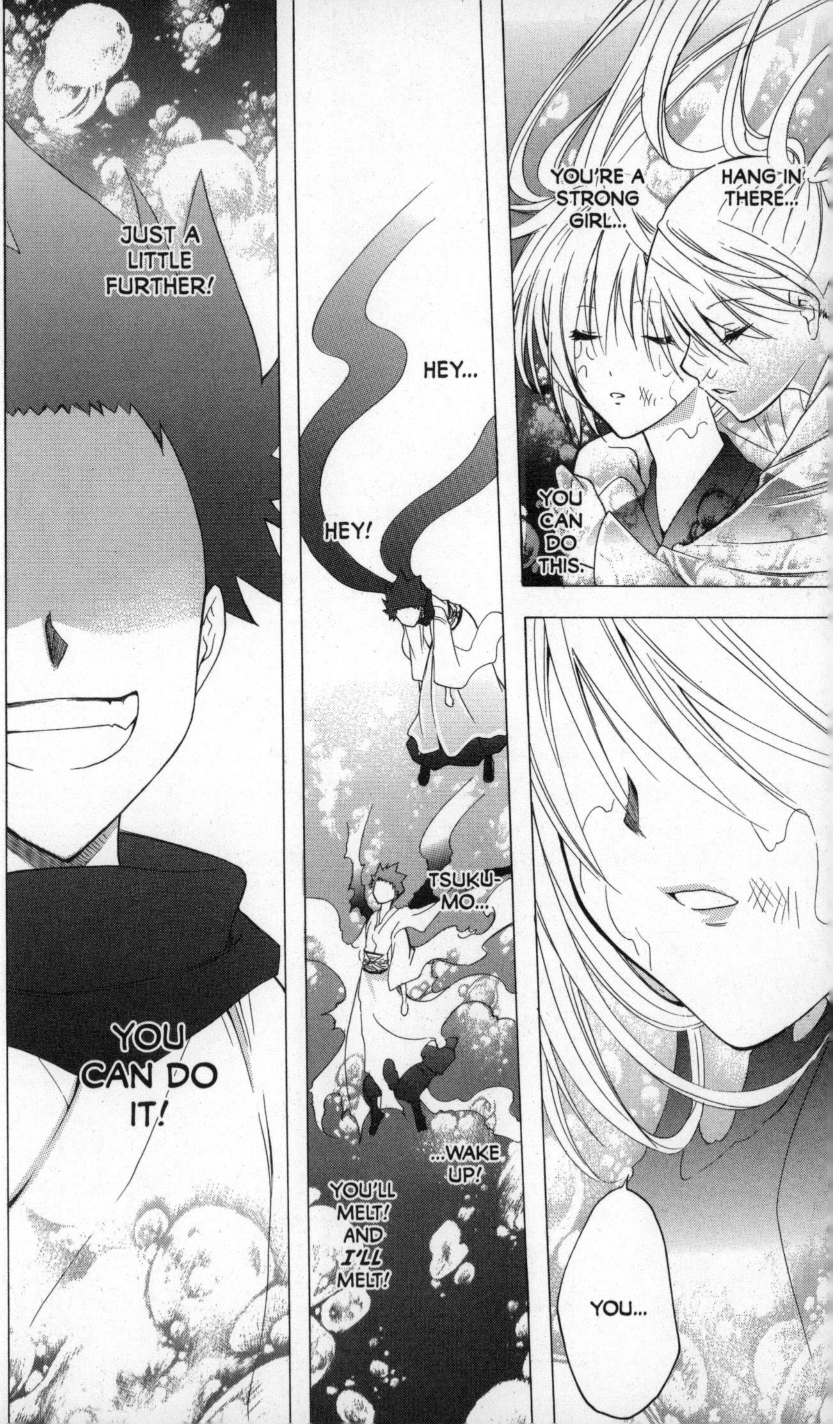
HANG IN THERE...
YOU'RE A STRONG GIRL...
YOU CAN DO THIS.
YOU...
HEY...
HEY!
TSUKU-MO...
...WAKE UP!
YOU'LL MELT! AND *I'LL* MELT!
JUST A LITTLE FURTHER!
YOU CAN DO IT!

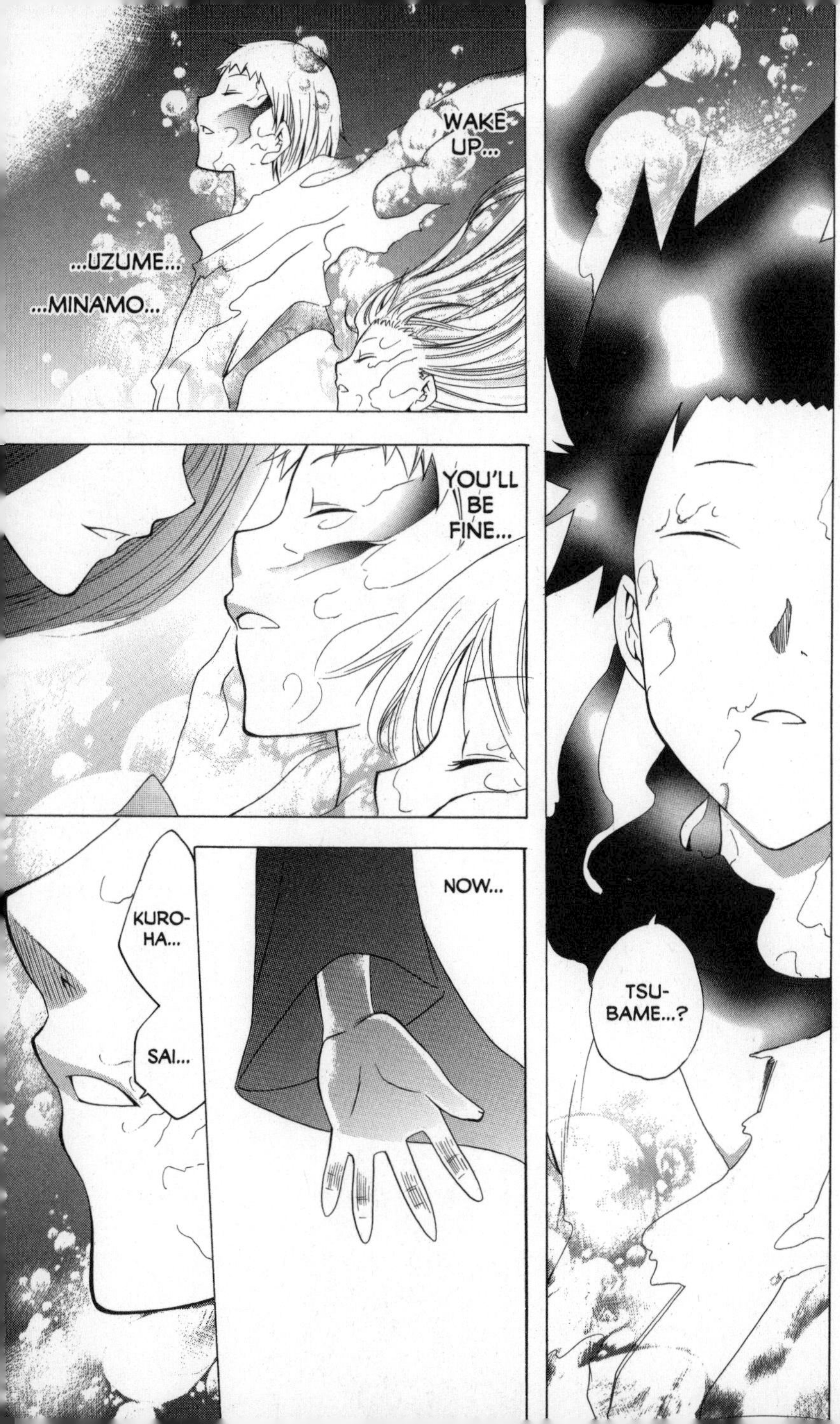
TSU-BAME...?
WAKE UP...
...UZUME...
...MINAMO...
YOU'LL BE FINE...
NOW...
KURO-HA...
SAI...

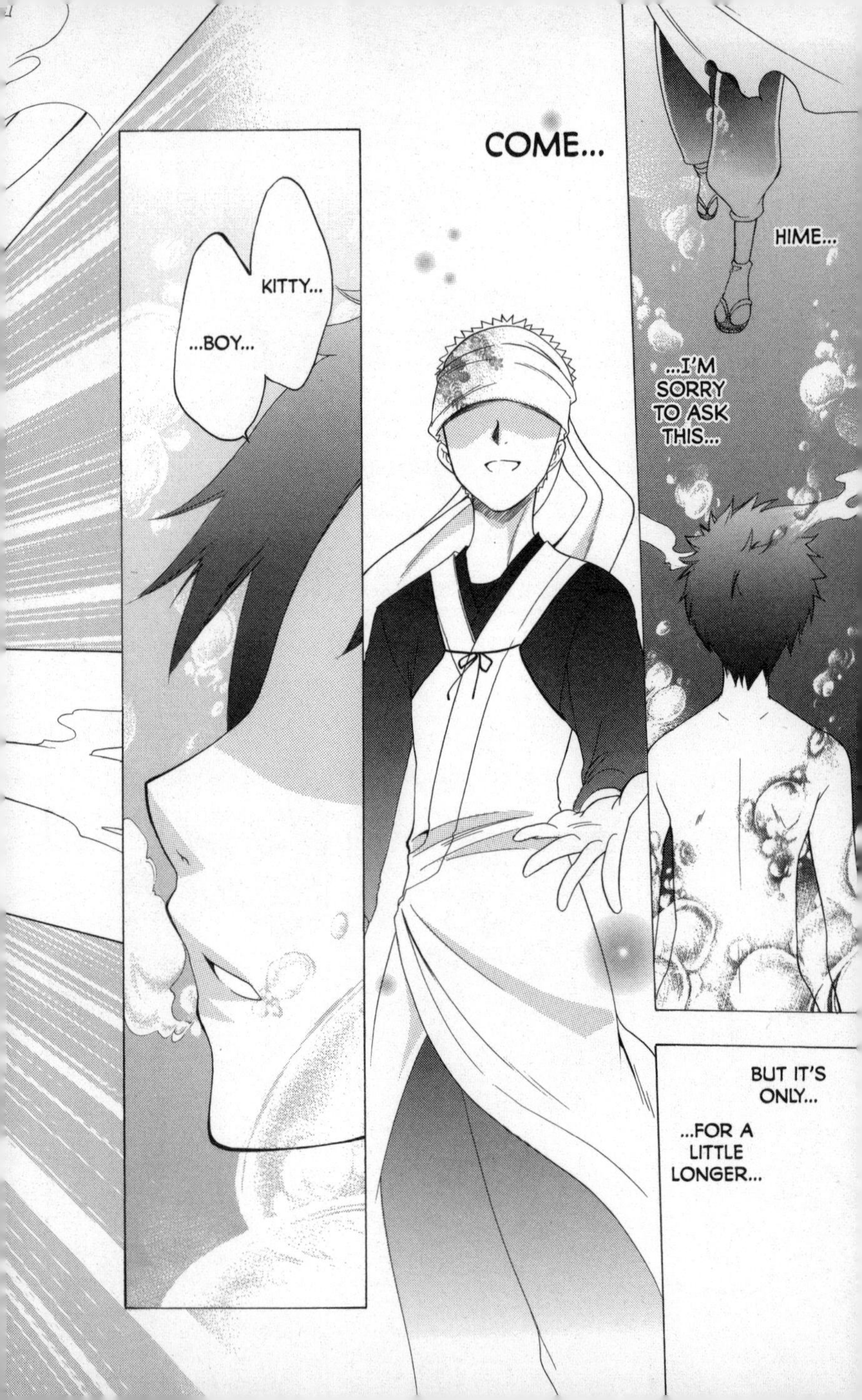
HIME...
...I'M SORRY TO ASK THIS...
BUT IT'S ONLY...
...FOR A LITTLE LONGER...
COME...
KITTY...
...BOY...

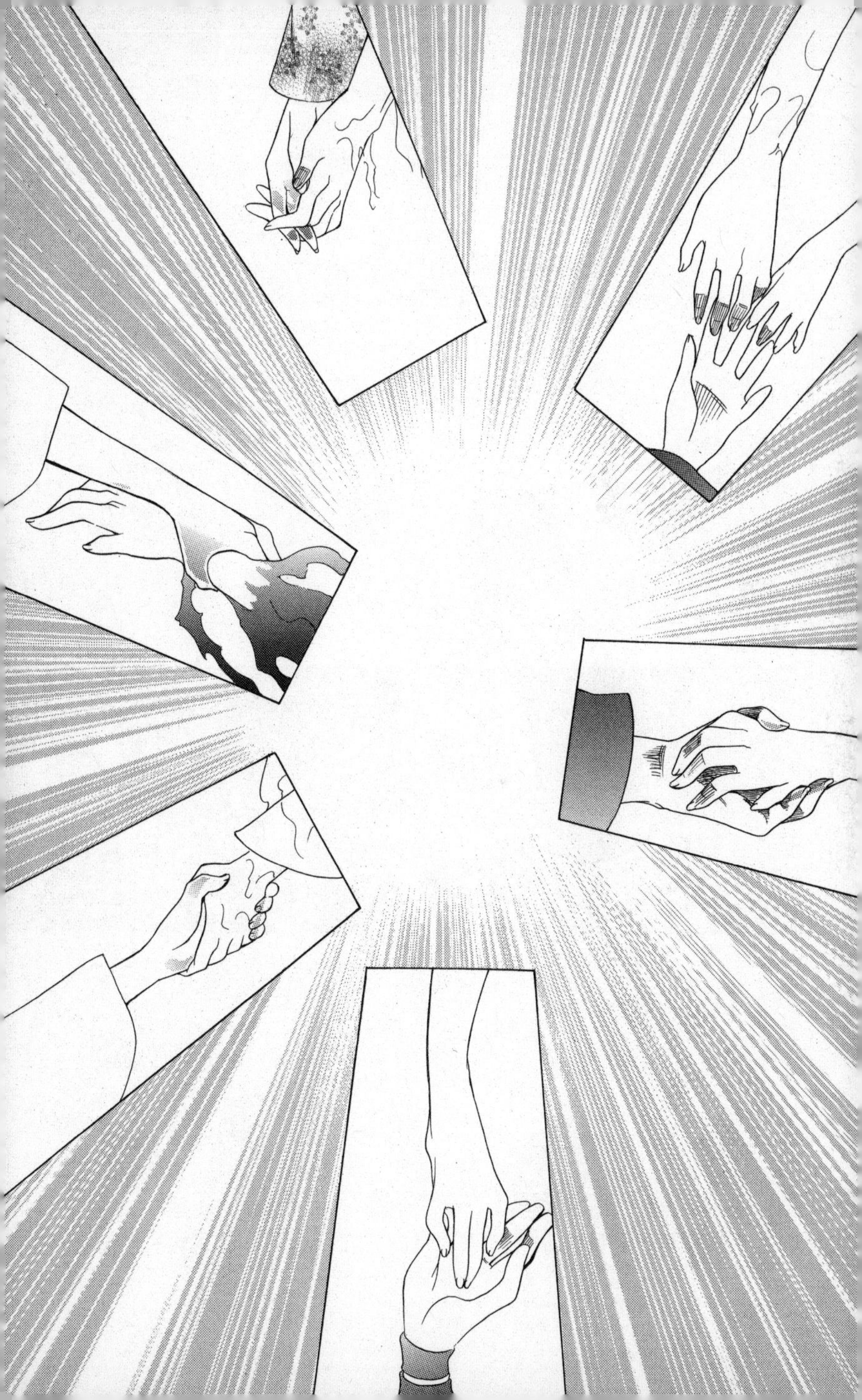

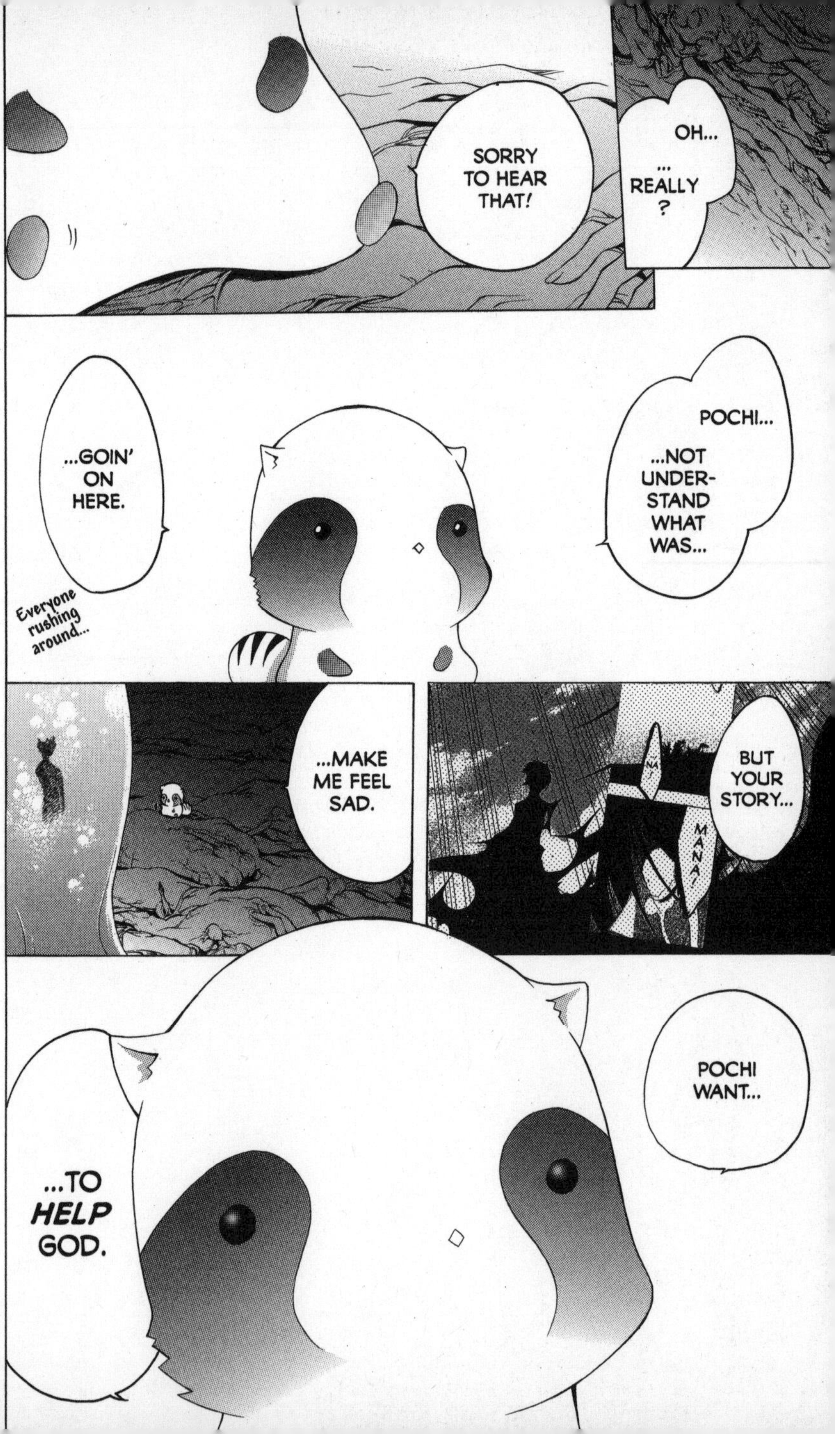
OH... ... REALLY?
SORRY TO HEAR THAT!
POCHI... ...NOT UNDERSTAND WHAT WAS...
...GOIN' ON HERE.
Everyone rushing around...
NA
MANA!
BUT YOUR STORY...
...MAKE ME FEEL SAD.
POCHI WANT...
...TO ***HELP*** GOD.

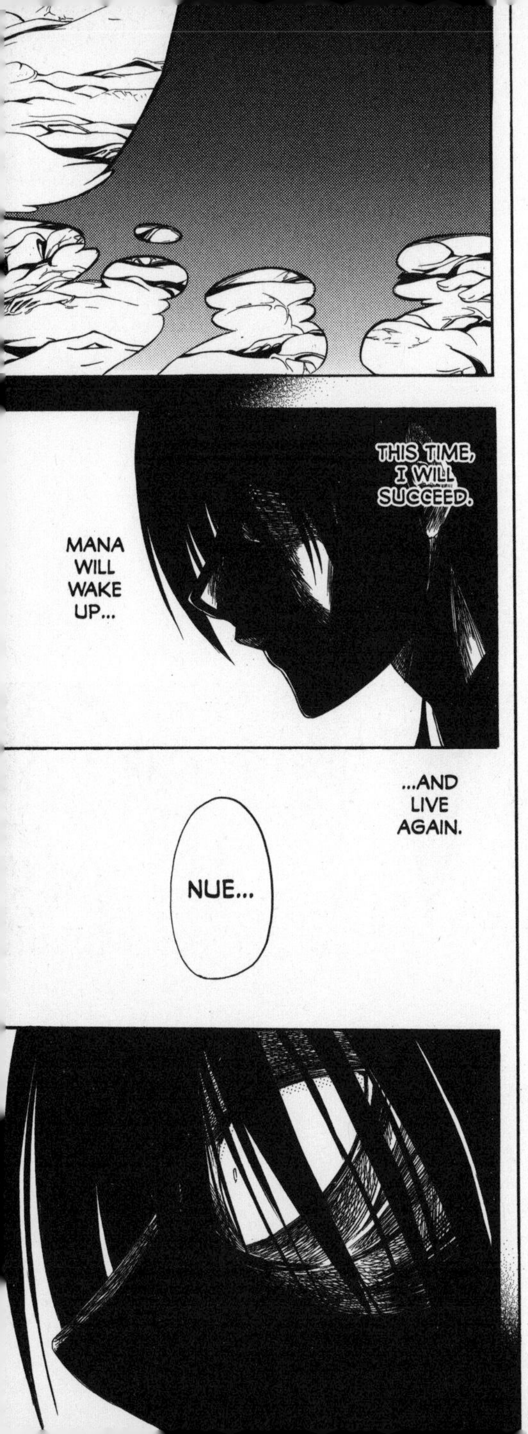
THIS TIME, I WILL SUCCEED.
MANA WILL WAKE UP...
...AND LIVE AGAIN.
NUE...

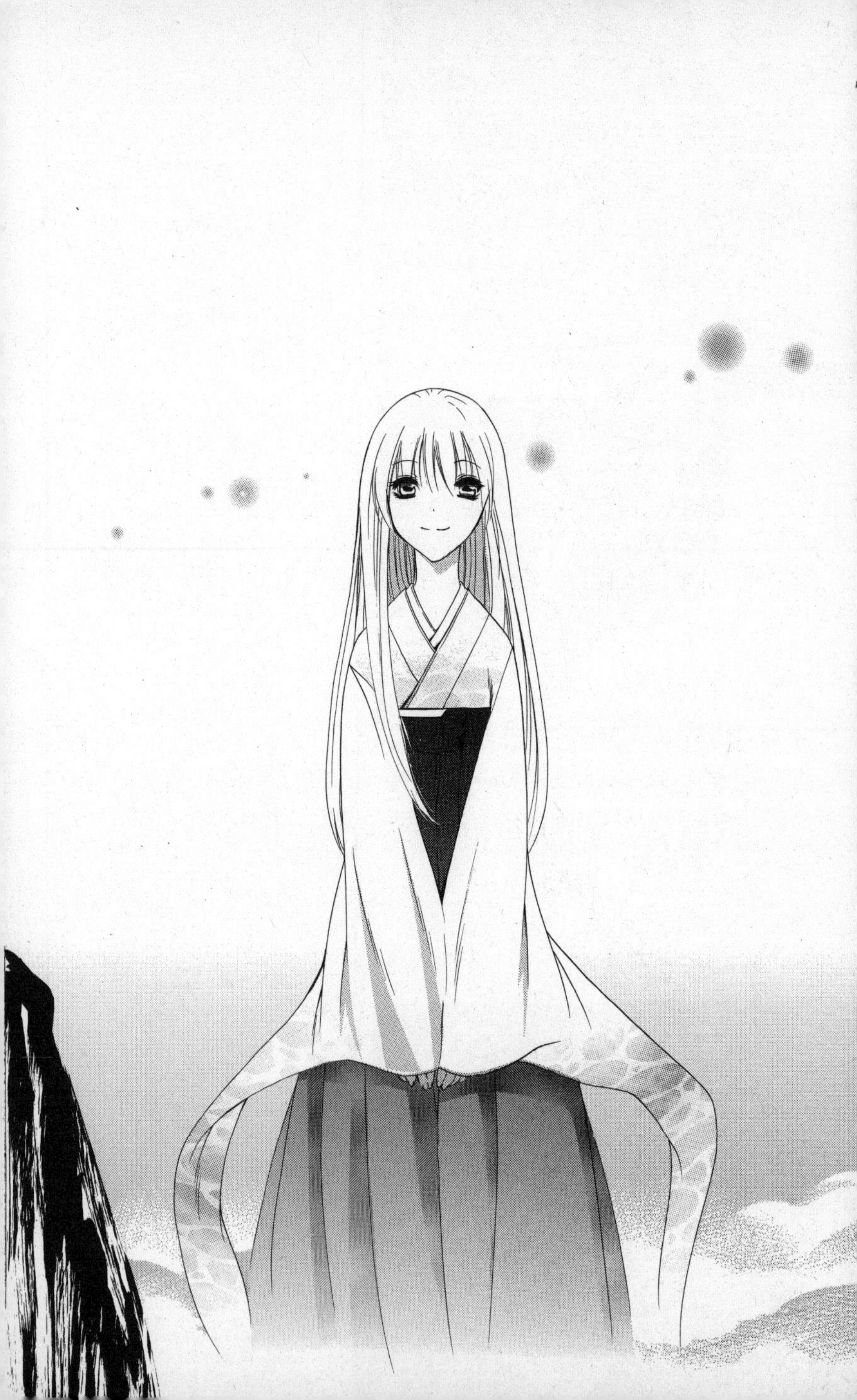

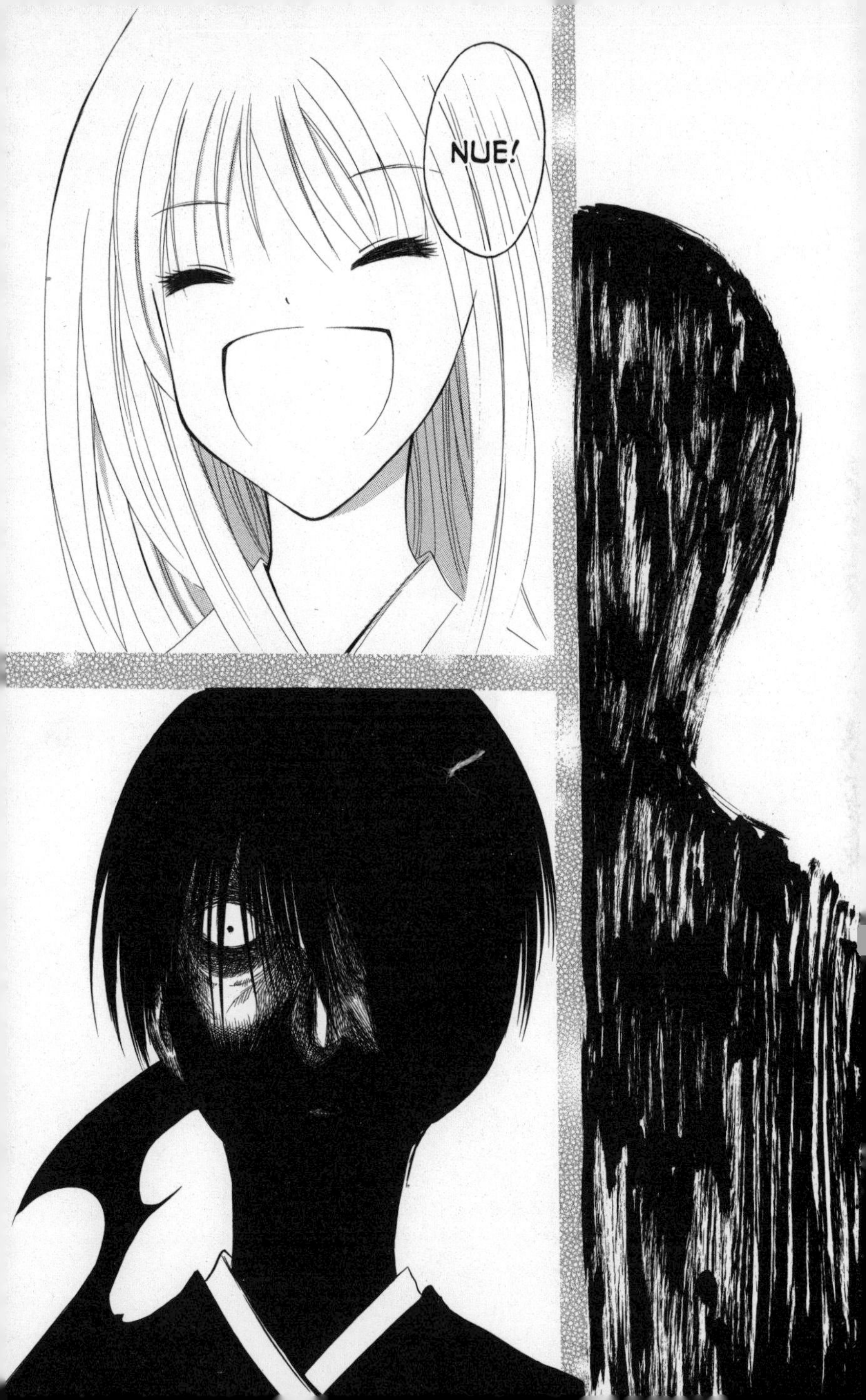
NUE!

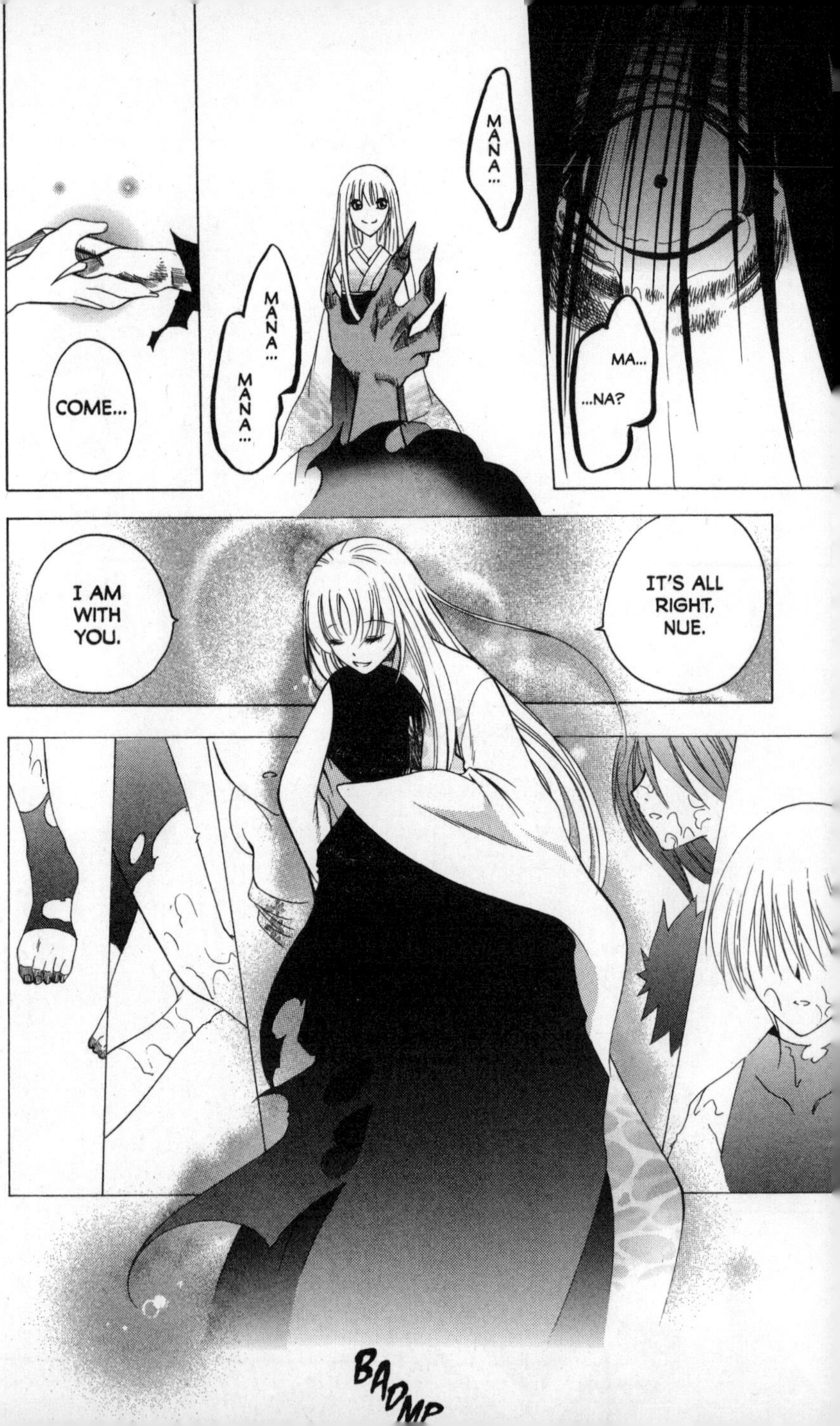
MA... ...NA?
MANA...
MANA... MANA...
COME...
IT'S ALL RIGHT, NUE.
I AM WITH YOU.
BADOMP

BADOMP

Chapter 219
Free

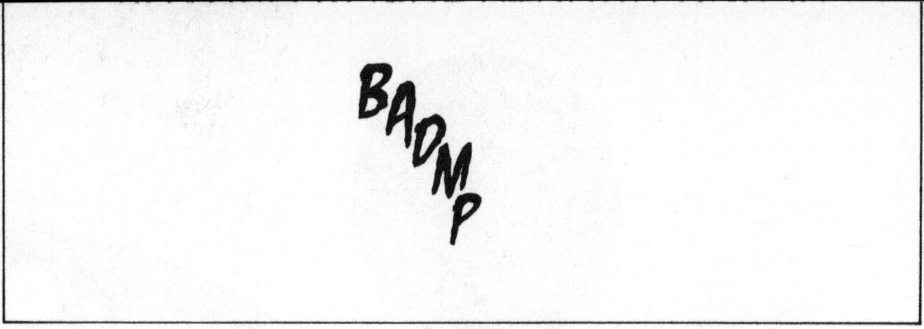

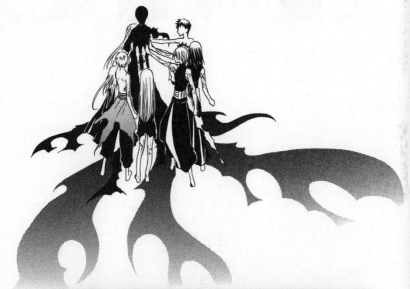

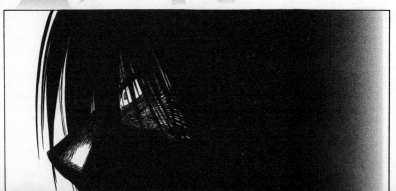

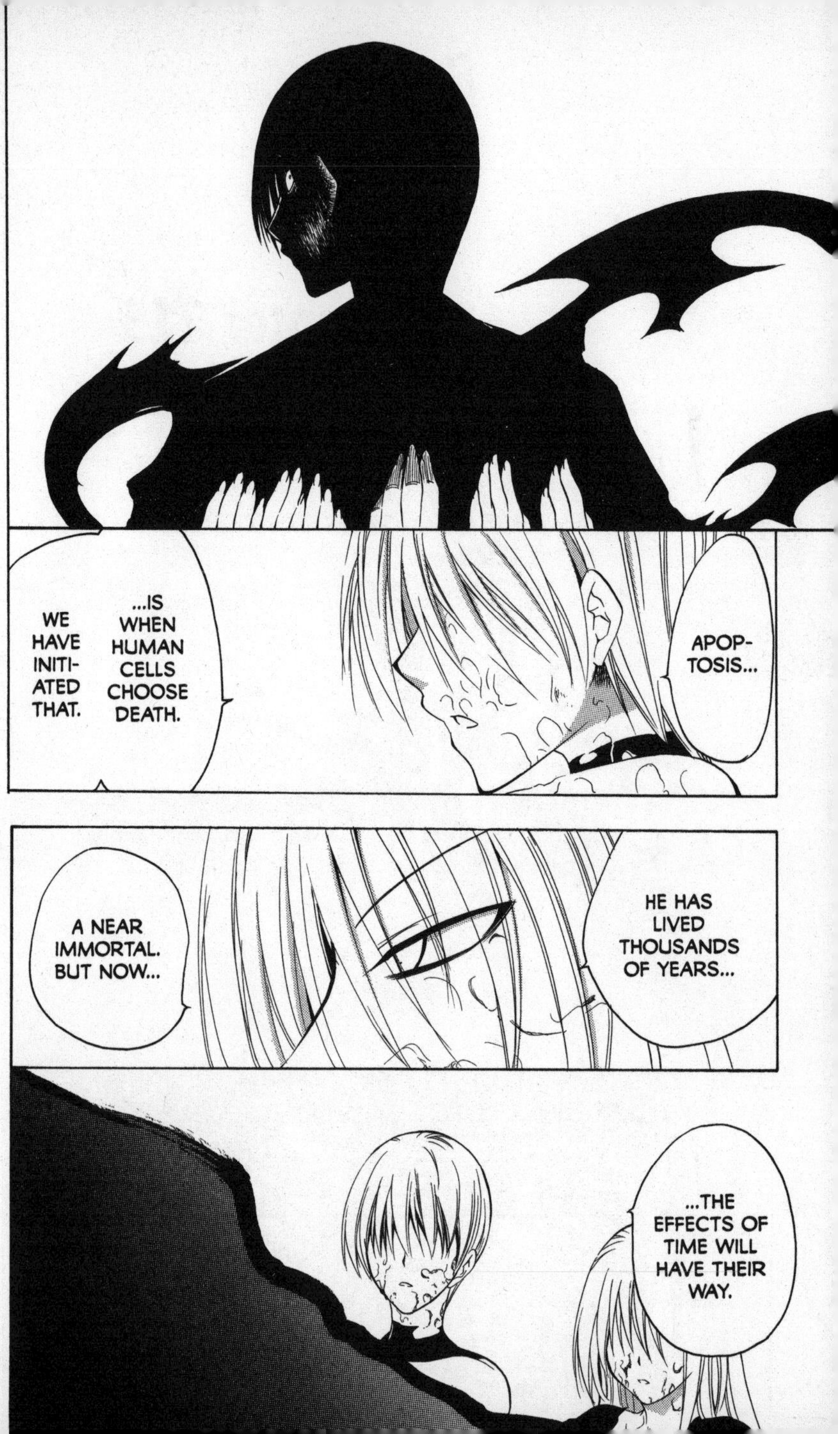
APOPTOSIS...
...IS WHEN HUMAN CELLS CHOOSE DEATH.
WE HAVE INITIATED THAT.
HE HAS LIVED THOUSANDS OF YEARS...
A NEAR IMMORTAL. BUT NOW...
...THE EFFECTS OF TIME WILL HAVE THEIR WAY.

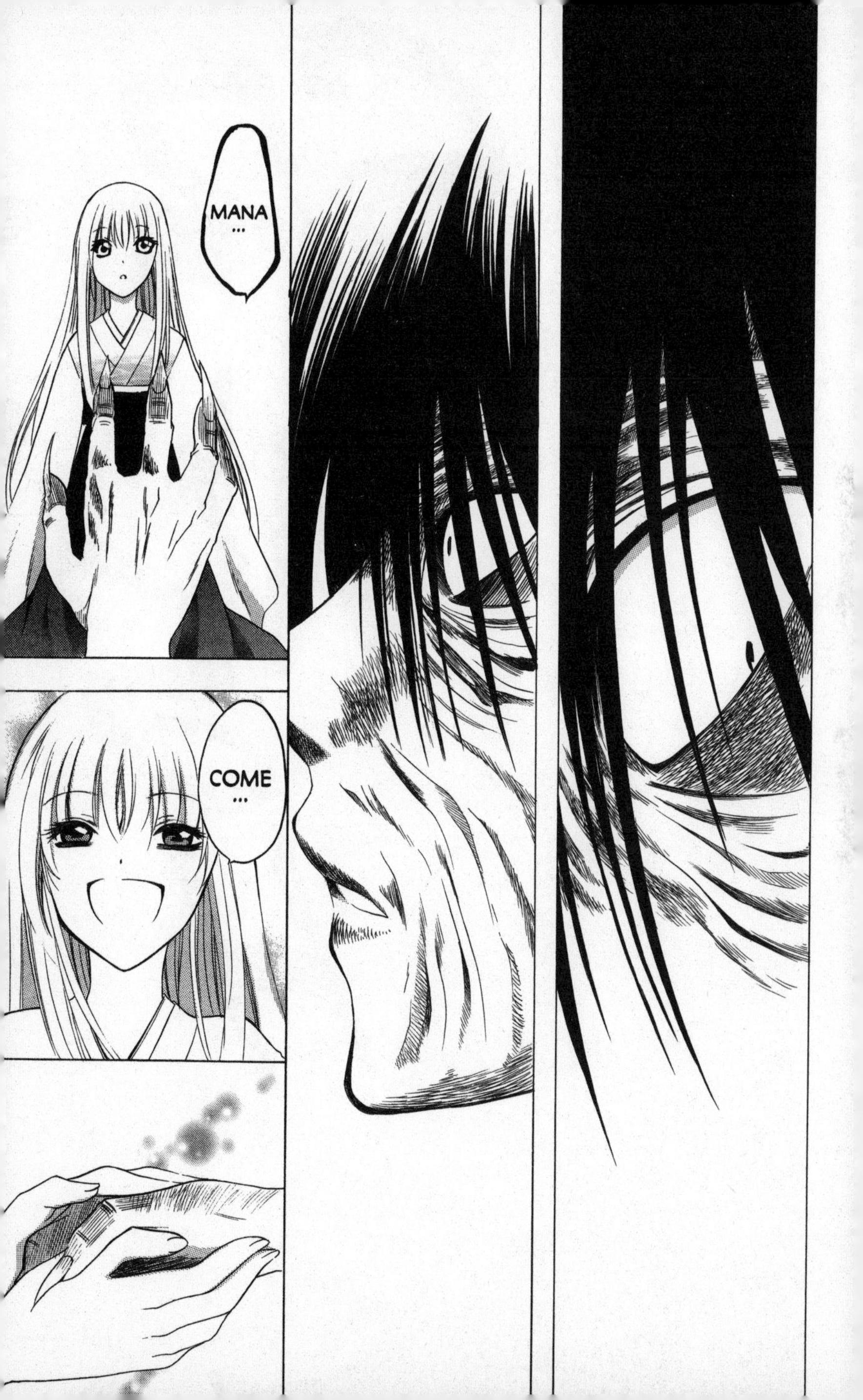
MANA...
COME...

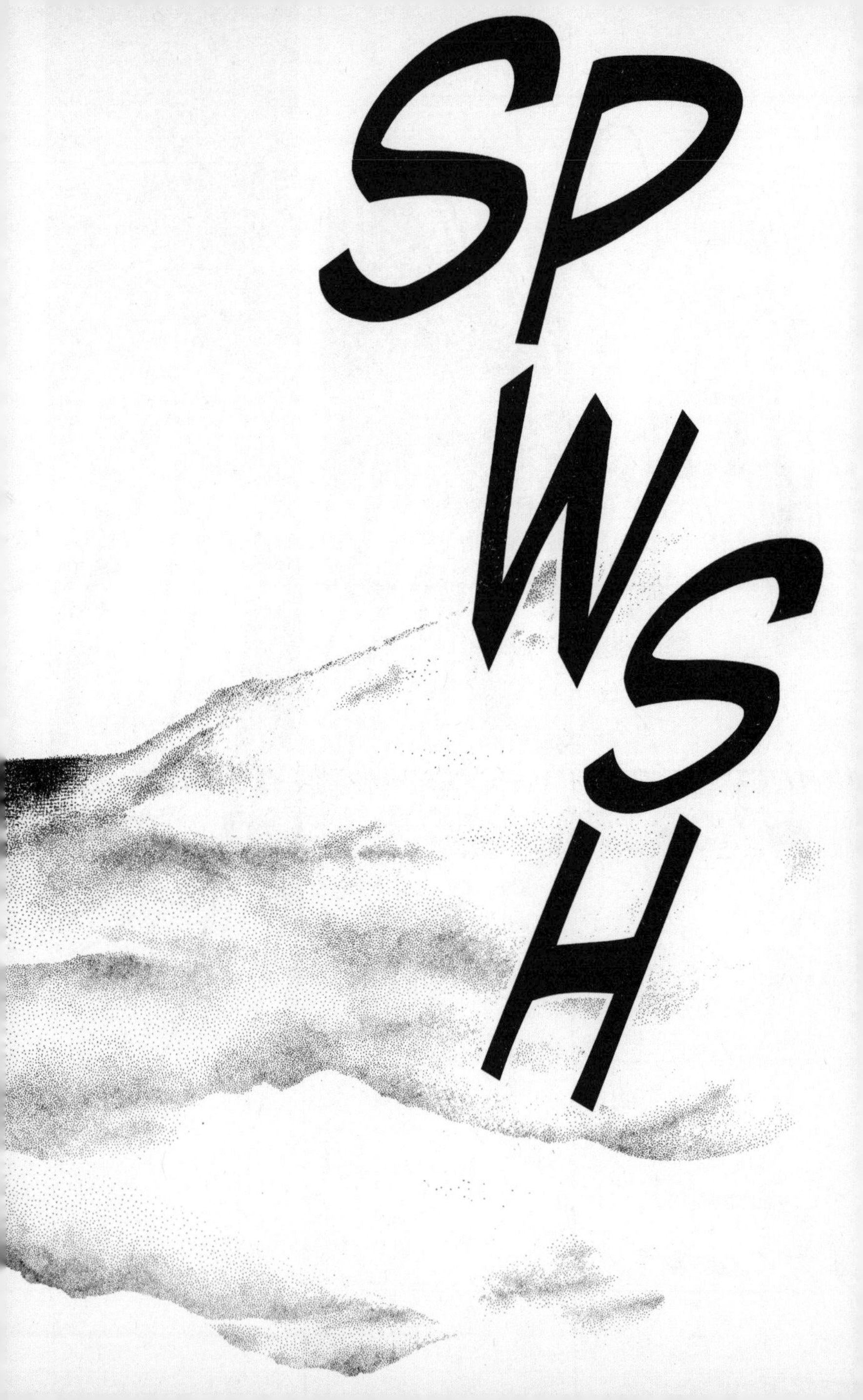
SPWSH

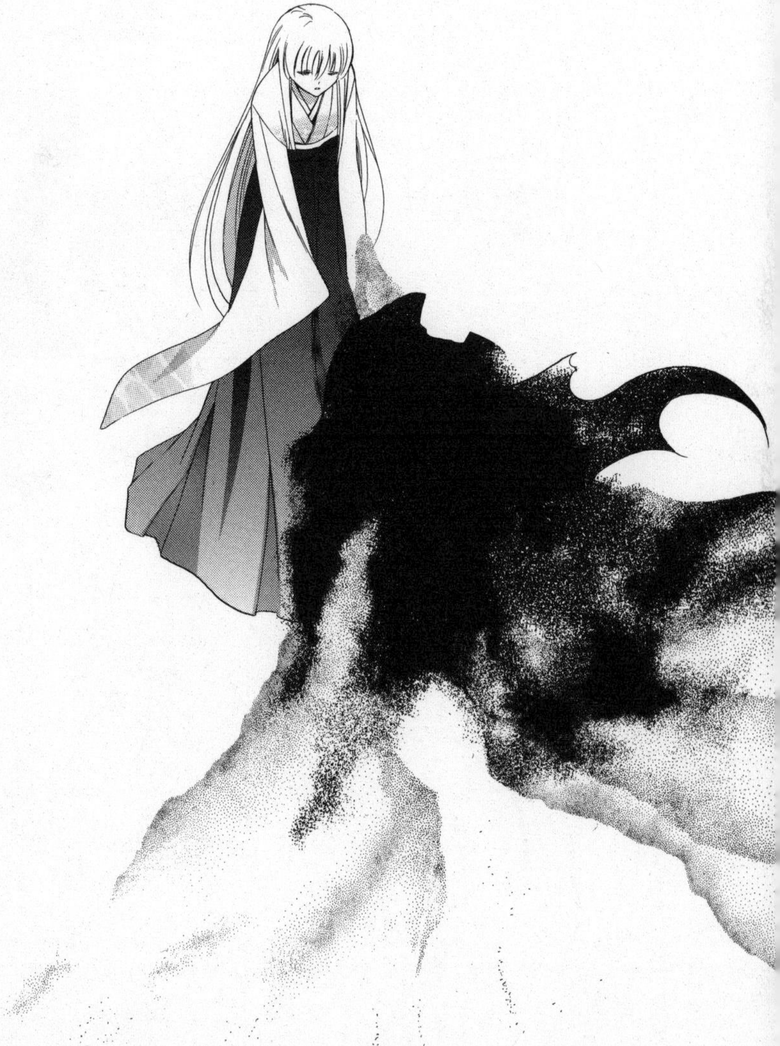

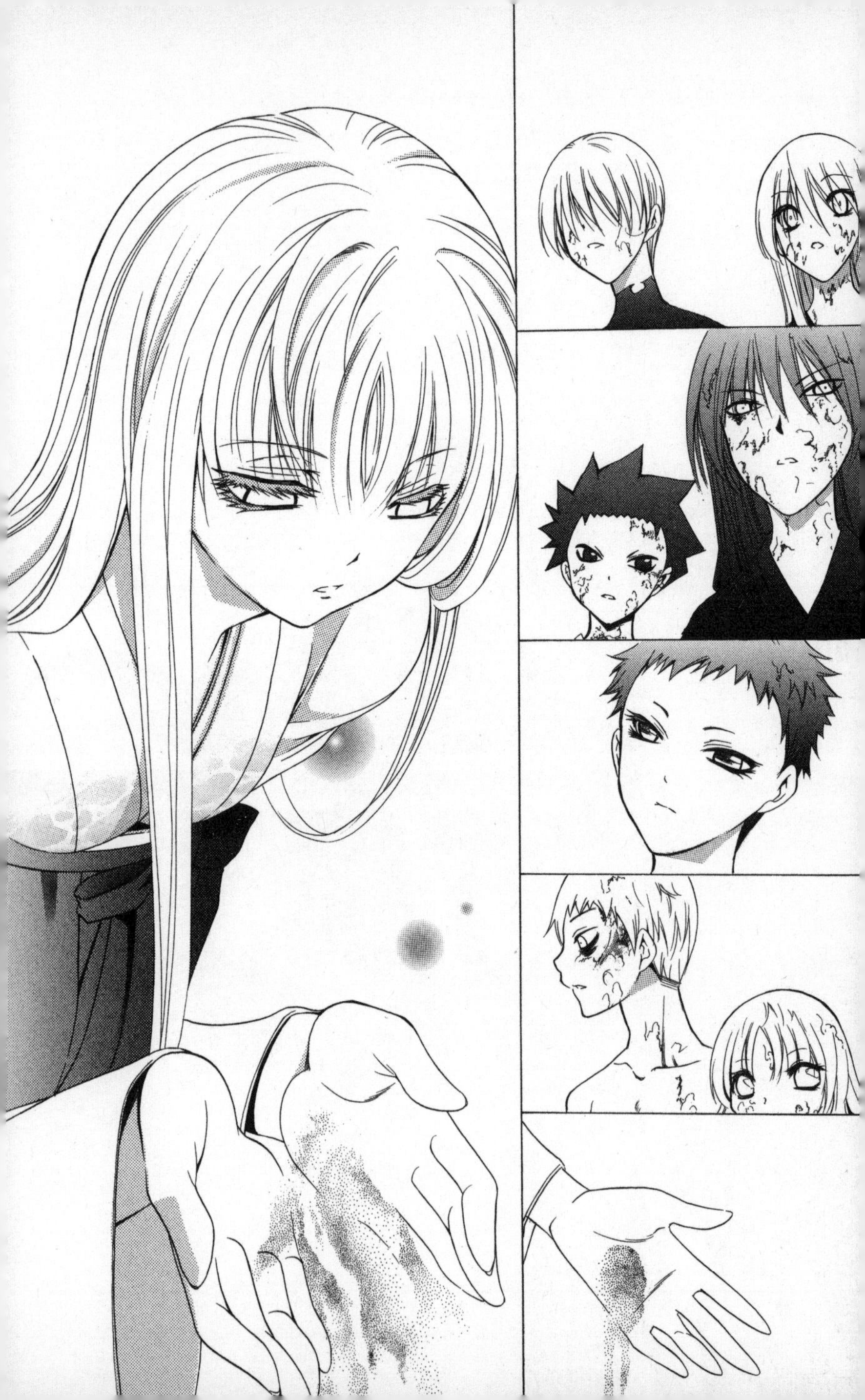

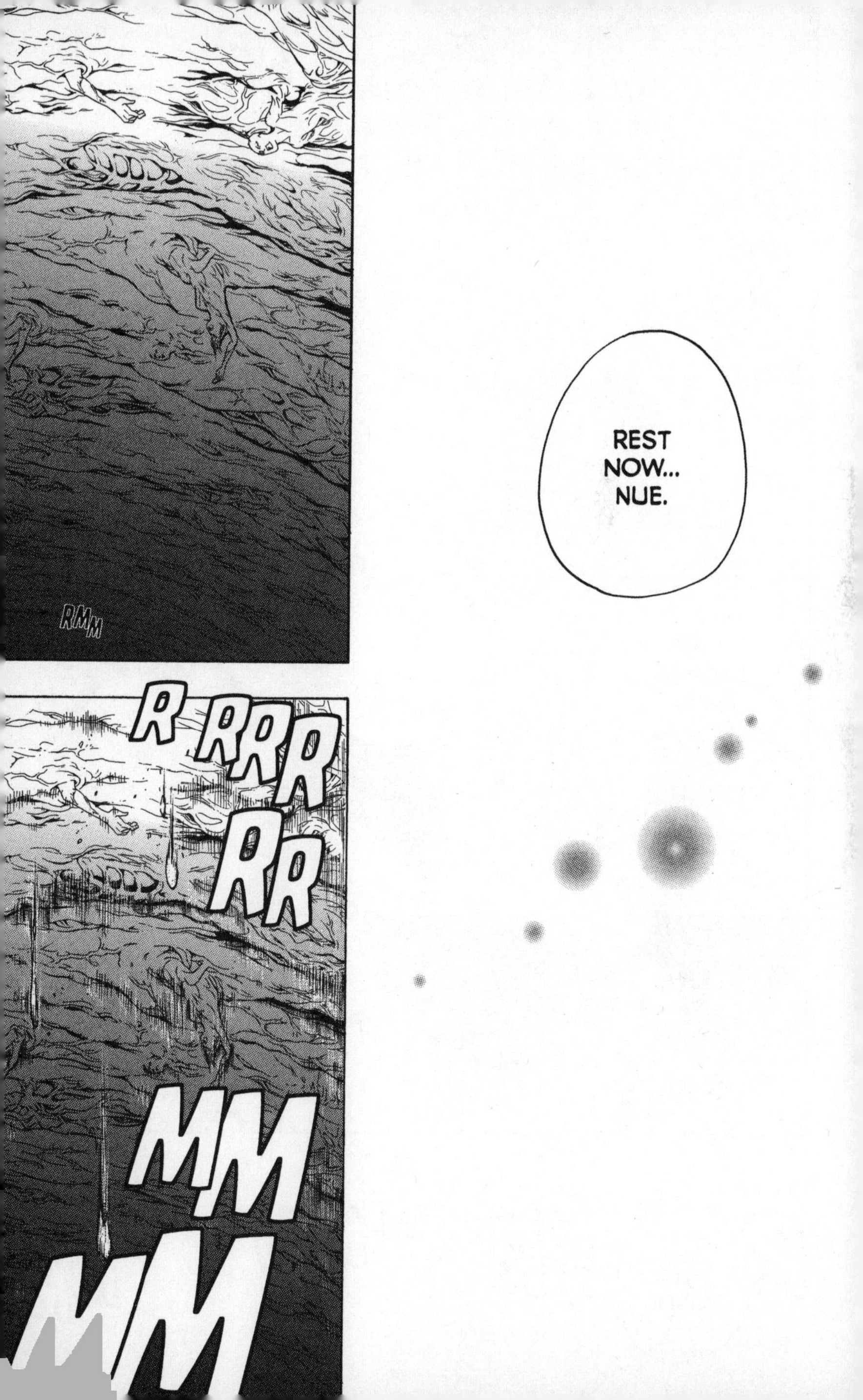
REST NOW... NUE.
RMM
R RRRR
RR
MM
MM

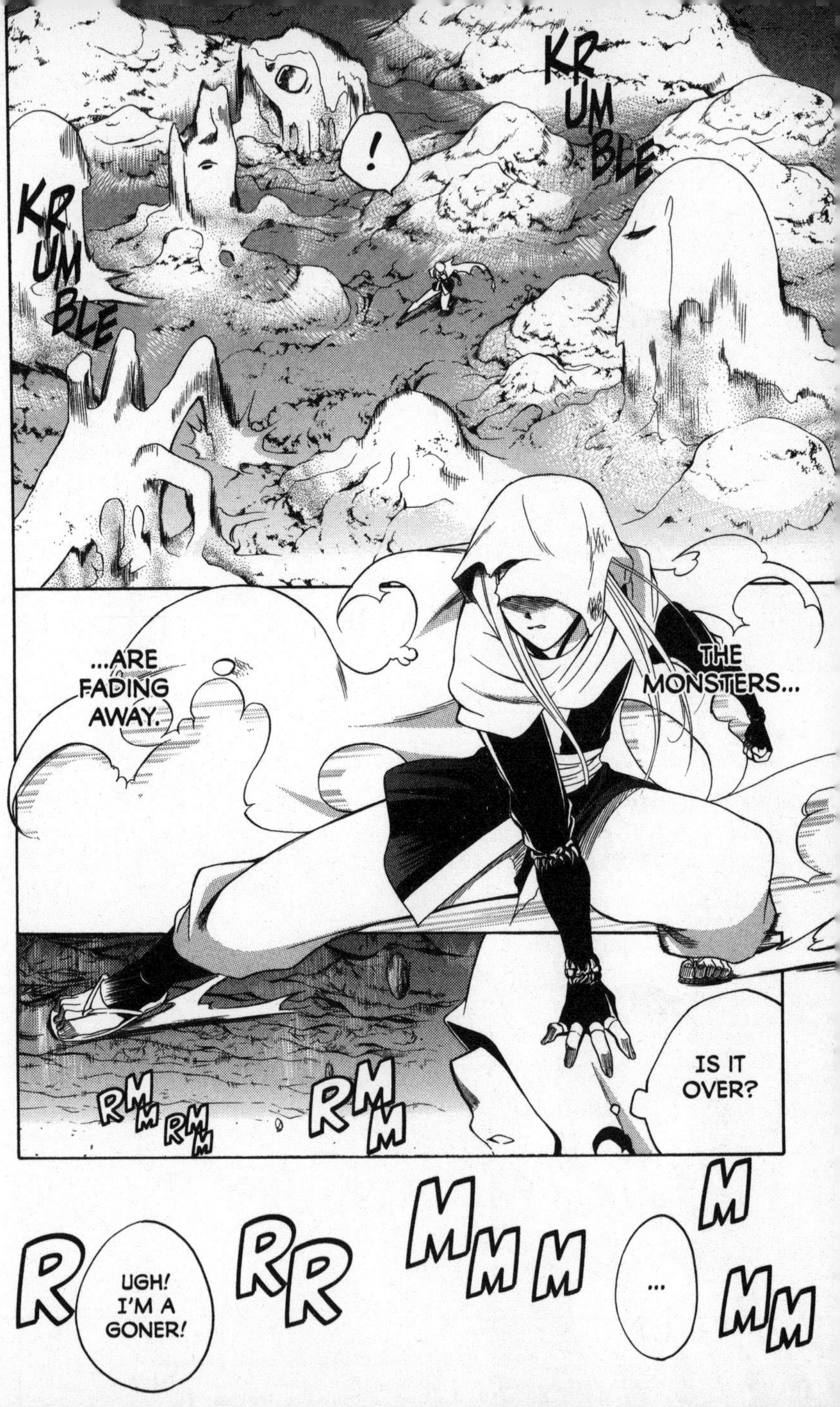
KRUMBLE
!
KRUMBLE
THE MONSTERS...
...ARE FADING AWAY.
IS IT OVER?
RMM
RMM RMM
...
UGH! I'M A GONER!
RRRMMMMMMMM

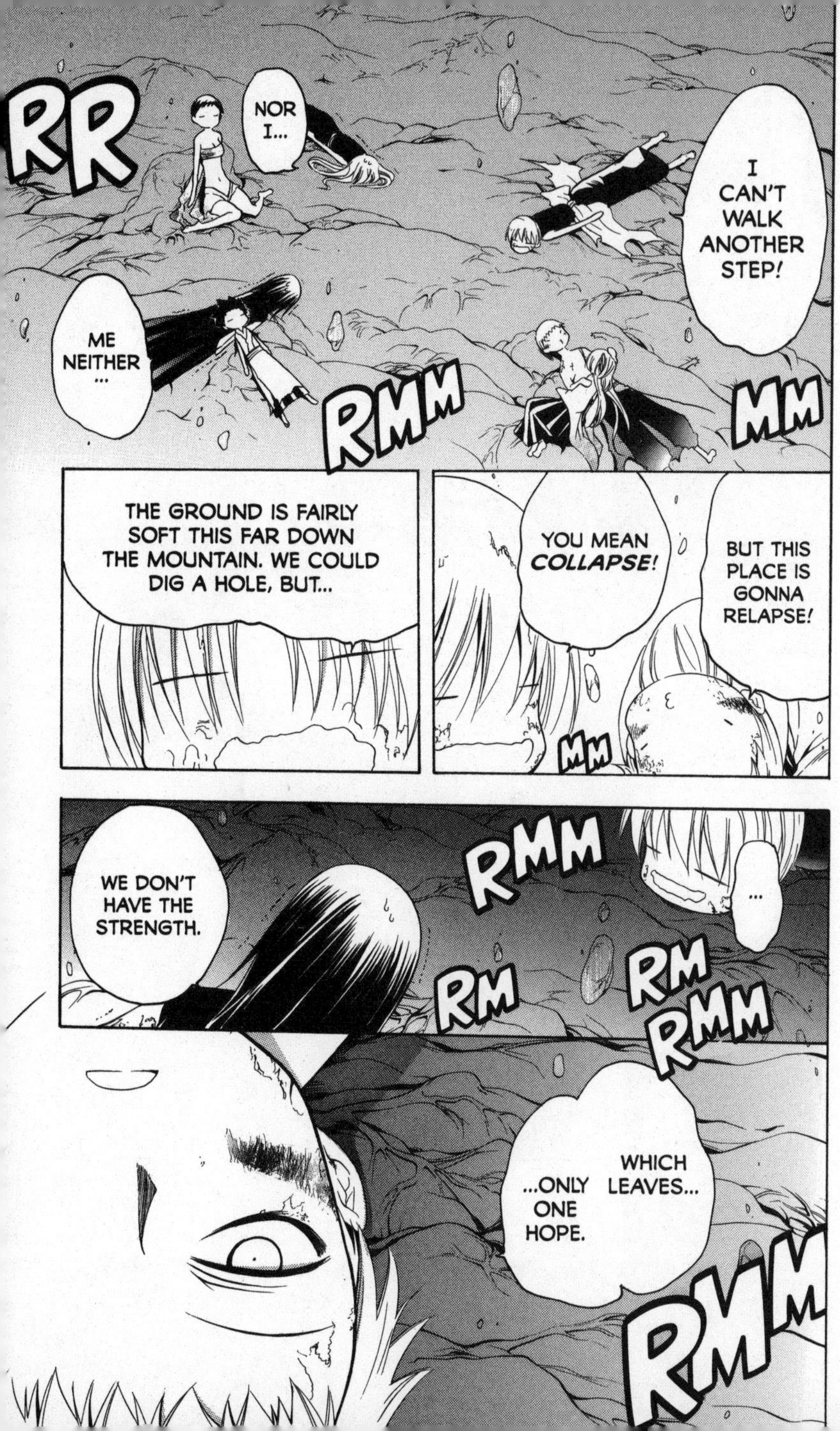
I CAN'T WALK ANOTHER STEP!
NOR I...
RR
ME NEITHER...
RMM
MM
BUT THIS PLACE IS GONNA RELAPSE!
YOU MEAN *COLLAPSE*!
MM
THE GROUND IS FAIRLY SOFT THIS FAR DOWN THE MOUNTAIN. WE COULD DIG A HOLE, BUT...
...
RMM
RM RMM
RM
WE DON'T HAVE THE STRENGTH.
WHICH LEAVES...
...ONLY ONE HOPE.
RMMM

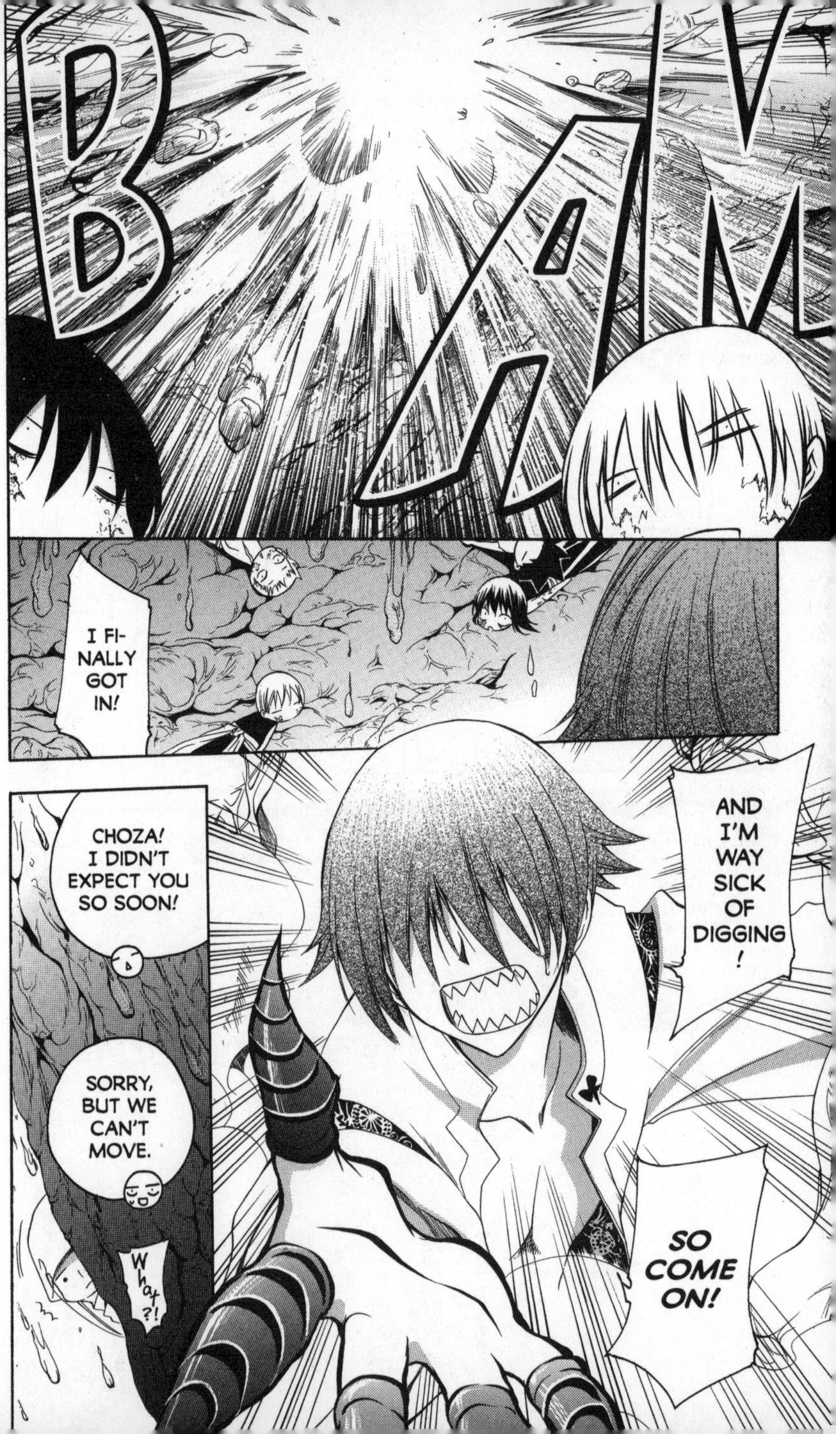
BAM
I FI-
NALLY
GOT
IN!
AND I'M WAY SICK OF DIGGING!
SO COME ON!
CHOZA! I DIDN'T EXPECT YOU SO SOON!
SORRY, BUT WE CAN'T MOVE.
What?!

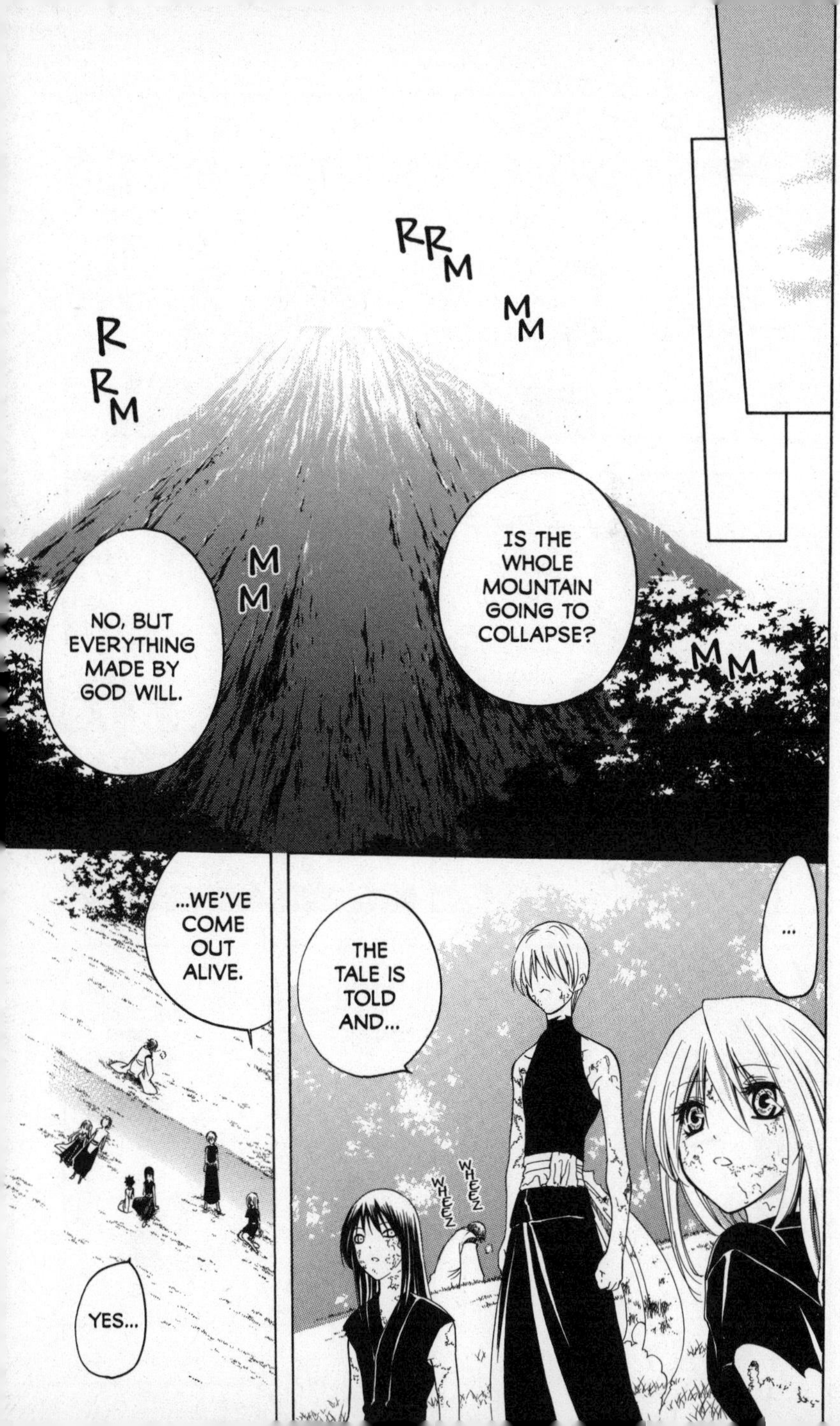
RRMM
MM
RRM
IS THE WHOLE MOUNTAIN GOING TO COLLAPSE?
MM
MM
NO, BUT EVERYTHING MADE BY GOD WILL.
...
THE TALE IS TOLD AND...
WHEEZ
WHEEZ
...WE'VE COME OUT ALIVE.
YES...

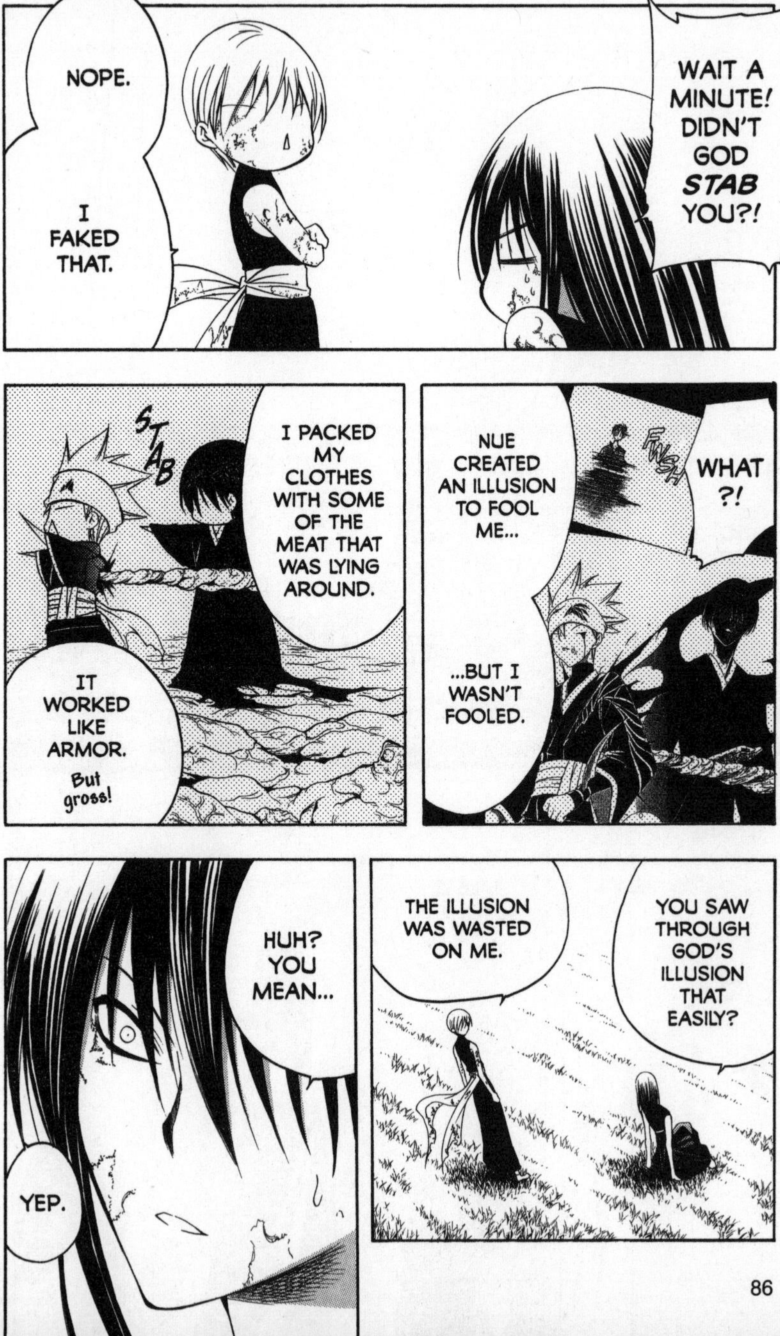
WAIT A MINUTE! DIDN'T GOD STAB YOU?!
NOPE.
I FAKED THAT.
WHAT?!
FWSH
NUE CREATED AN ILLUSION TO FOOL ME...
...BUT I WASN'T FOOLED.
STAB
I PACKED MY CLOTHES WITH SOME OF THE MEAT THAT WAS LYING AROUND.
IT WORKED LIKE ARMOR.
But gross!
YOU SAW THROUGH GOD'S ILLUSION THAT EASILY?
THE ILLUSION WAS WASTED ON ME.
HUH? YOU MEAN...
YEP.

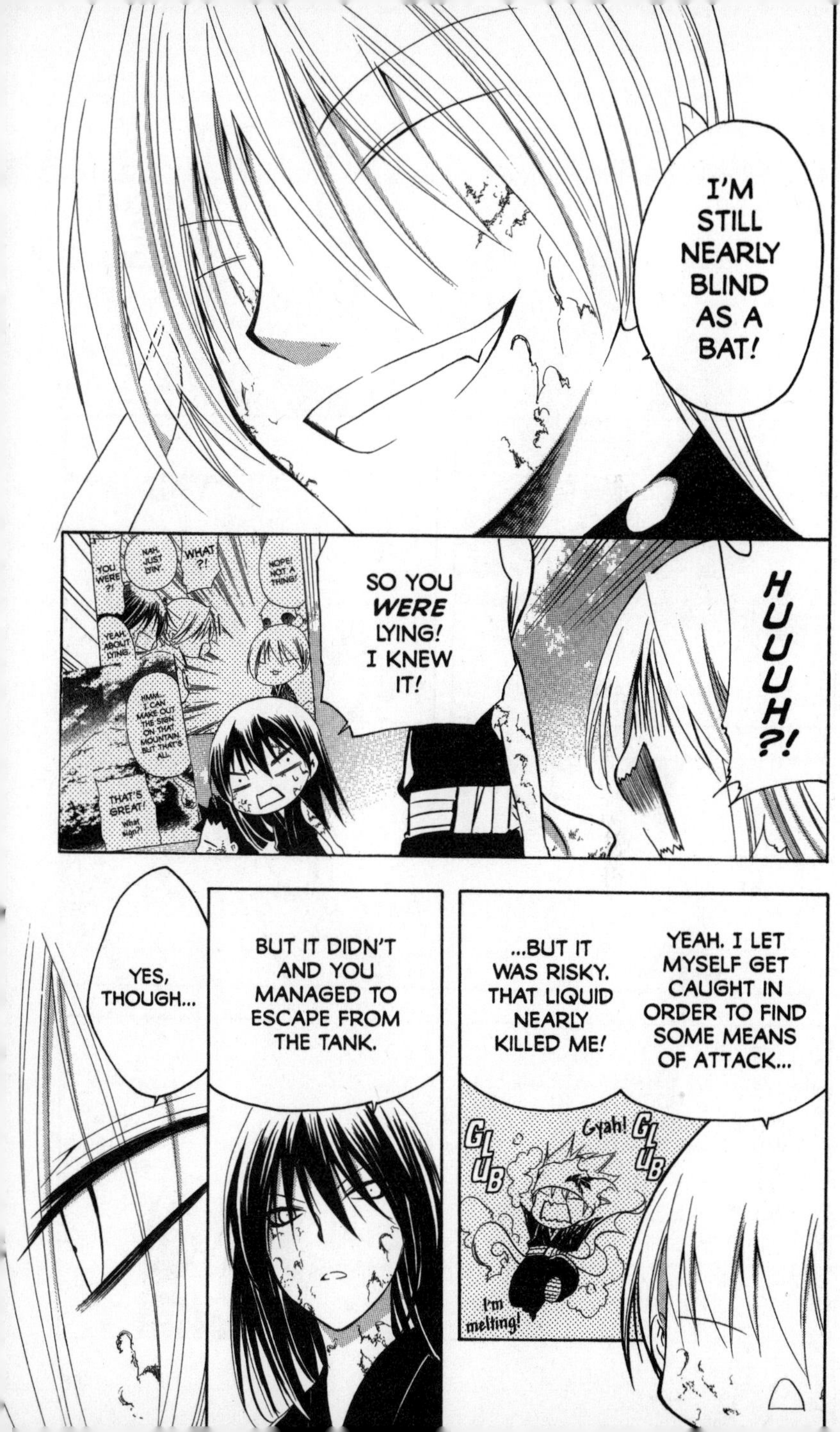
I'M STILL NEARLY BLIND AS A BAT!
HUUUUH?!
SO YOU *WERE* LYING! I KNEW IT!
NOPE! NOT A THING!
WHAT?!
NAH, JUST LYIN'.
YOU WERE?!
YEAH. ABOUT LYING.
HMM... I CAN MAKE OUT THE SIGN ON THAT MOUNTAIN, BUT THAT'S ALL.
THAT'S GREAT!
What sign?!
YEAH. I LET MYSELF GET CAUGHT IN ORDER TO FIND SOME MEANS OF ATTACK...
...BUT IT WAS RISKY. THAT LIQUID NEARLY KILLED ME!
GLUB
Gyah!
GLUB
I'm melting!
BUT IT DIDN'T AND YOU MANAGED TO ESCAPE FROM THE TANK.
YES, THOUGH...

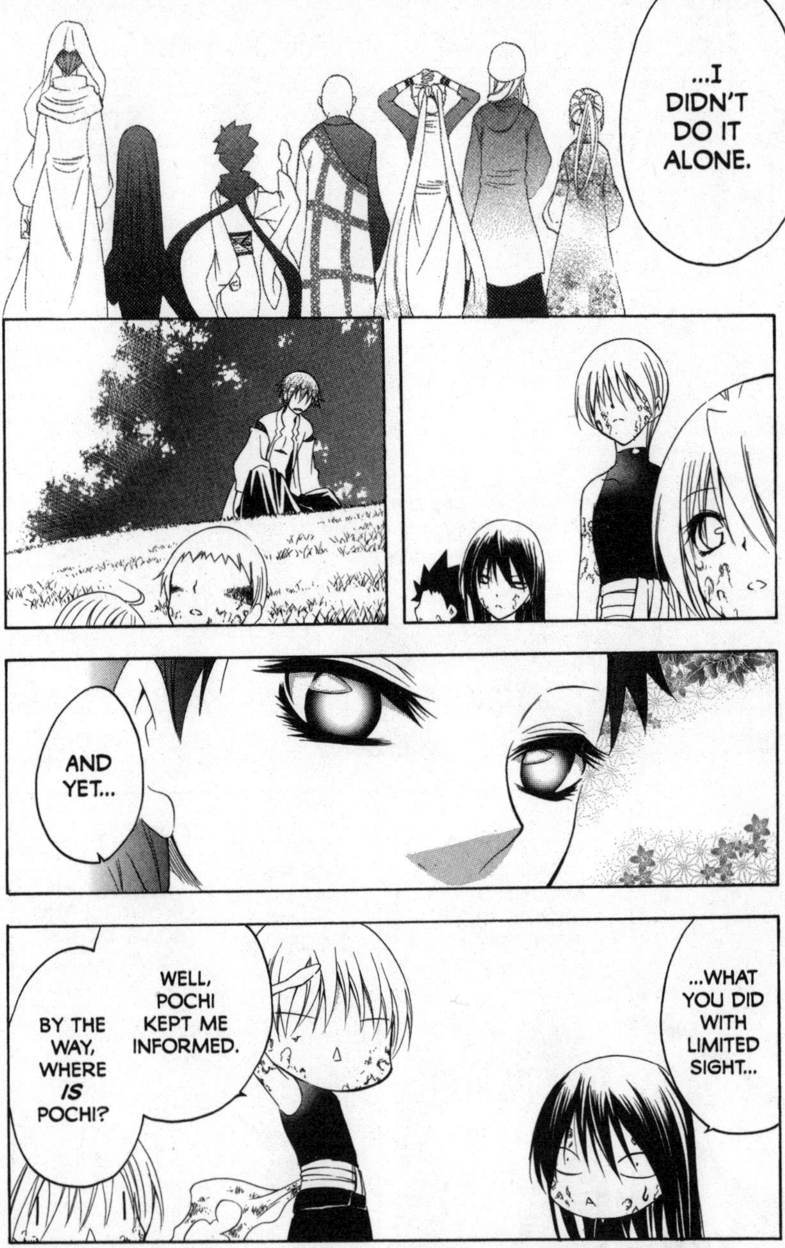
...I DIDN'T DO IT ALONE.
AND YET...
...WHAT YOU DID WITH LIMITED SIGHT...
WELL, POCHI KEPT ME INFORMED.
BY THE WAY, WHERE *IS* POCHI?

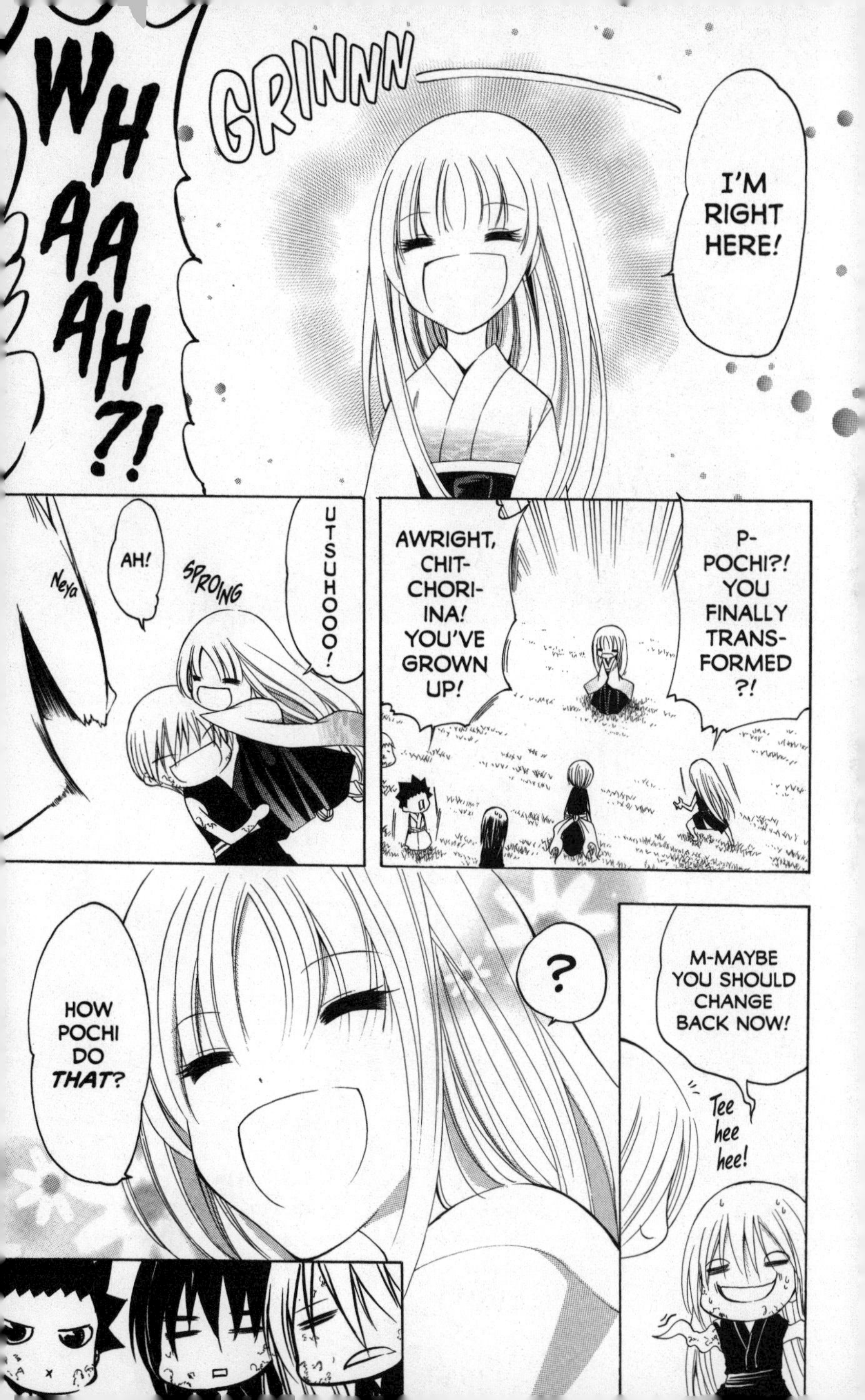
I'M RIGHT HERE!
GRINNN
WHAAAH?!
P-POCHI?! YOU FINALLY TRANS-FORMED?!
AWRIGHT, CHIT-CHORI-INA! YOU'VE GROWN UP!
UTSUHOOOO!
SPROING
AH!
Neya
M-MAYBE YOU SHOULD CHANGE BACK NOW!
Tee hee hee!
?
HOW POCHI DO *THAT*?

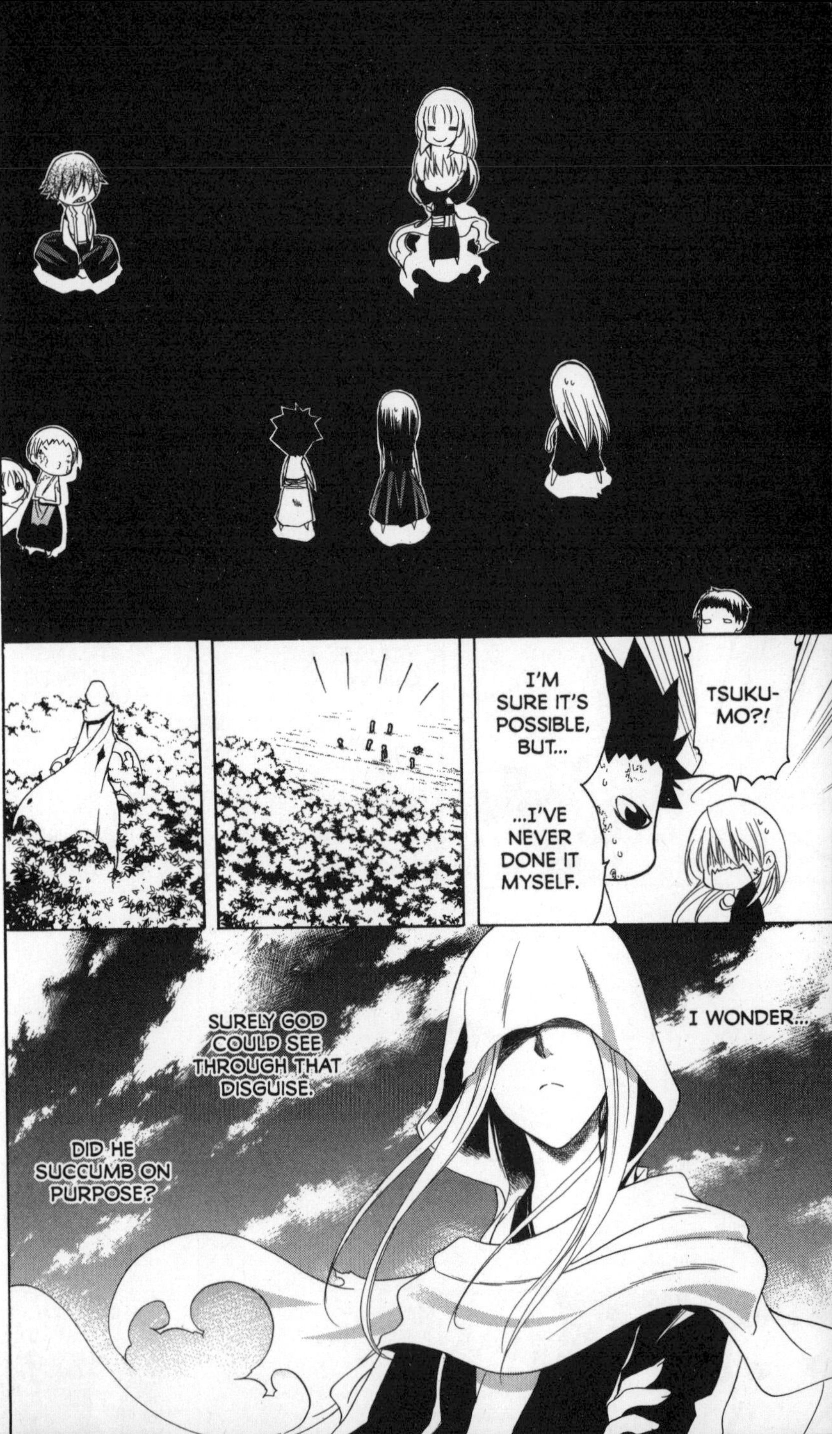
TSUKU-MO?!
I'M SURE IT'S POSSIBLE, BUT...
...I'VE NEVER DONE IT MYSELF.
I WONDER...
SURELY GOD COULD SEE THROUGH THAT DISGUISE.
DID HE SUCCUMB ON PURPOSE?

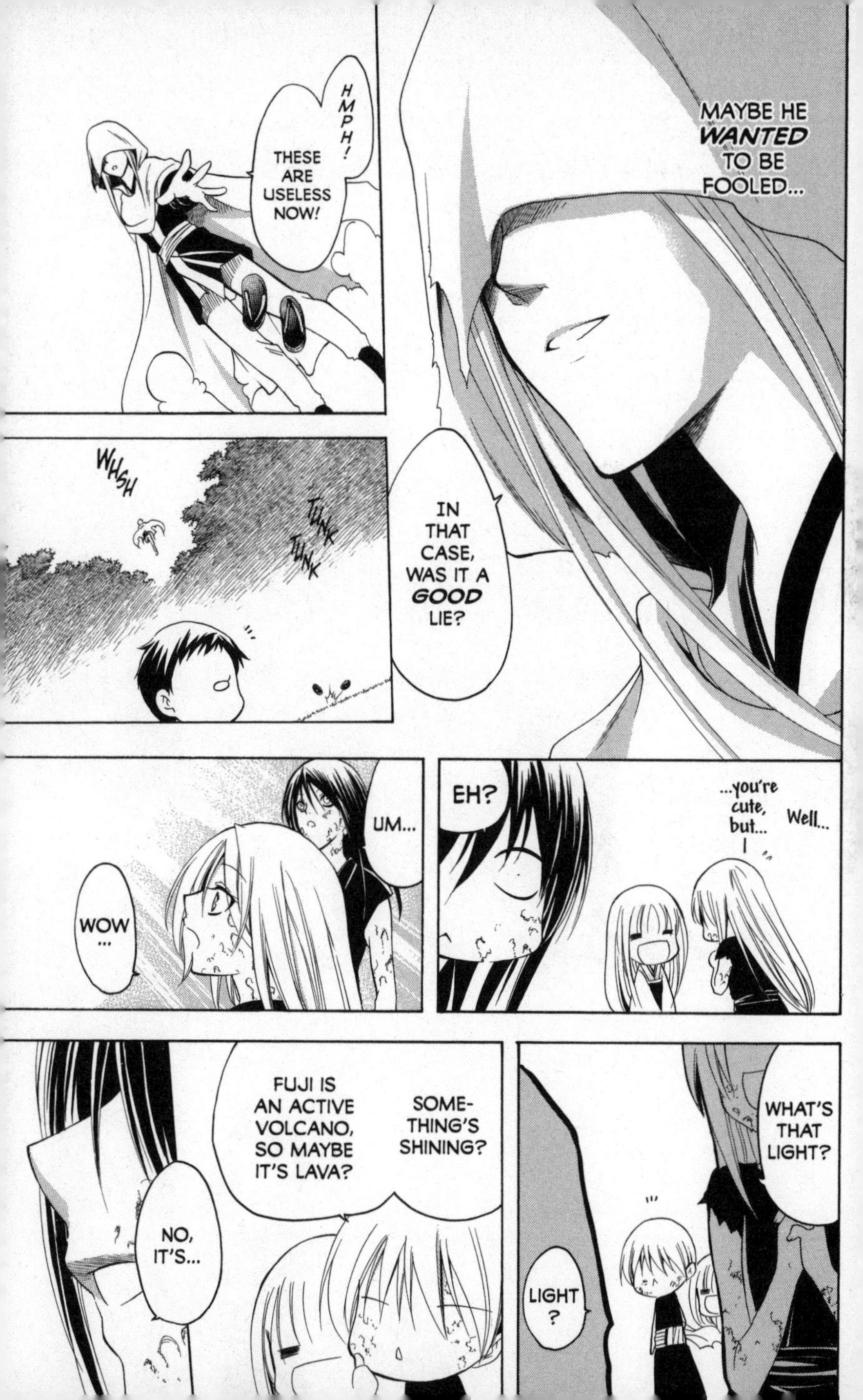
MAYBE HE *WANTED* TO BE FOOLED...
IN THAT CASE, WAS IT A *GOOD* LIE?
HMPH!
THESE ARE USELESS NOW!
WHSH
TUNK TUNK
Well...
...you're cute, but... I
EH?
UM...
WOW...
WHAT'S THAT LIGHT?
LIGHT?
SOME-THING'S SHINING?
FUJI IS AN ACTIVE VOLCANO, SO MAYBE IT'S LAVA?
NO, IT'S...

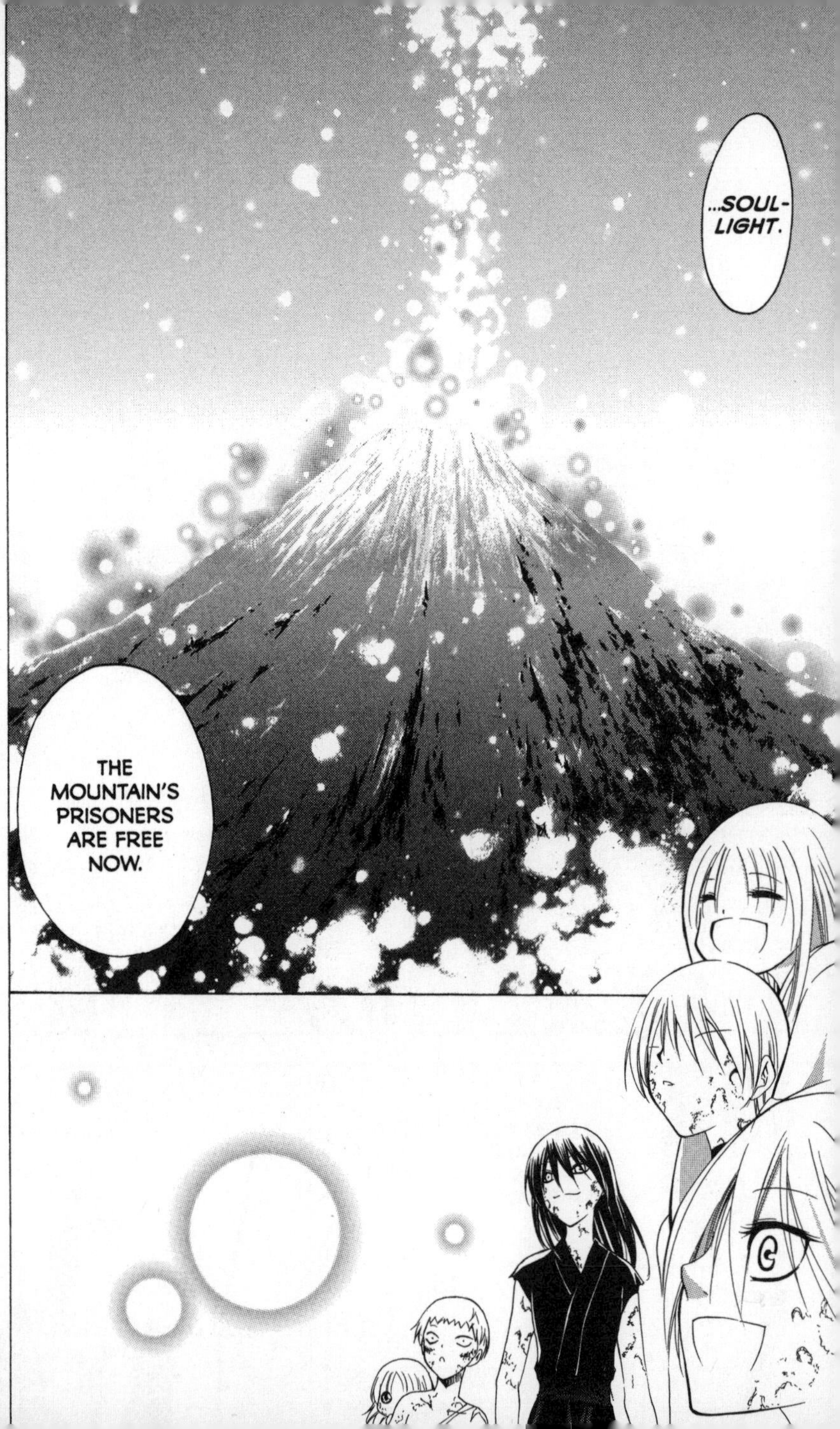
...SOUL-
LIGHT.
THE MOUNTAIN'S PRISONERS ARE FREE NOW.

Chapter 220
The Treasure of God

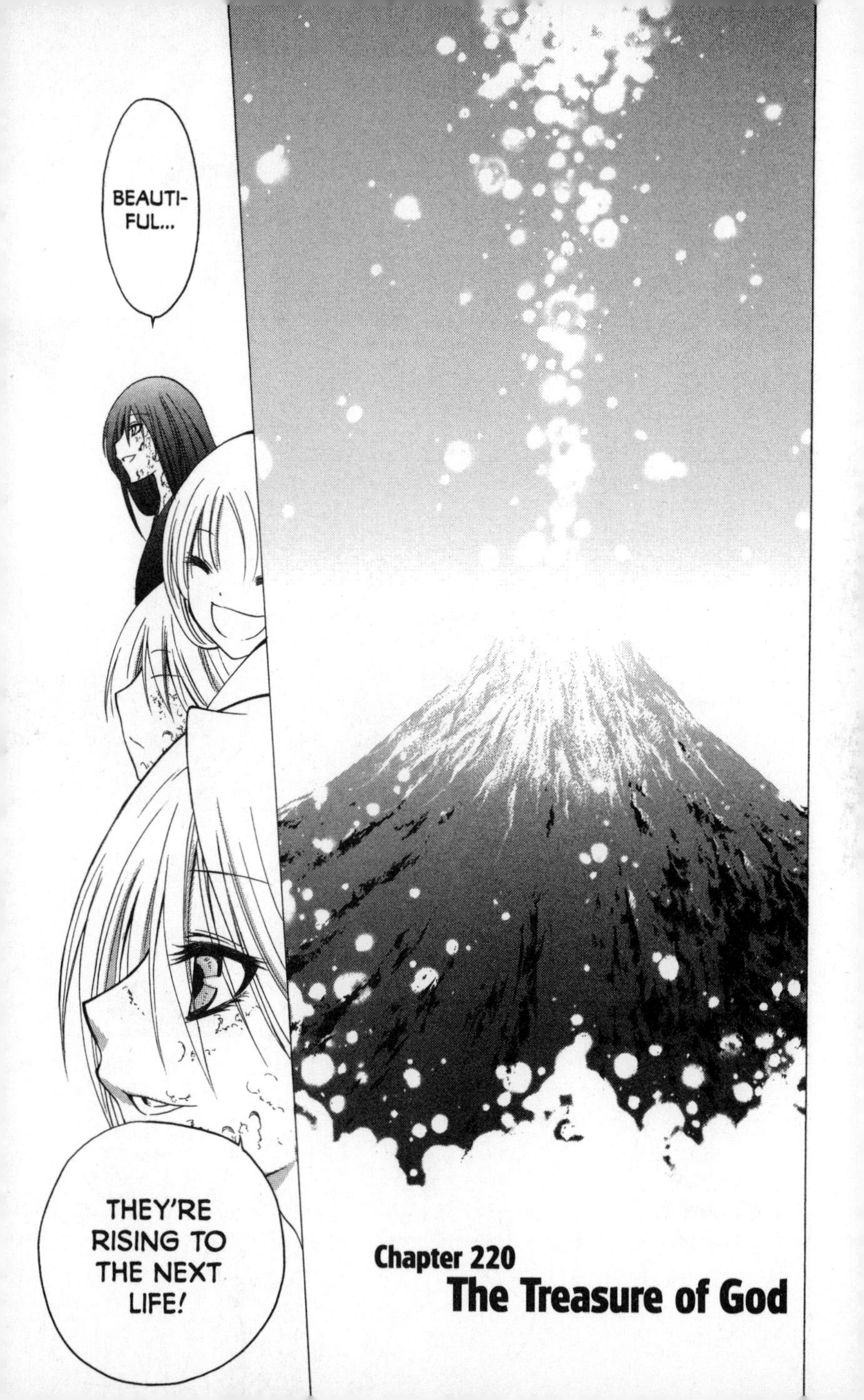
BEAUTI-FUL...
THEY'RE RISING TO THE NEXT LIFE!

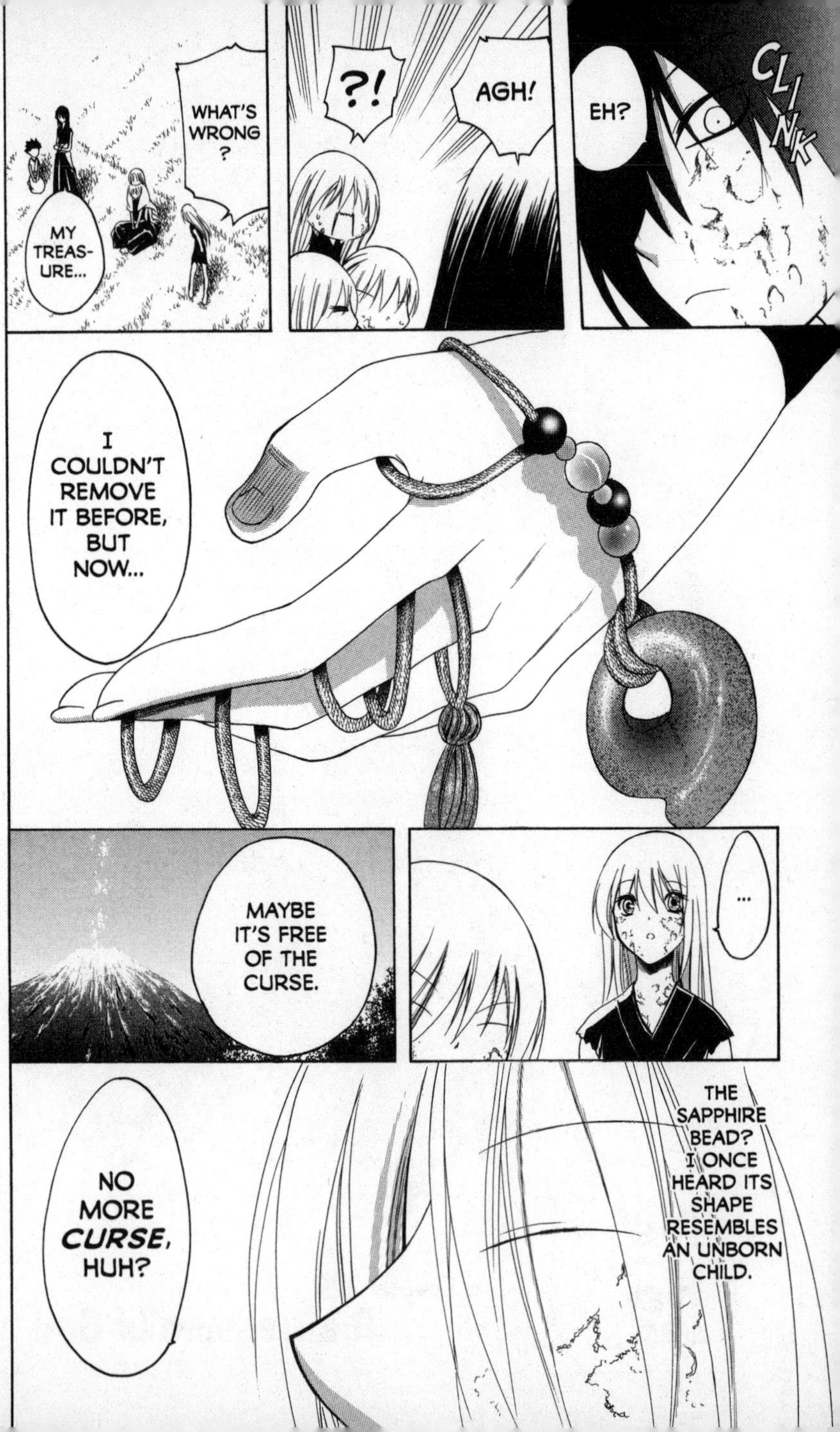

EH?
CLINK
AGH!
?!
WHAT'S WRONG?
MY TREASURE...
I COULDN'T REMOVE IT BEFORE, BUT NOW...
...
MAYBE IT'S FREE OF THE CURSE.
THE SAPPHIRE BEAD? I ONCE HEARD ITS SHAPE RESEMBLES AN UNBORN CHILD.
NO MORE *CURSE*, HUH?

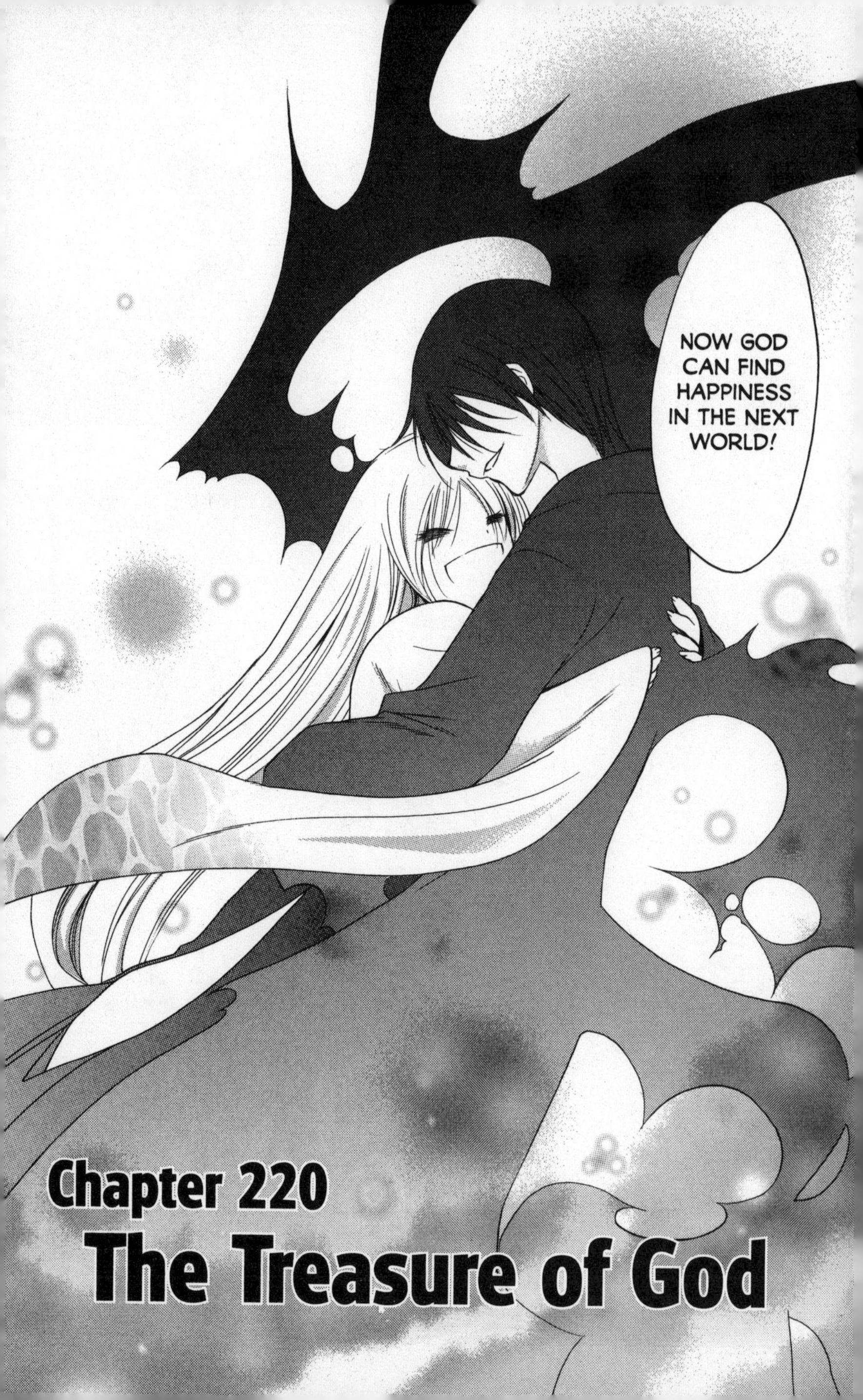
NOW GOD CAN FIND HAPPINESS IN THE NEXT WORLD!

Chapter 220
The Treasure of God

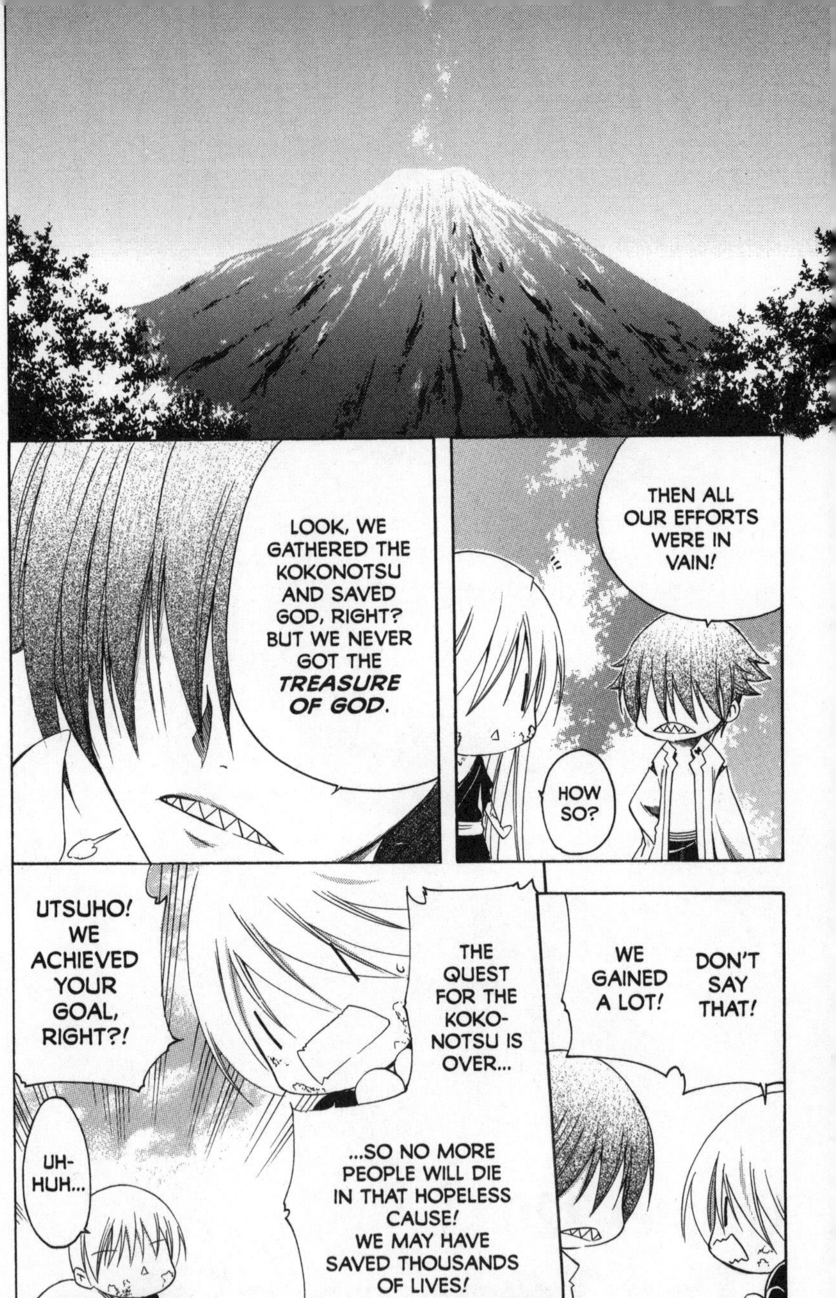
THEN ALL OUR EFFORTS WERE IN VAIN!
HOW SO?
LOOK, WE GATHERED THE KOKONOTSU AND SAVED GOD, RIGHT? BUT WE NEVER GOT THE *TREASURE OF GOD*.
DON'T SAY THAT!
WE GAINED A LOT!
THE QUEST FOR THE KOKO-NOTSU IS OVER...
...SO NO MORE PEOPLE WILL DIE IN THAT HOPELESS CAUSE! WE MAY HAVE SAVED THOUSANDS OF LIVES!
UTSUHO! WE ACHIEVED YOUR GOAL, RIGHT?!
UH-HUH...

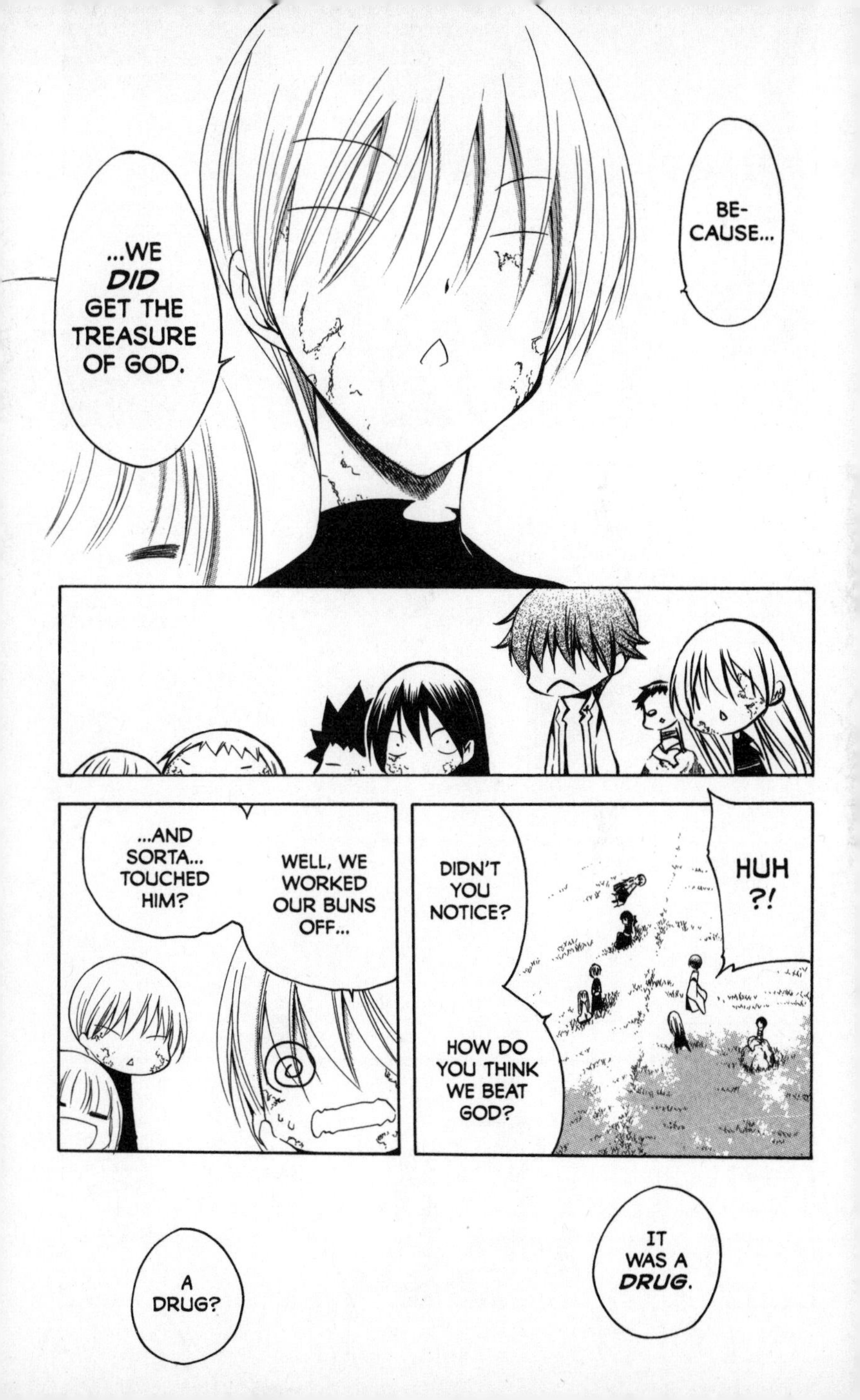
BE-CAUSE...
...WE *DID* GET THE TREASURE OF GOD.
HUH ?!
DIDN'T YOU NOTICE?
HOW DO YOU THINK WE BEAT GOD?
WELL, WE WORKED OUR BUNS OFF...
...AND SORTA... TOUCHED HIM?
IT WAS A *DRUG*.
A DRUG?

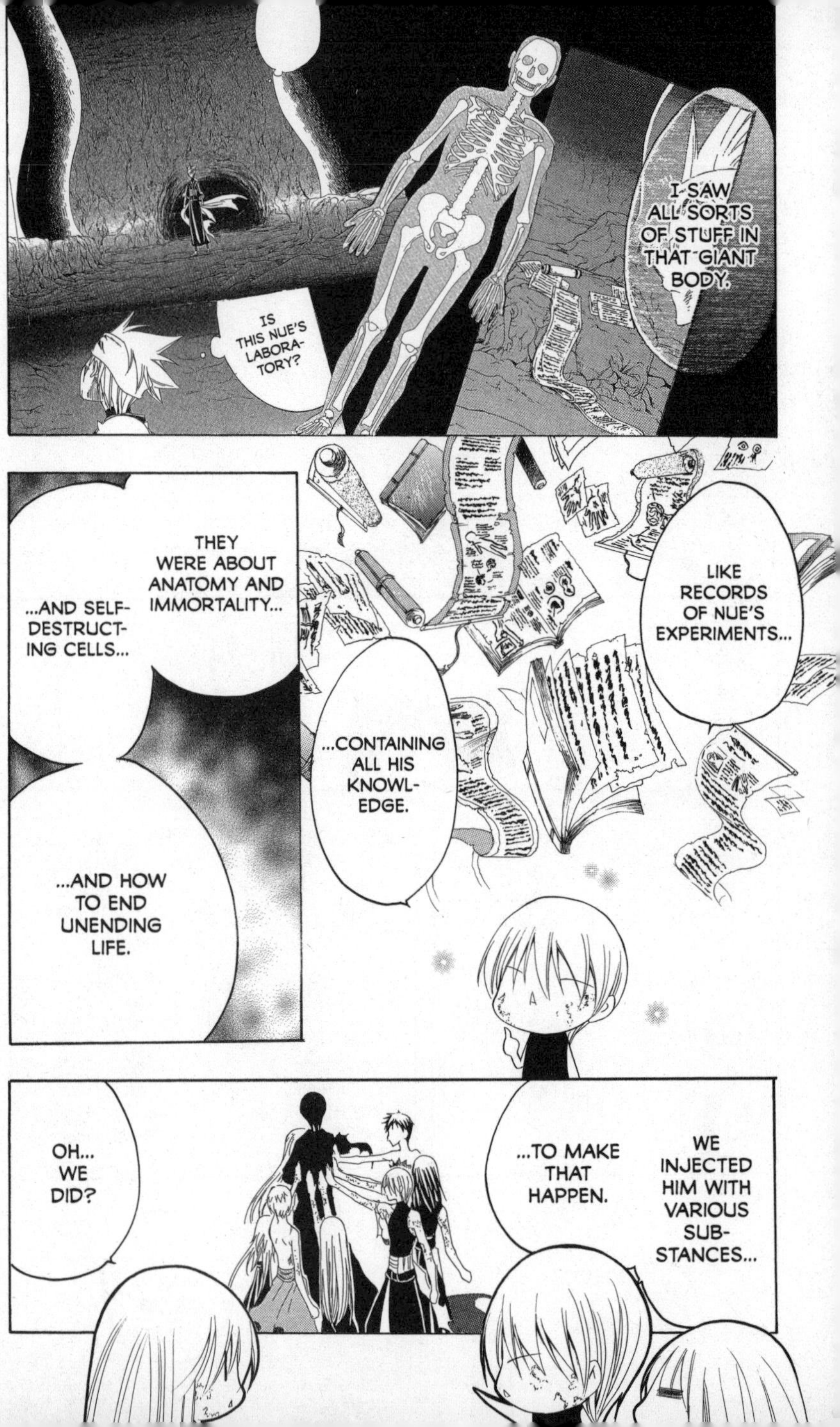
I SAW ALL SORTS OF STUFF IN THAT GIANT BODY.
IS THIS NUE'S LABORATORY?
LIKE RECORDS OF NUE'S EXPERIMENTS...
...CONTAINING ALL HIS KNOWLEDGE.
THEY WERE ABOUT ANATOMY AND IMMORTALITY...
...AND SELF-DESTRUCTING CELLS...
...AND HOW TO END UNENDING LIFE.
WE INJECTED HIM WITH VARIOUS SUBSTANCES...
...TO MAKE THAT HAPPEN.
OH... WE DID?

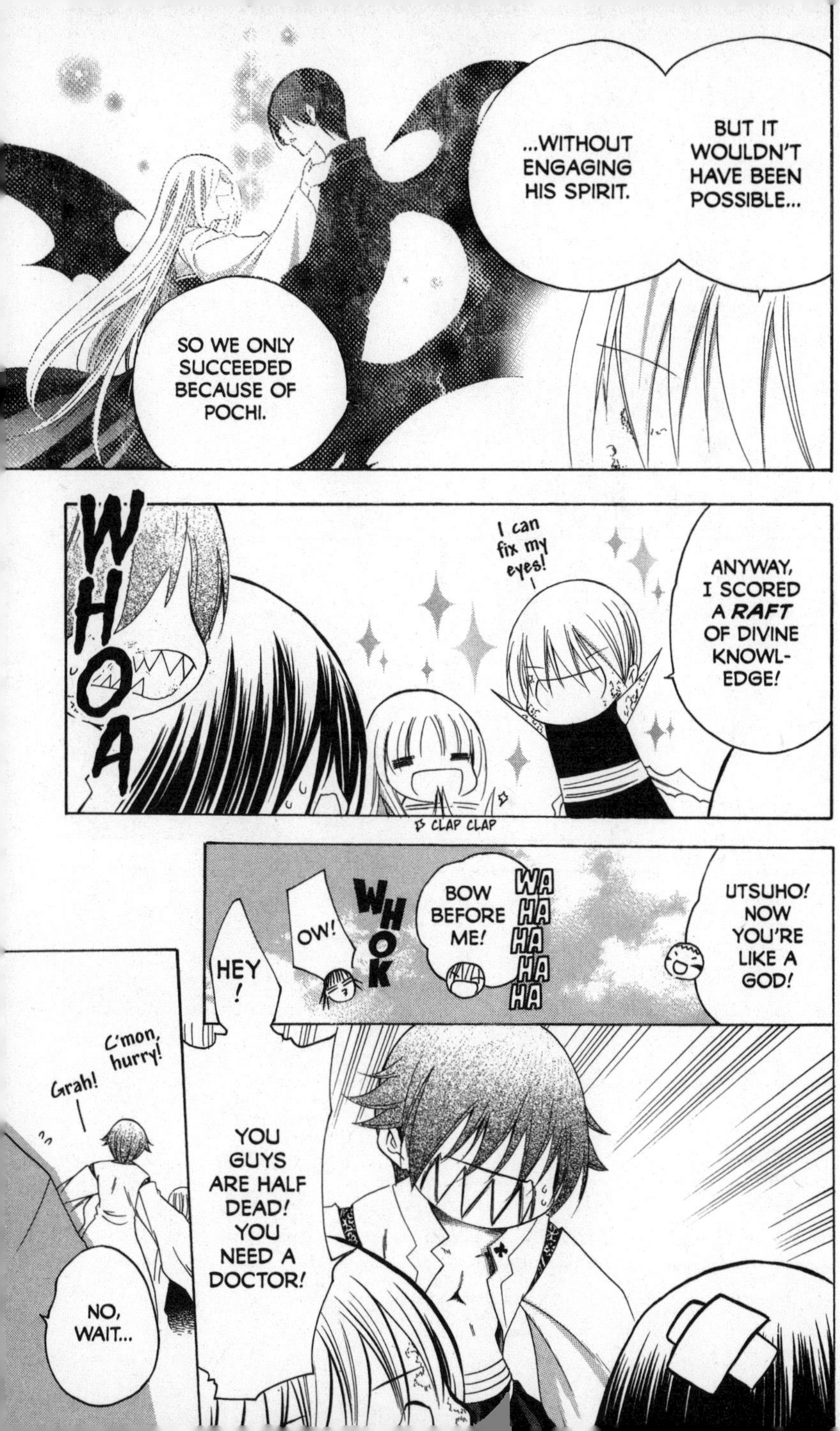
BUT IT WOULDN'T HAVE BEEN POSSIBLE...
...WITHOUT ENGAGING HIS SPIRIT.
SO WE ONLY SUCCEEDED BECAUSE OF POCHI.
ANYWAY, I SCORED A RAFT OF DIVINE KNOWL-EDGE!
I can fix my eyes!
WHOA
CLAP CLAP
UTSUHO! NOW YOU'RE LIKE A GOD!
WA HA HA HA HA
BOW BEFORE ME!
WHOK
OW!
HEY!
YOU GUYS ARE HALF DEAD! YOU NEED A DOCTOR!
C'mon, hurry!
Grah!
NO, WAIT...

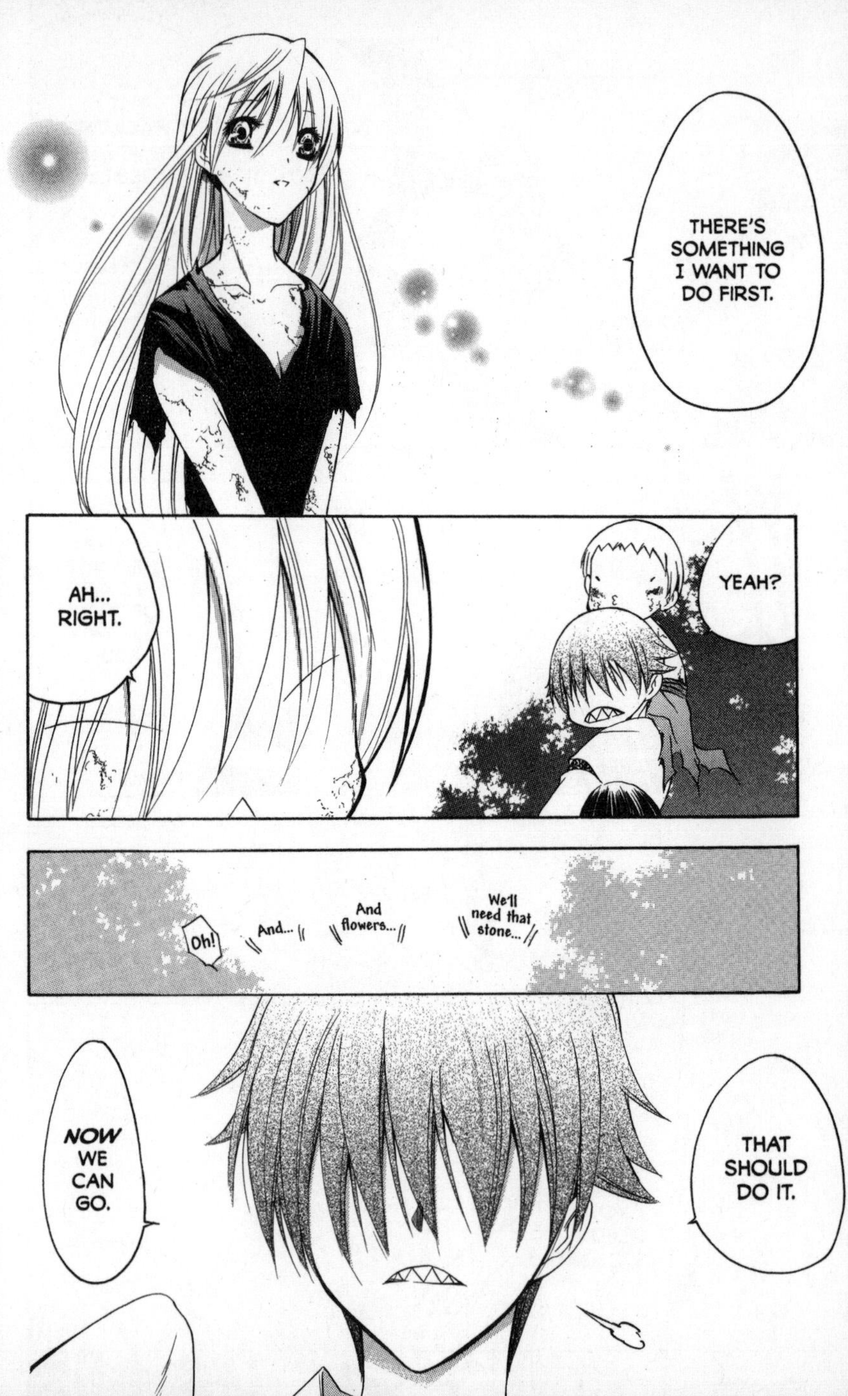
THERE'S SOMETHING I WANT TO DO FIRST.
YEAH?
AH... RIGHT.
We'll need that stone...
And flowers...
And...
Oh!
THAT SHOULD DO IT.
NOW WE CAN GO.

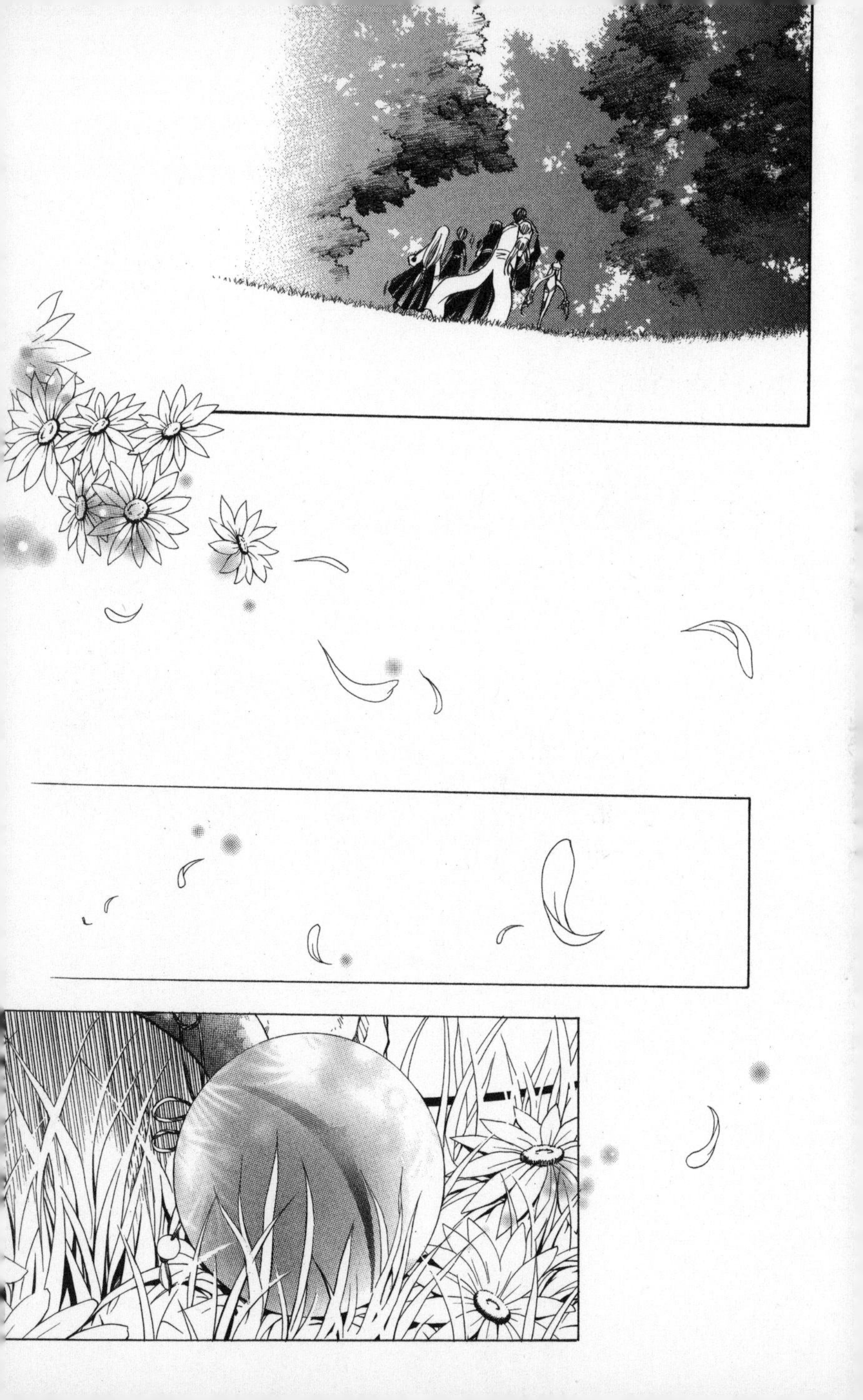

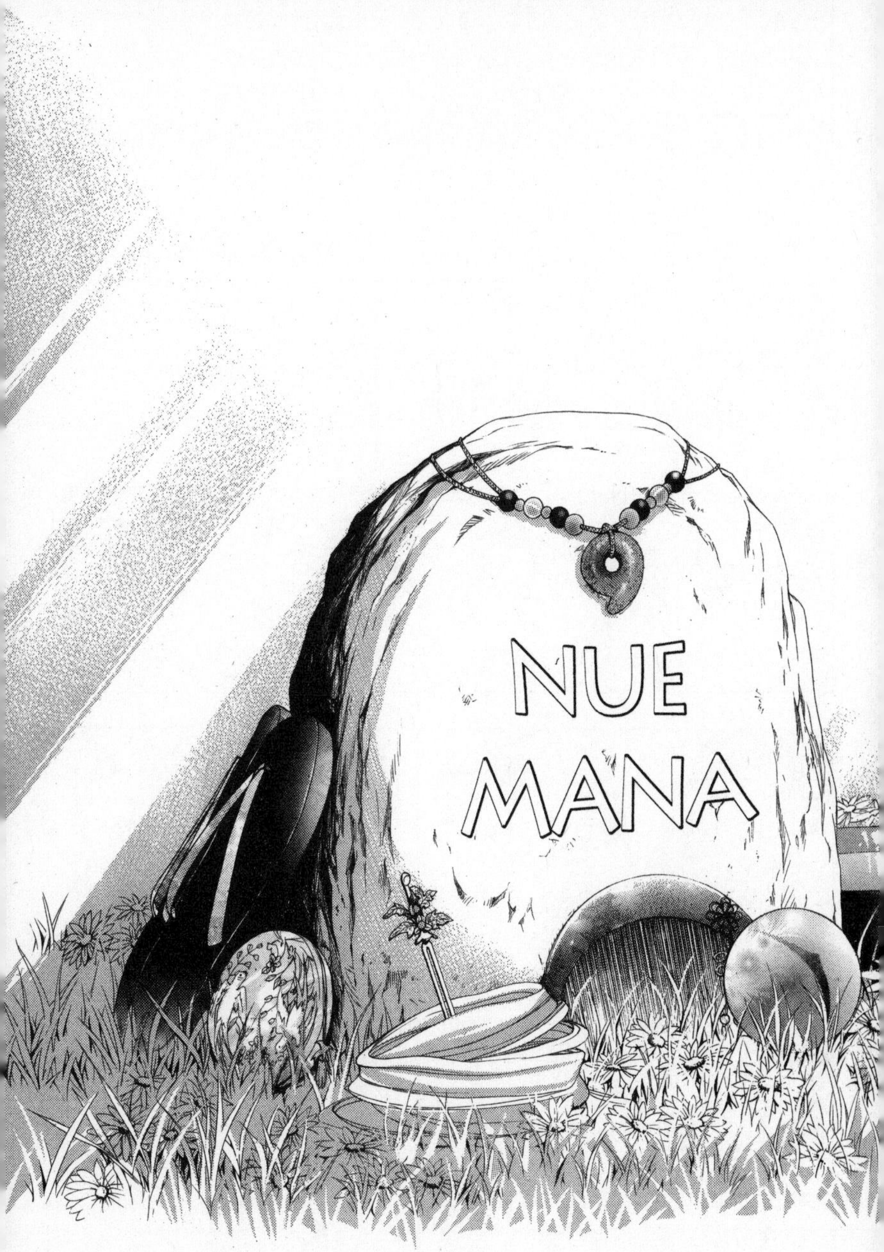
NUE
MANA

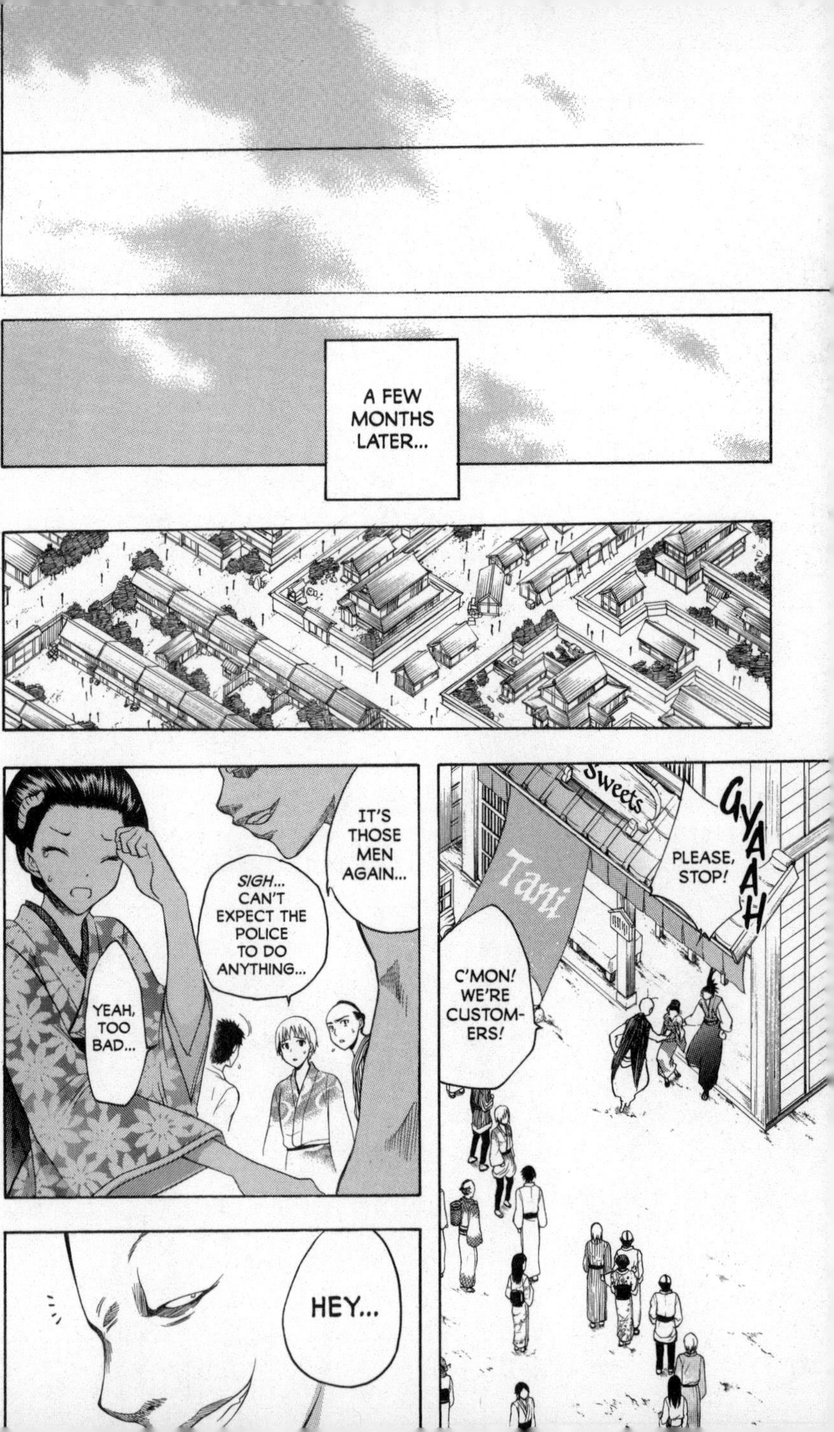
A FEW MONTHS LATER...
Sweets
Tani
GYAAH
PLEASE, STOP!
C'MON! WE'RE CUSTOM-ERS!
IT'S THOSE MEN AGAIN...
SIGH... CAN'T EXPECT THE POLICE TO DO ANYTHING...
YEAH, TOO BAD...
HEY...

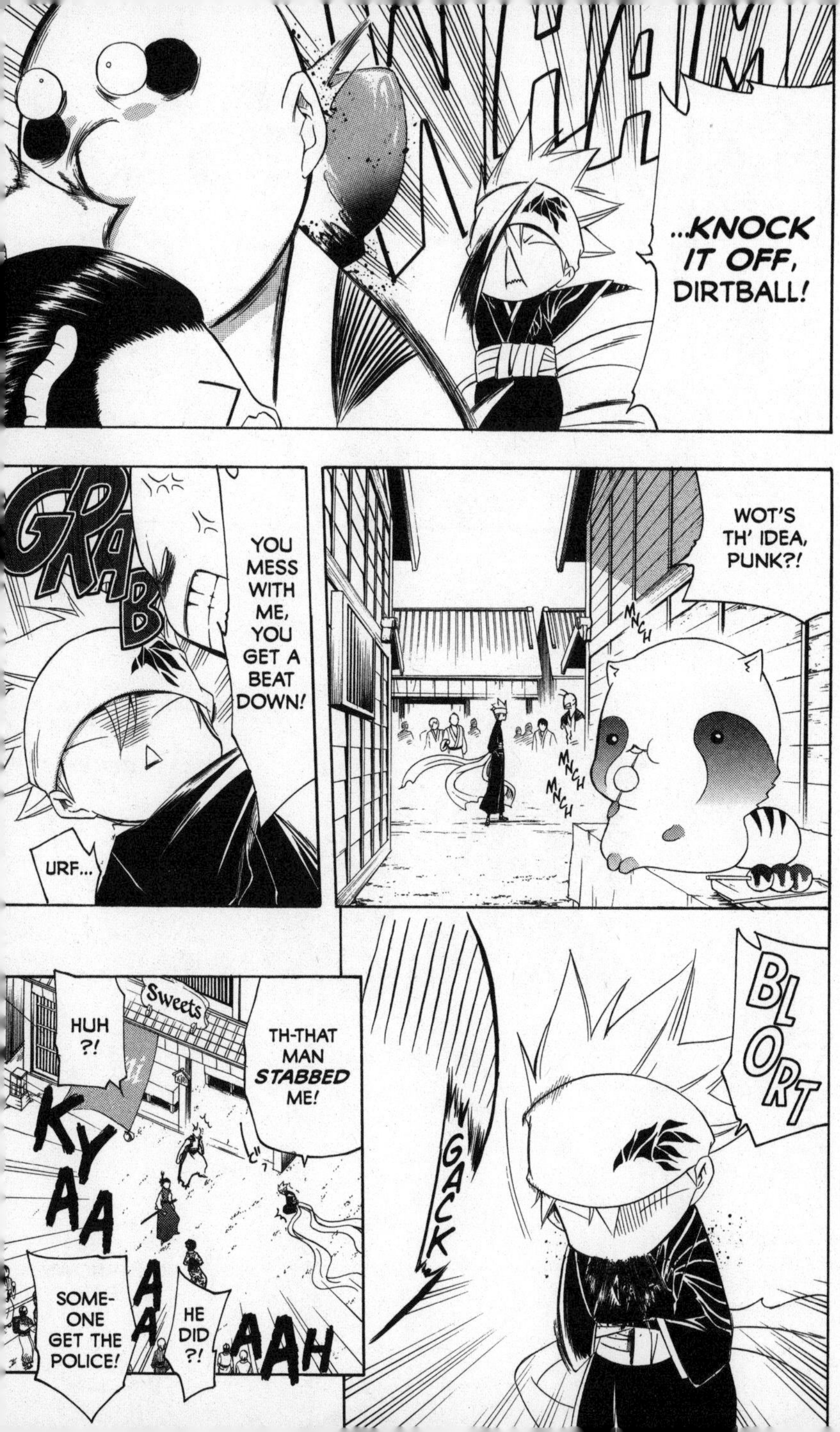

...KNOCK IT OFF, DIRTBALL!
WOT'S TH' IDEA, PUNK?!
MNCH
MNCH
MNCH
MNCH
GRAB
YOU MESS WITH ME, YOU GET A BEAT DOWN!
URF...
BLORT
GACK
TH-THAT MAN STABBED ME!
HUH ?!
Sweets
KYAAAAAH
HE DID ?!
SOME-ONE GET THE POLICE!

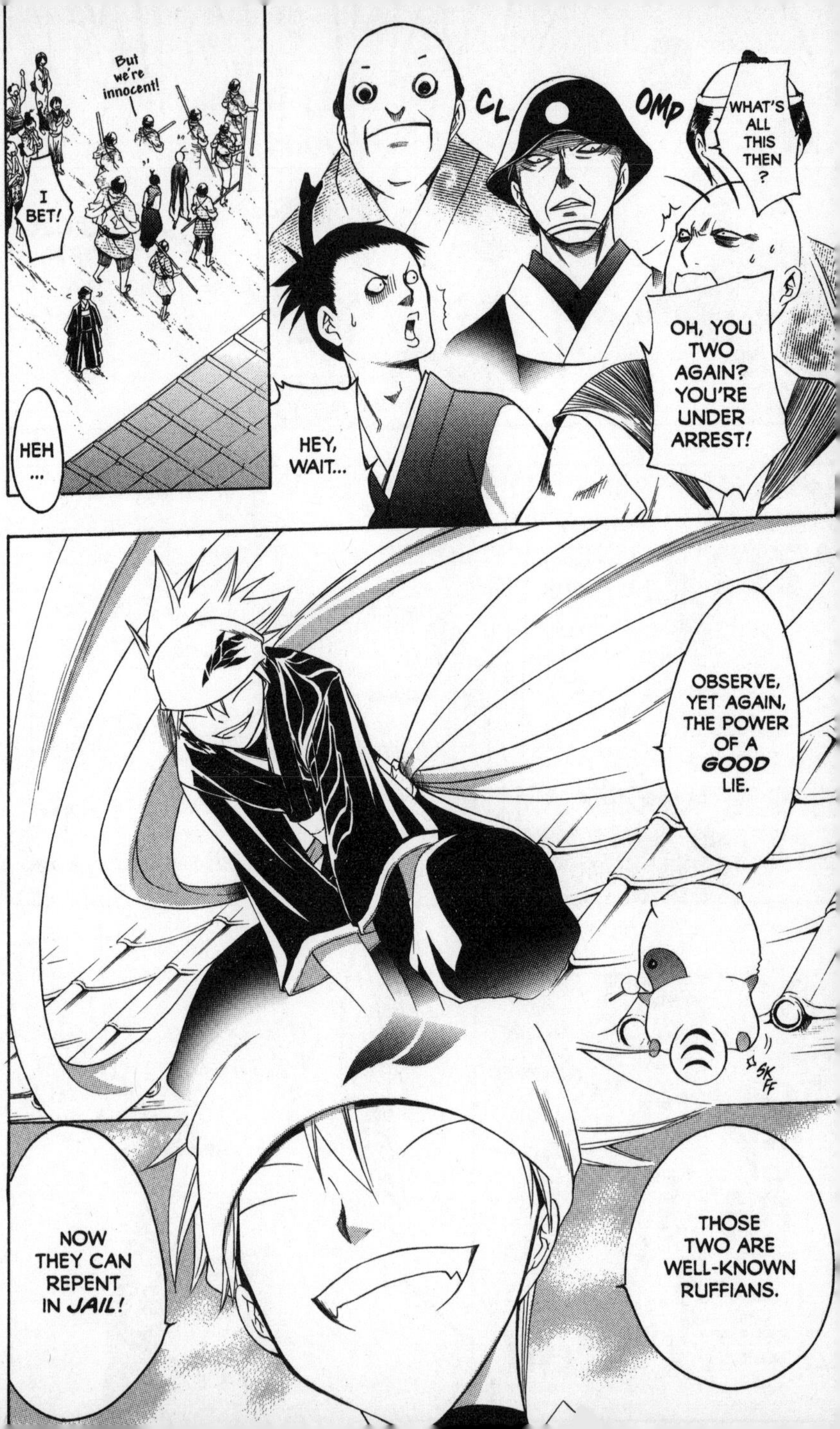
CL
OMP
WHAT'S ALL THIS THEN?
OH, YOU TWO AGAIN? YOU'RE UNDER ARREST!
HEY, WAIT...
But we're innocent!
I BET!
HEH...
OBSERVE, YET AGAIN, THE POWER OF A GOOD LIE.
SKFF
THOSE TWO ARE WELL-KNOWN RUFFIANS.
NOW THEY CAN REPENT IN JAIL!

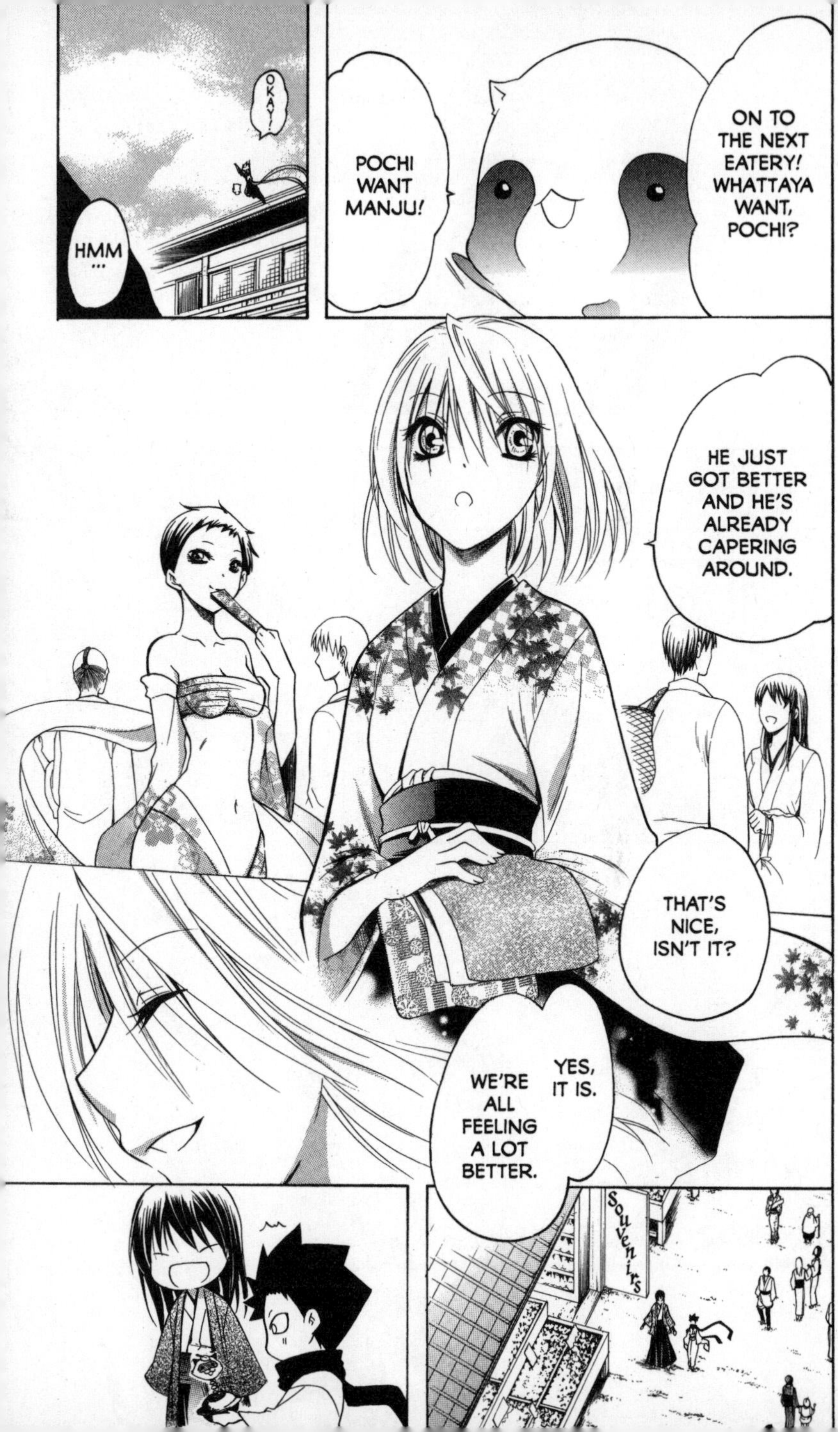
ON TO THE NEXT EATERY! WHATTAYA WANT, POCHI?
POCHI WANT MANJU!
OKAY!
HMM...
HE JUST GOT BETTER AND HE'S ALREADY CAPERING AROUND.
THAT'S NICE, ISN'T IT?
YES, IT IS.
WE'RE ALL FEELING A LOT BETTER.
Souvenirs

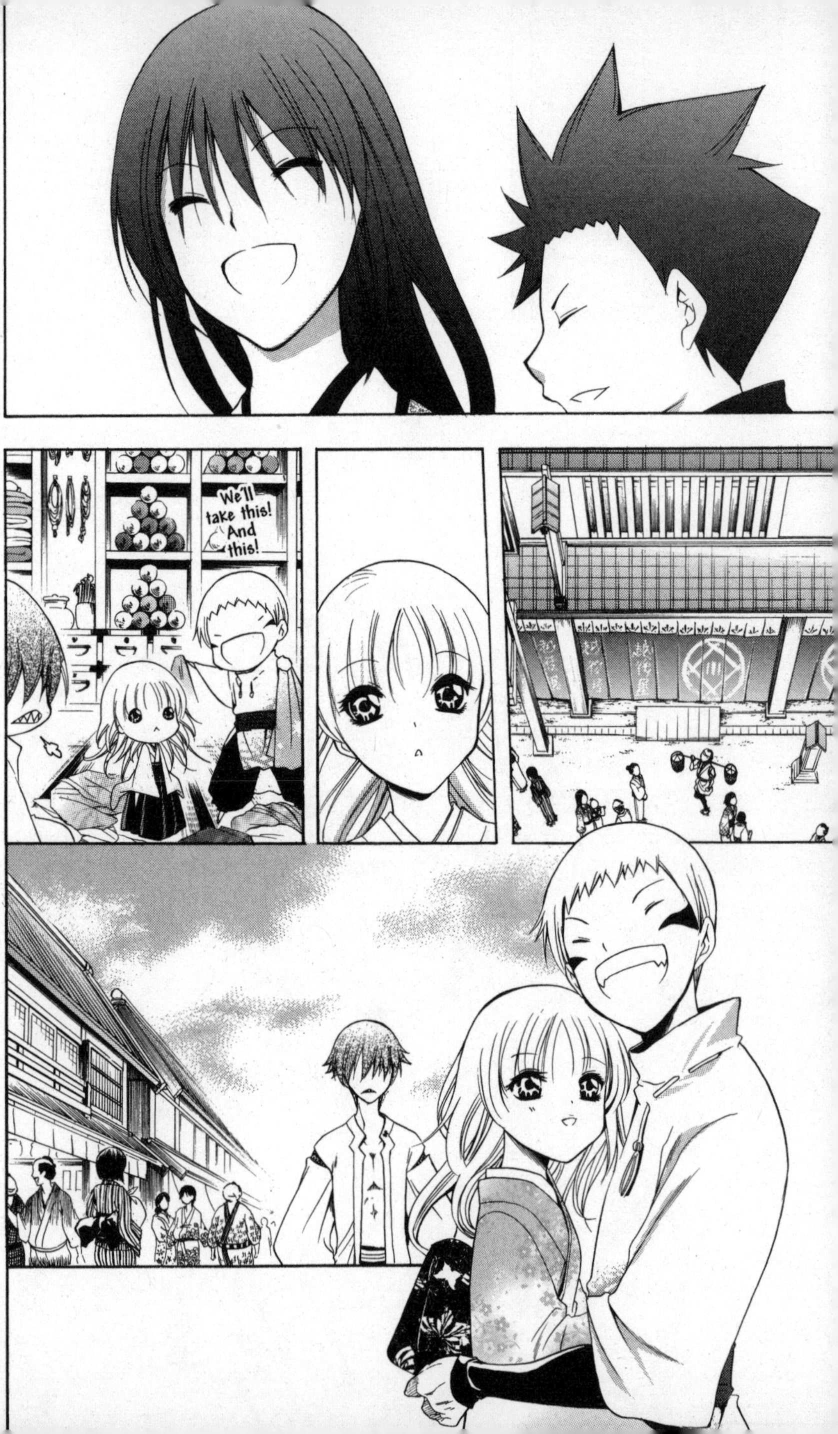
We'll take this! And this!

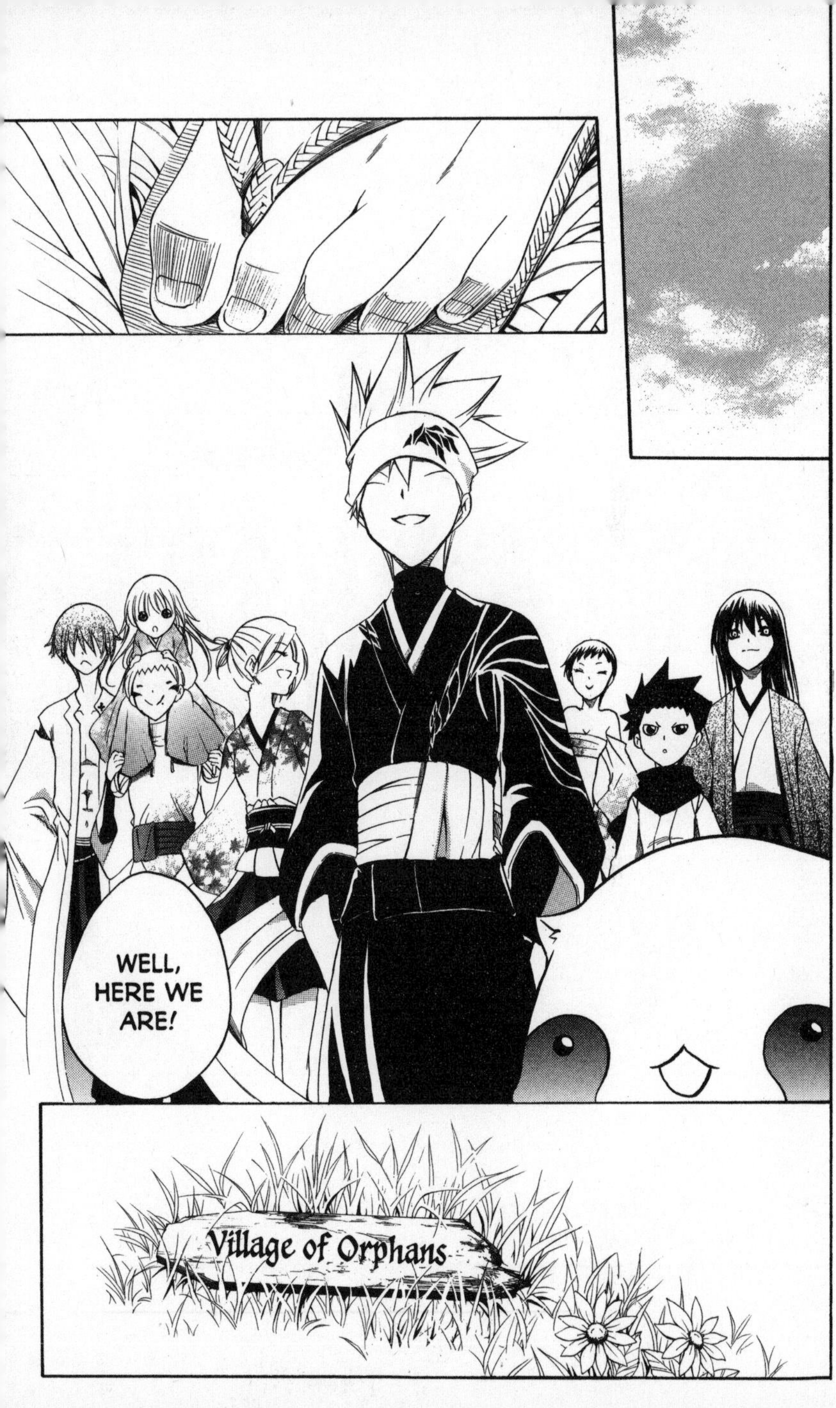
WELL, HERE WE ARE!
Village of Orphans

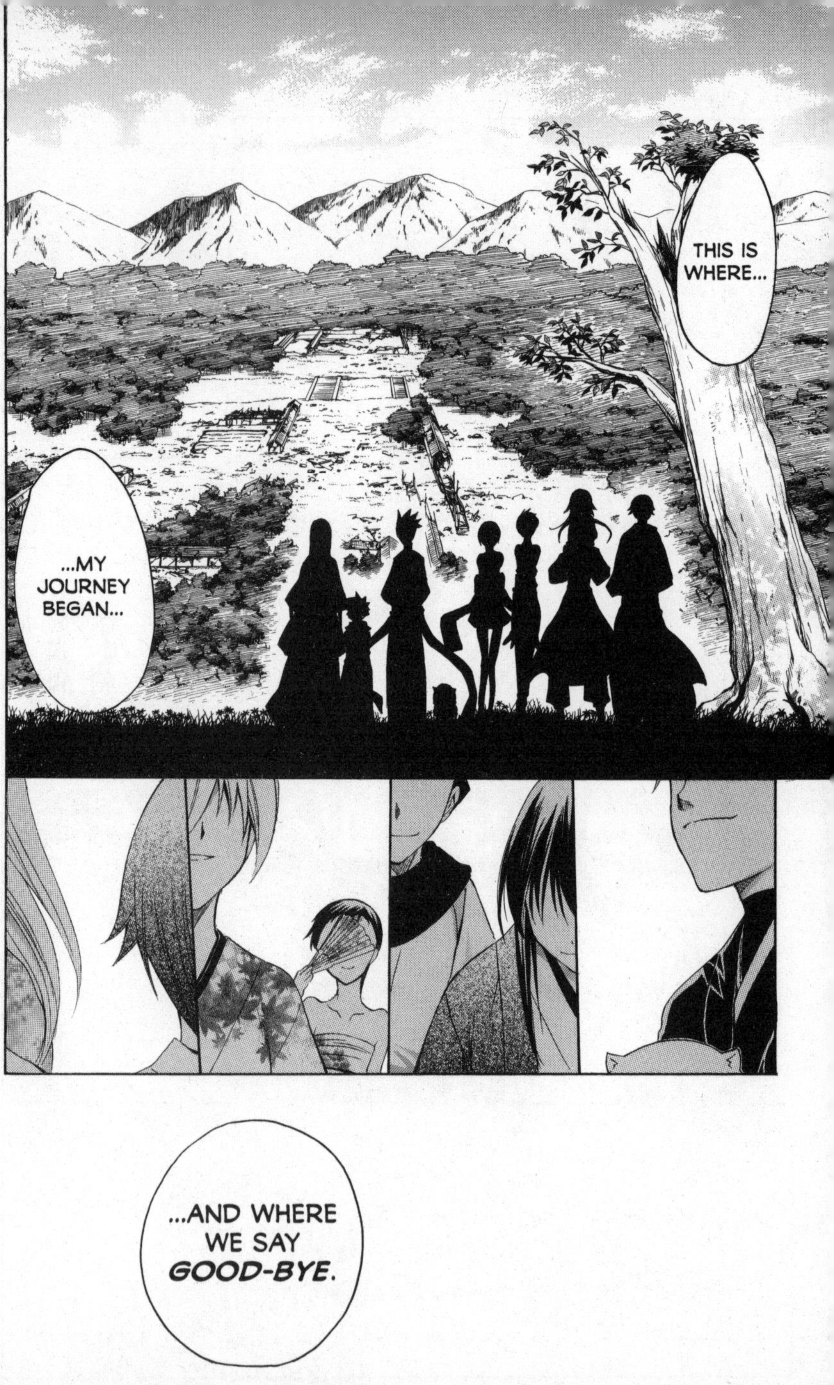
THIS IS WHERE...
...MY JOURNEY BEGAN...
...AND WHERE WE SAY *GOOD-BYE*.

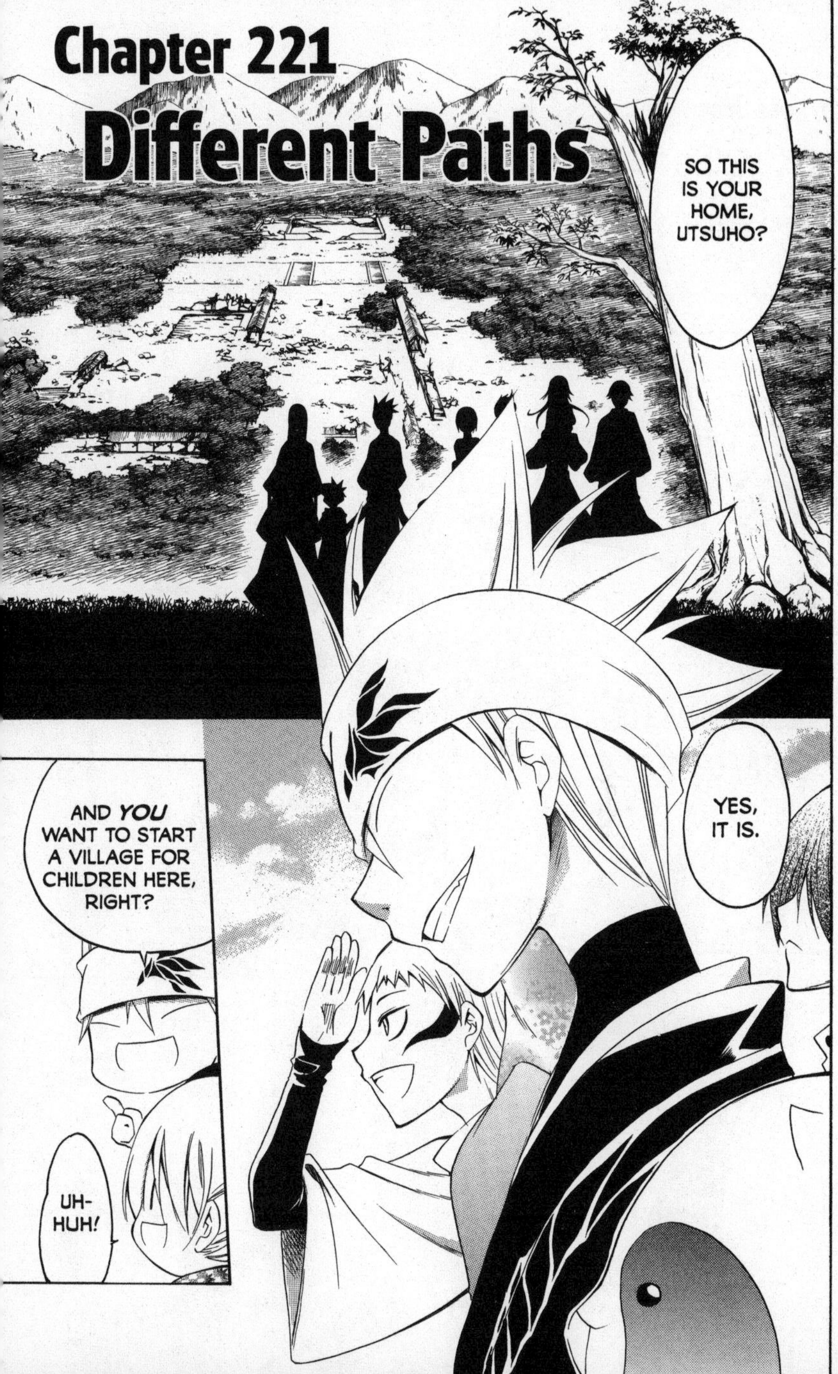
Chapter 221
Different Paths
SO THIS IS YOUR HOME, UTSUHO?
YES, IT IS.
AND *YOU* WANT TO START A VILLAGE FOR CHILDREN HERE, RIGHT?
UH-HUH!

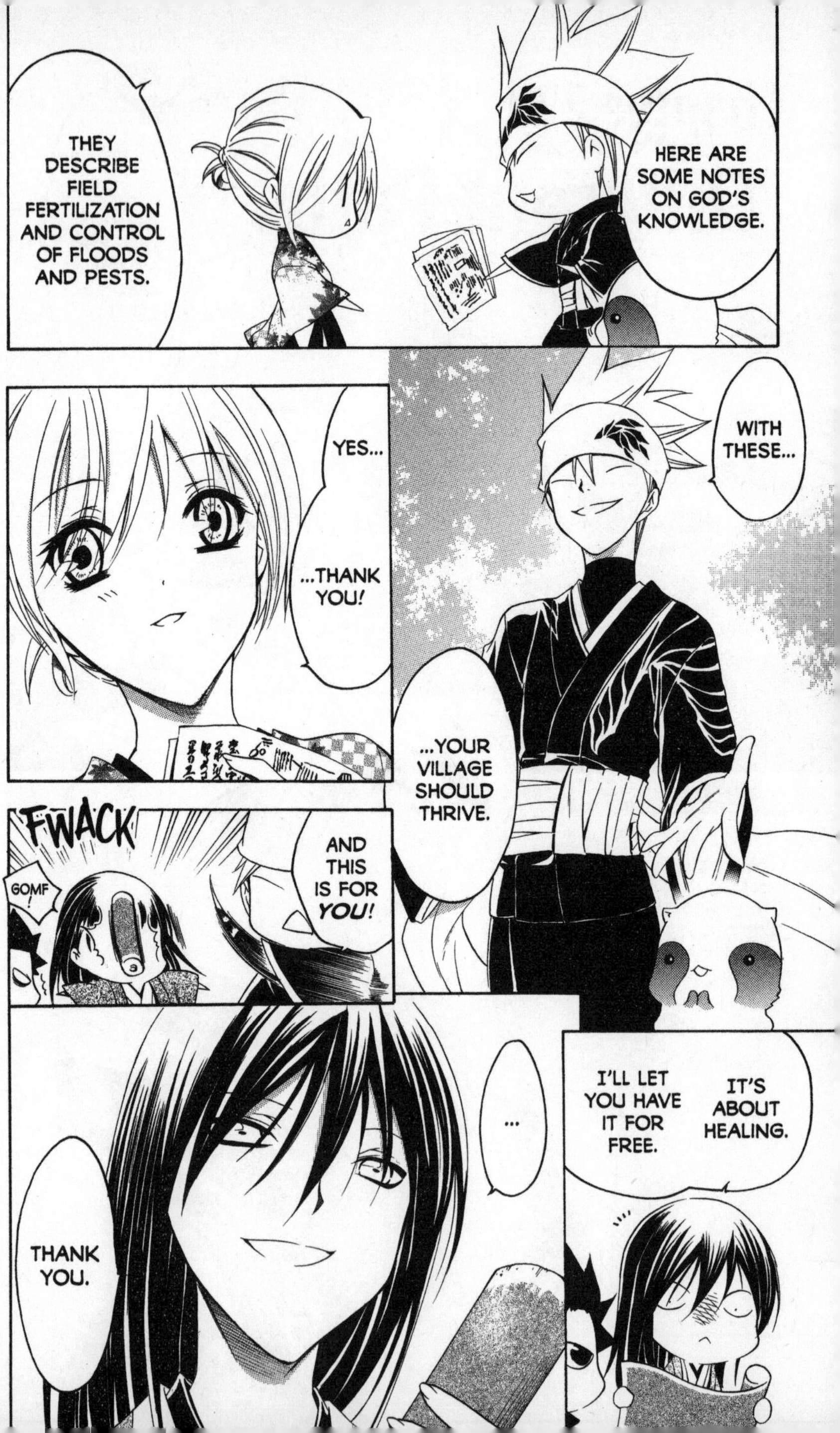
HERE ARE SOME NOTES ON GOD'S KNOWLEDGE.
THEY DESCRIBE FIELD FERTILIZATION AND CONTROL OF FLOODS AND PESTS.
WITH THESE...
...YOUR VILLAGE SHOULD THRIVE.
YES...
...THANK YOU!
FWACK
AND THIS IS FOR *YOU*!
GOMF!
IT'S ABOUT HEALING.
I'LL LET YOU HAVE IT FOR FREE.
...
THANK YOU.

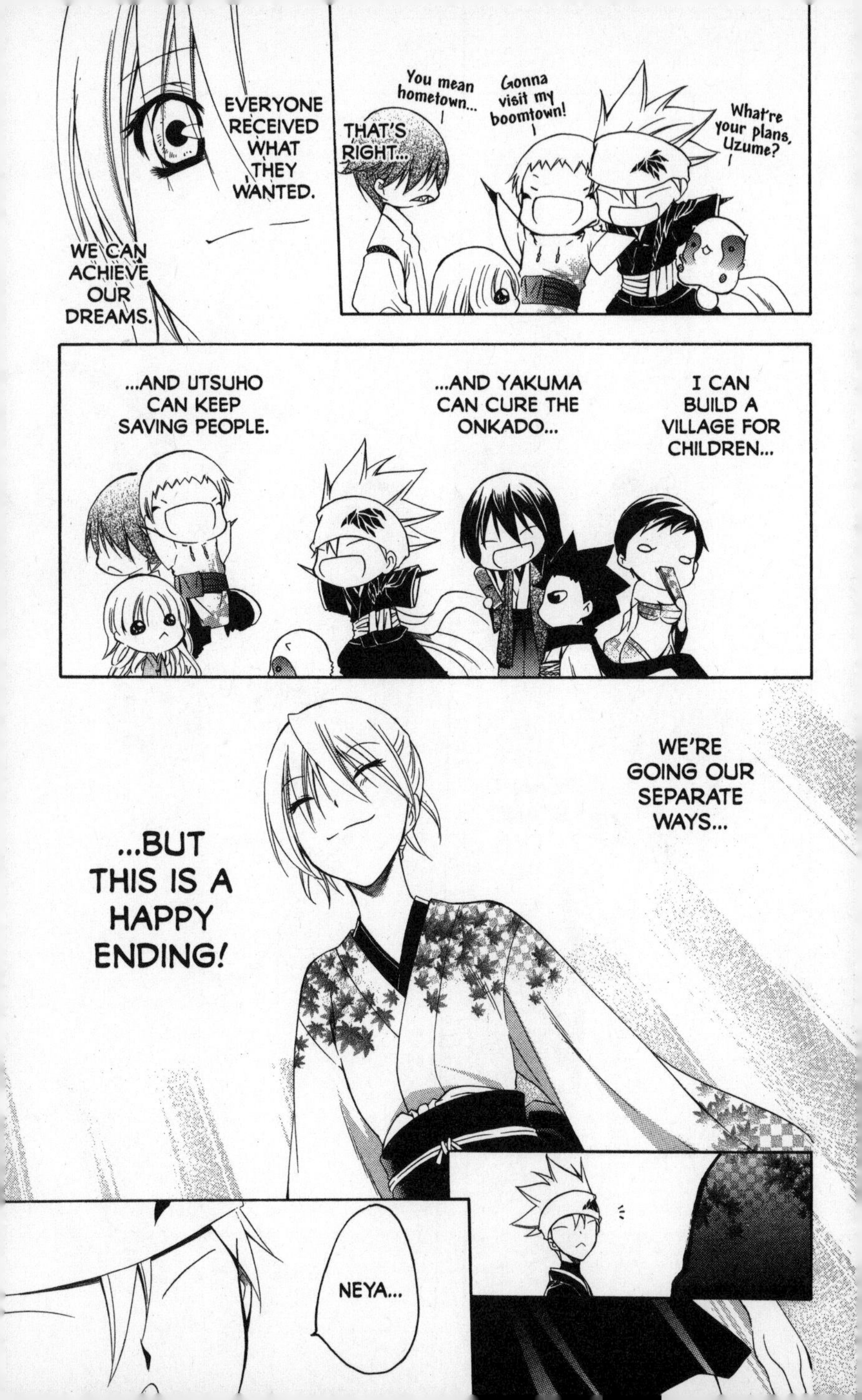
What're your plans, Uzume?
Gonna visit my boomtown!
You mean hometown...
THAT'S RIGHT...
EVERYONE RECEIVED WHAT THEY WANTED.
WE CAN ACHIEVE OUR DREAMS.
I CAN BUILD A VILLAGE FOR CHILDREN...
...AND YAKUMA CAN CURE THE ONKADO...
...AND UTSUHO CAN KEEP SAVING PEOPLE.
WE'RE GOING OUR SEPARATE WAYS...
...BUT THIS IS A HAPPY ENDING!
NEYA...

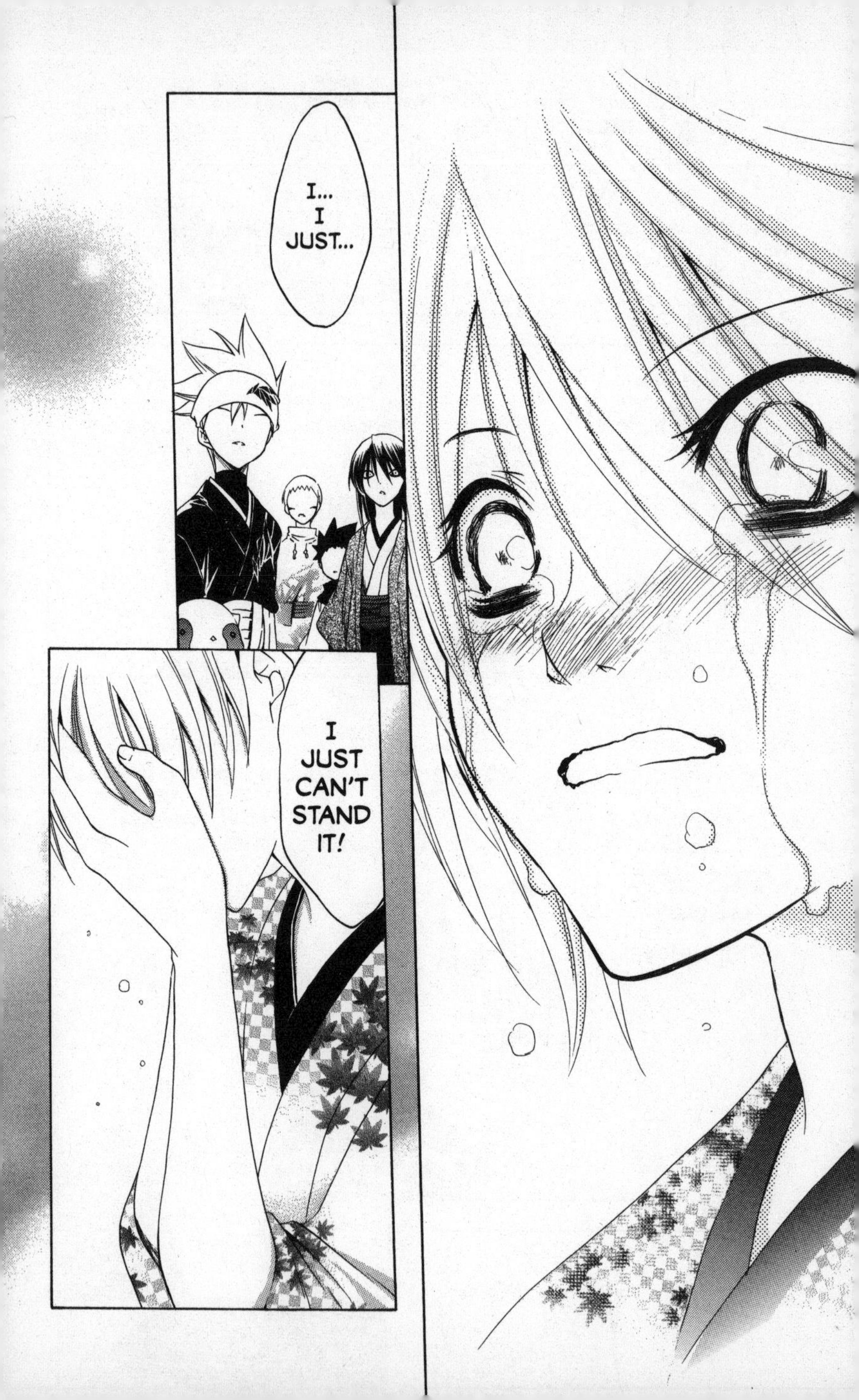
I... I JUST...
I JUST CAN'T STAND IT!

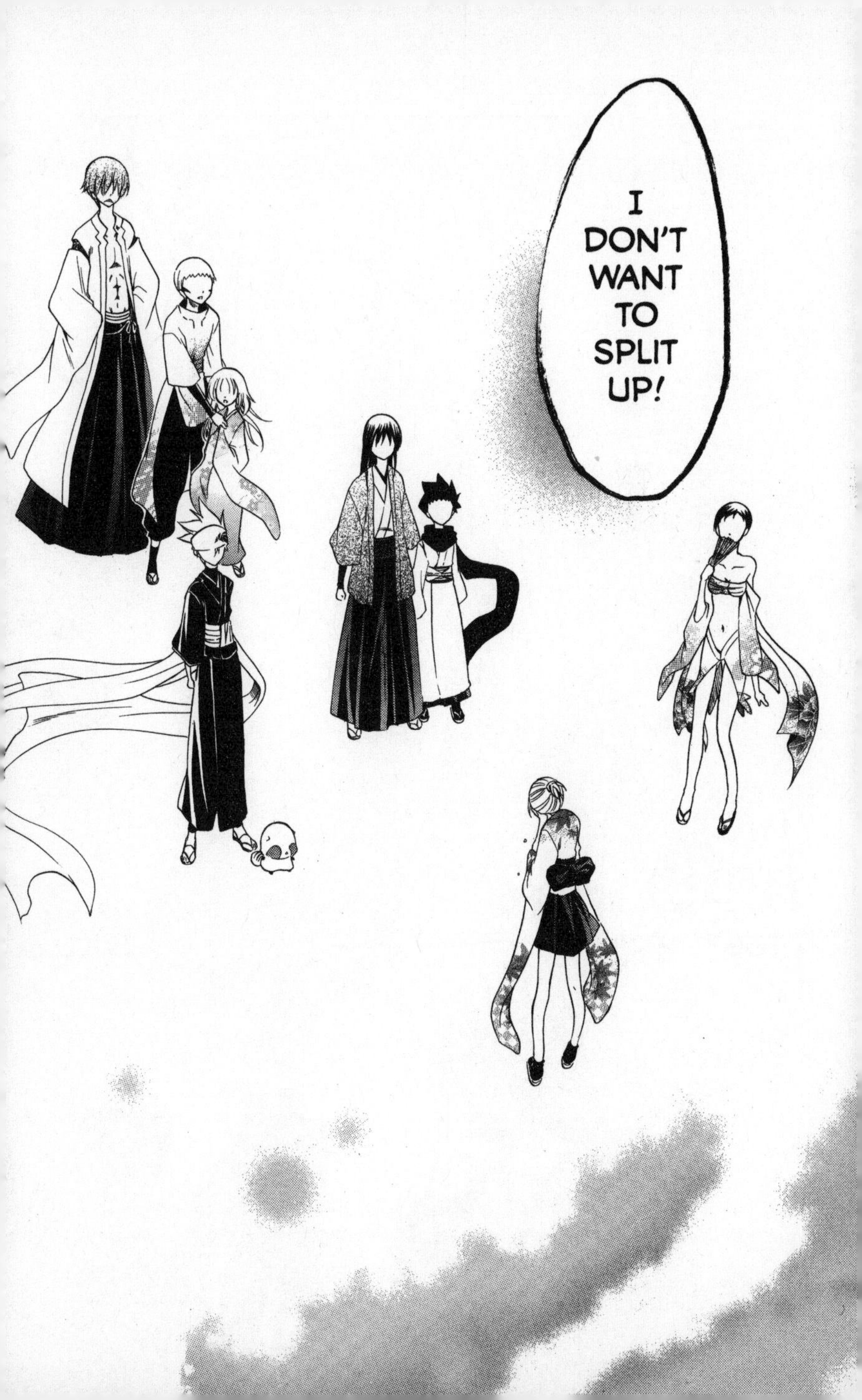
I DON'T WANT TO SPLIT UP!

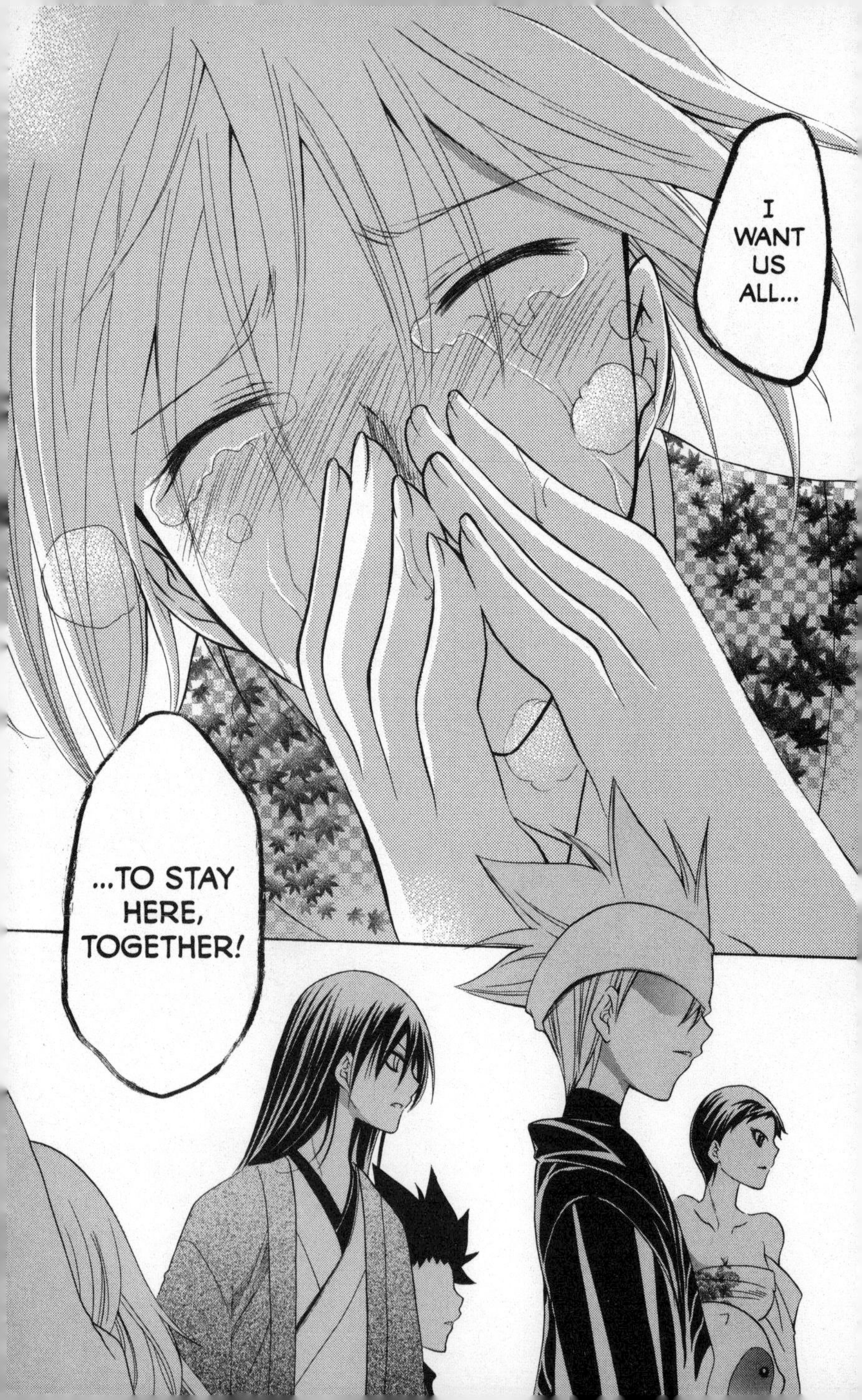
I WANT US ALL...
...TO STAY HERE, TOGETHER!

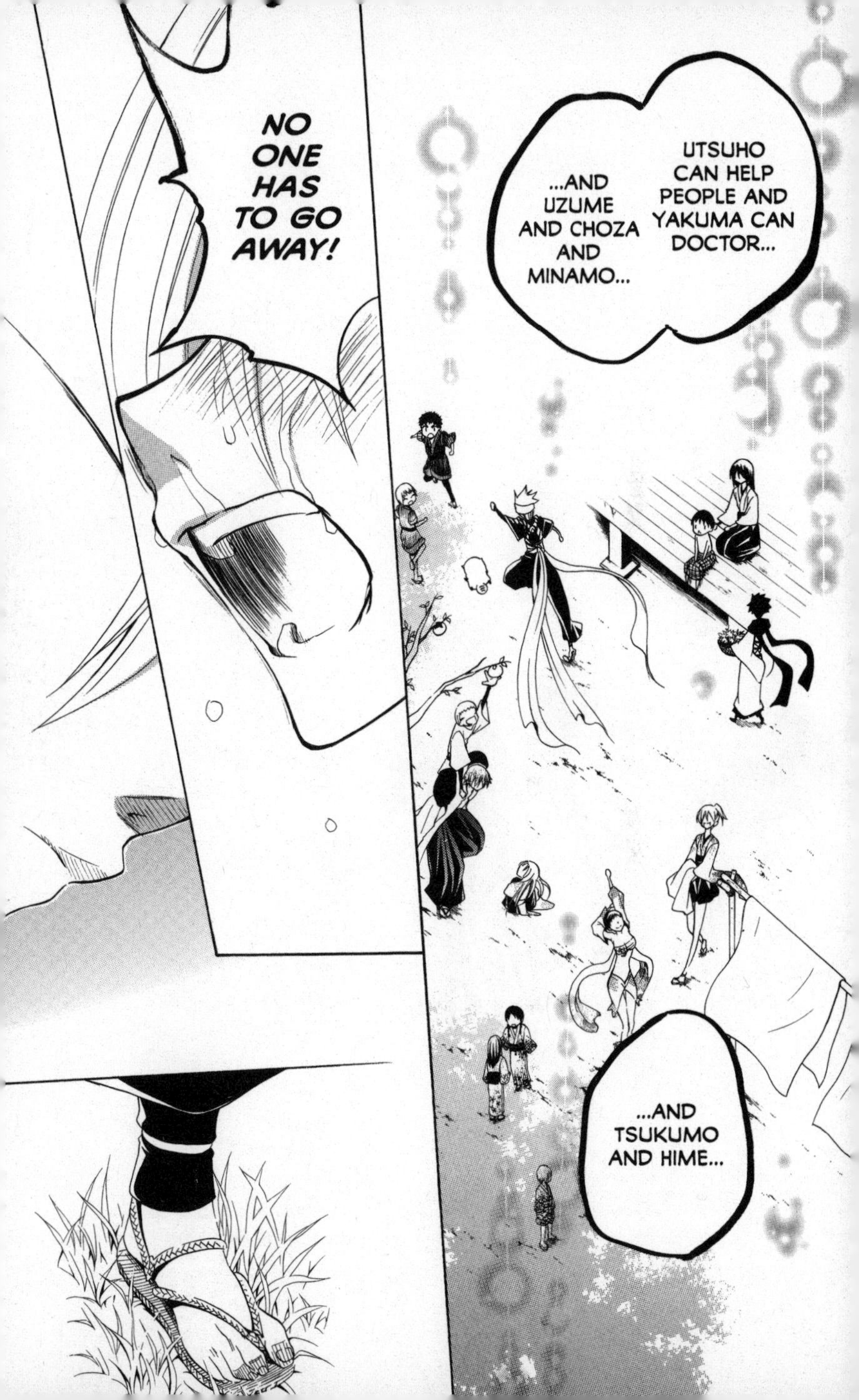
UTSUHO CAN HELP PEOPLE AND YAKUMA CAN DOCTOR...
...AND UZUME AND CHOZA AND MINAMO...
...AND TSUKUMO AND HIME...
NO ONE HAS TO GO AWAY!

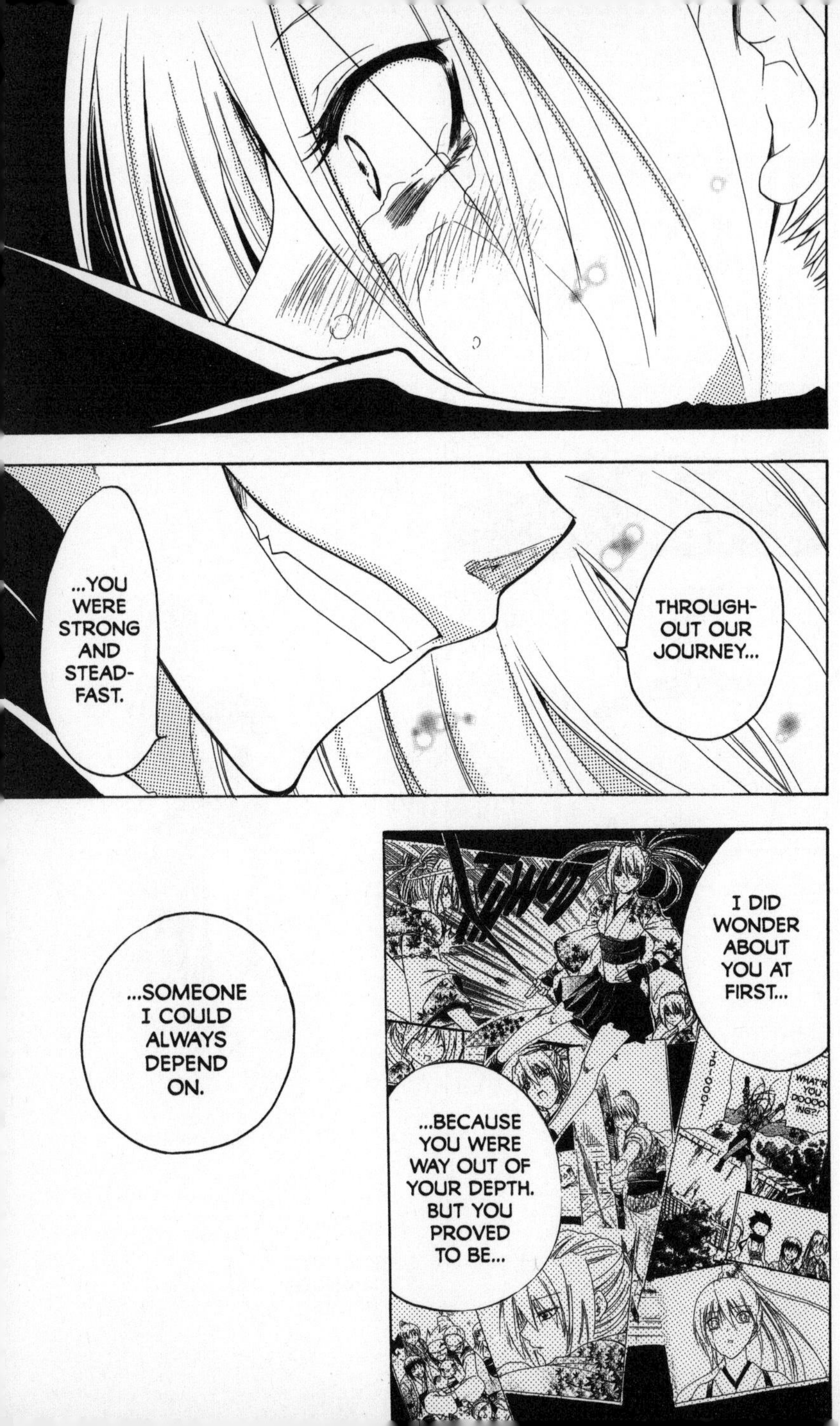
THROUGH-OUT OUR JOURNEY...
...YOU WERE STRONG AND STEAD-FAST.
I DID WONDER ABOUT YOU AT FIRST...
IDIOOOT!
WHAT'R YOU DOOOOO ING?!
...BECAUSE YOU WERE WAY OUT OF YOUR DEPTH. BUT YOU PROVED TO BE...
...SOMEONE I COULD ALWAYS DEPEND ON.

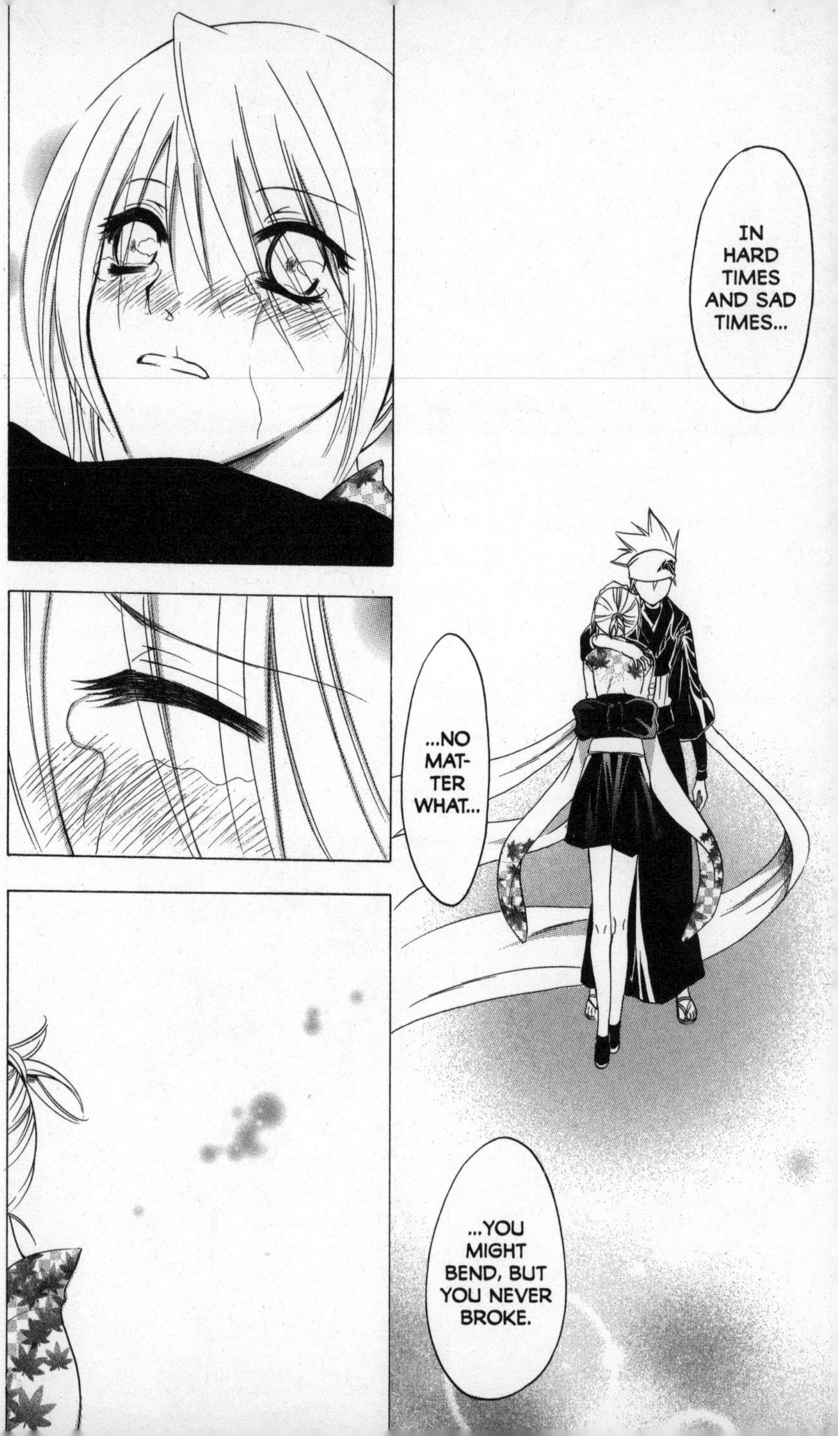
IN HARD TIMES AND SAD TIMES...
...NO MATTER WHAT...
...YOU MIGHT BEND, BUT YOU NEVER BROKE.

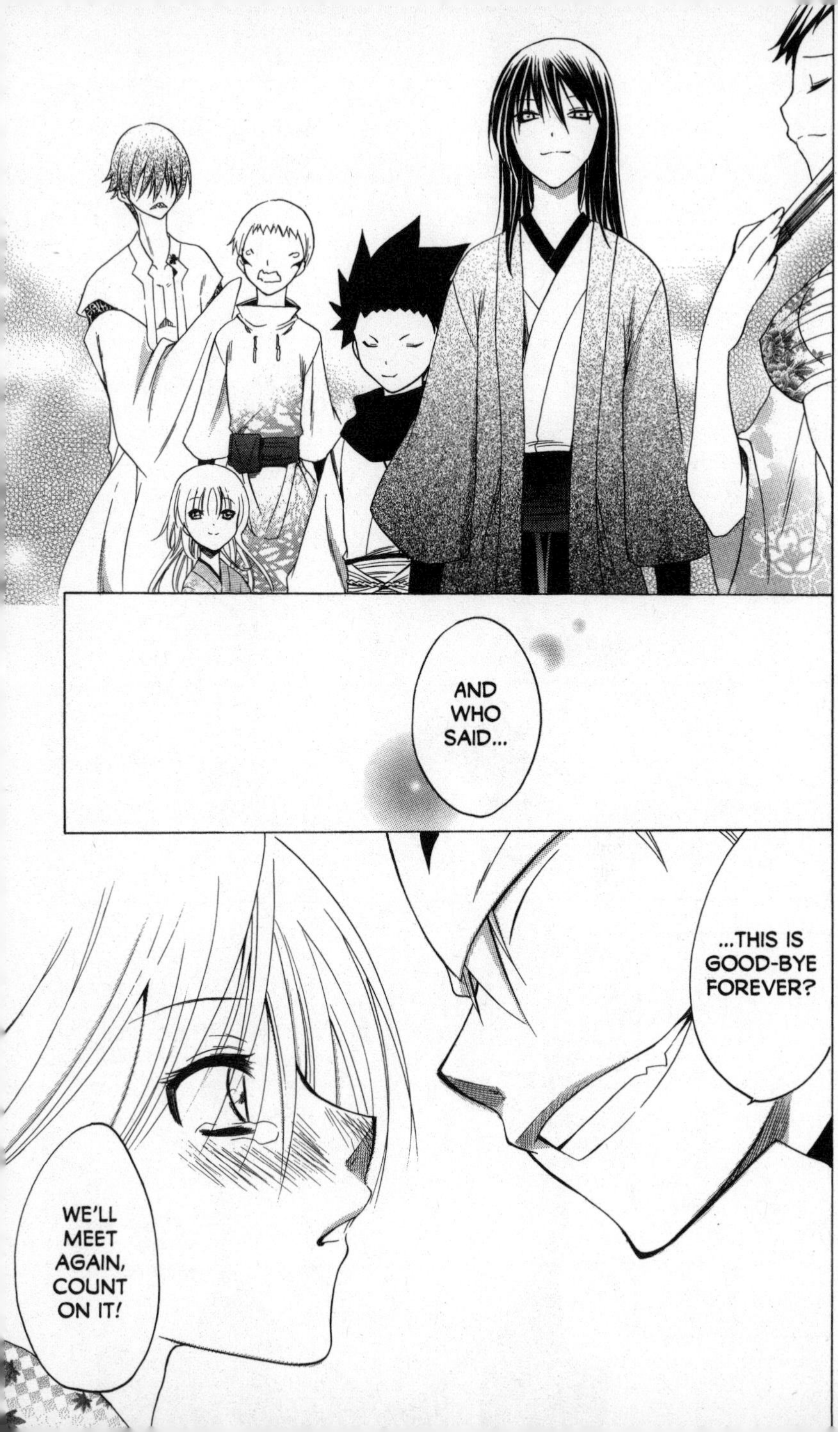
AND WHO SAID...
...THIS IS GOOD-BYE FOREVER?
WE'LL MEET AGAIN, COUNT ON IT!

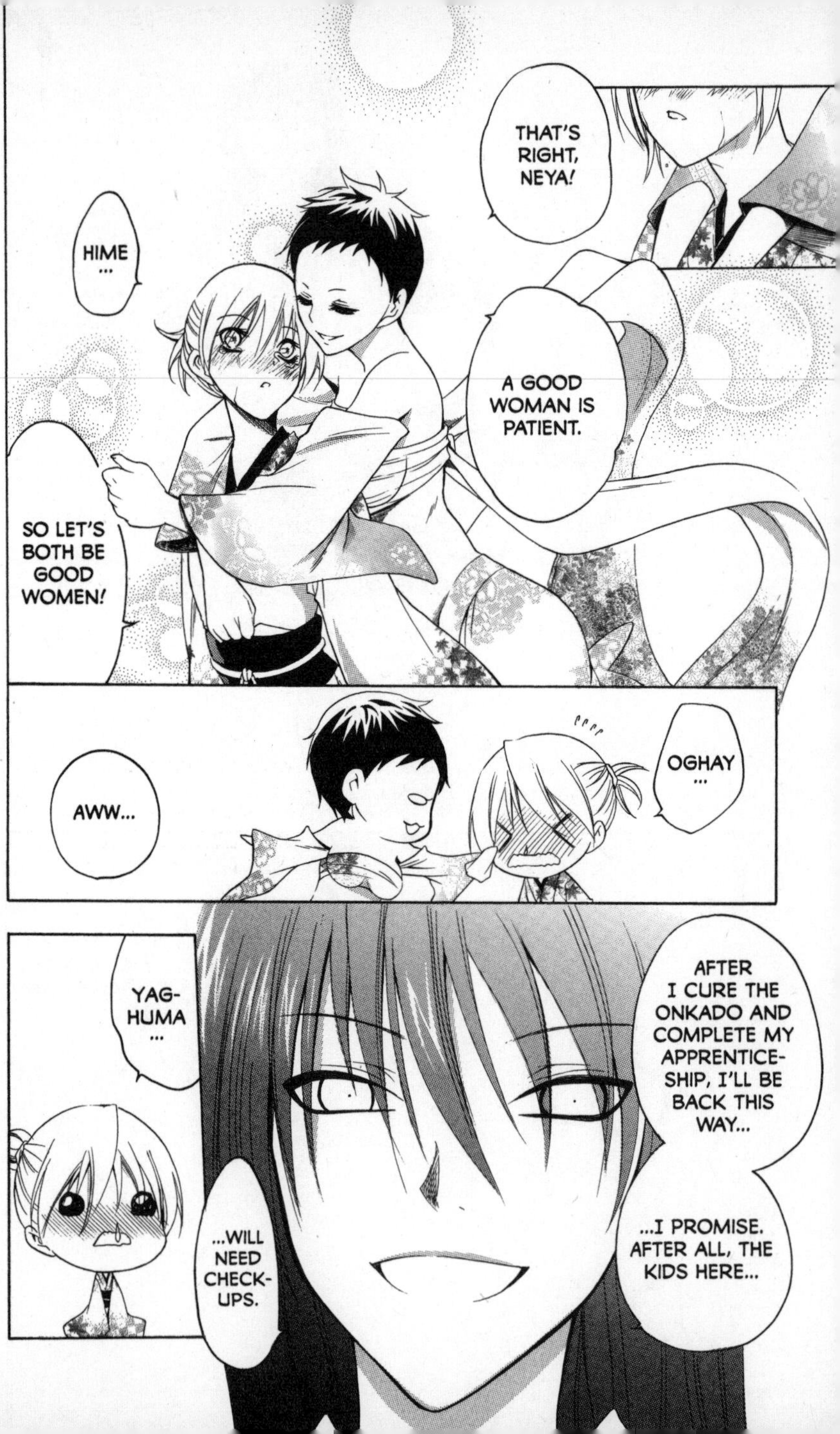
THAT'S RIGHT, NEYA!
HIME...
A GOOD WOMAN IS PATIENT.
SO LET'S BOTH BE GOOD WOMEN!
OGHAY...
AWW...
AFTER I CURE THE ONKADO AND COMPLETE MY APPRENTICE-SHIP, I'LL BE BACK THIS WAY...
YAG-HUMA...
...I PROMISE. AFTER ALL, THE KIDS HERE...
...WILL NEED CHECK-UPS.

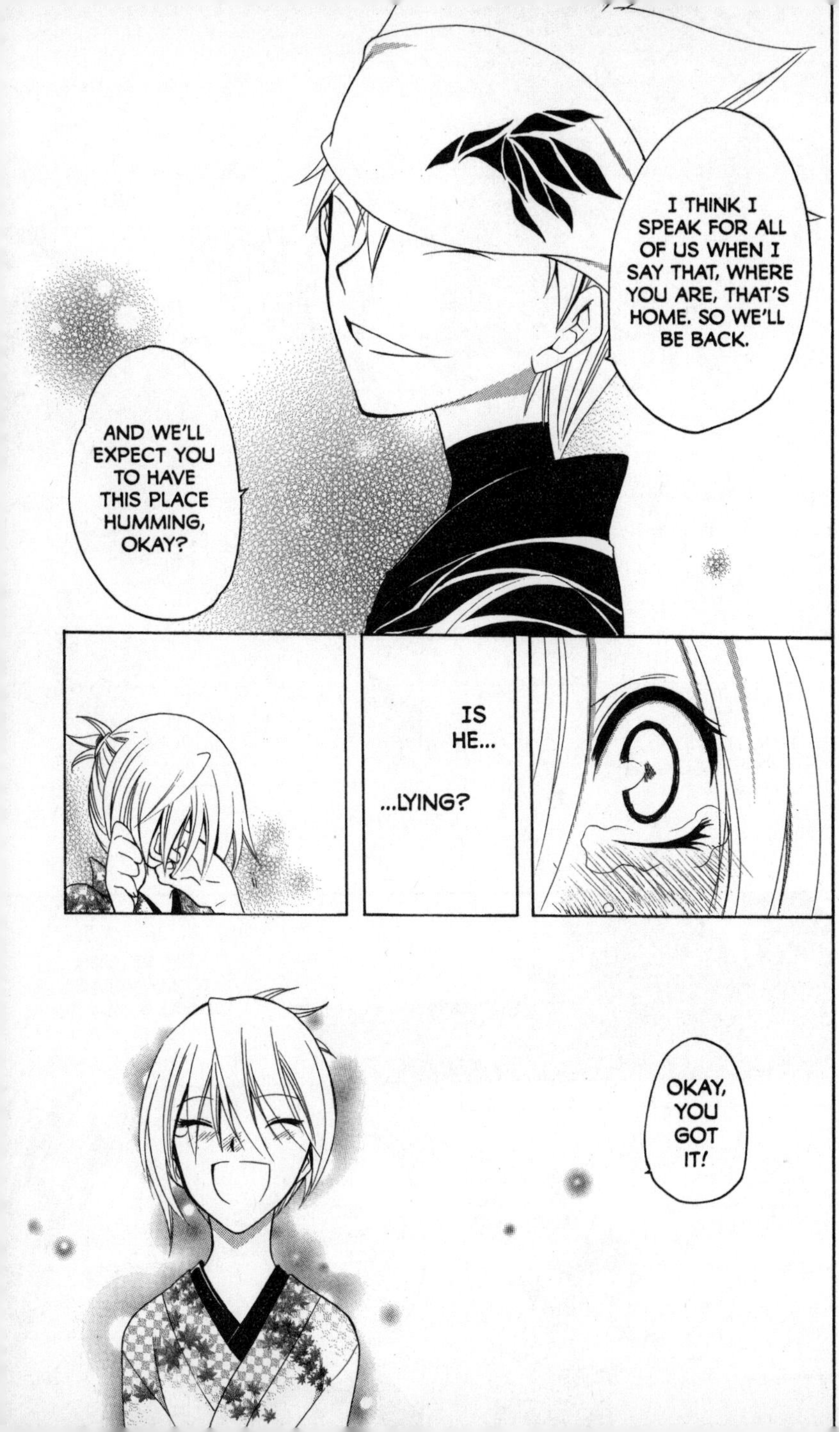
I THINK I SPEAK FOR ALL OF US WHEN I SAY THAT, WHERE YOU ARE, THAT'S HOME. SO WE'LL BE BACK.
AND WE'LL EXPECT YOU TO HAVE THIS PLACE HUMMING, OKAY?
IS HE...
...LYING?
OKAY, YOU GOT IT!

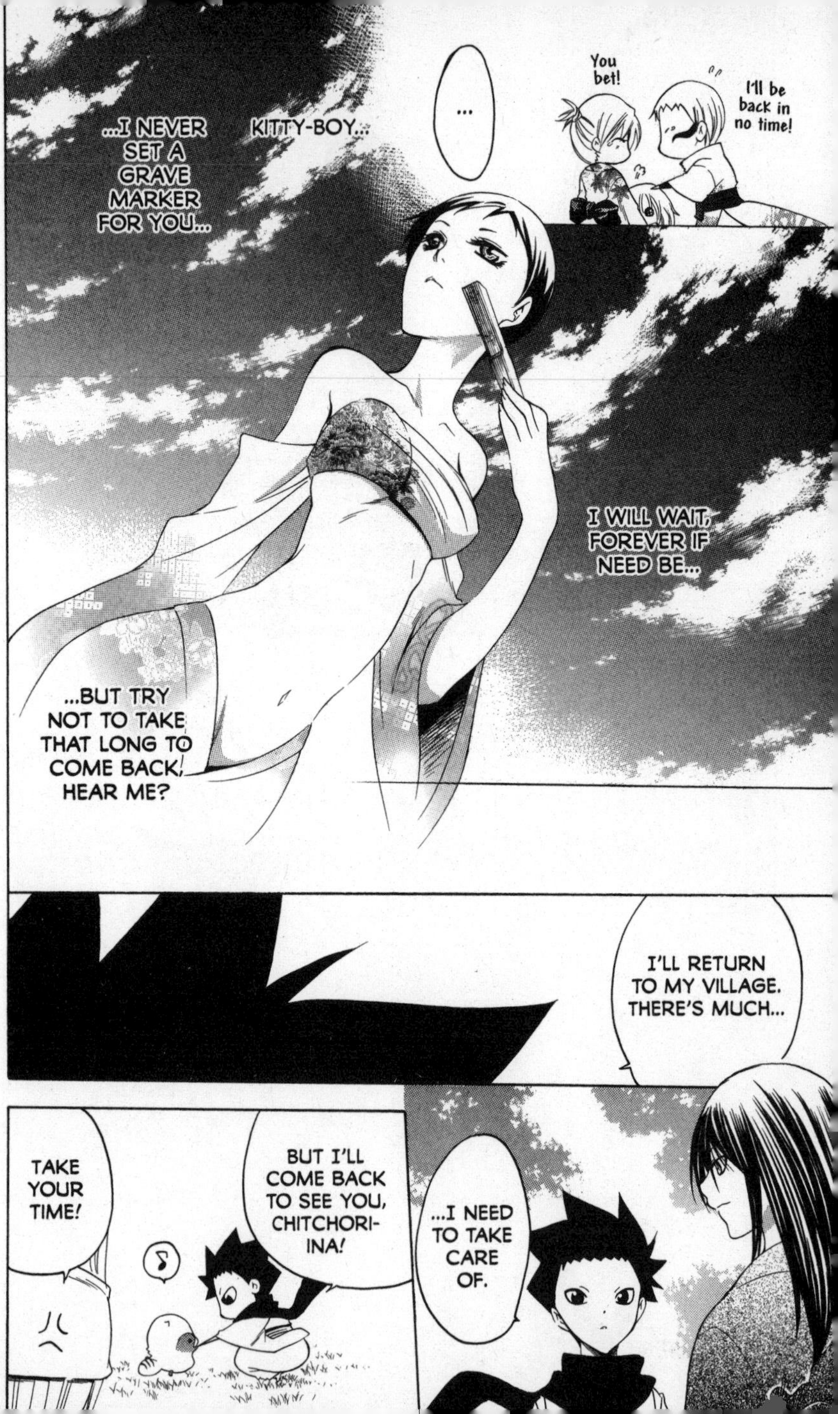
I'll be back in no time!
You bet!
...
KITTY-BOY...
...I NEVER SET A GRAVE MARKER FOR YOU...
I WILL WAIT, FOREVER IF NEED BE...
...BUT TRY NOT TO TAKE THAT LONG TO COME BACK, HEAR ME?
I'LL RETURN TO MY VILLAGE. THERE'S MUCH...
...I NEED TO TAKE CARE OF.
BUT I'LL COME BACK TO SEE YOU, CHITCHORI-INA!
♪
TAKE YOUR TIME!

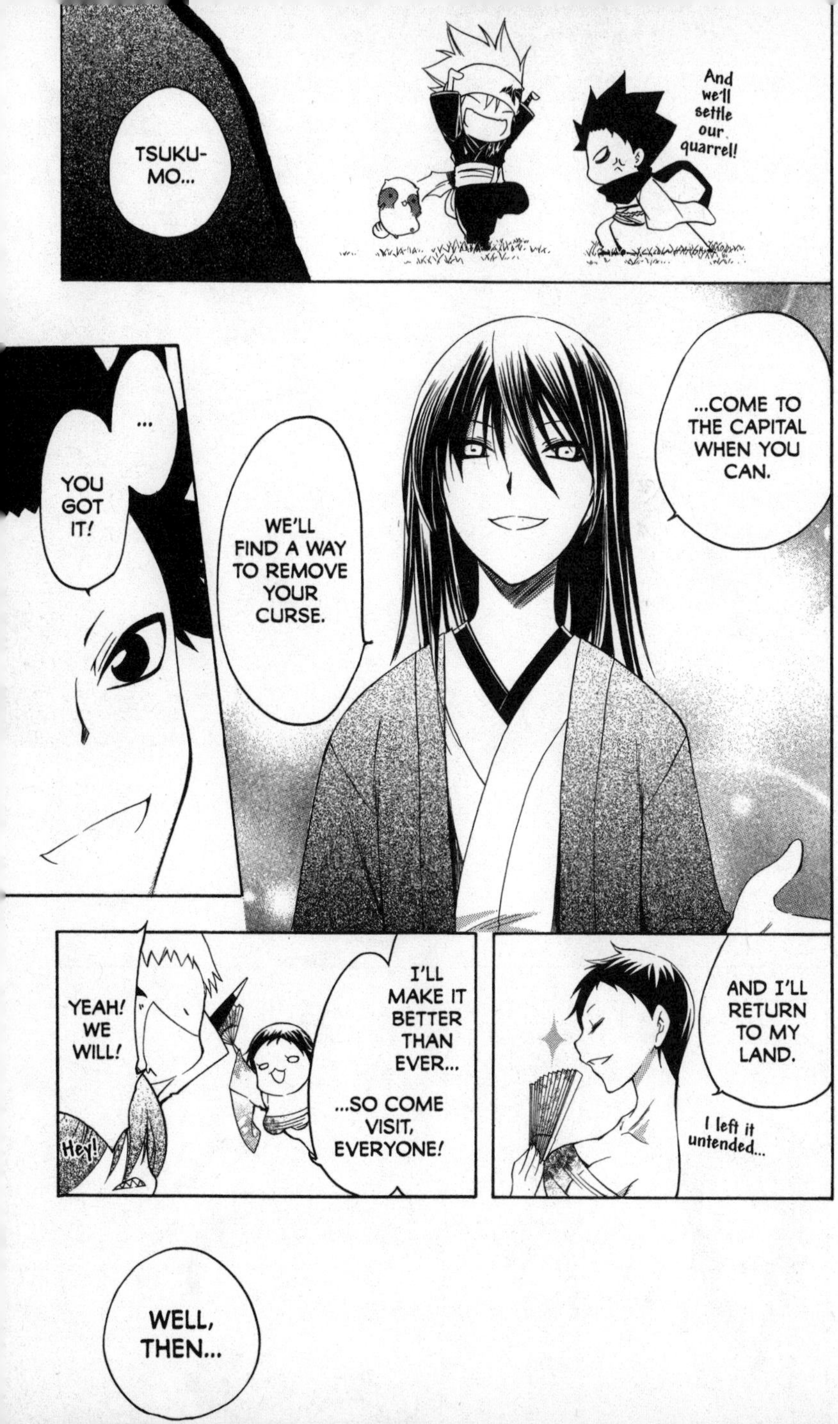
And we'll settle our quarrel!
TSUKU-MO...
...COME TO THE CAPITAL WHEN YOU CAN.
WE'LL FIND A WAY TO REMOVE YOUR CURSE.
...
YOU GOT IT!
AND I'LL RETURN TO MY LAND.
I left it untended...
I'LL MAKE IT BETTER THAN EVER...
...SO COME VISIT, EVERYONE!
YEAH! WE WILL!
Hey!
WELL, THEN...

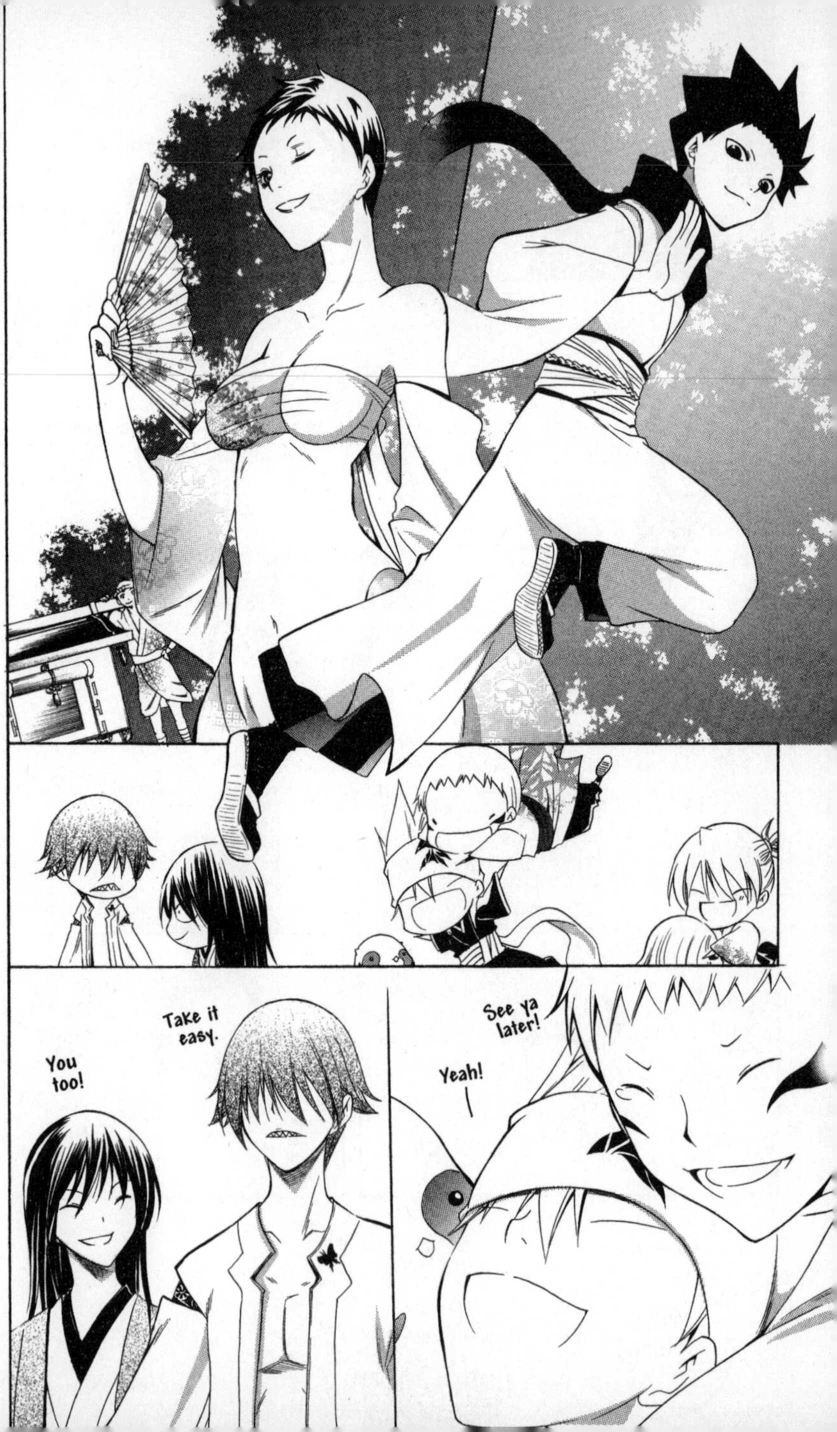
See ya later!
Yeah!
Take it easy.
You too!

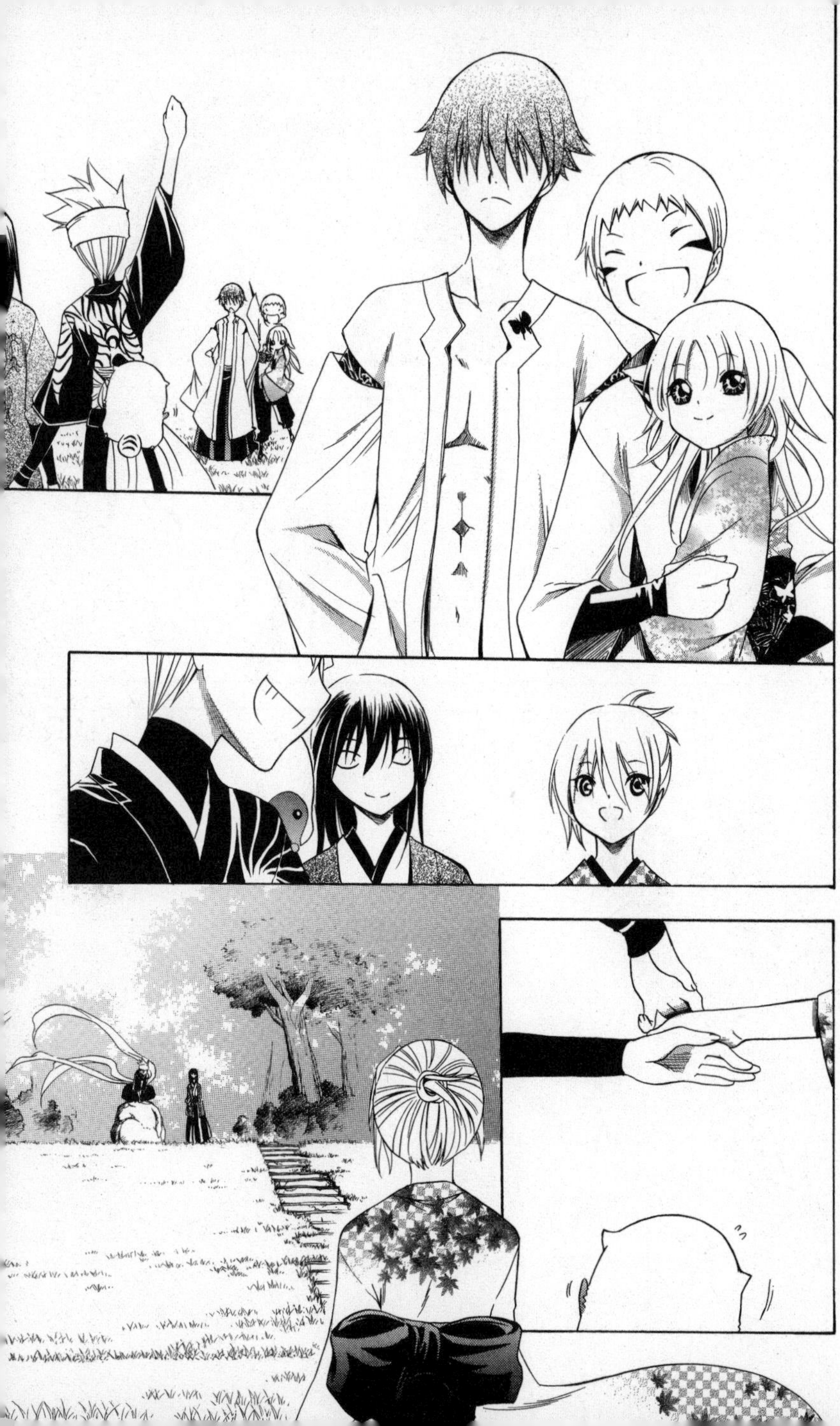

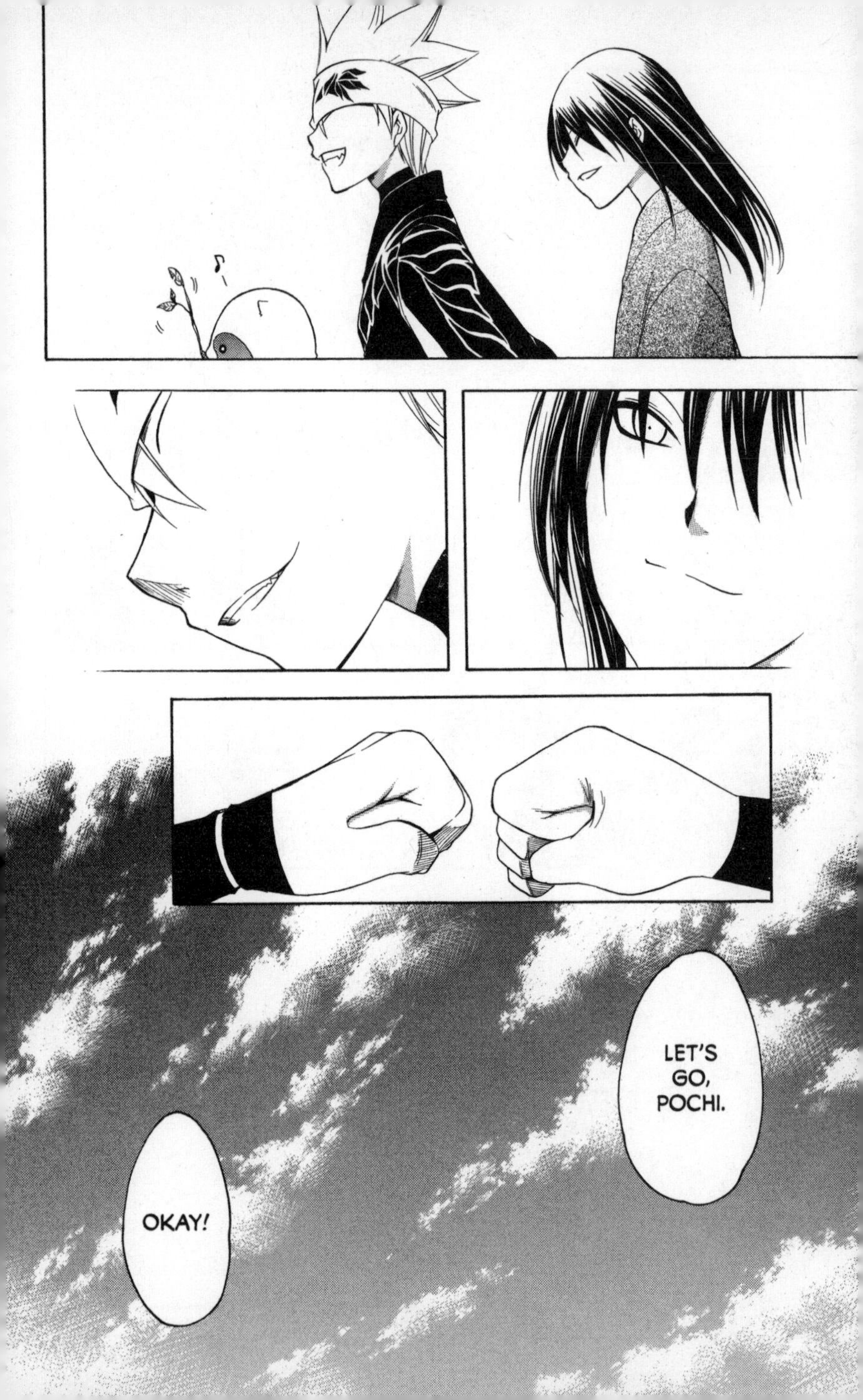
LET'S GO, POCHI.
OKAY!

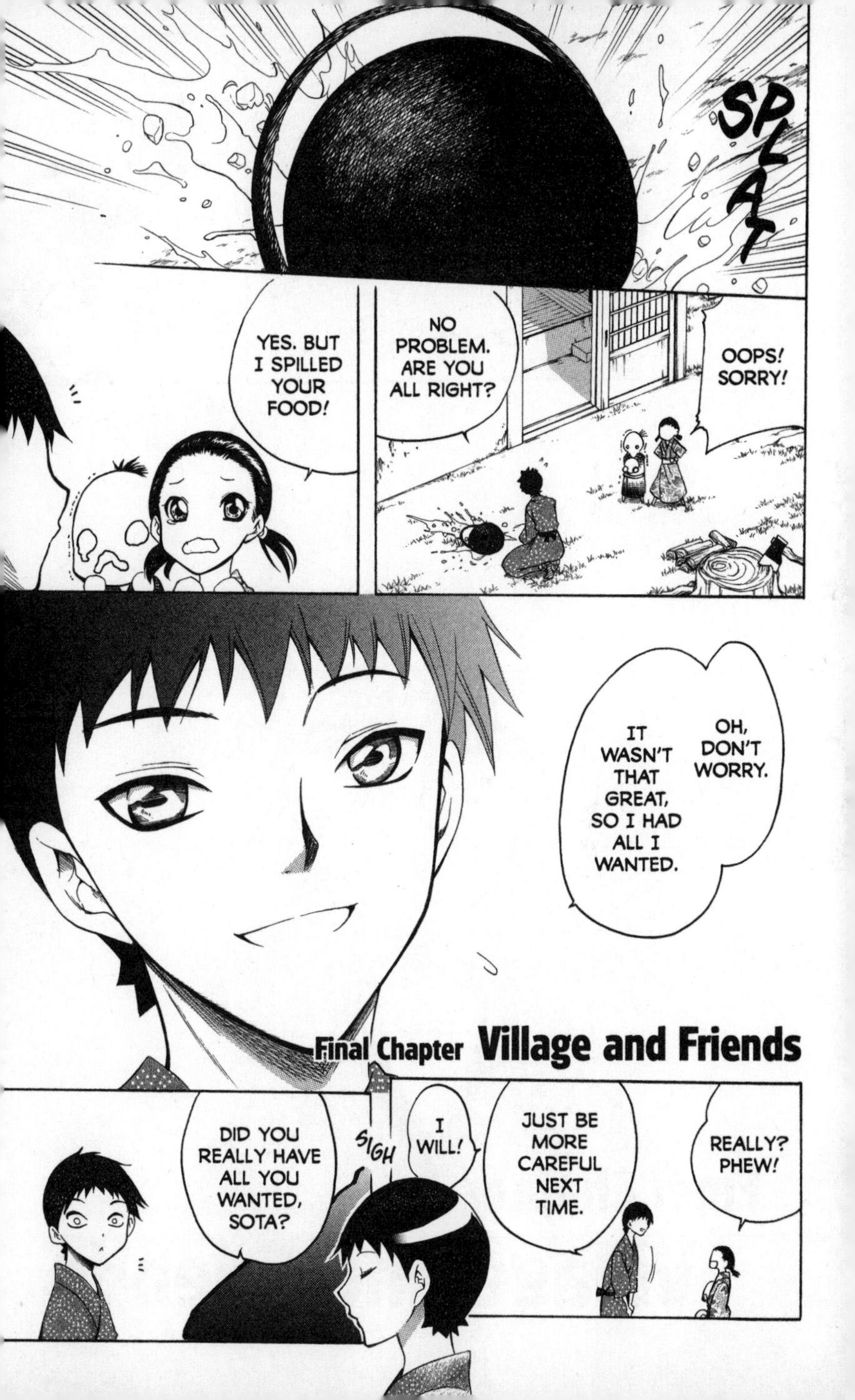
SPLAT
OOPS! SORRY!
NO PROBLEM. ARE YOU ALL RIGHT?
YES. BUT I SPILLED YOUR FOOD!
OH, DON'T WORRY.
IT WASN'T THAT GREAT, SO I HAD ALL I WANTED.
Final Chapter Village and Friends
REALLY? PHEW!
JUST BE MORE CAREFUL NEXT TIME.
I WILL!
SIGH
DID YOU REALLY HAVE ALL YOU WANTED, SOTA?

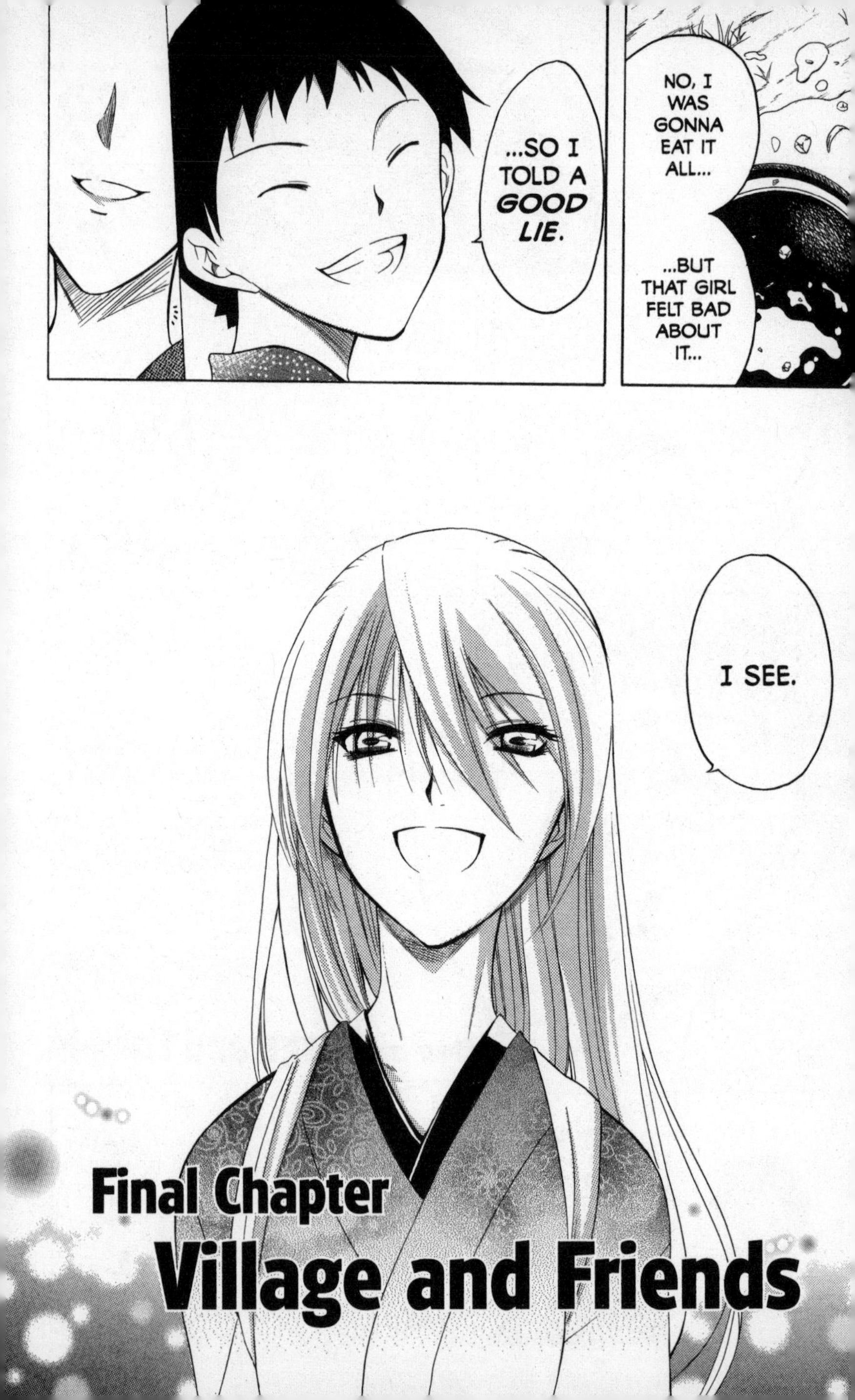
NO, I WAS GONNA EAT IT ALL...
...BUT THAT GIRL FELT BAD ABOUT IT...
...SO I TOLD A *GOOD LIE*.
I SEE.

Final Chapter
Village and Friends

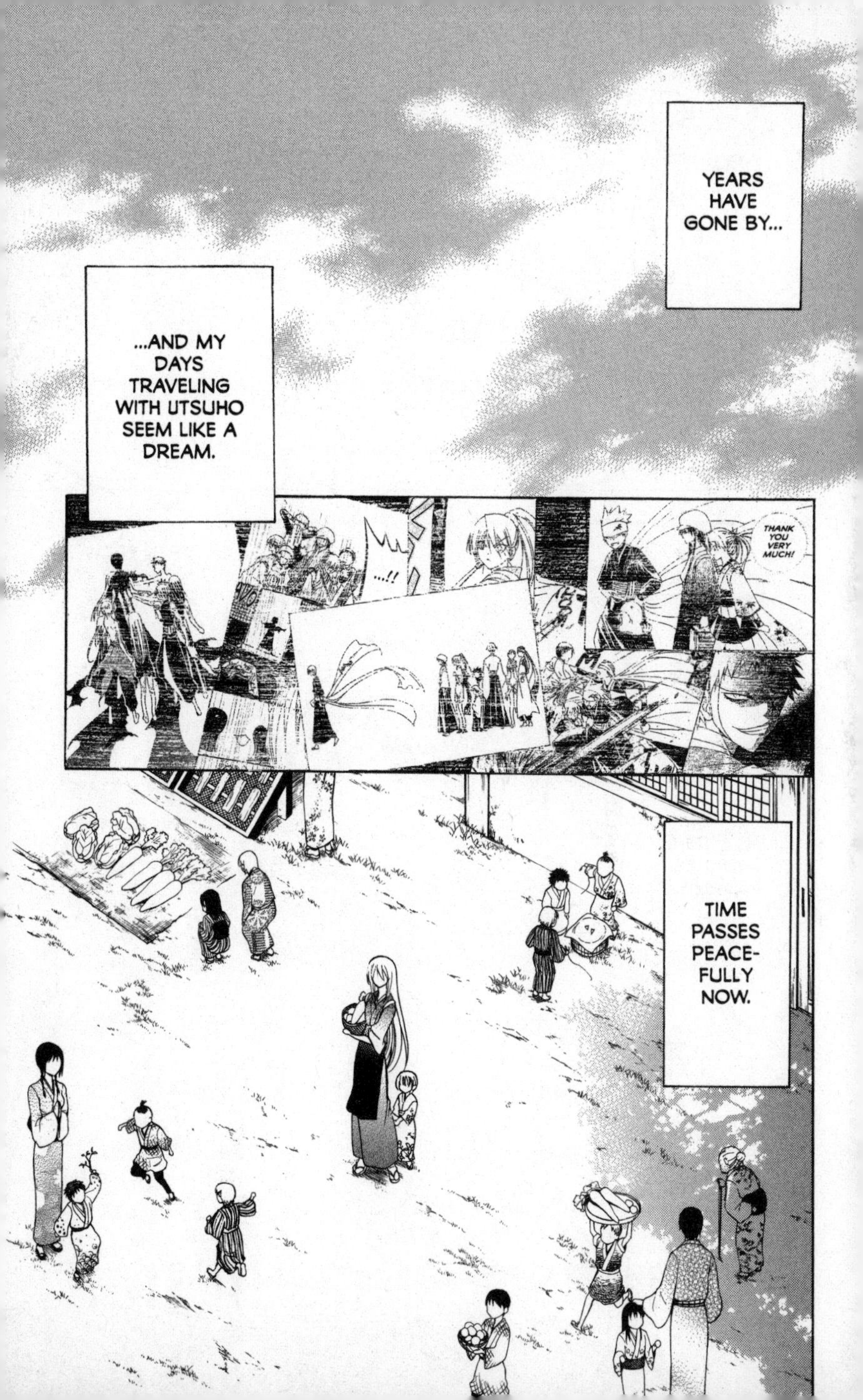
YEARS HAVE GONE BY...
...AND MY DAYS TRAVELING WITH UTSUHO SEEM LIKE A DREAM.
THANK YOU VERY MUCH!
...!!
TIME PASSES PEACE-FULLY NOW.

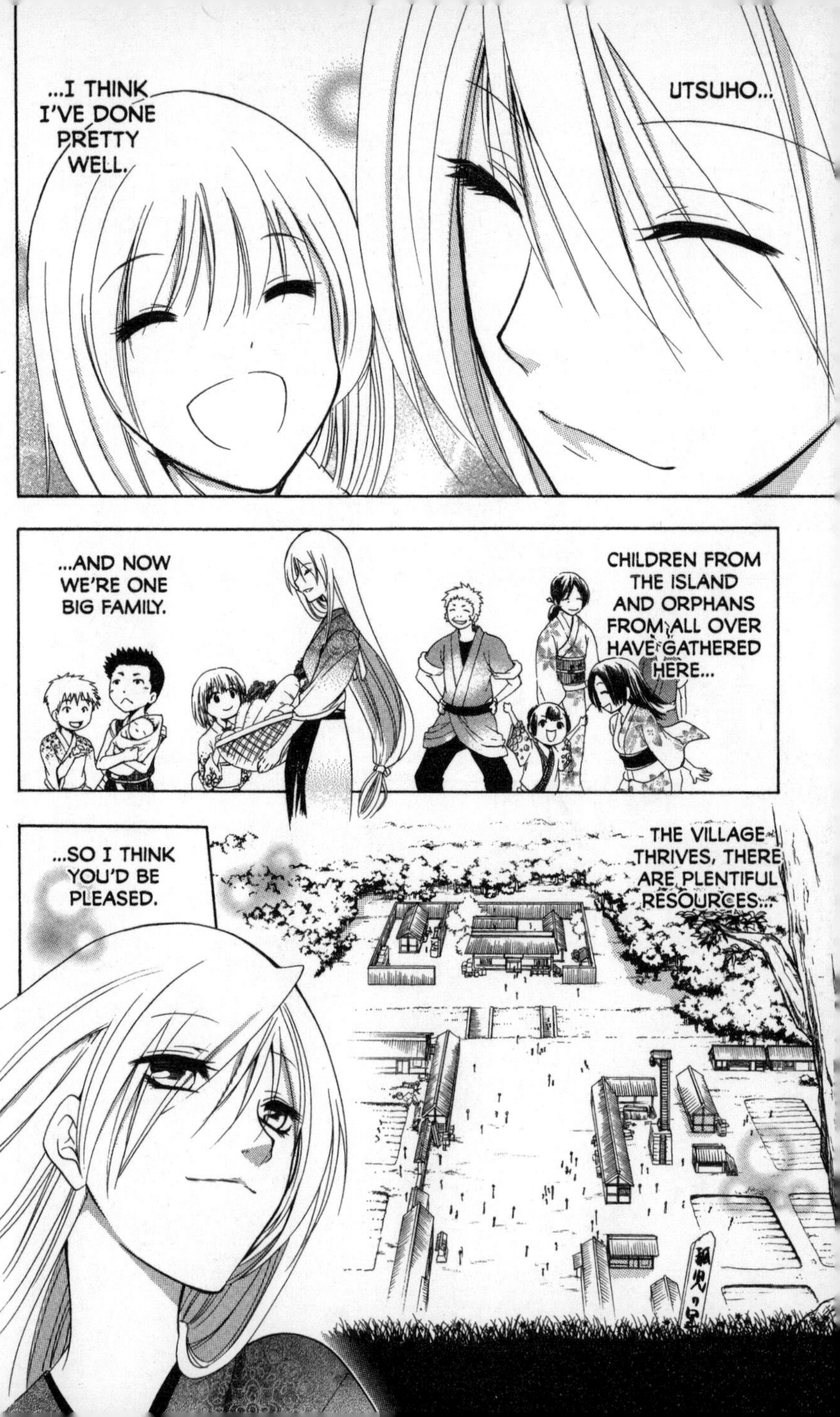
UTSUHO...
...I THINK I'VE DONE PRETTY WELL.
CHILDREN FROM THE ISLAND AND ORPHANS FROM ALL OVER HAVE GATHERED HERE...
...AND NOW WE'RE ONE BIG FAMILY.
THE VILLAGE THRIVES, THERE ARE PLENTIFUL RESOURCES...
...SO I THINK YOU'D BE PLEASED.

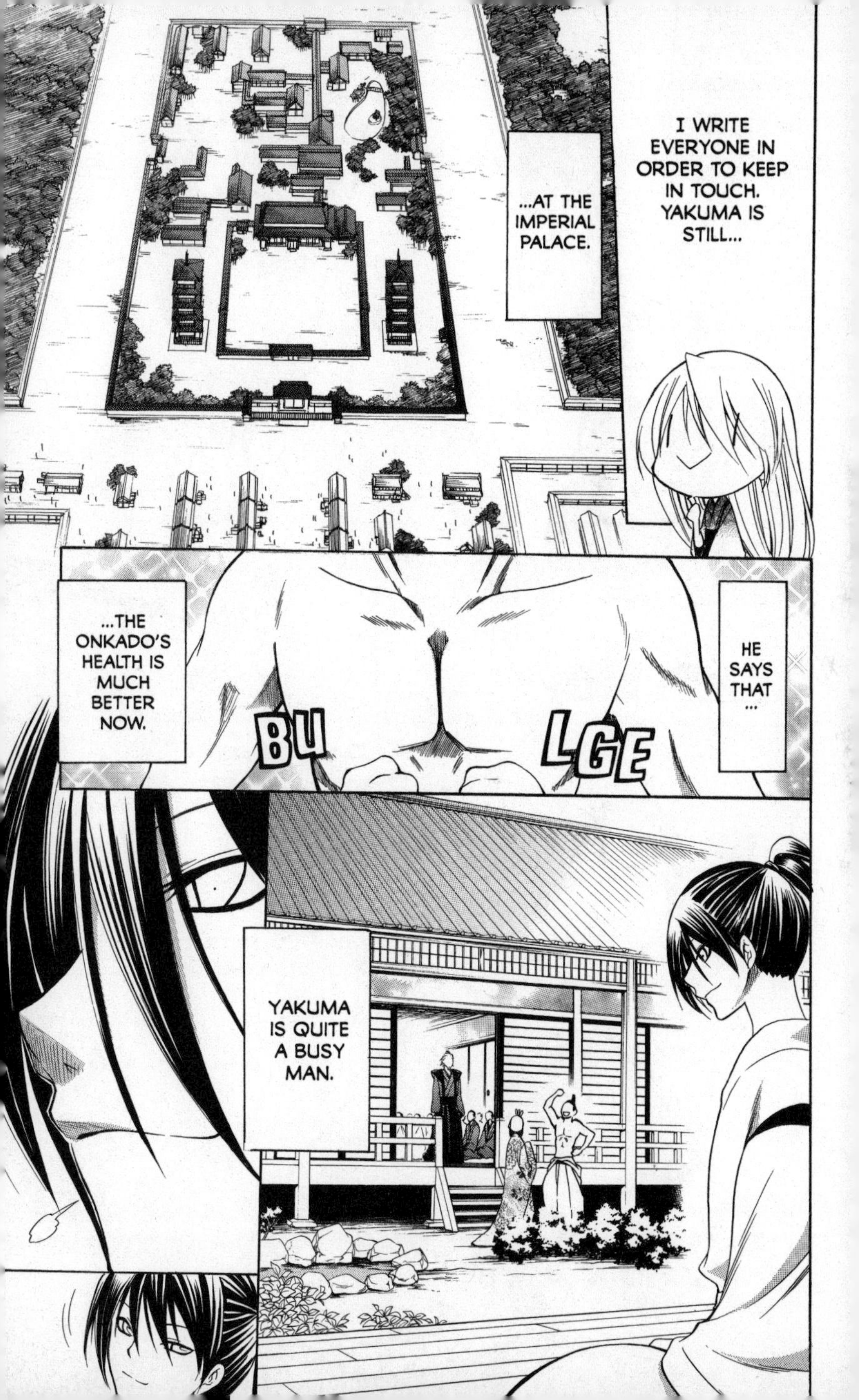
I WRITE EVERYONE IN ORDER TO KEEP IN TOUCH. YAKUMA IS STILL...
...AT THE IMPERIAL PALACE.
HE SAYS THAT...
BULGE
...THE ONKADO'S HEALTH IS MUCH BETTER NOW.
YAKUMA IS QUITE A BUSY MAN.

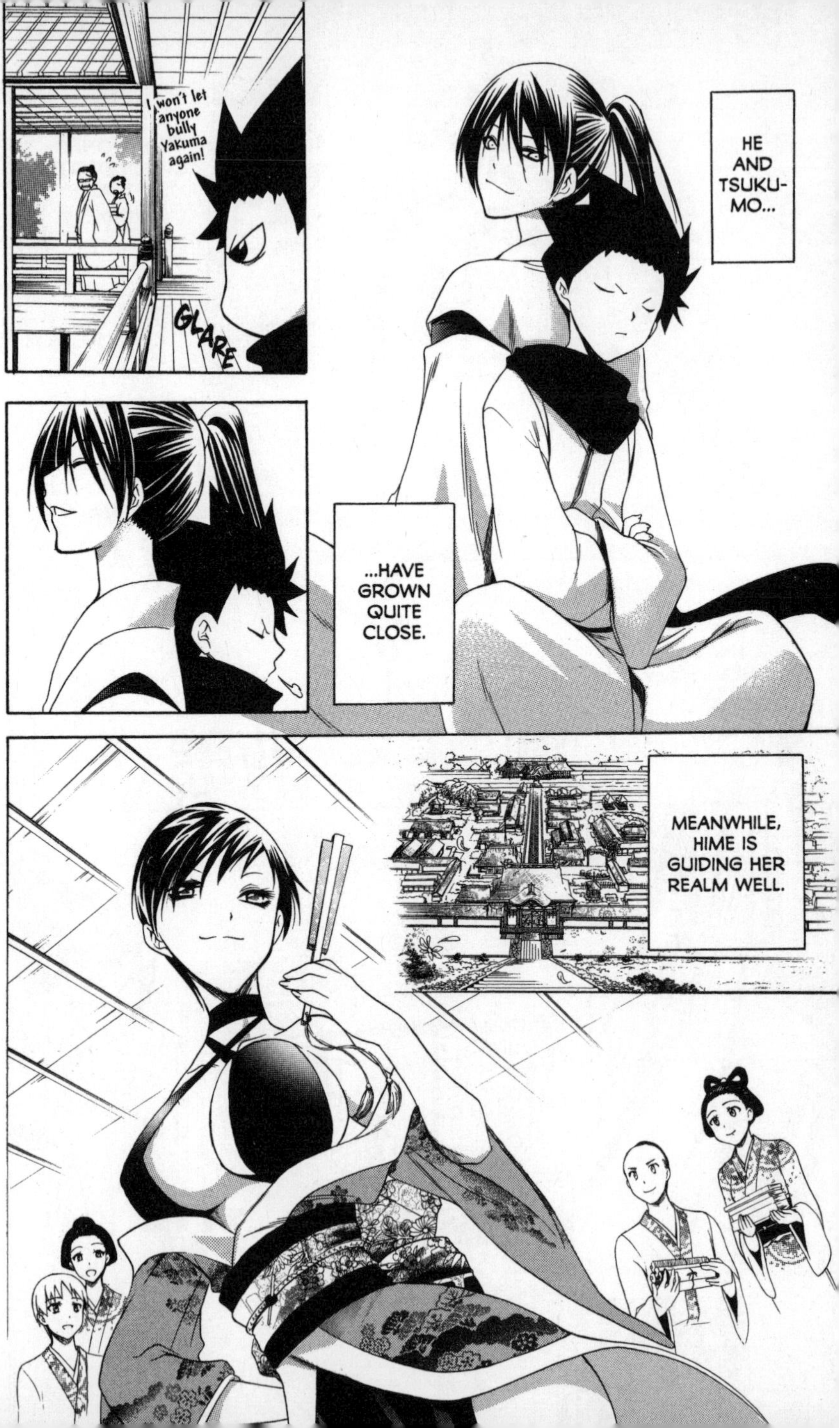
HE AND TSUKUMO...
...HAVE GROWN QUITE CLOSE.
I won't let anyone bully Yakuma again!
GLARE
MEANWHILE, HIME IS GUIDING HER REALM WELL.

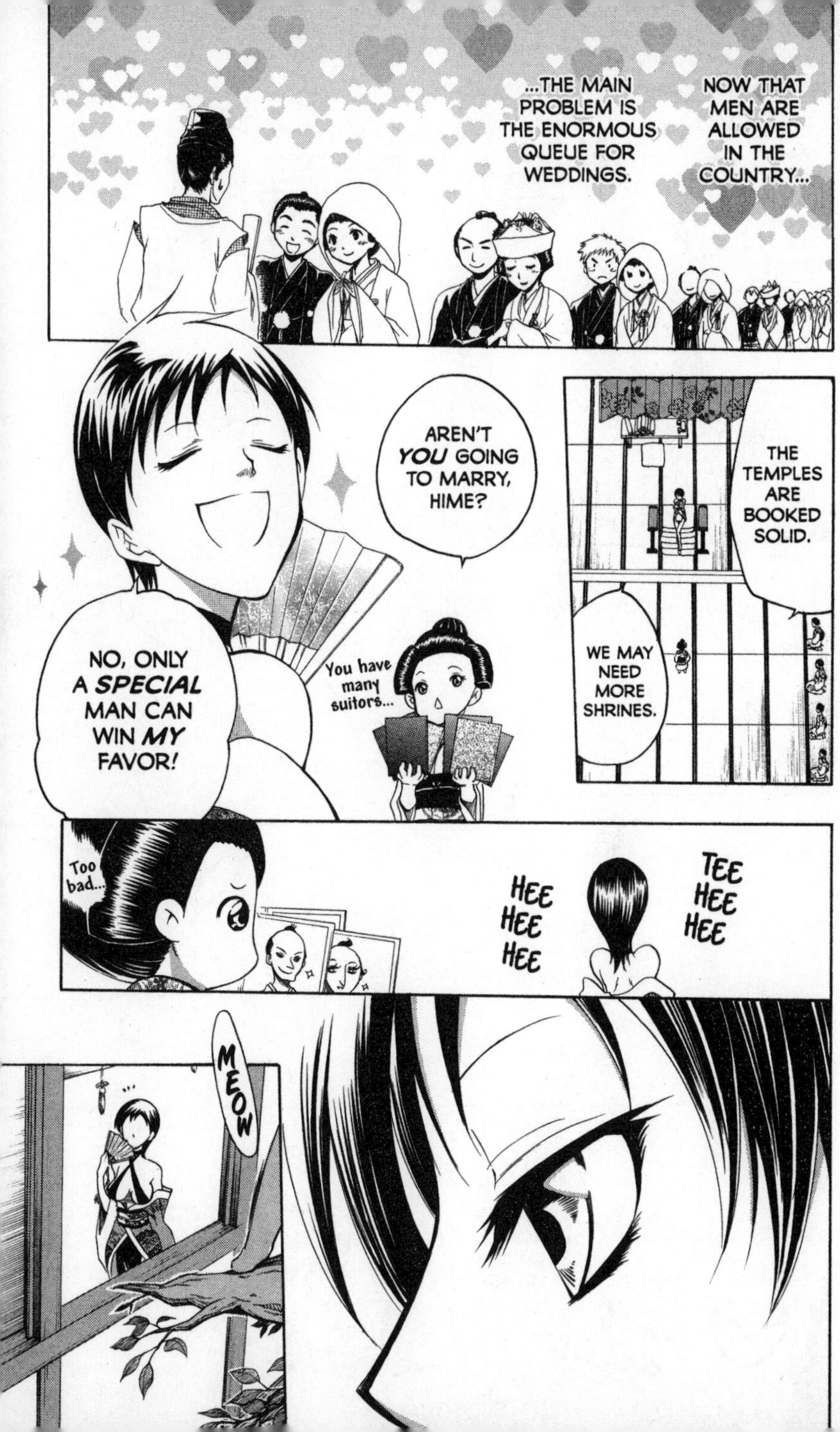
NOW THAT MEN ARE ALLOWED IN THE COUNTRY...
...THE MAIN PROBLEM IS THE ENORMOUS QUEUE FOR WEDDINGS.
THE TEMPLES ARE BOOKED SOLID.
WE MAY NEED MORE SHRINES.
AREN'T *YOU* GOING TO MARRY, HIME?
NO, ONLY A *SPECIAL* MAN CAN WIN *MY* FAVOR!
You have many suitors...
TEE HEE HEE
HEE HEE HEE
Too bad...
MEOW

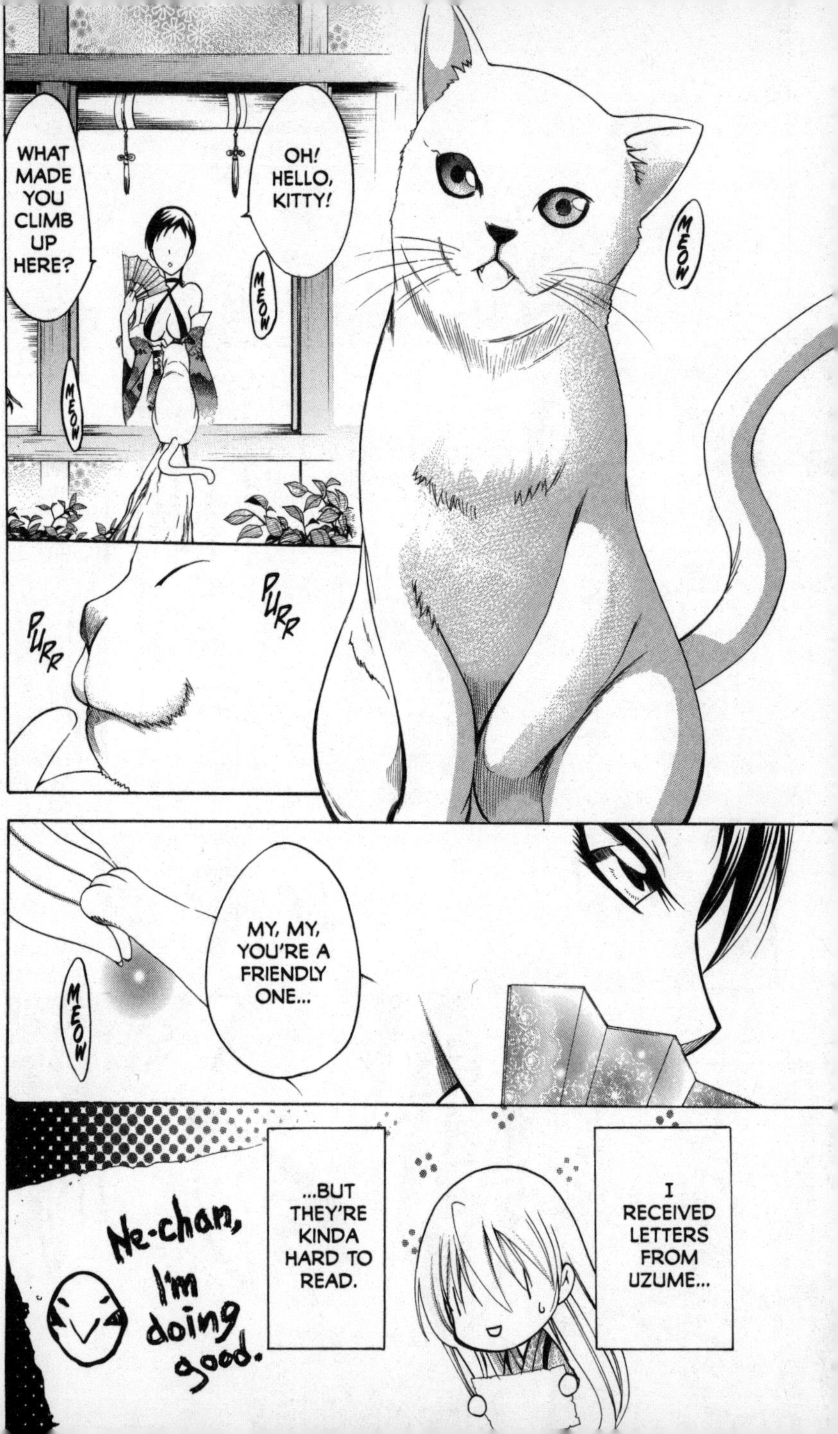
MEOW
OH! HELLO, KITTY!
MEOW
WHAT MADE YOU CLIMB UP HERE?
MEOW
PURR
PURR
MY, MY, YOU'RE A FRIENDLY ONE...
MEOW
I RECEIVED LETTERS FROM UZUME...
...BUT THEY'RE KINDA HARD TO READ.
Ne-chan, I'm doing good.

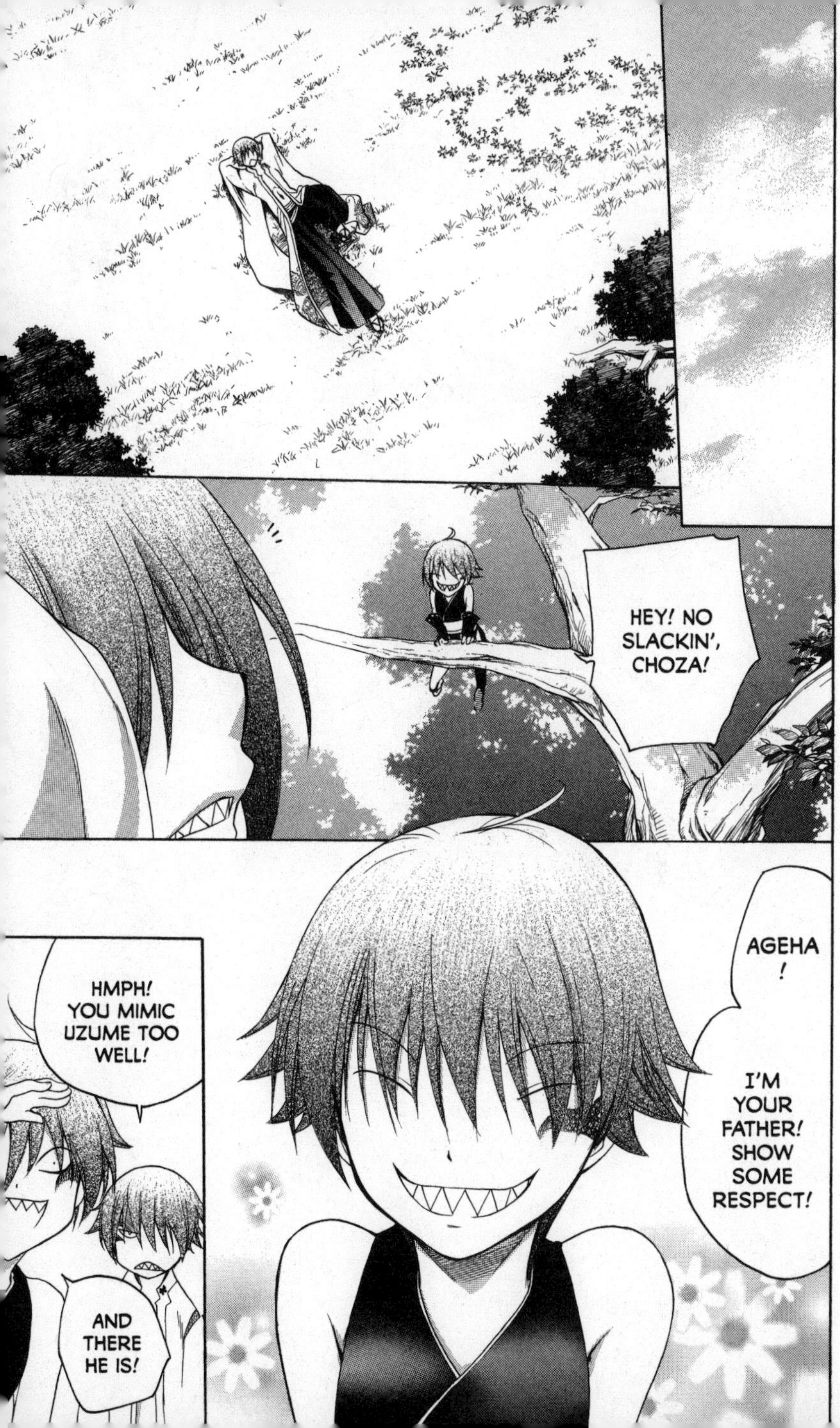
HEY! NO SLACKIN', CHOZA!
AGEHA!
I'M YOUR FATHER! SHOW SOME RESPECT!
HMPH! YOU MIMIC UZUME TOO WELL!
AND THERE HE IS!

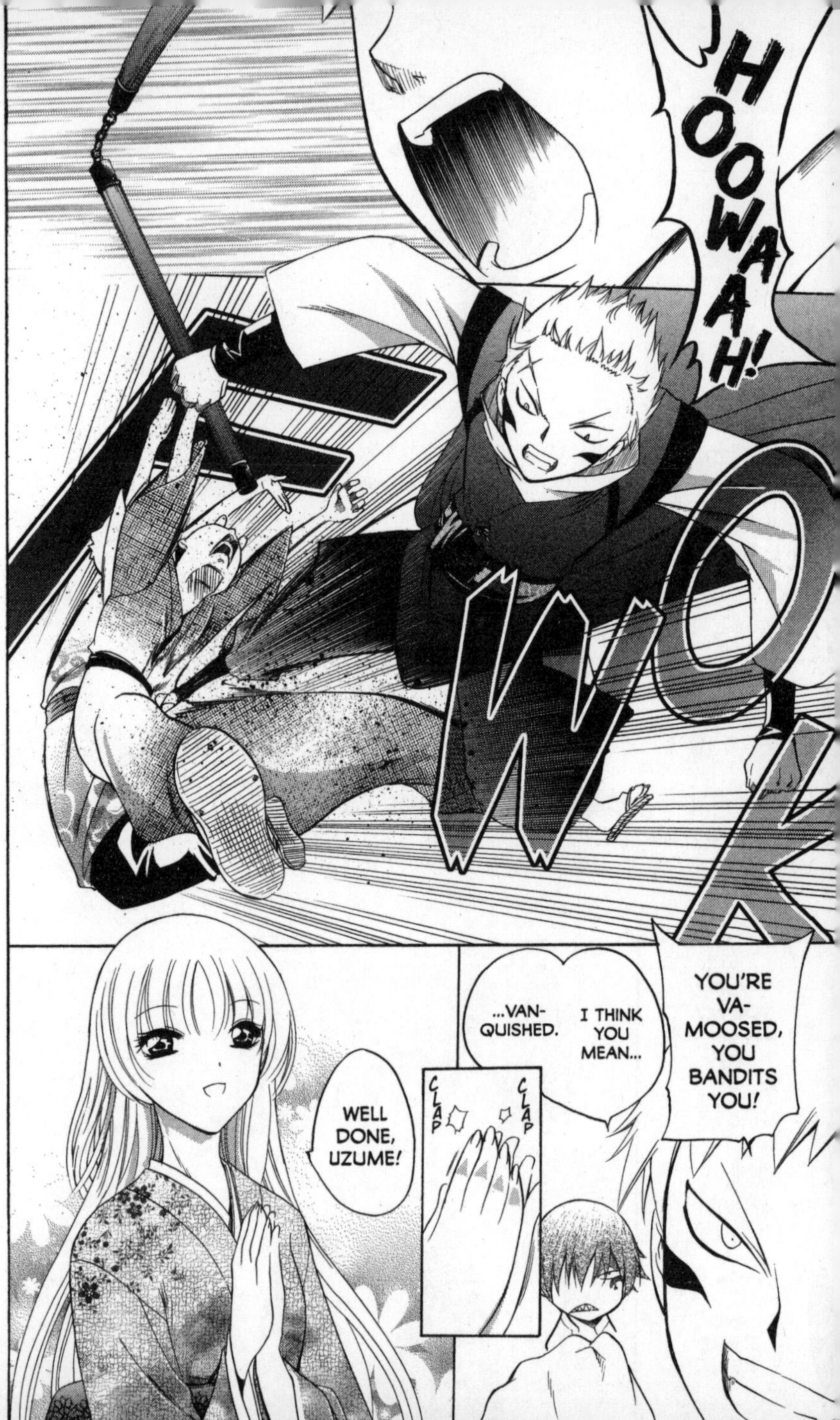
HOOOWAAH!
WHACK
YOU'RE VA-MOOSED, YOU BANDITS YOU!
I THINK YOU MEAN...
...VAN-QUISHED.
CLAP CLAP
WELL DONE, UZUME!

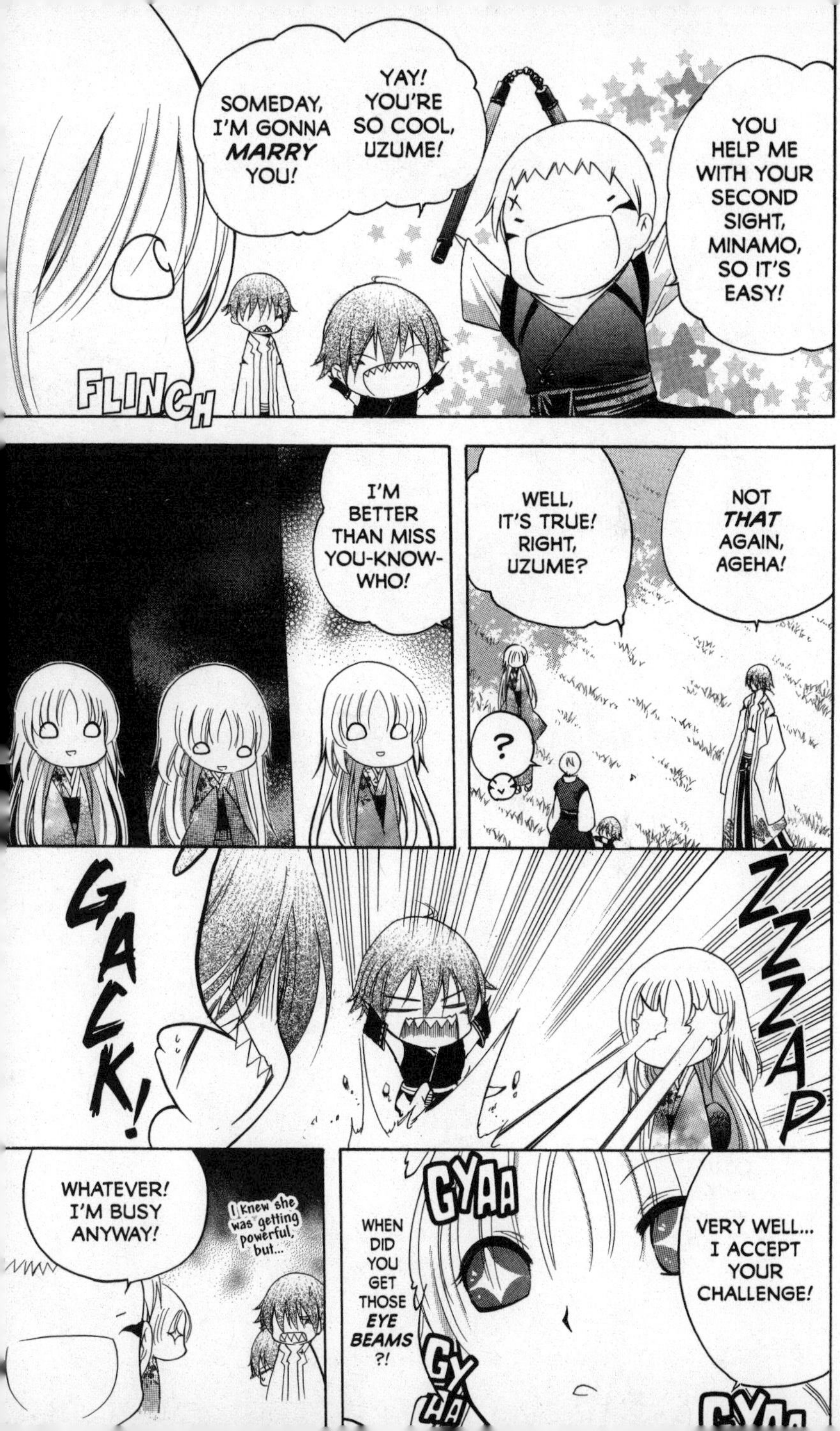
YOU HELP ME WITH YOUR SECOND SIGHT, MINAMO, SO IT'S EASY!
YAY! YOU'RE SO COOL, UZUME!
SOMEDAY, I'M GONNA *MARRY* YOU!
FLINCH
NOT *THAT* AGAIN, AGEHA!
WELL, IT'S TRUE! RIGHT, UZUME?
?
I'M BETTER THAN MISS YOU-KNOW-WHO!
ZZZAP
GACK!
VERY WELL... I ACCEPT YOUR CHALLENGE!
GYAA
WHEN DID YOU GET THOSE *EYE BEAMS*?!
GYAA
I knew she was getting powerful, but...
WHATEVER! I'M BUSY ANYWAY!

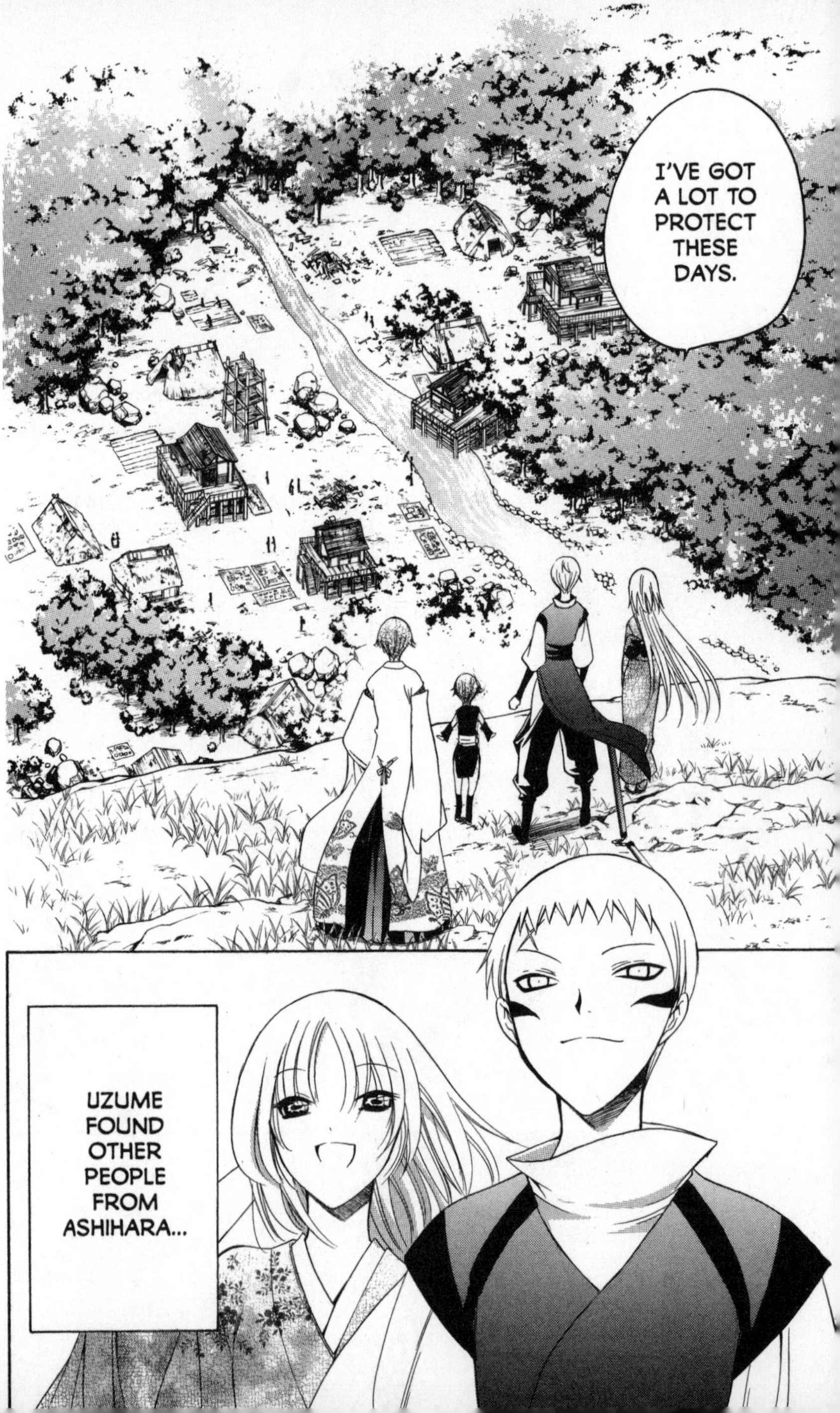
I'VE GOT A LOT TO PROTECT THESE DAYS.
UZUME FOUND OTHER PEOPLE FROM ASHIHARA...

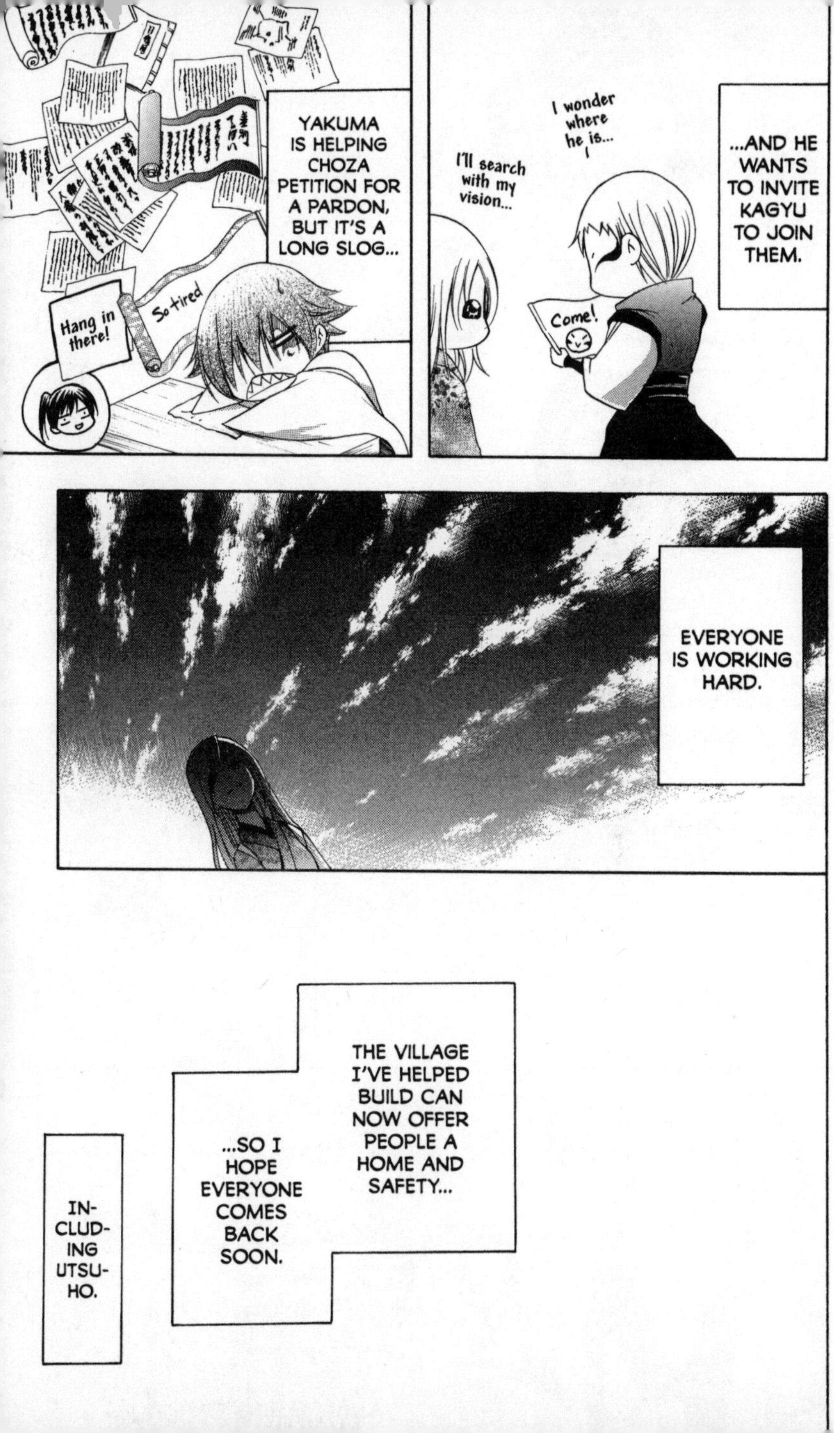
...AND HE WANTS TO INVITE KAGYU TO JOIN THEM.
I wonder where he is...
I'll search with my vision...
Come!
YAKUMA IS HELPING CHOZA PETITION FOR A PARDON, BUT IT'S A LONG SLOG...
So tired
Hang in there!
EVERYONE IS WORKING HARD.
THE VILLAGE I'VE HELPED BUILD CAN NOW OFFER PEOPLE A HOME AND SAFETY...
...SO I HOPE EVERYONE COMES BACK SOON.
IN-CLUD-ING UTSU-HO.

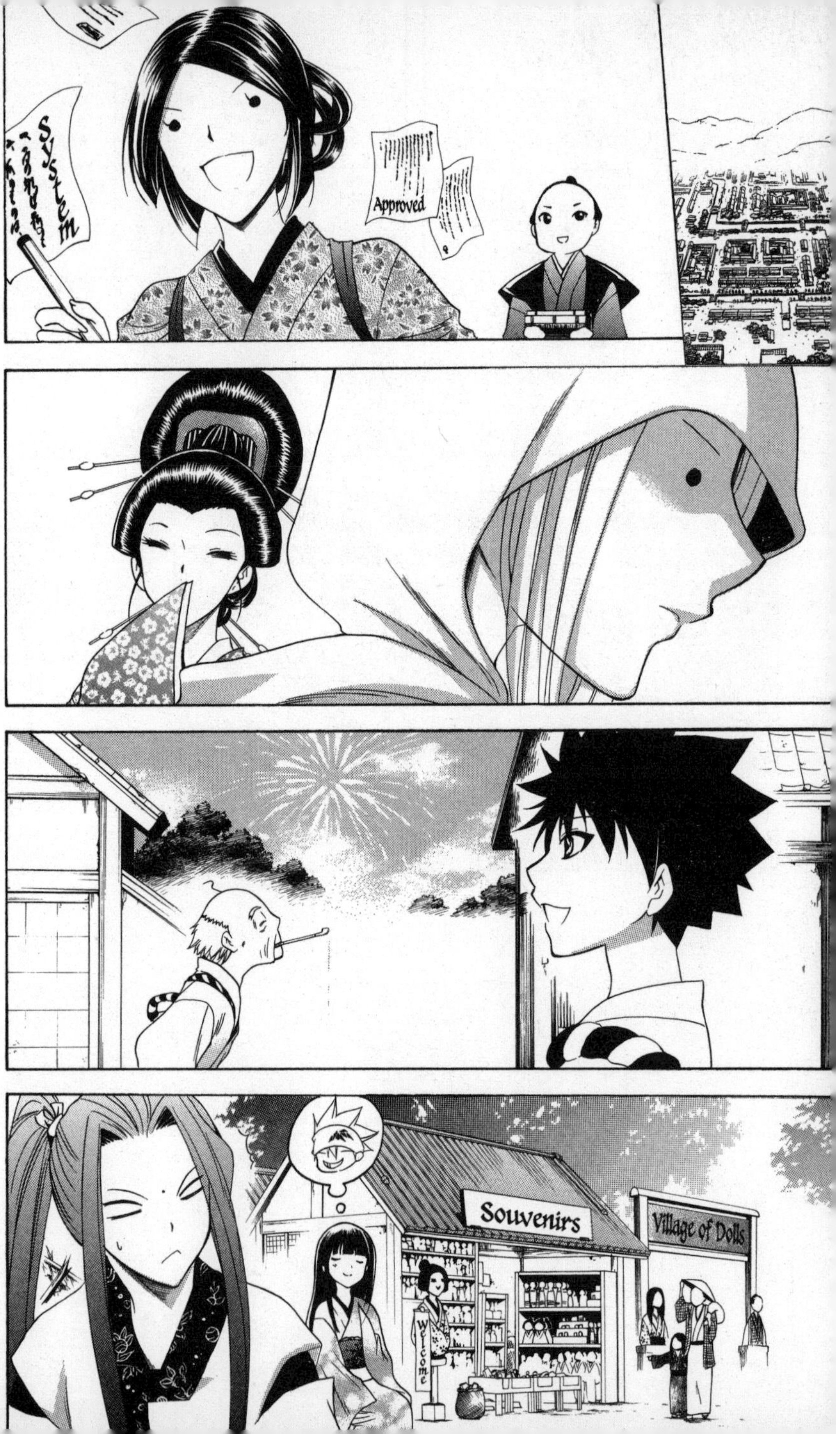
System
Approved
Village of Dolls
Souvenirs
Welcome

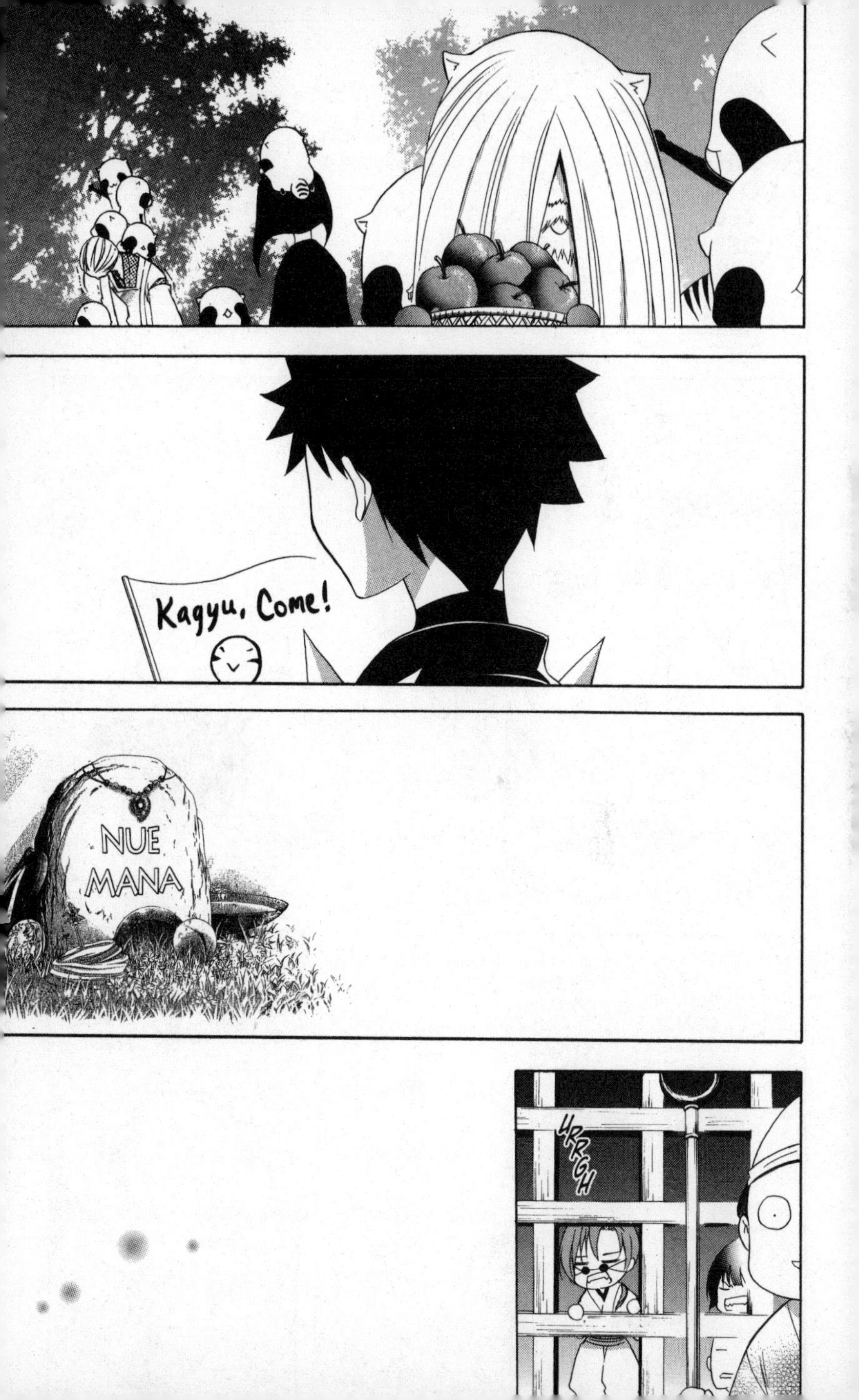
Kagyu, Come!
NUE
MANA
URRGH

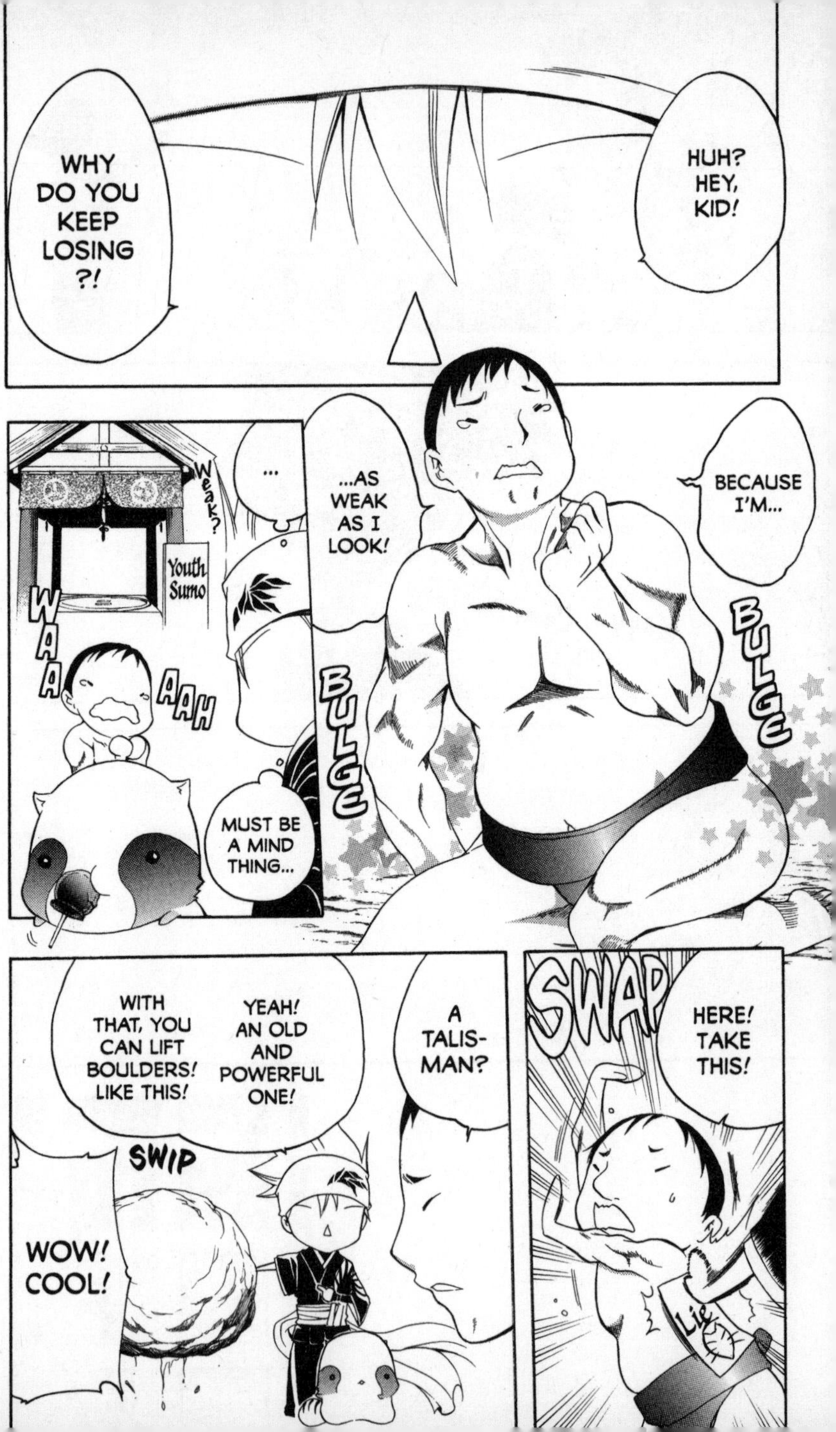
HUH? HEY, KID!
WHY DO YOU KEEP LOSING ?!
BECAUSE I'M...
BULGE
BULGE
...AS WEAK AS I LOOK!
...
Weak?
Youth Sumo
WAAA
AAAH
MUST BE A MIND THING...
SWAP
HERE! TAKE THIS!
Lie
A TALIS-MAN?
YEAH! AN OLD AND POWERFUL ONE!
WITH THAT, YOU CAN LIFT BOULDERS! LIKE THIS!
SWIP
WOW! COOL!

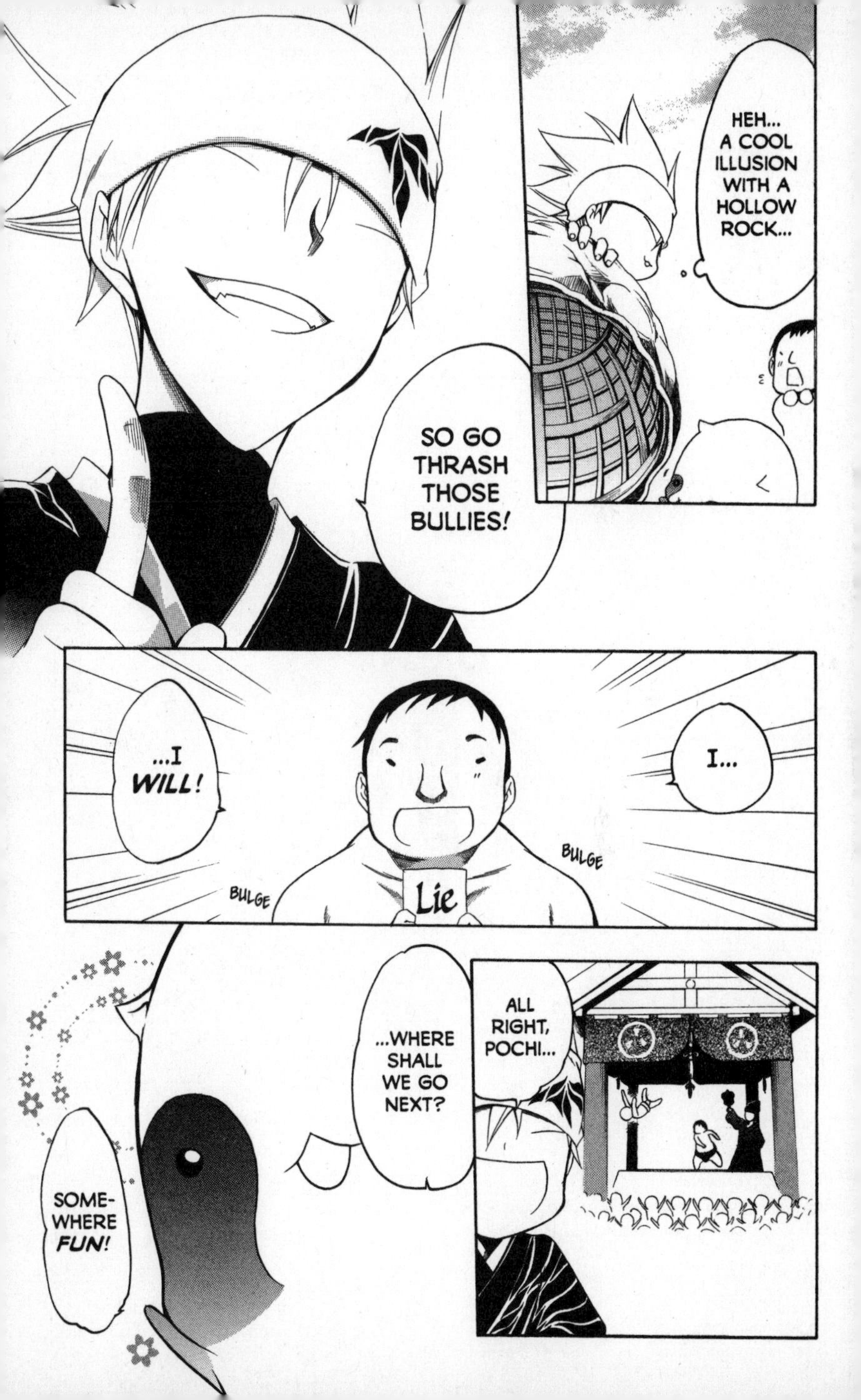
HEH... A COOL ILLUSION WITH A HOLLOW ROCK...
SO GO THRASH THOSE BULLIES!
I...
...I *WILL*!
BULGE
Lie
BULGE
ALL RIGHT, POCHI...
...WHERE SHALL WE GO NEXT?
SOME-WHERE *FUN*!

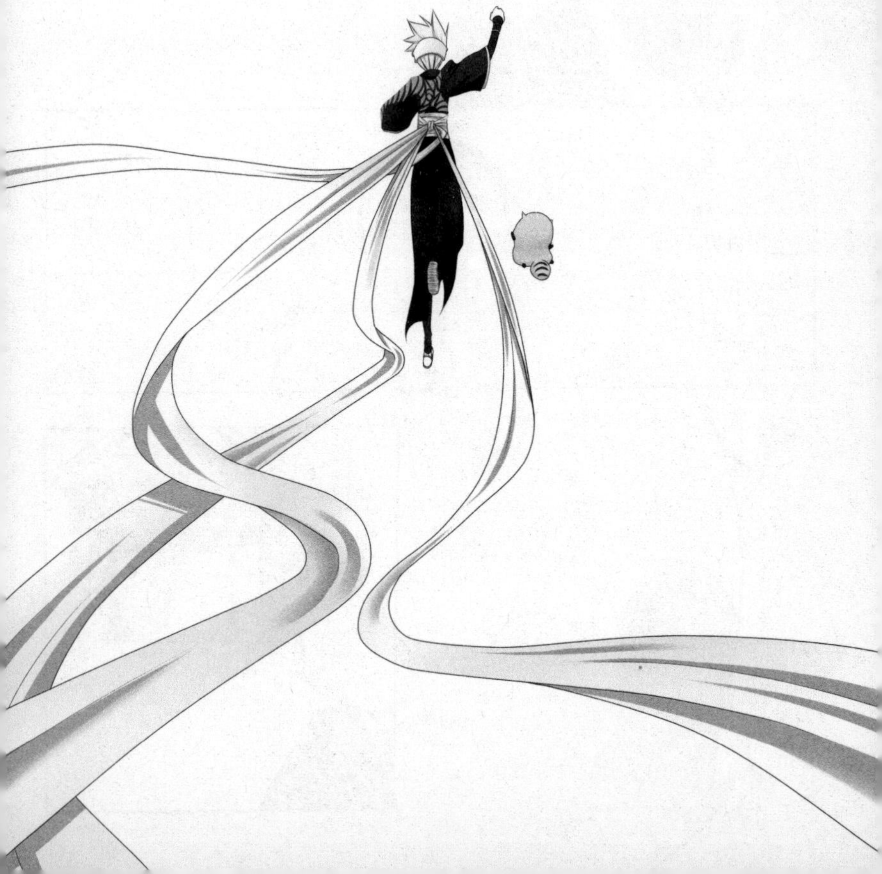

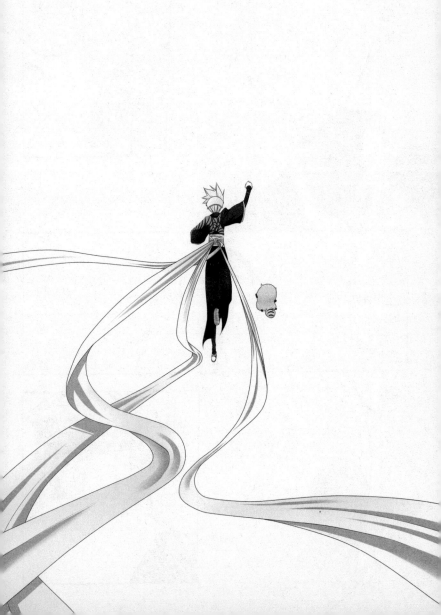

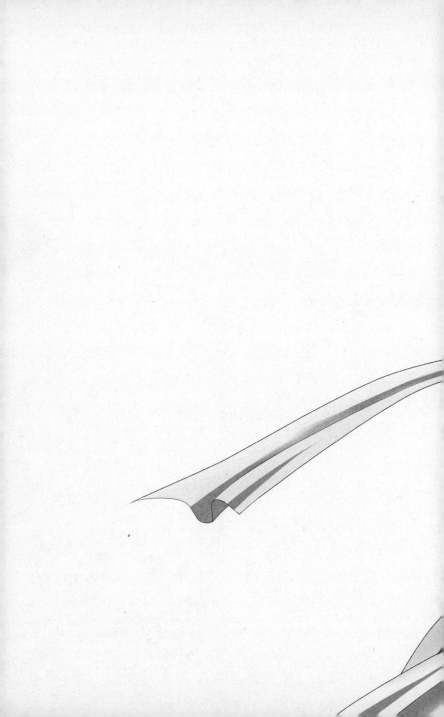

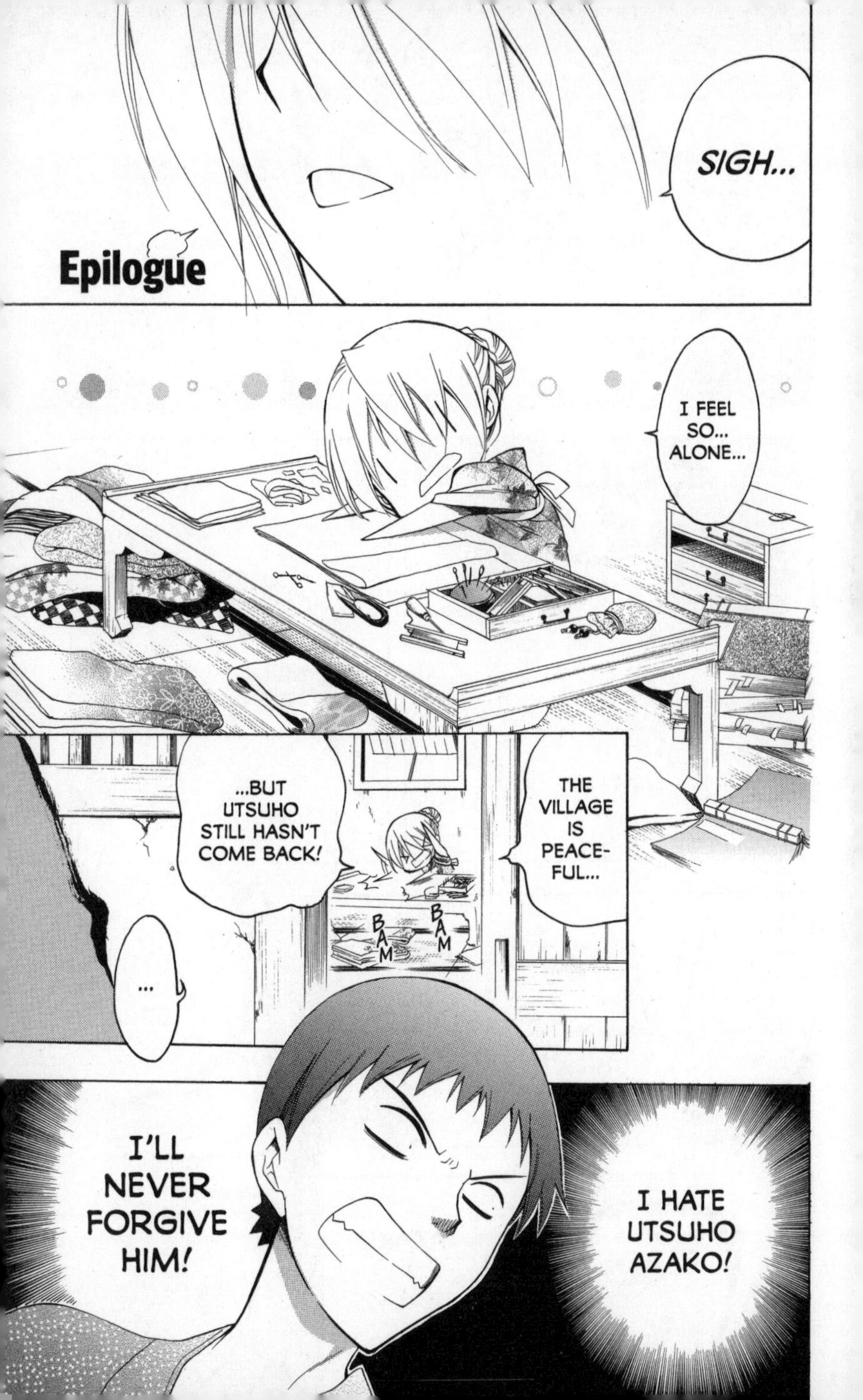
SIGH...
Epilogue
I FEEL SO... ALONE...
THE VILLAGE IS PEACE-FUL...
...BUT UTSUHO STILL HASN'T COME BACK!
BAM
BAM
...
I HATE UTSUHO AZAKO!
I'LL NEVER FORGIVE HIM!

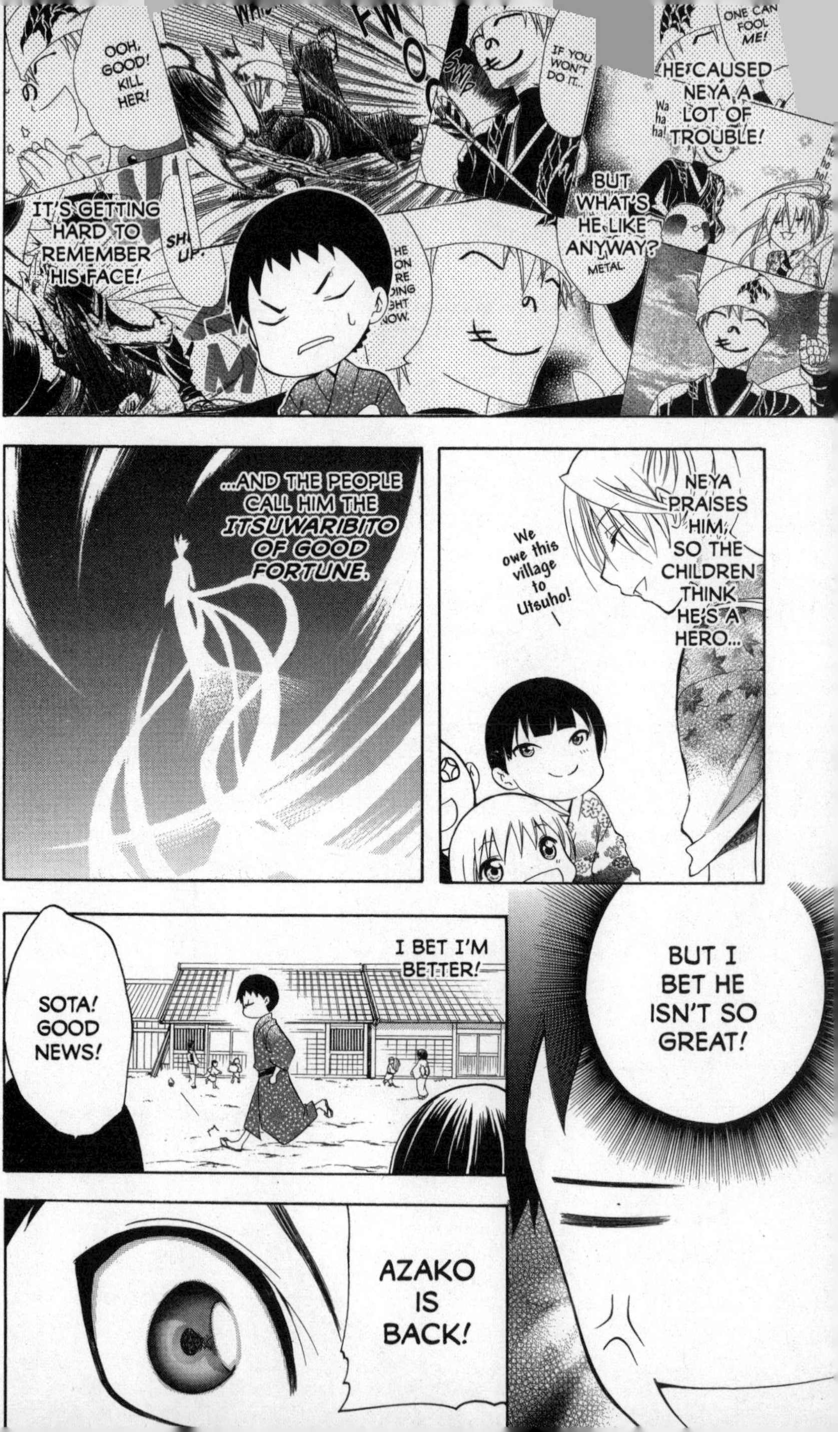
ONE CAN FOOL ME!
HE CAUSED NEYA A LOT OF TROUBLE!
Wa ha ha!
IF YOU WON'T DO IT...
OOH, GOOD! KILL HER!
BUT WHAT'S HE LIKE ANYWAY?
METAL
SHUT UP!
IT'S GETTING HARD TO REMEMBER HIS FACE!
NEYA PRAISES HIM, SO THE CHILDREN THINK HE'S A HERO...
We owe this village to Utsuho!
...AND THE PEOPLE CALL HIM THE ITSUWARIBITO OF GOOD FORTUNE.
BUT I BET HE ISN'T SO GREAT!
I BET I'M BETTER!
SOTA! GOOD NEWS!
AZAKO IS BACK!

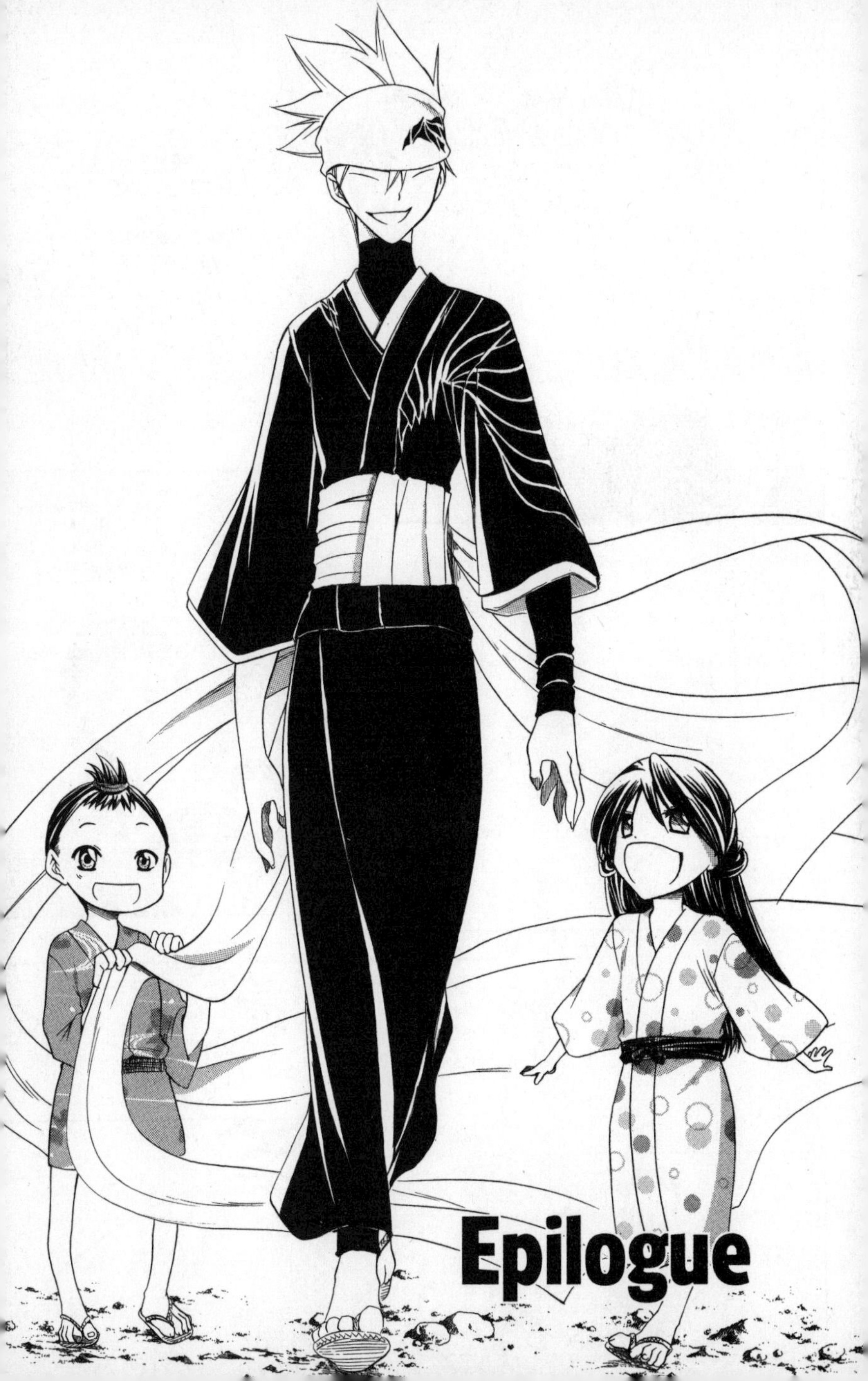
Epilogue

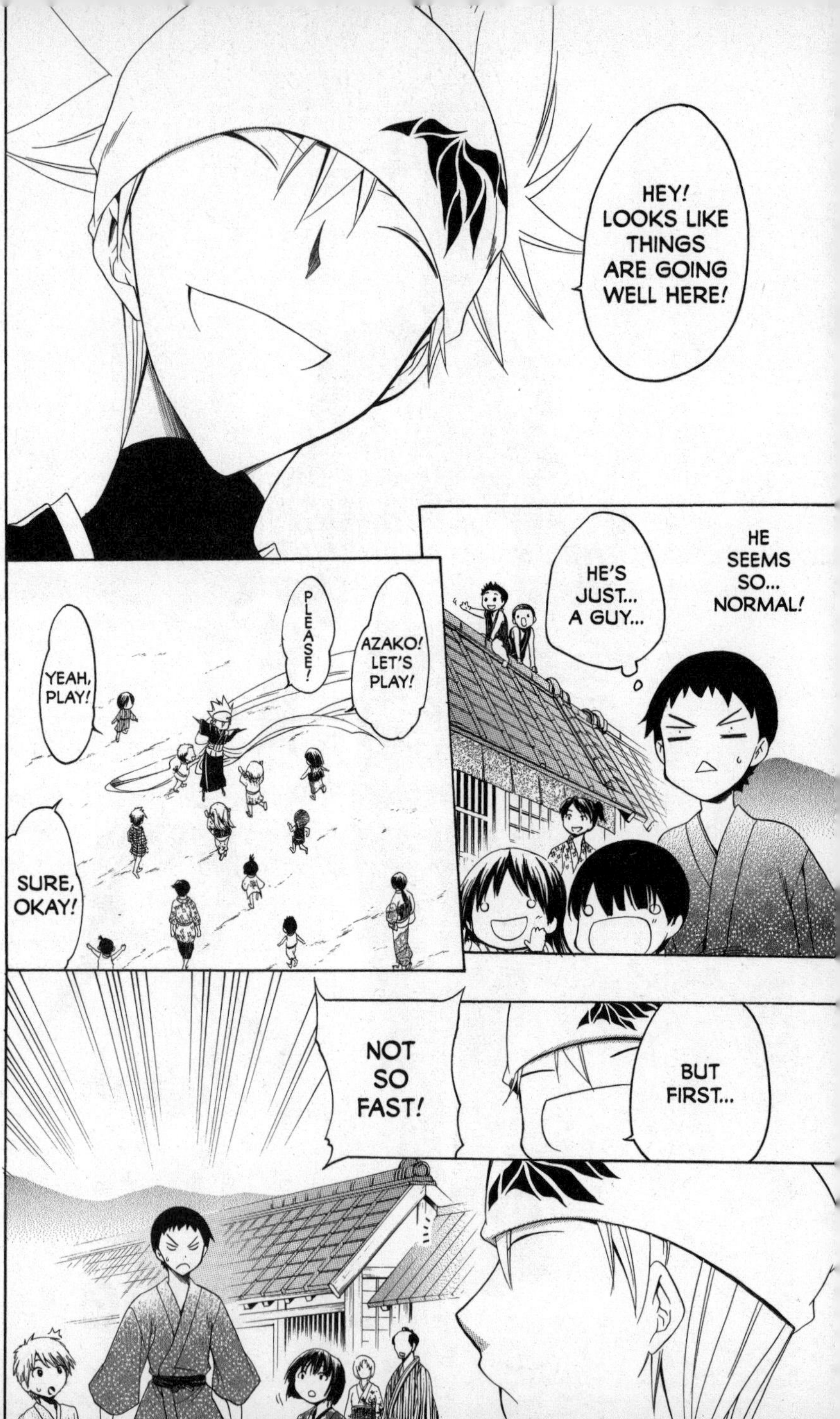
HEY! LOOKS LIKE THINGS ARE GOING WELL HERE!
HE SEEMS SO... NORMAL!
HE'S JUST... A GUY...
AZAKO! LET'S PLAY!
PLEASE!
YEAH, PLAY!
SURE, OKAY!
BUT FIRST...
NOT SO FAST!

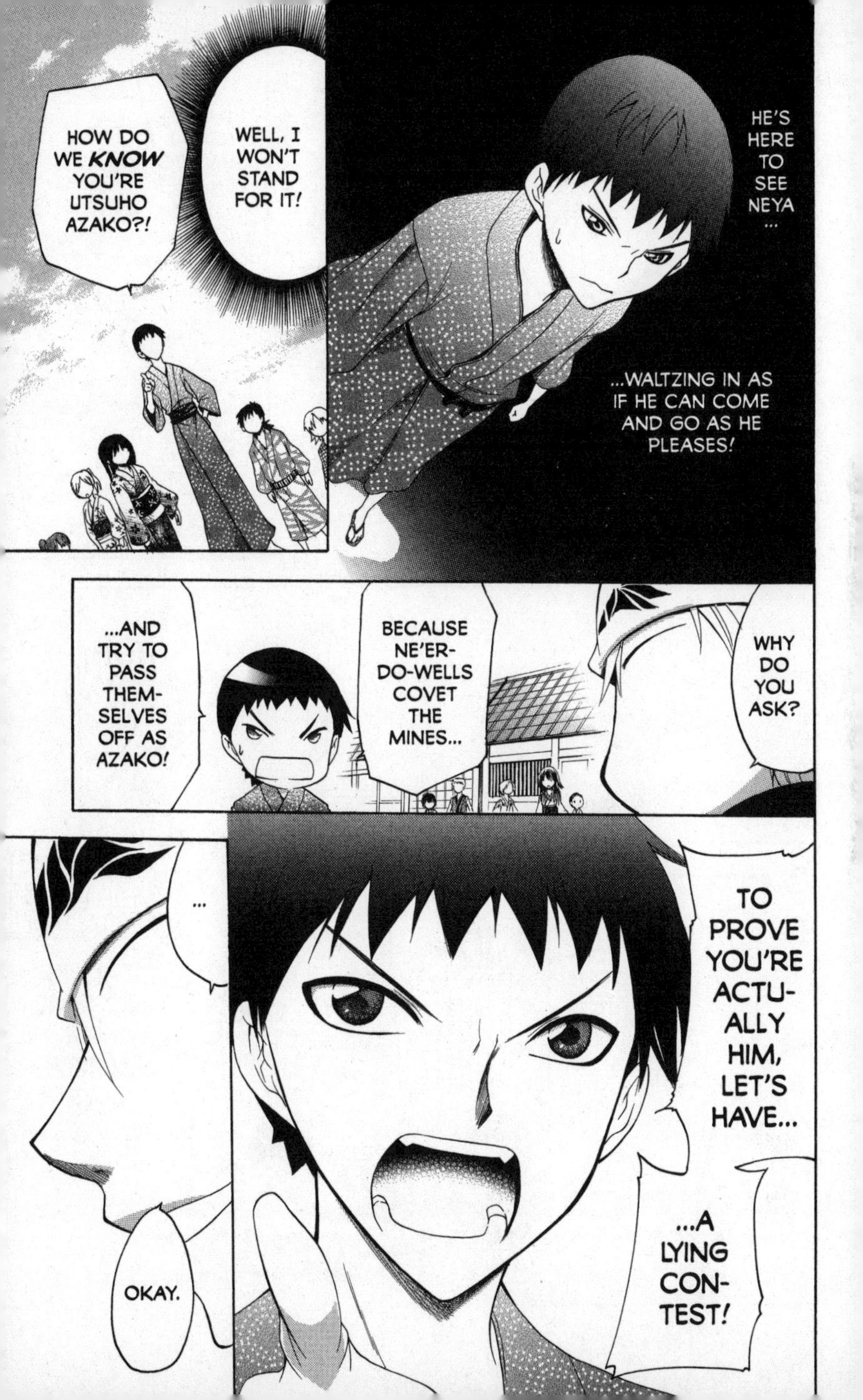
HE'S HERE TO SEE NEYA...
...WALTZING IN AS IF HE CAN COME AND GO AS HE PLEASES!
WELL, I WON'T STAND FOR IT!
HOW DO WE ***KNOW*** YOU'RE UTSUHO AZAKO?!
WHY DO YOU ASK?
BECAUSE NE'ER-DO-WELLS COVET THE MINES...
...AND TRY TO PASS THEMSELVES OFF AS AZAKO!
TO PROVE YOU'RE ACTUALLY HIM, LET'S HAVE...
...A LYING CONTEST!
...
OKAY.

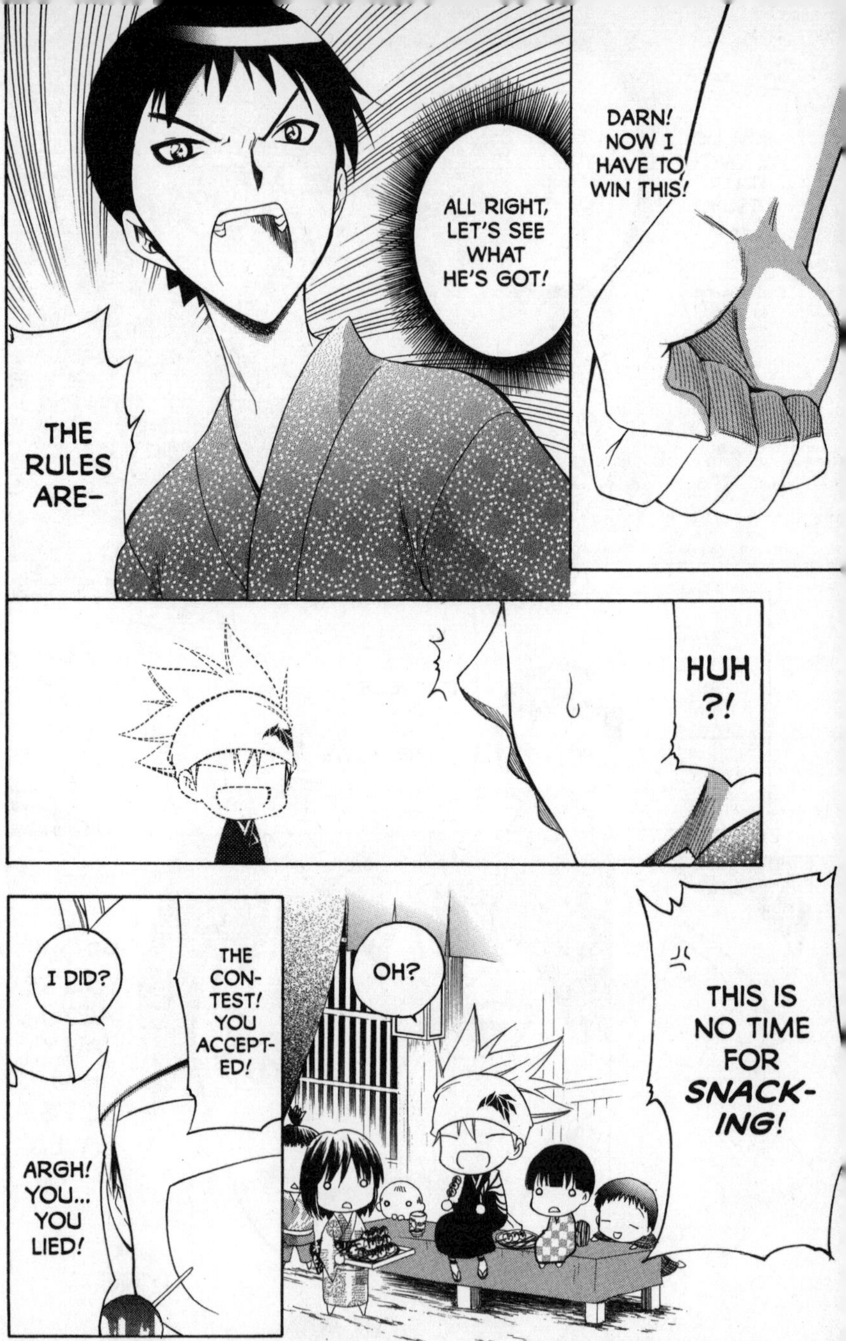
DARN! NOW I HAVE TO WIN THIS!
ALL RIGHT, LET'S SEE WHAT HE'S GOT!
THE RULES ARE–
HUH ?!
THIS IS NO TIME FOR *SNACKING!*
OH?
THE CONTEST! YOU ACCEPTED!
I DID?
ARGH! YOU... YOU LIED!

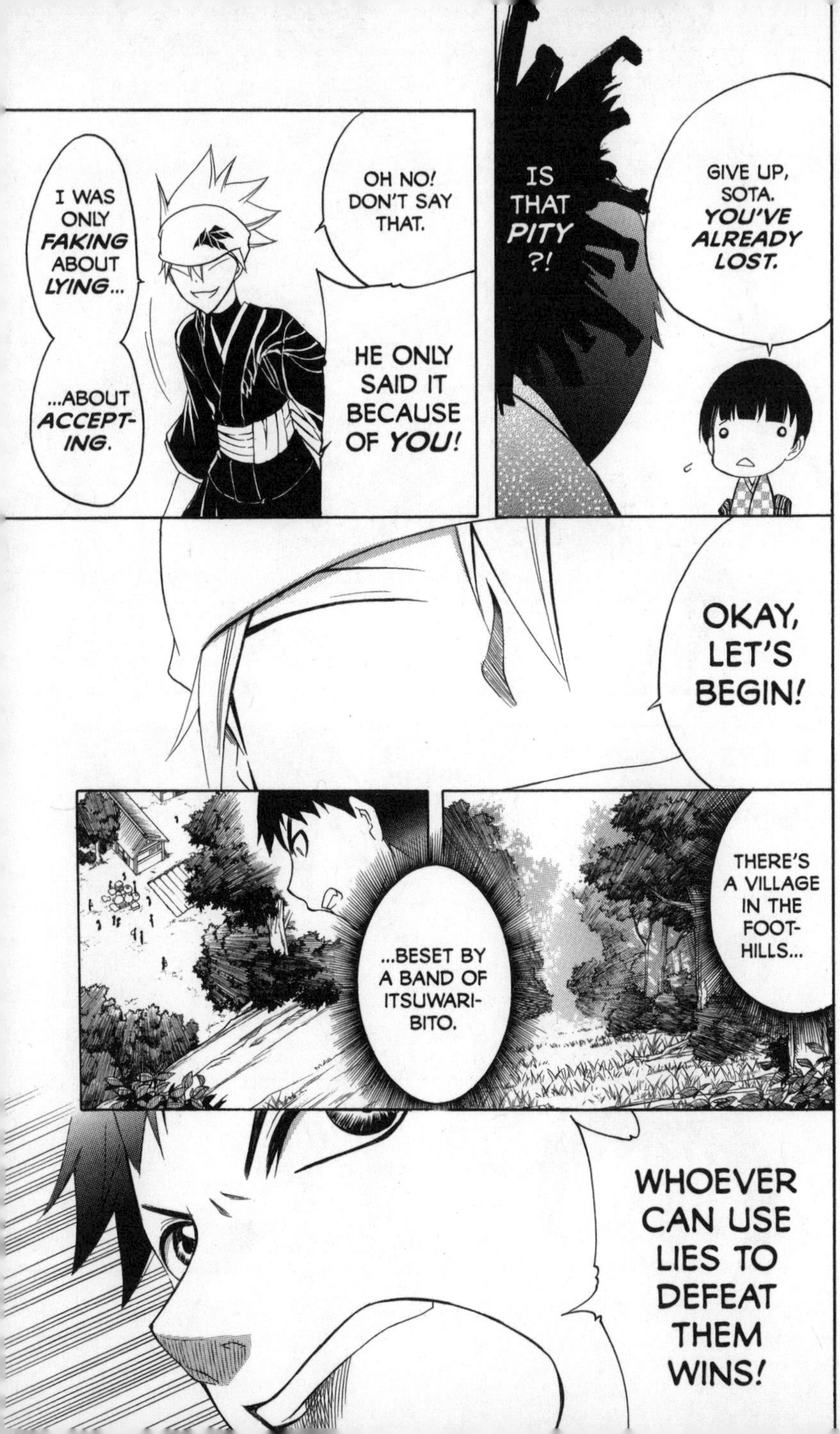
GIVE UP, SOTA. YOU'VE ALREADY LOST.
IS THAT PITY?!
OH NO! DON'T SAY THAT.
HE ONLY SAID IT BECAUSE OF YOU!
I WAS ONLY FAKING ABOUT LYING...
...ABOUT ACCEPTING.
OKAY, LET'S BEGIN!
THERE'S A VILLAGE IN THE FOOTHILLS...
...BESET BY A BAND OF ITSUWARIBITO.
WHOEVER CAN USE LIES TO DEFEAT THEM WINS!

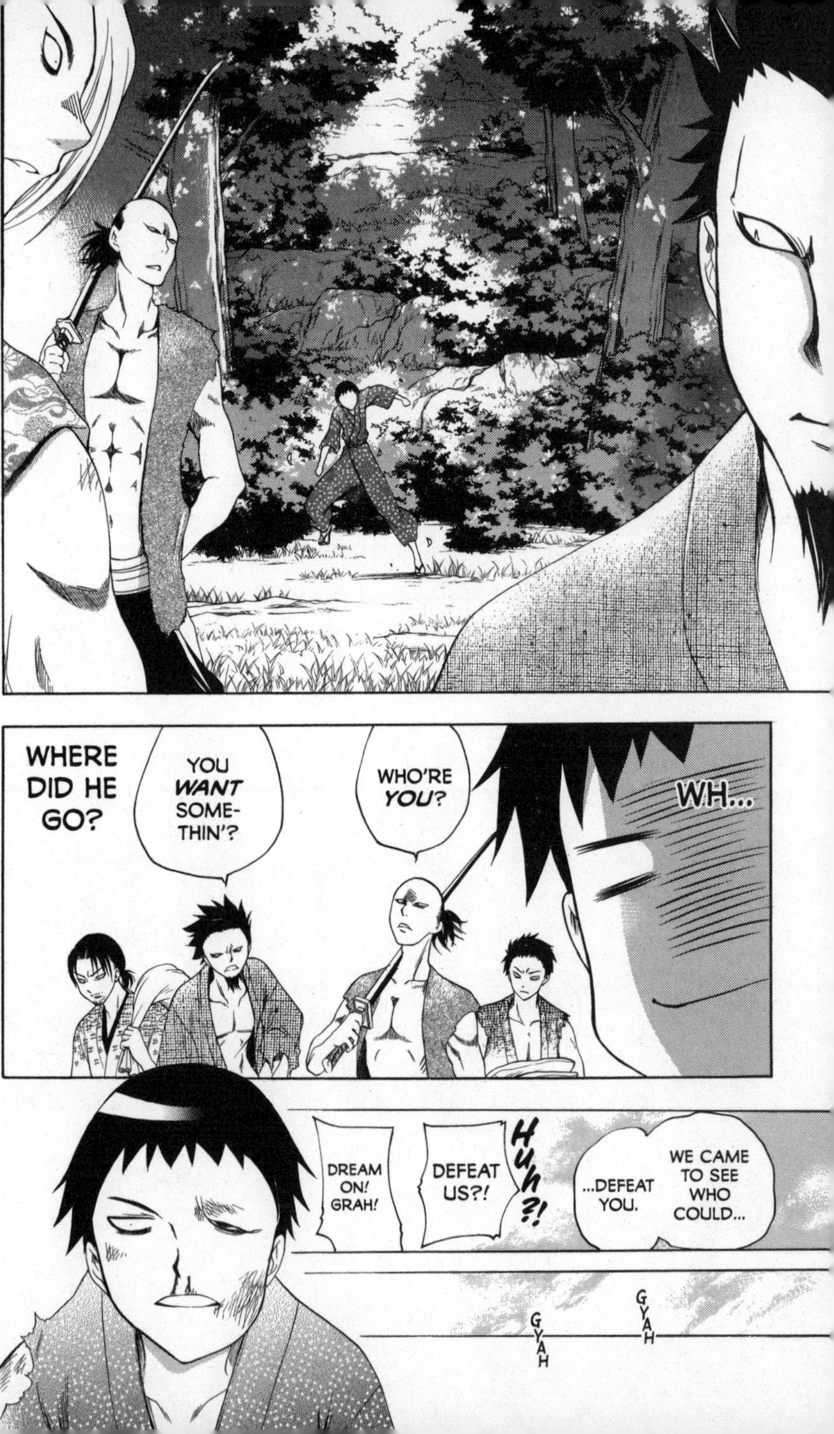
WH...
WHO'RE YOU?
YOU WANT SOME-THIN'?
WHERE DID HE GO?
WE CAME TO SEE WHO COULD...
...DEFEAT YOU.
HUH?!
DEFEAT US?!
DREAM ON! GRAH!
GYAH
GYAH

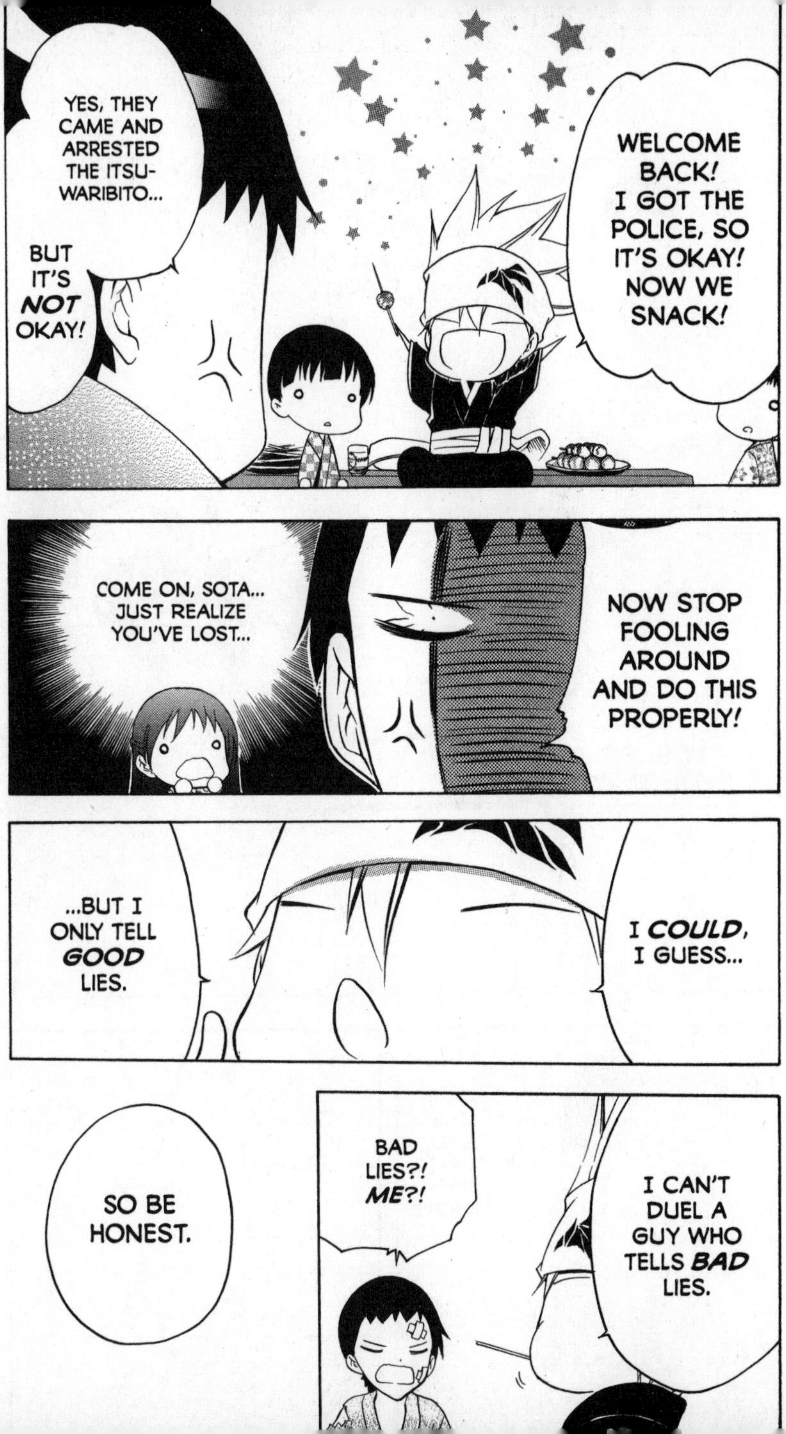
WELCOME BACK! I GOT THE POLICE, SO IT'S OKAY! NOW WE SNACK!
YES, THEY CAME AND ARRESTED THE ITSU-WARIBITO...
BUT IT'S NOT OKAY!
NOW STOP FOOLING AROUND AND DO THIS PROPERLY!
COME ON, SOTA... JUST REALIZE YOU'VE LOST...
I COULD, I GUESS...
...BUT I ONLY TELL GOOD LIES.
I CAN'T DUEL A GUY WHO TELLS BAD LIES.
BAD LIES?! ME?!
SO BE HONEST.

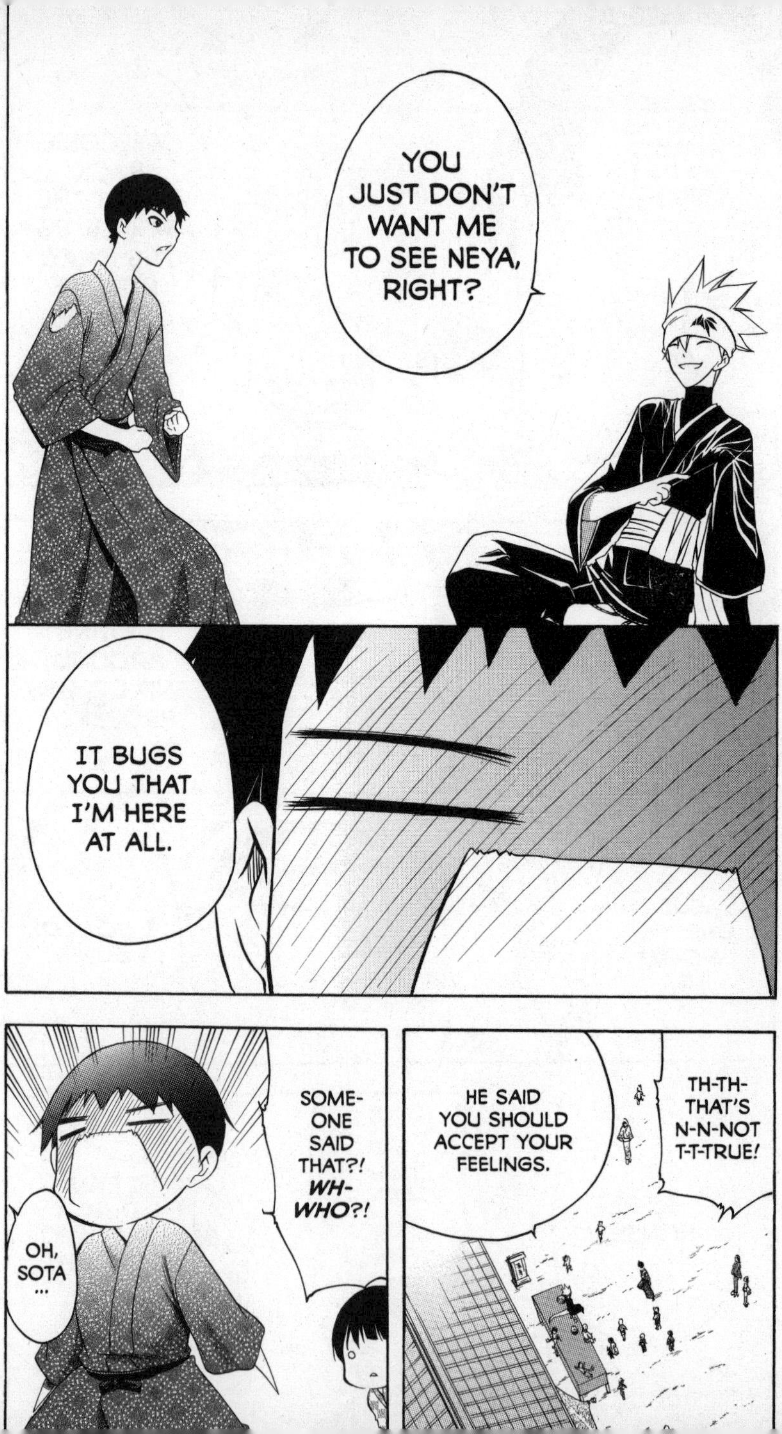
YOU JUST DON'T WANT ME TO SEE NEYA, RIGHT?
IT BUGS YOU THAT I'M HERE AT ALL.
TH-TH-THAT'S N-N-NOT T-T-TRUE!
HE SAID YOU SHOULD ACCEPT YOUR FEELINGS.
SOME-ONE SAID THAT?! *WH-WHO*?!
OH, SOTA...

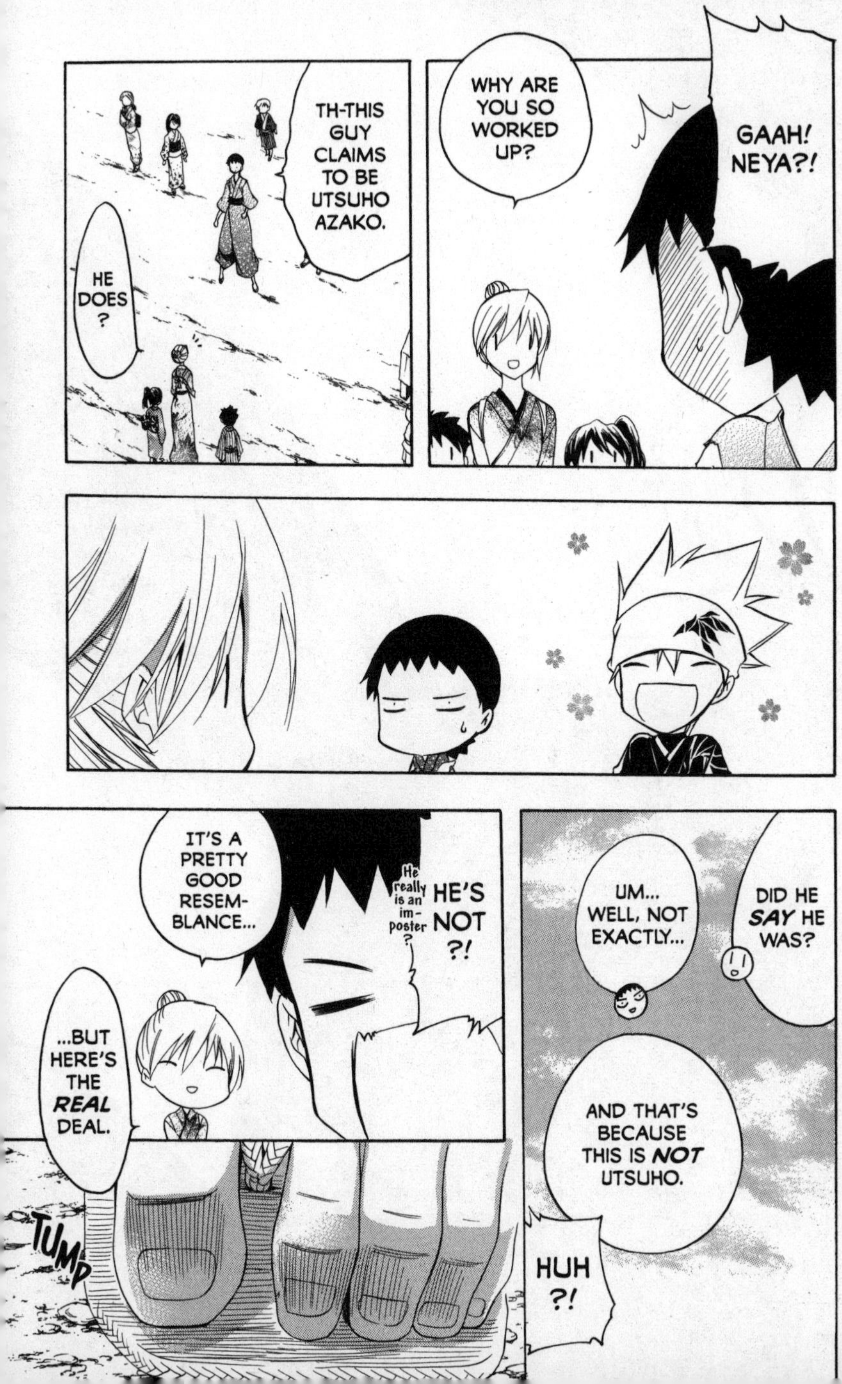
GAAH! NEYA?!
WHY ARE YOU SO WORKED UP?
TH-THIS GUY CLAIMS TO BE UTSUHO AZAKO.
HE DOES?
DID HE *SAY* HE WAS?
UM... WELL, NOT EXACTLY...
AND THAT'S BECAUSE THIS IS *NOT* UTSUHO.
HUH?!
HE'S NOT?!
He really is an im-poster?
IT'S A PRETTY GOOD RESEM-BLANCE...
...BUT HERE'S THE *REAL* DEAL.
TUMP

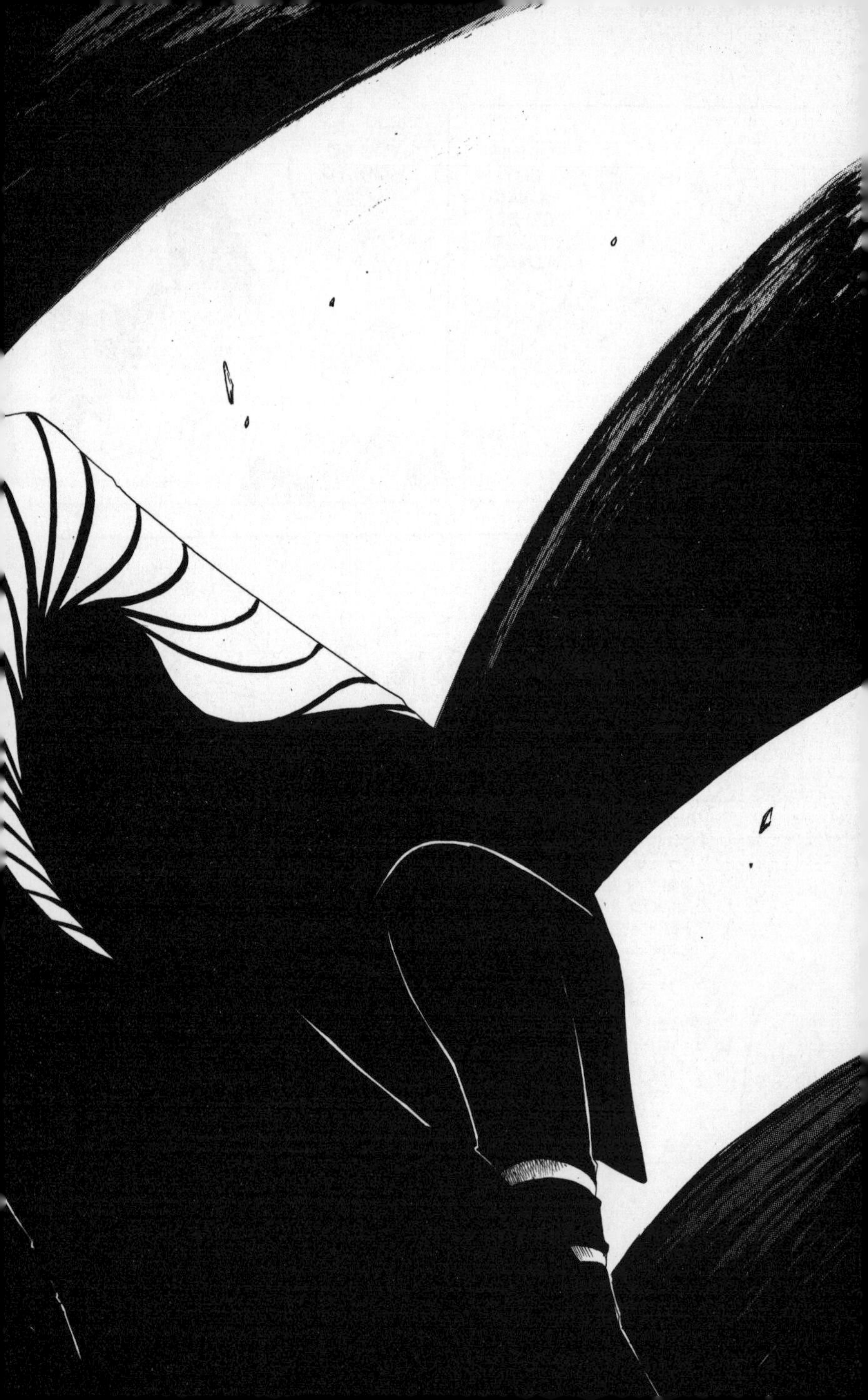

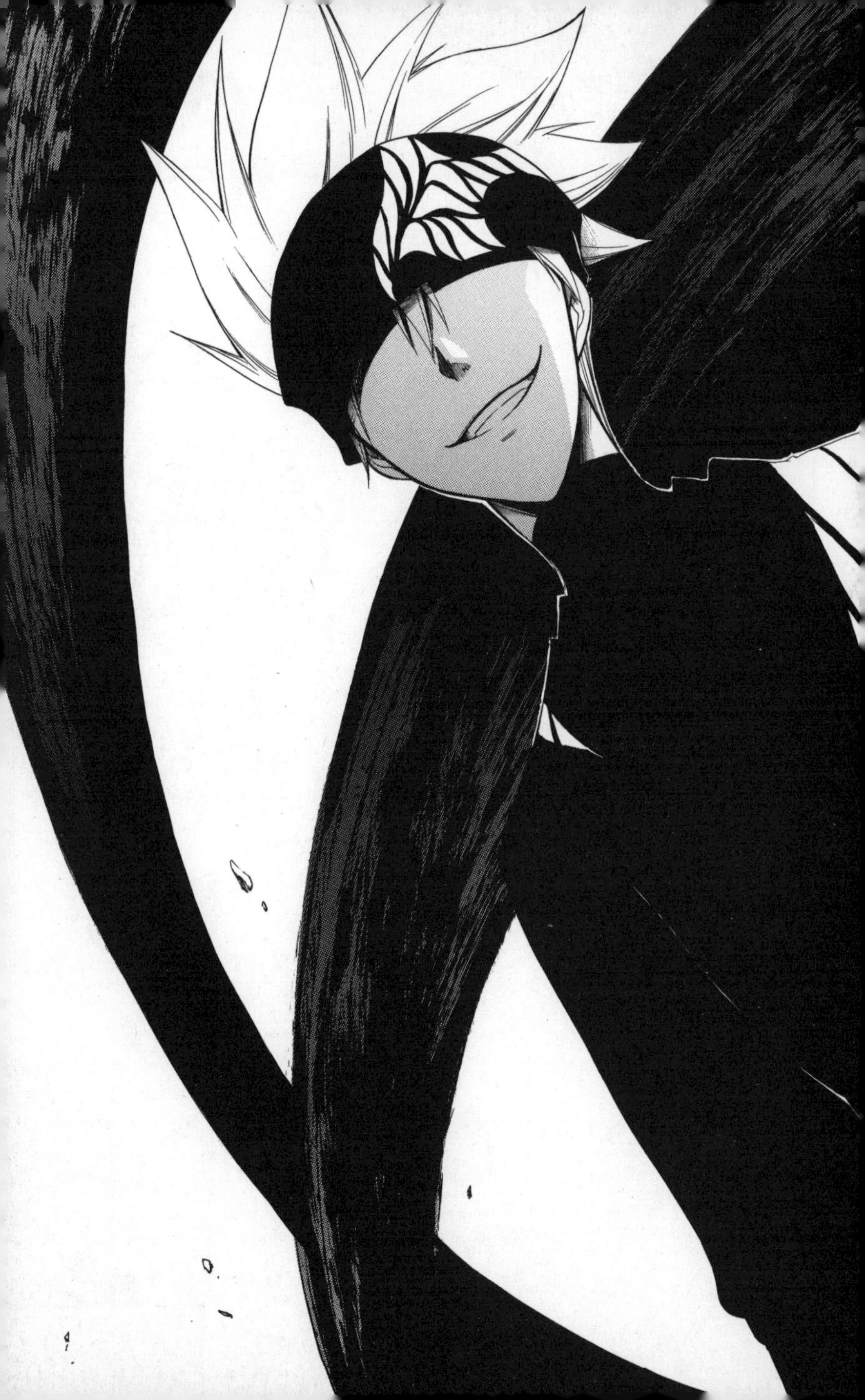

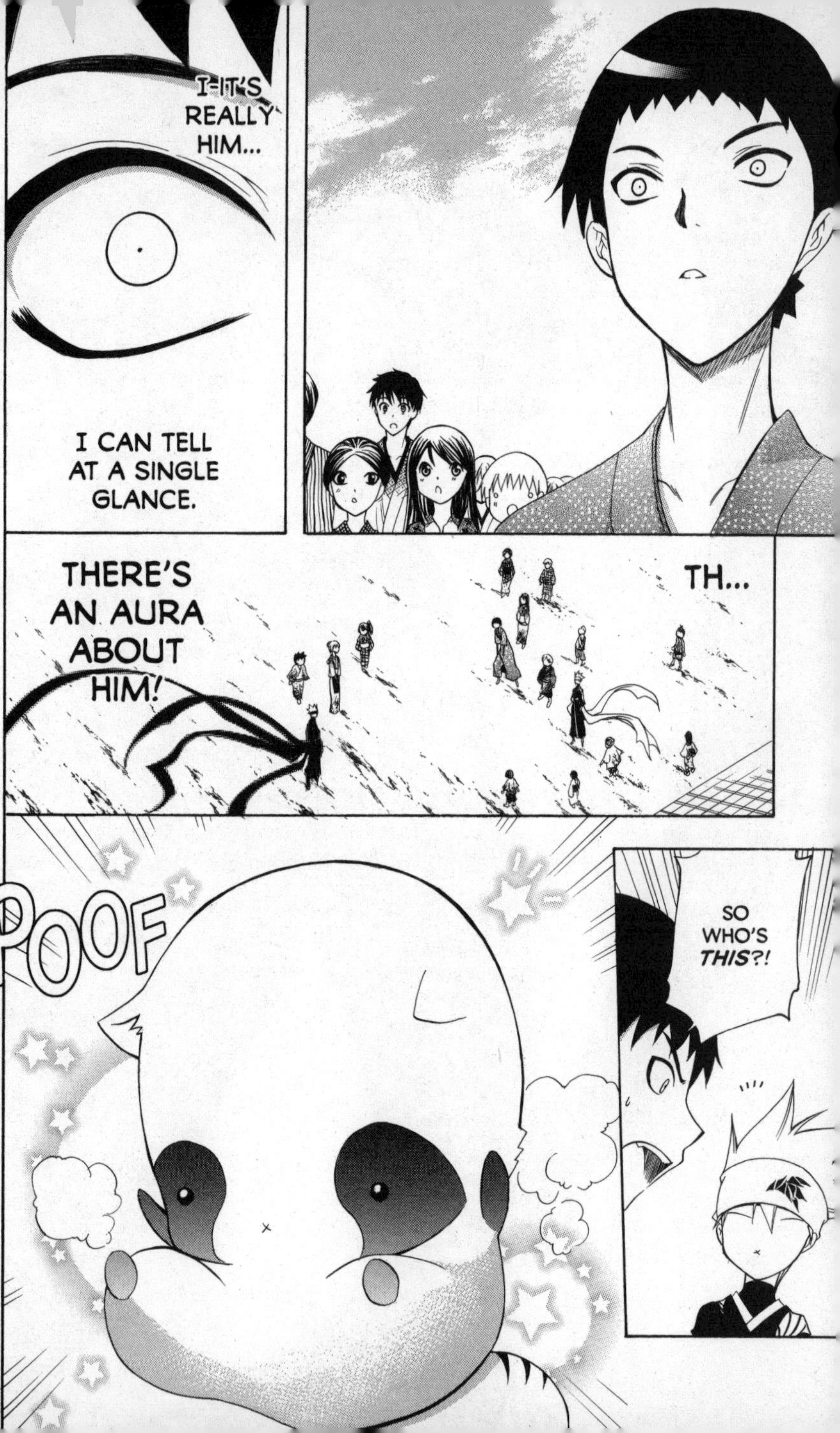
I-IT'S REALLY HIM...
I CAN TELL AT A SINGLE GLANCE.
TH...
THERE'S AN AURA ABOUT HIM!
SO WHO'S *THIS*?!
POOF

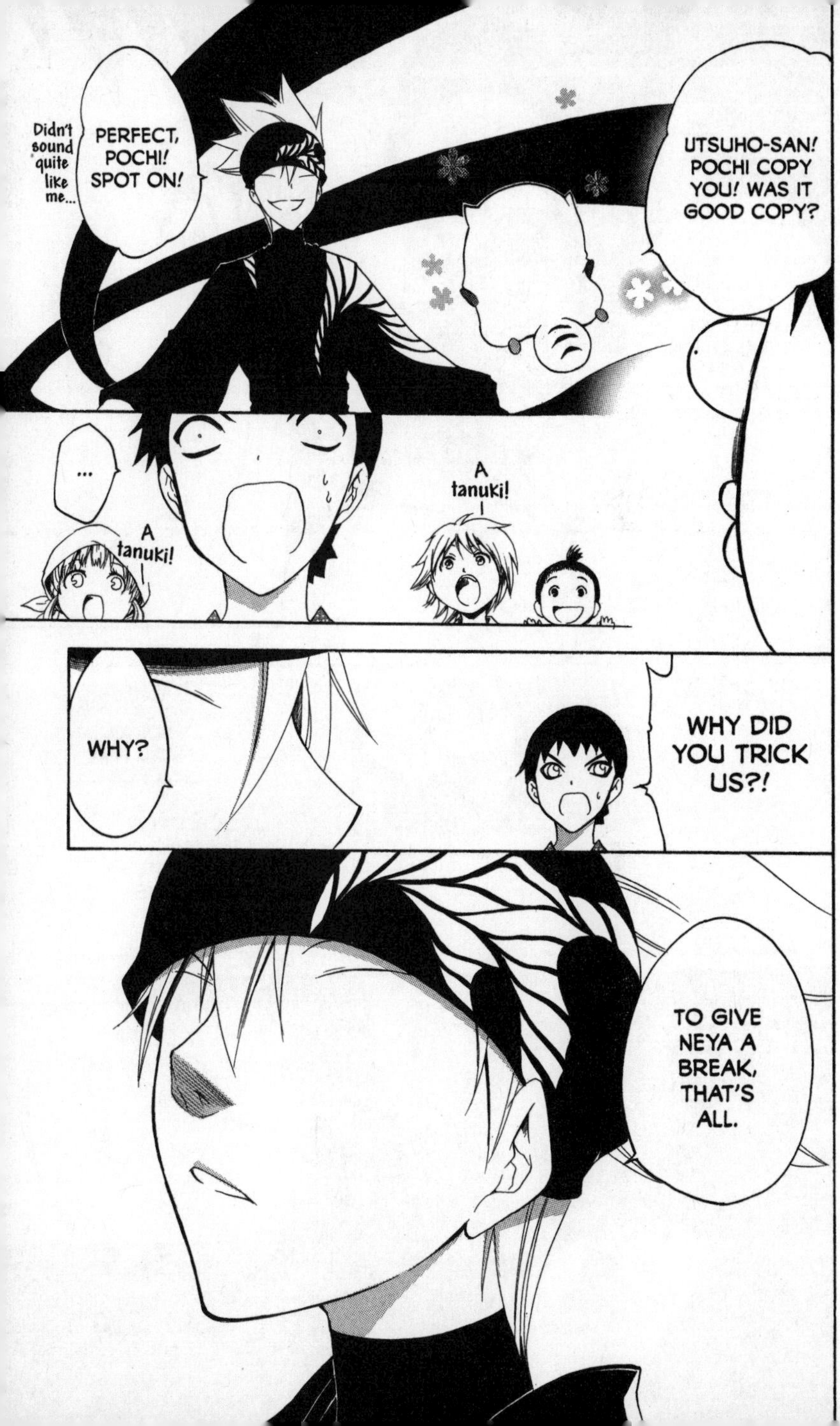
UTSUHO-SAN! POCHI COPY YOU! WAS IT GOOD COPY?
PERFECT, POCHI! SPOT ON!
Didn't sound quite like me...
A tanuki!
...
A tanuki!
WHY DID YOU TRICK US?!
WHY?
TO GIVE NEYA A BREAK, THAT'S ALL.

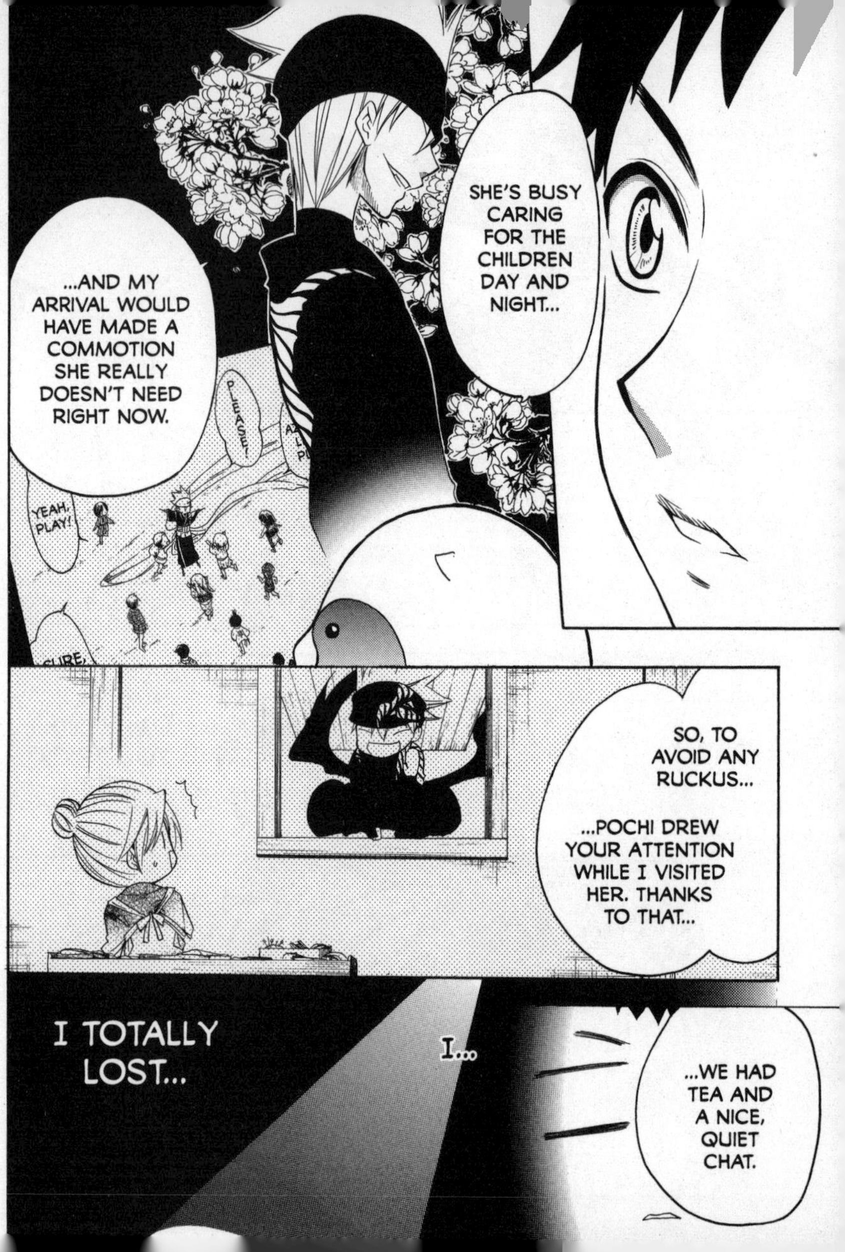
SHE'S BUSY CARING FOR THE CHILDREN DAY AND NIGHT...
...AND MY ARRIVAL WOULD HAVE MADE A COMMOTION SHE REALLY DOESN'T NEED RIGHT NOW.
PLEASE!
YEAH, PLAY!
SO, TO AVOID ANY RUCKUS...
...POCHI DREW YOUR ATTENTION WHILE I VISITED HER. THANKS TO THAT...
...WE HAD TEA AND A NICE, QUIET CHAT.
I...
I TOTALLY LOST...

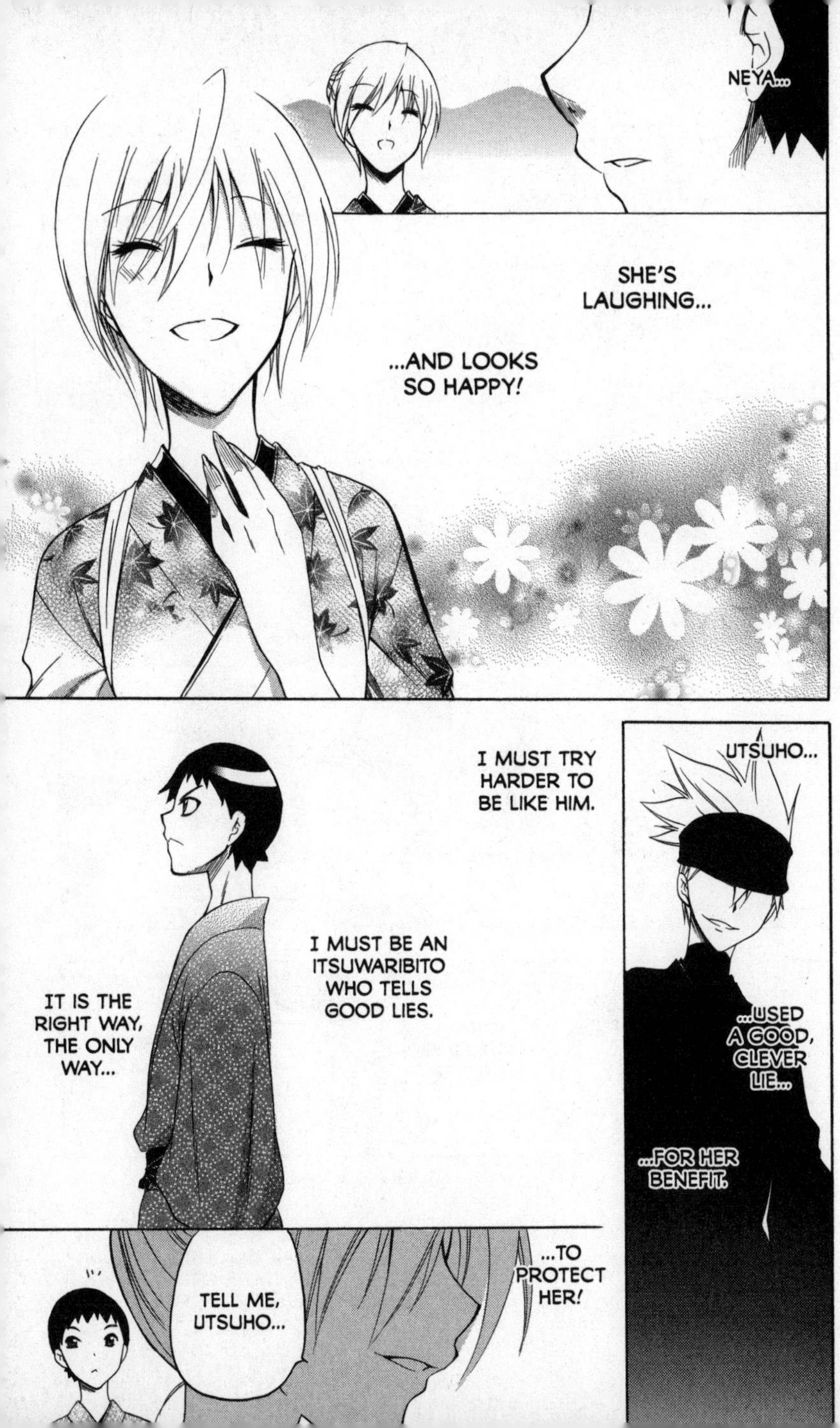
NEYA...
SHE'S LAUGHING...
...AND LOOKS SO HAPPY!
UTSUHO...
...USED A GOOD, CLEVER LIE...
...FOR HER BENEFIT.
I MUST TRY HARDER TO BE LIKE HIM.
I MUST BE AN ITSUWARIBITO WHO TELLS GOOD LIES.
IT IS THE RIGHT WAY, THE ONLY WAY...
...TO PROTECT HER!
TELL ME, UTSUHO...

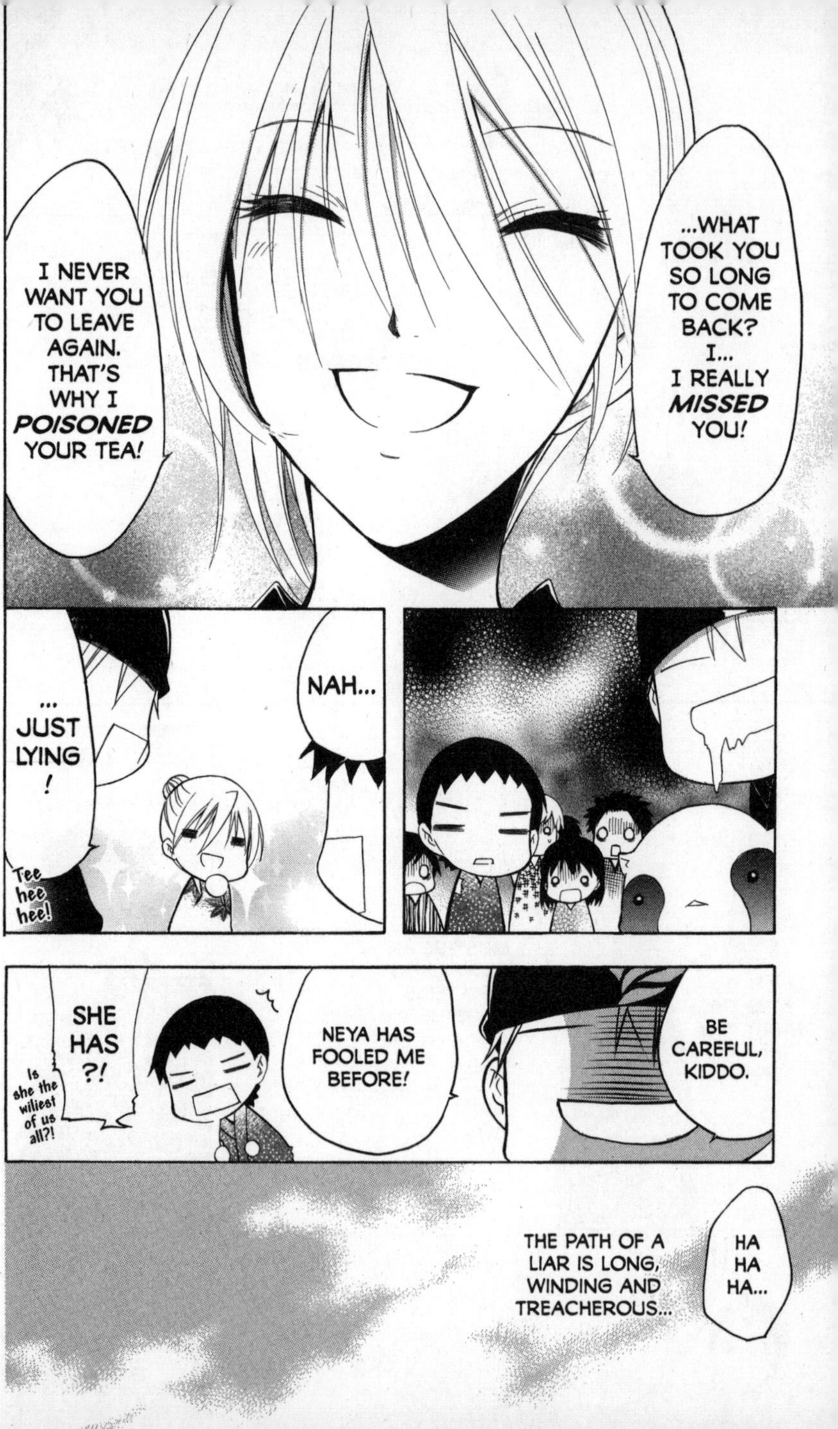
...WHAT TOOK YOU SO LONG TO COME BACK? I... I REALLY *MISSED* YOU!
I NEVER WANT YOU TO LEAVE AGAIN. THAT'S WHY I *POISONED* YOUR TEA!
NAH...
... JUST LYING!
Tee hee hee!
BE CAREFUL, KIDDO.
NEYA HAS FOOLED ME BEFORE!
SHE HAS?!
Is she the wiliest of us all?!
HA HA HA...
THE PATH OF A LIAR IS LONG, WINDING AND TREACHEROUS...

Special Bonus Manga

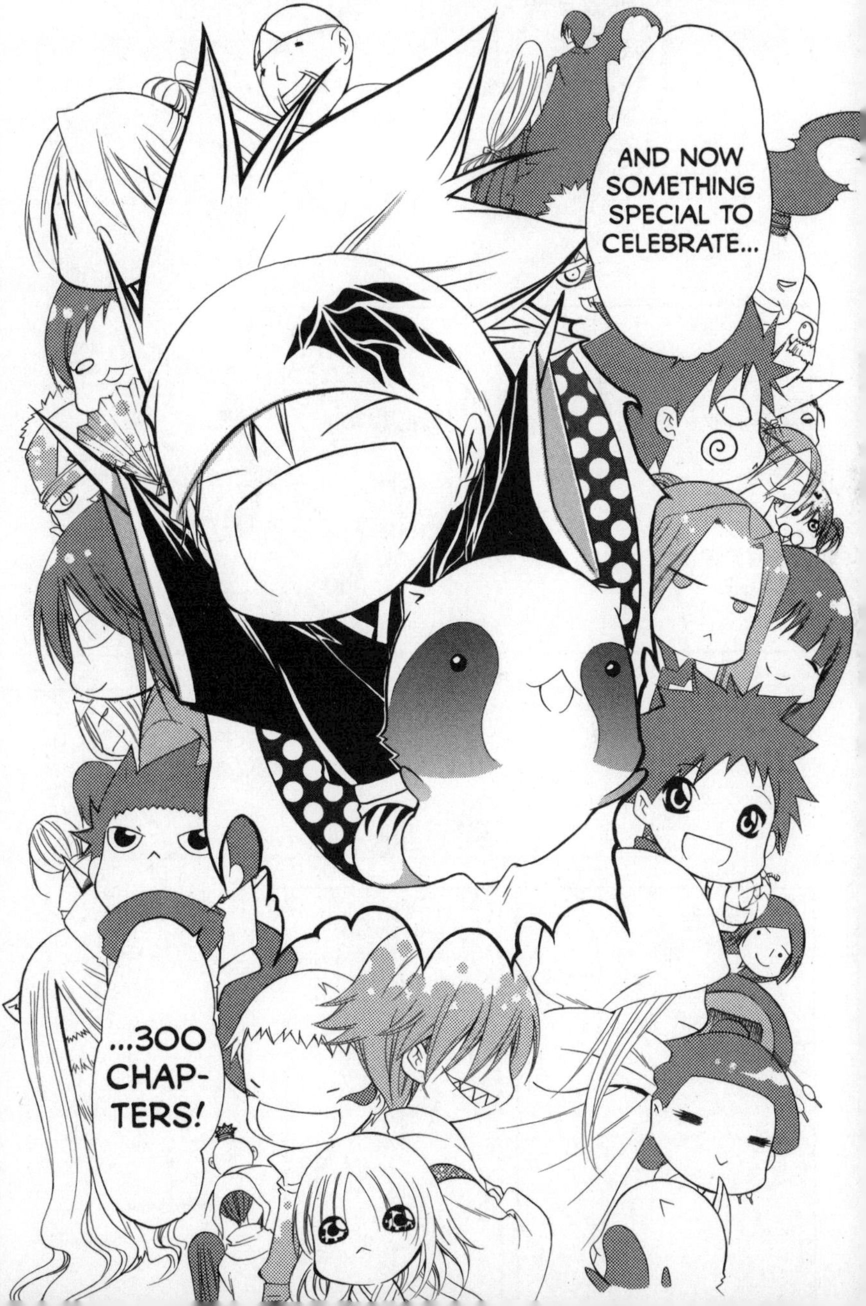

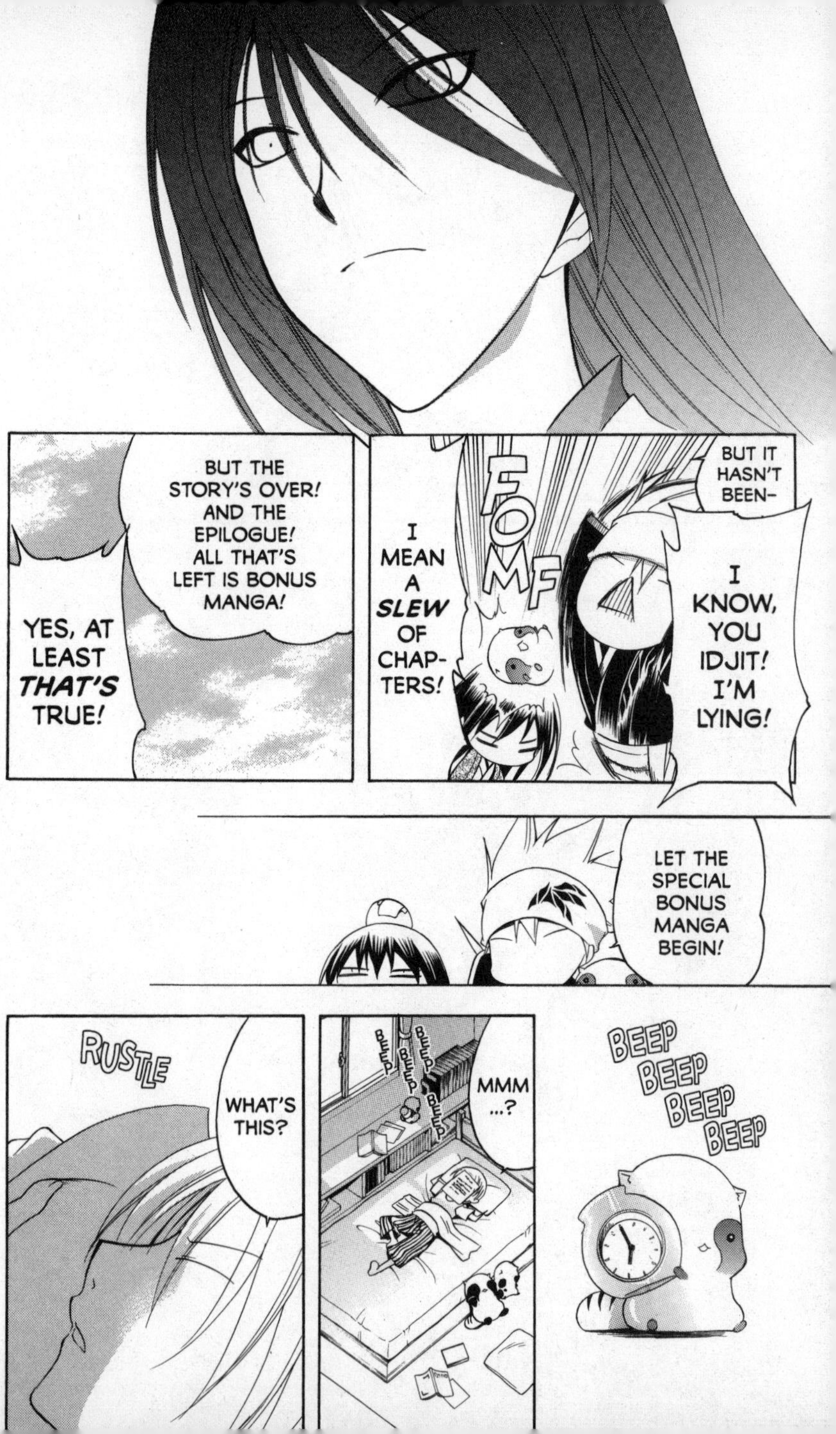
BUT IT HASN'T BEEN–
I KNOW, YOU IDJIT! I'M LYING!
FOMF
I MEAN A *SLEW* OF CHAPTERS!
BUT THE STORY'S OVER! AND THE EPILOGUE! ALL THAT'S LEFT IS BONUS MANGA!
YES, AT LEAST *THAT'S* TRUE!
LET THE SPECIAL BONUS MANGA BEGIN!
BEEP BEEP BEEP BEEP
MMM ...?
BEEP BEEP BEEP BEEP
RUSTLE
WHAT'S THIS?

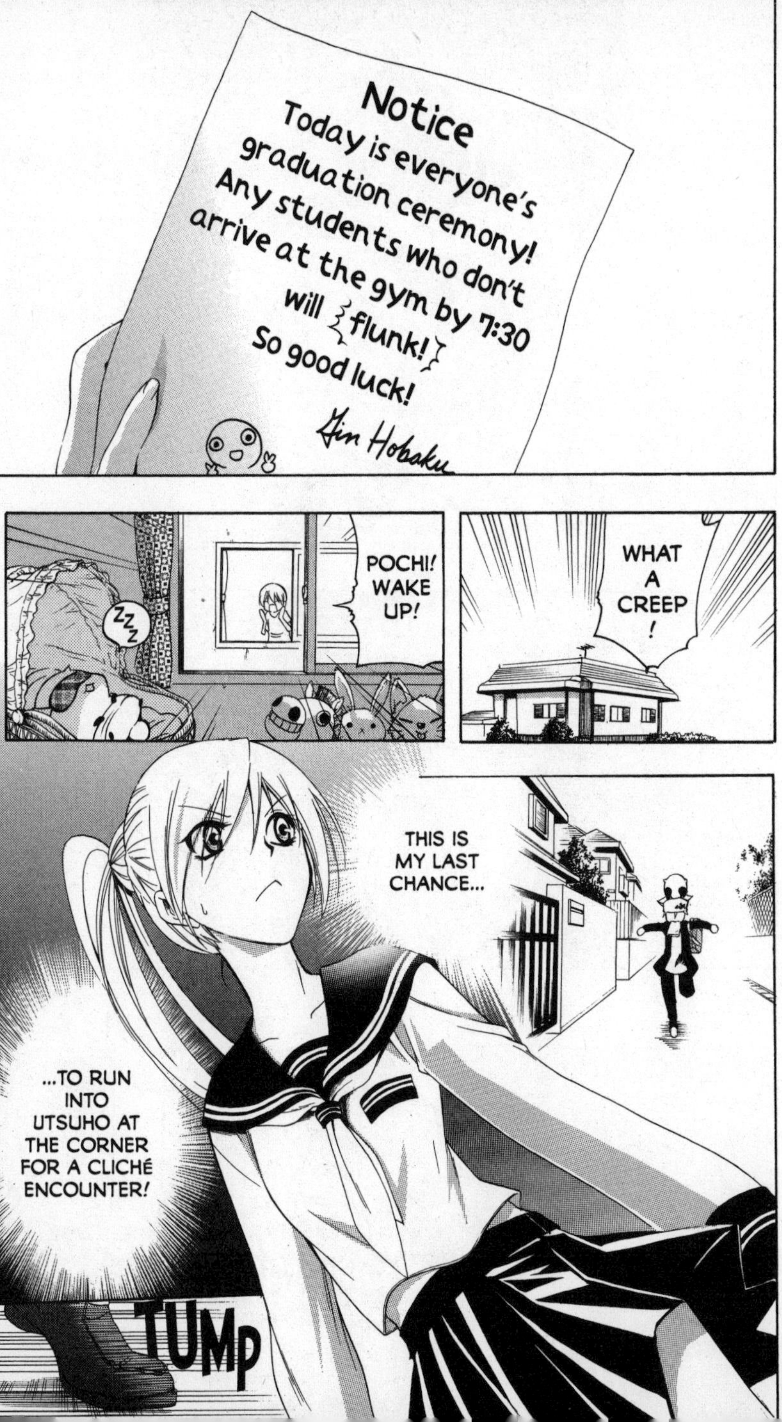
Notice
Today is everyone's graduation ceremony!
Any students who don't arrive at the gym by 7:30 will flunk!
So good luck!
Gin Hobaku
WHAT A CREEP!
POCHI! WAKE UP!
ZZZ
THIS IS MY LAST CHANCE...
...TO RUN INTO UTSUHO AT THE CORNER FOR A CLICHÉ ENCOUNTER!
TUMP

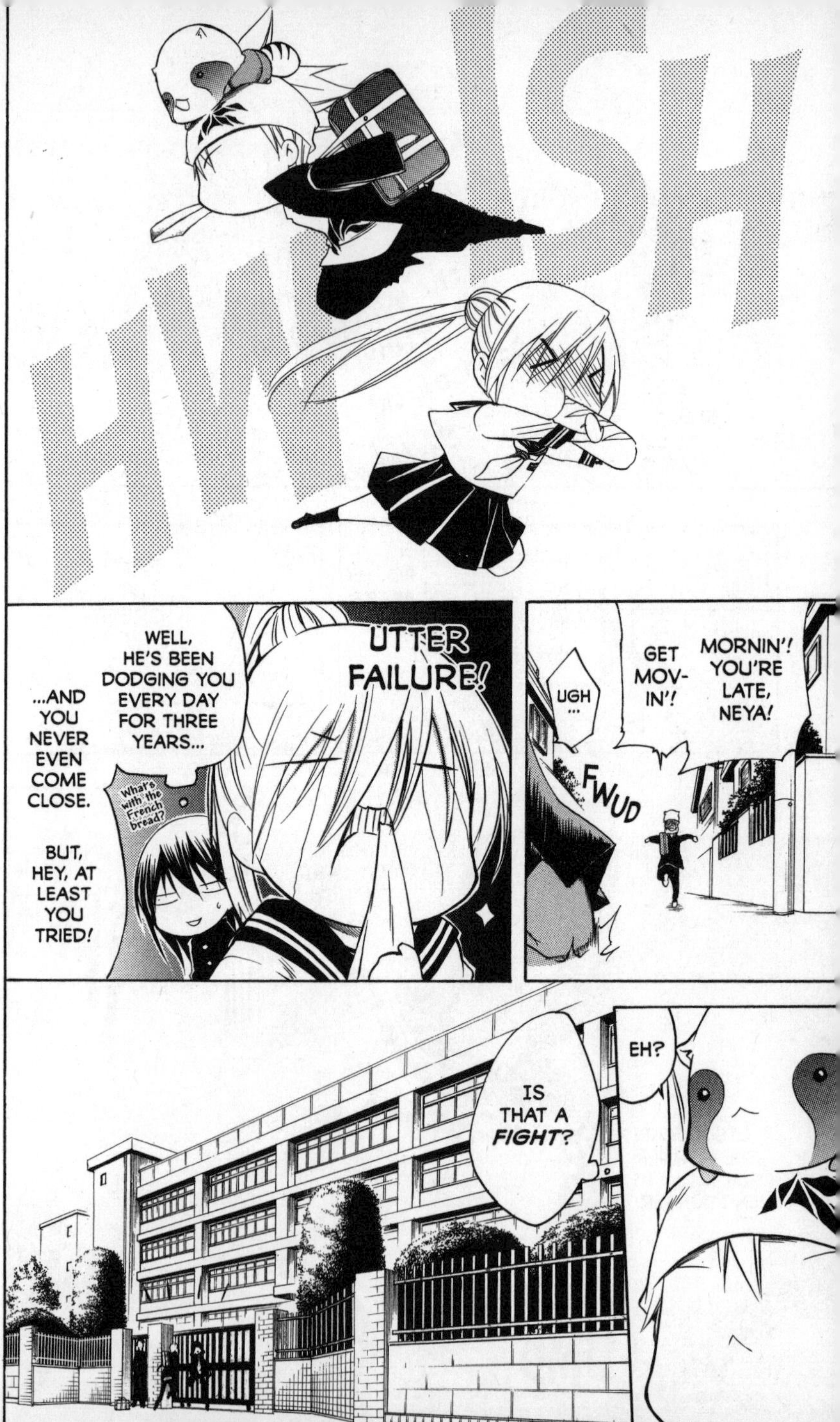
HWISH
MORNIN'! YOU'RE LATE, NEYA!
GET MOV-IN'!
UGH...
FWUD
UTTER FAILURE!
WELL, HE'S BEEN DODGING YOU EVERY DAY FOR THREE YEARS...
...AND YOU NEVER EVEN COME CLOSE.
What's with the French bread?
BUT, HEY, AT LEAST YOU TRIED!
EH?
IS THAT A *FIGHT*?

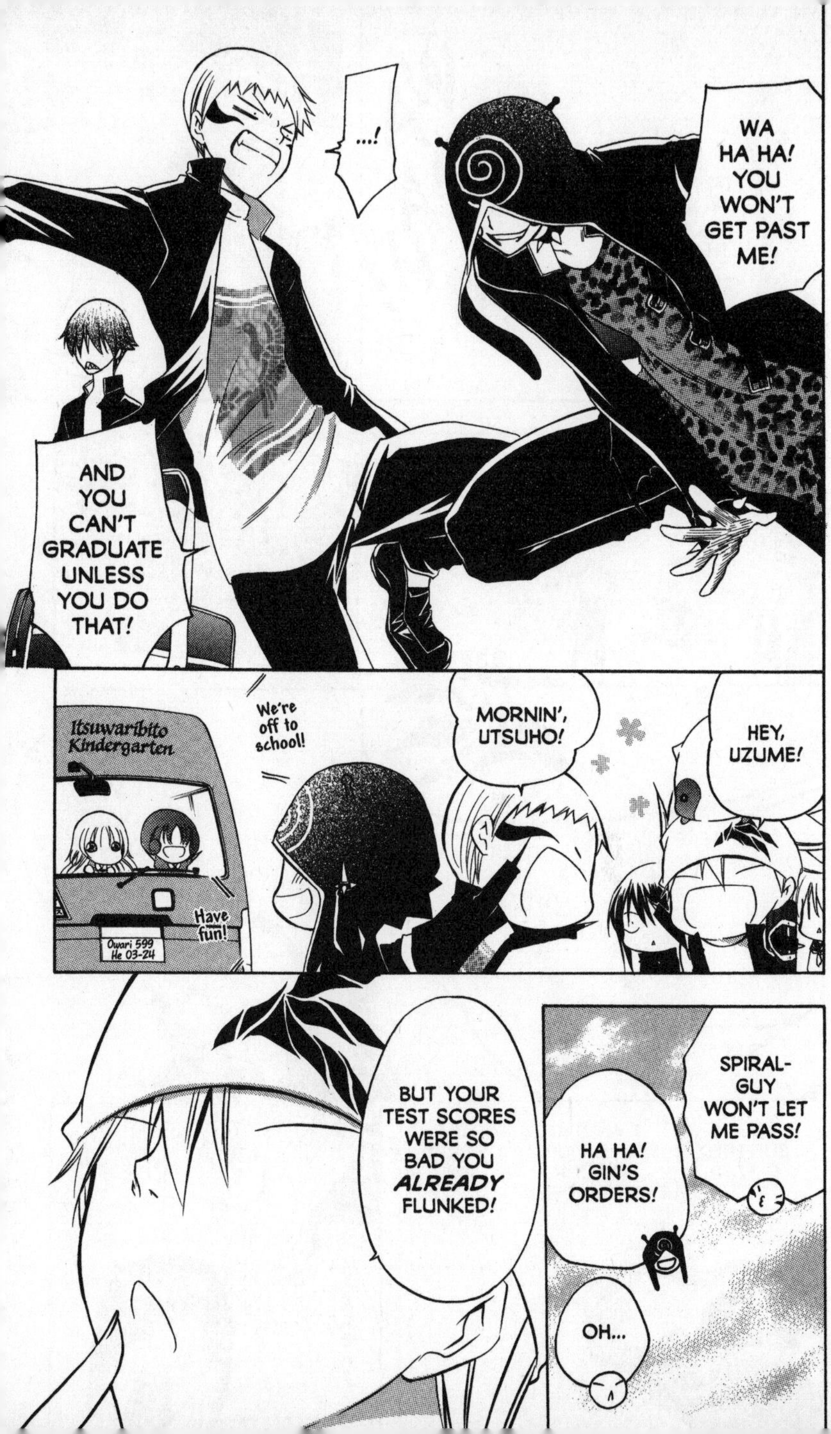
WA HA HA! YOU WON'T GET PAST ME!
...!
AND YOU CAN'T GRADUATE UNLESS YOU DO THAT!
HEY, UZUME!
MORNIN', UTSUHO!
We're off to school!
Itsuwaribito Kindergarten
Have fun!
Owari 599 He 03-24
SPIRAL-GUY WON'T LET ME PASS!
HA HA! GIN'S ORDERS!
OH...
BUT YOUR TEST SCORES WERE SO BAD YOU ALREADY FLUNKED!

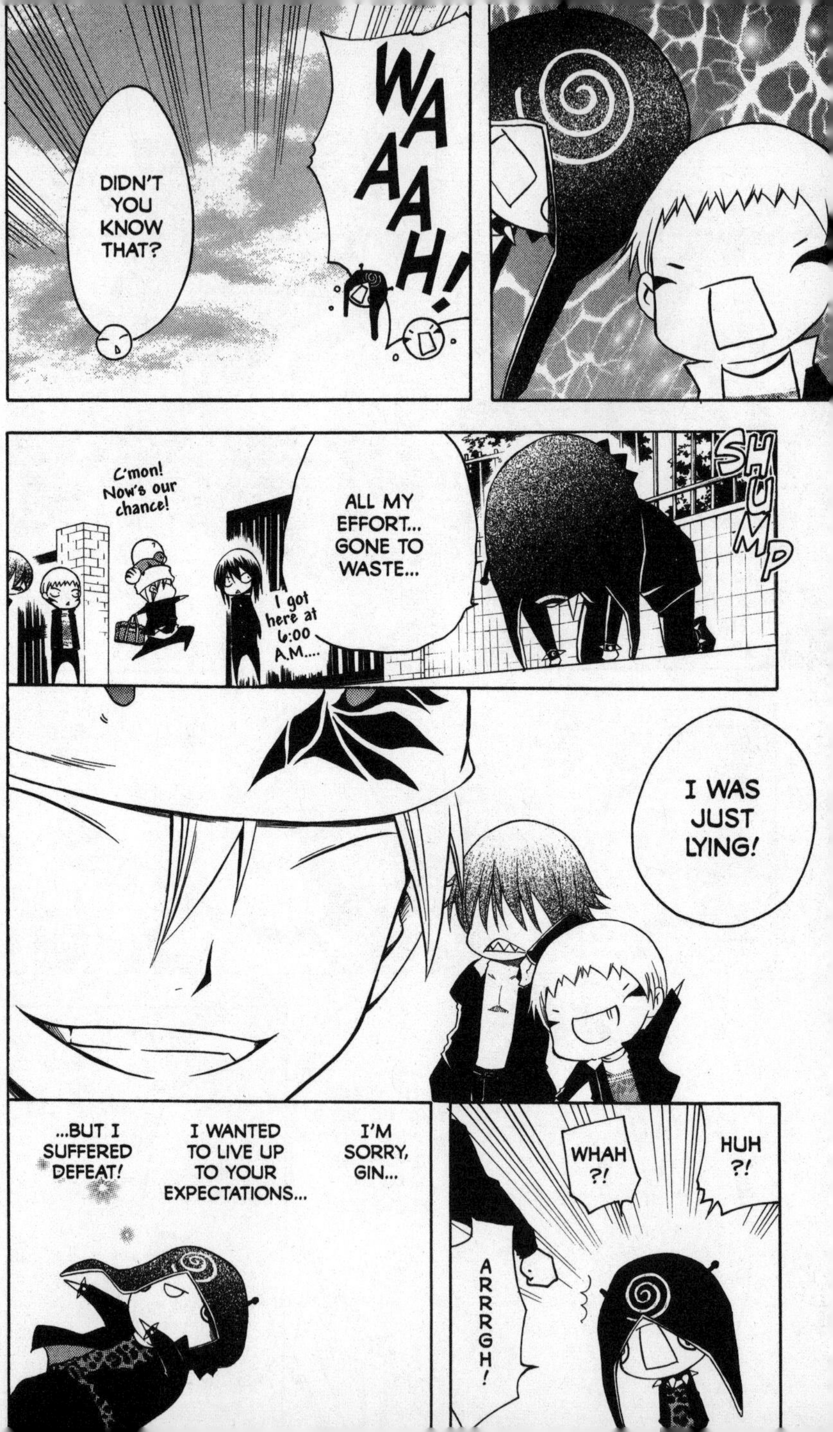
WAAAH!
DIDN'T YOU KNOW THAT?
SHUMP
ALL MY EFFORT... GONE TO WASTE...
I got here at 6:00 A.M....
C'mon! Now's our chance!
I WAS JUST LYING!
HUH ?!
WHAH ?!
ARRRGH!
I'M SORRY, GIN...
I WANTED TO LIVE UP TO YOUR EXPECTATIONS...
...BUT I SUFFERED DEFEAT!

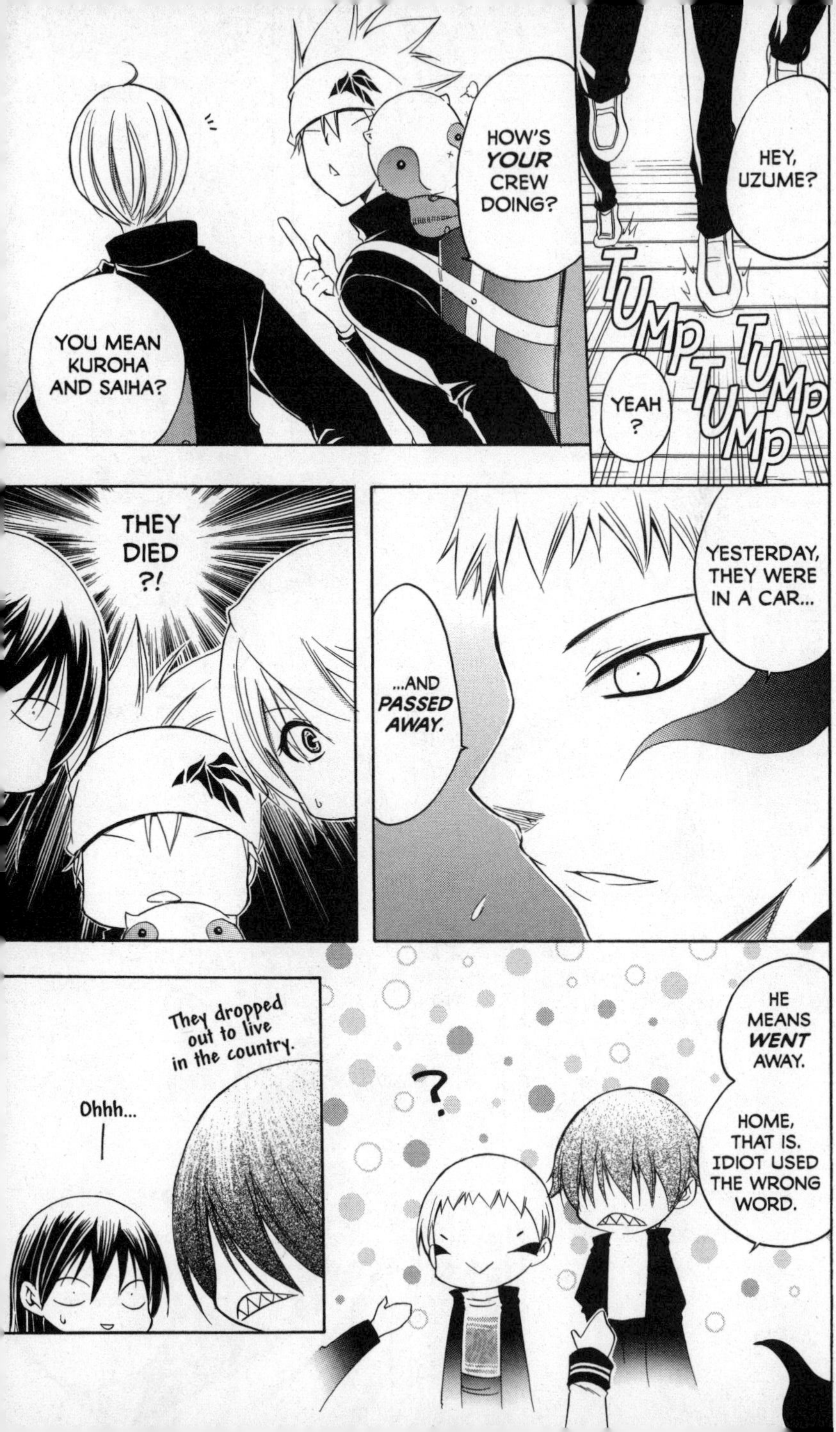
HEY, UZUME?
TUMP TUMP TUMP
YEAH?
HOW'S *YOUR* CREW DOING?
YOU MEAN KUROHA AND SAIHA?
YESTERDAY, THEY WERE IN A CAR...
...AND *PASSED AWAY.*
THEY DIED ?!
HE MEANS *WENT* AWAY.
HOME, THAT IS. IDIOT USED THE WRONG WORD.
?
They dropped out to live in the country.
Ohhh...

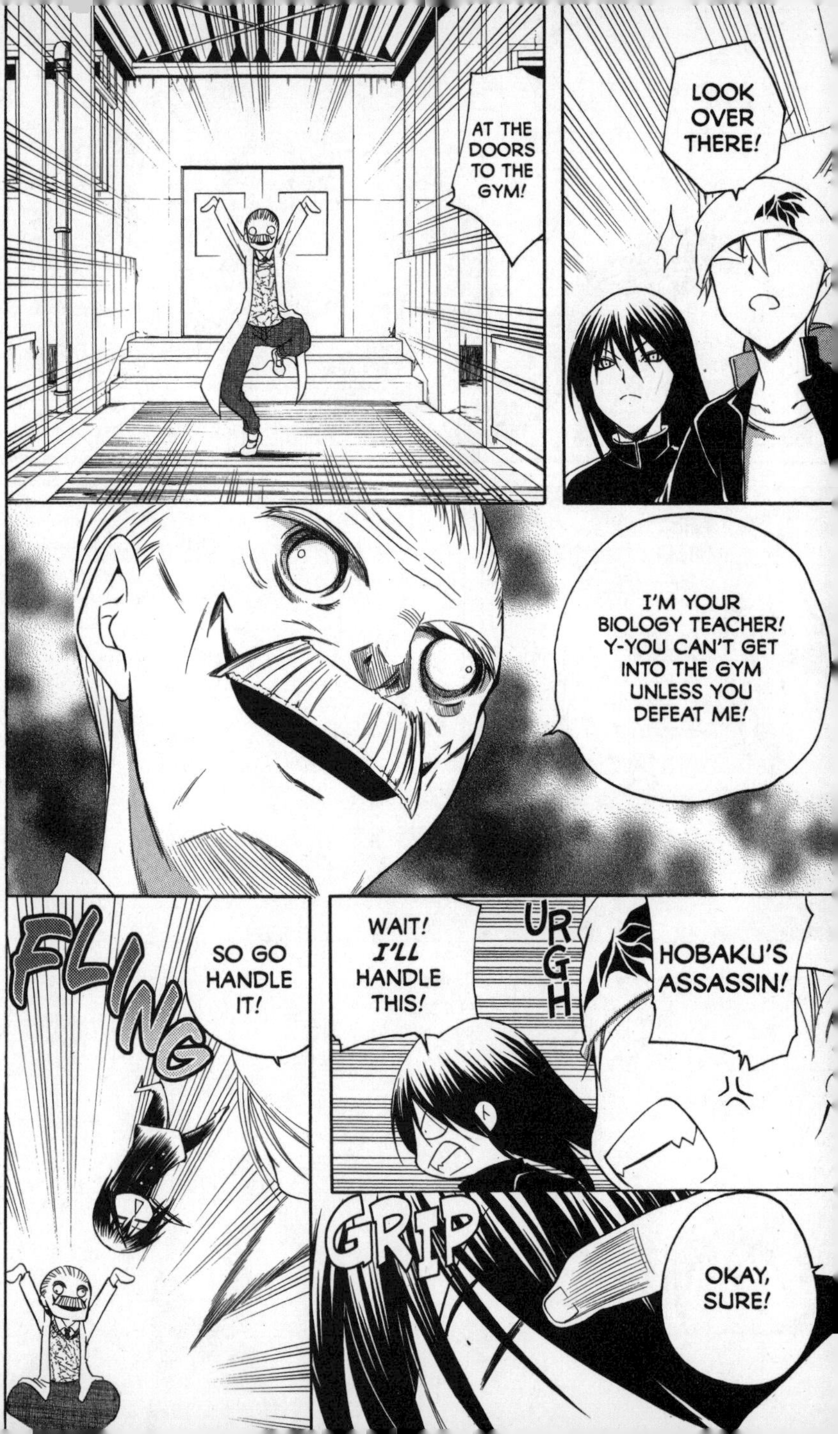
LOOK OVER THERE!
AT THE DOORS TO THE GYM!
I'M YOUR BIOLOGY TEACHER! Y-YOU CAN'T GET INTO THE GYM UNLESS YOU DEFEAT ME!
HOBAKU'S ASSASSIN!
URGH
WAIT! *I'LL* HANDLE THIS!
OKAY, SURE!
GRIP
SO GO HANDLE IT!
FLING

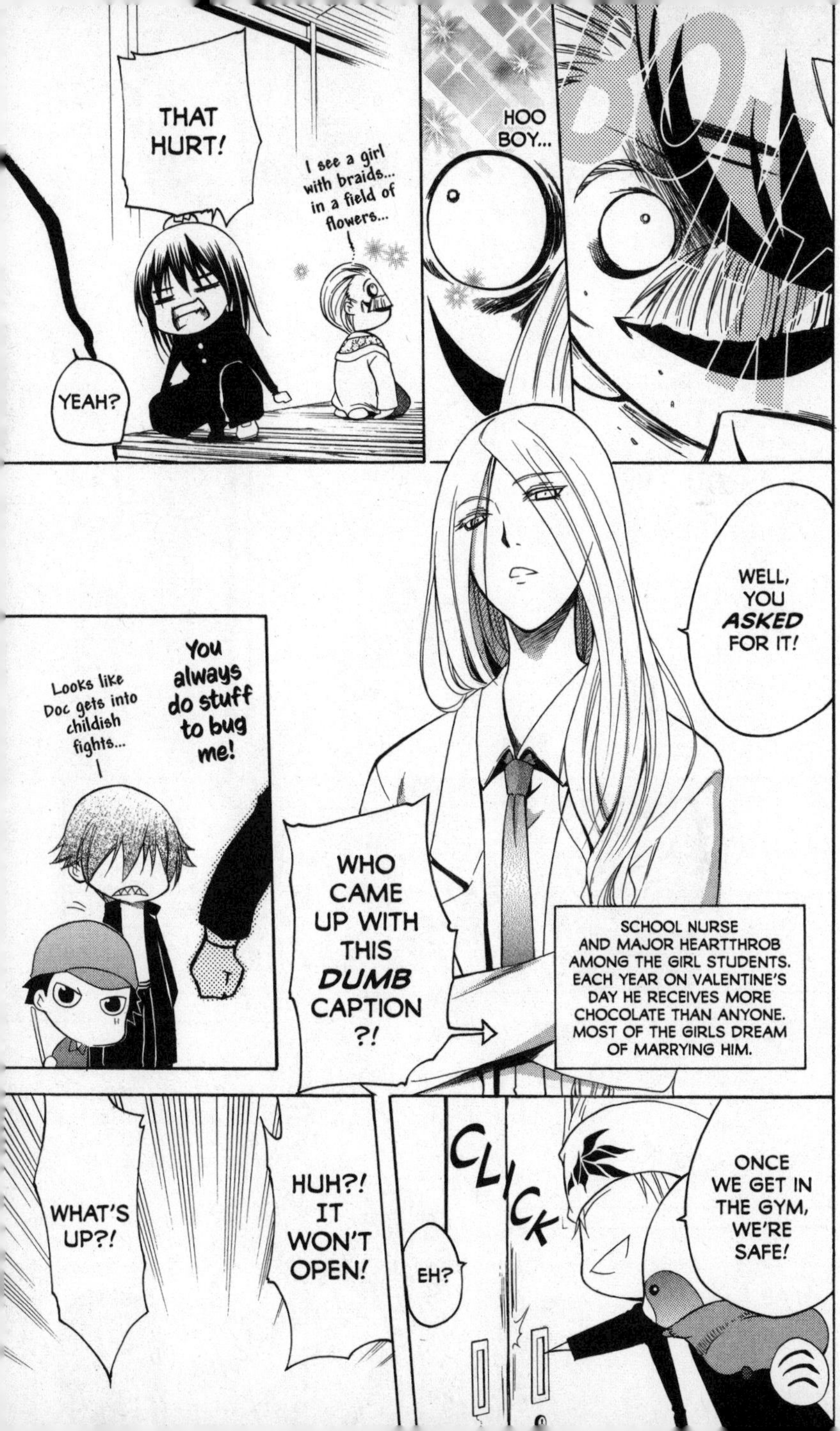
HOO BOY...
THAT HURT!
I see a girl with braids... in a field of flowers...
YEAH?
WELL, YOU *ASKED* FOR IT!
SCHOOL NURSE AND MAJOR HEARTTHROB AMONG THE GIRL STUDENTS. EACH YEAR ON VALENTINE'S DAY HE RECEIVES MORE CHOCOLATE THAN ANYONE. MOST OF THE GIRLS DREAM OF MARRYING HIM.
WHO CAME UP WITH THIS *DUMB* CAPTION?!
You always do stuff to bug me!
Looks like Doc gets into childish fights...
ONCE WE GET IN THE GYM, WE'RE SAFE!
CLICK
EH?
HUH?! IT WON'T OPEN!
WHAT'S UP?!

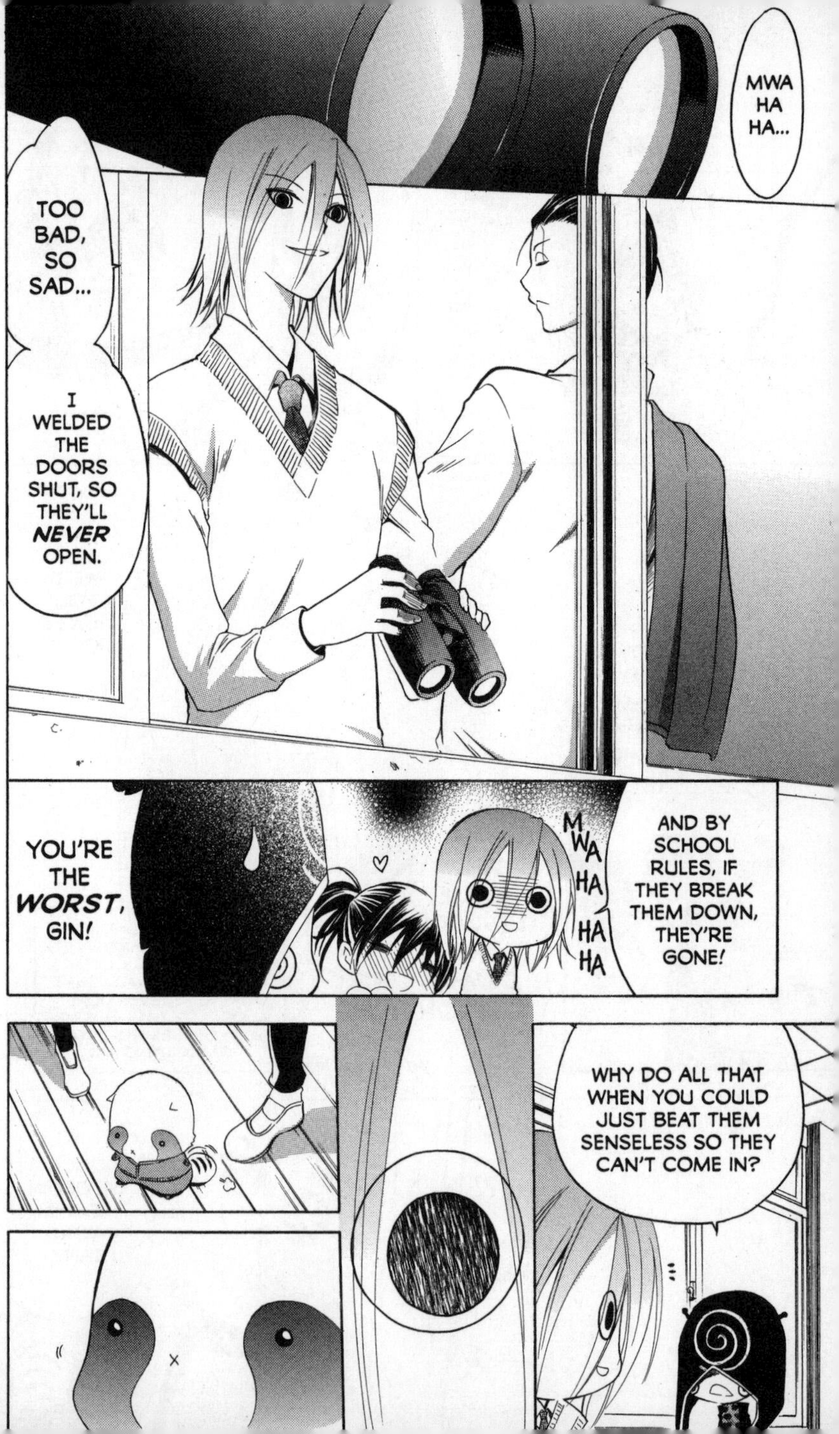
MWA HA HA...
TOO BAD, SO SAD...
I WELDED THE DOORS SHUT, SO THEY'LL *NEVER* OPEN.
AND BY SCHOOL RULES, IF THEY BREAK THEM DOWN, THEY'RE GONE!
MWA HA HA HA
YOU'RE THE *WORST*, GIN!
WHY DO ALL THAT WHEN YOU COULD JUST BEAT THEM SENSELESS SO THEY CAN'T COME IN?

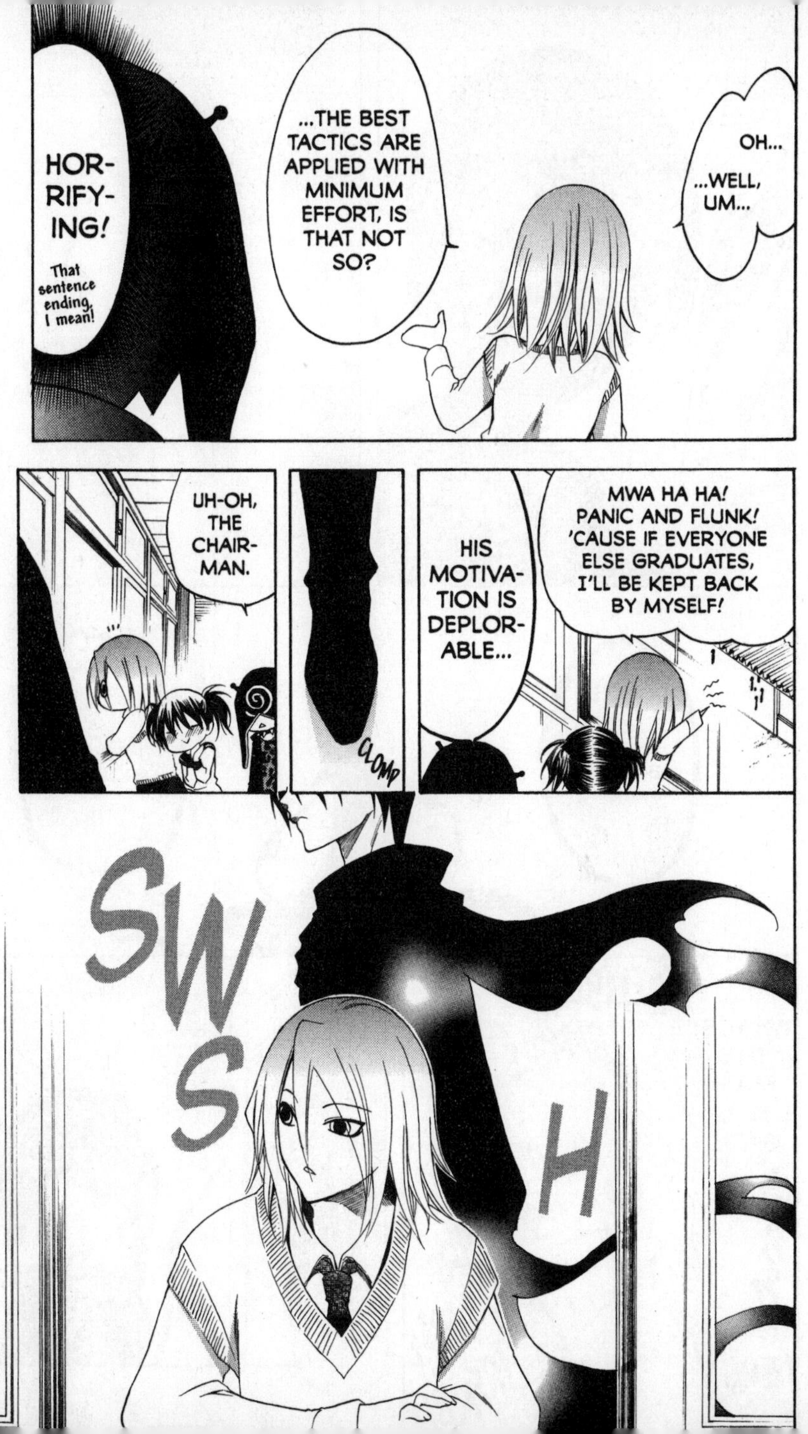

OH...
...WELL, UM...
...THE BEST TACTICS ARE APPLIED WITH MINIMUM EFFORT, IS THAT NOT SO?
HOR-RIFY-ING!
That sentence ending, I mean!
MWA HA HA! PANIC AND FLUNK! 'CAUSE IF EVERYONE ELSE GRADUATES, I'LL BE KEPT BACK BY MYSELF!
HIS MOTIVA-TION IS DEPLOR-ABLE...
CLOMP
UH-OH, THE CHAIR-MAN.
SWSH

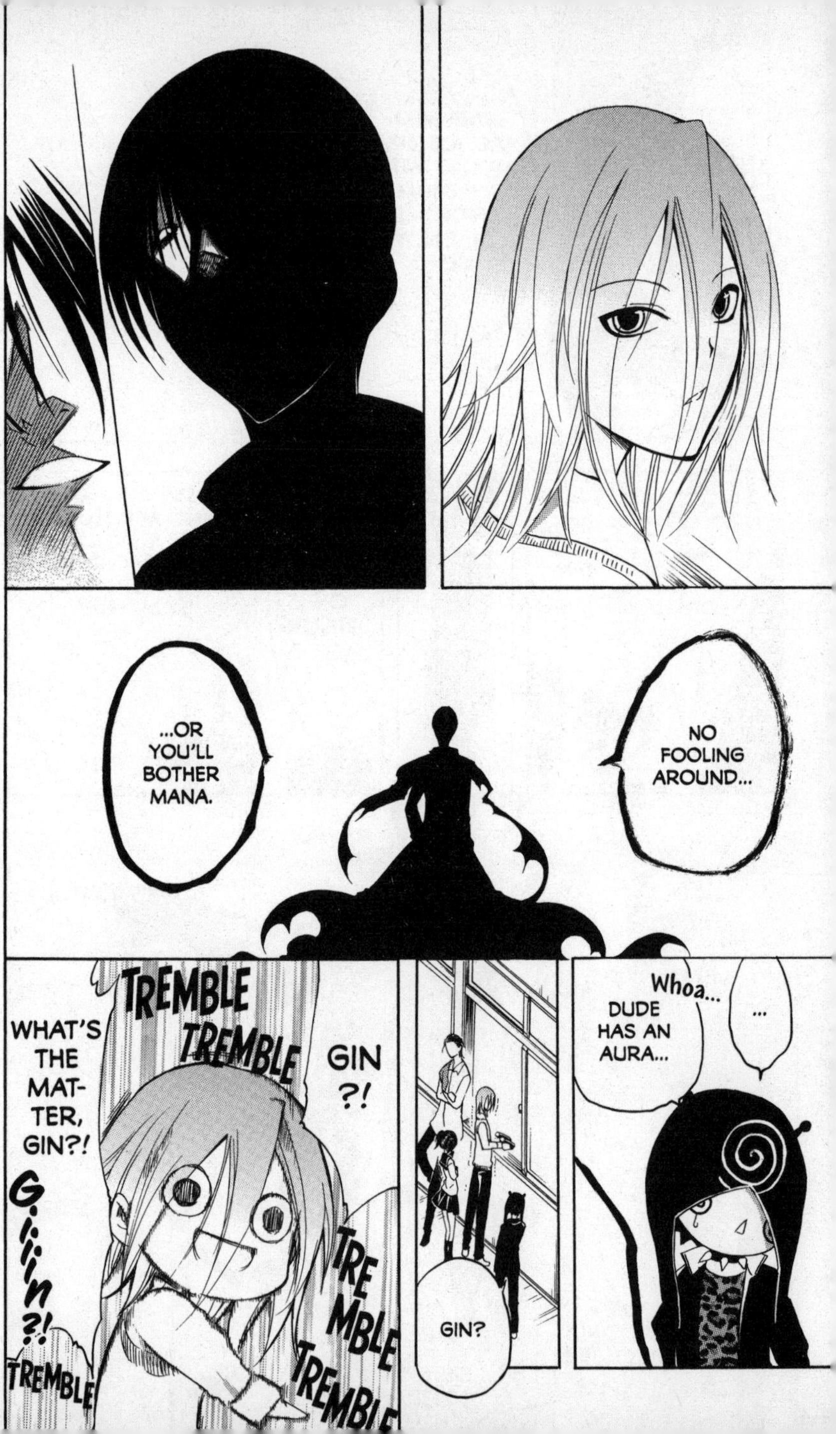
NO FOOLING AROUND...
...OR YOU'LL BOTHER MANA.
...
Whoa...
DUDE HAS AN AURA...
GIN?
GIN ?!
TREMBLE
TREMBLE
WHAT'S THE MAT-TER, GIN?!
TRE MBLE
TREMBLE
Giiin?!
TREMBLE

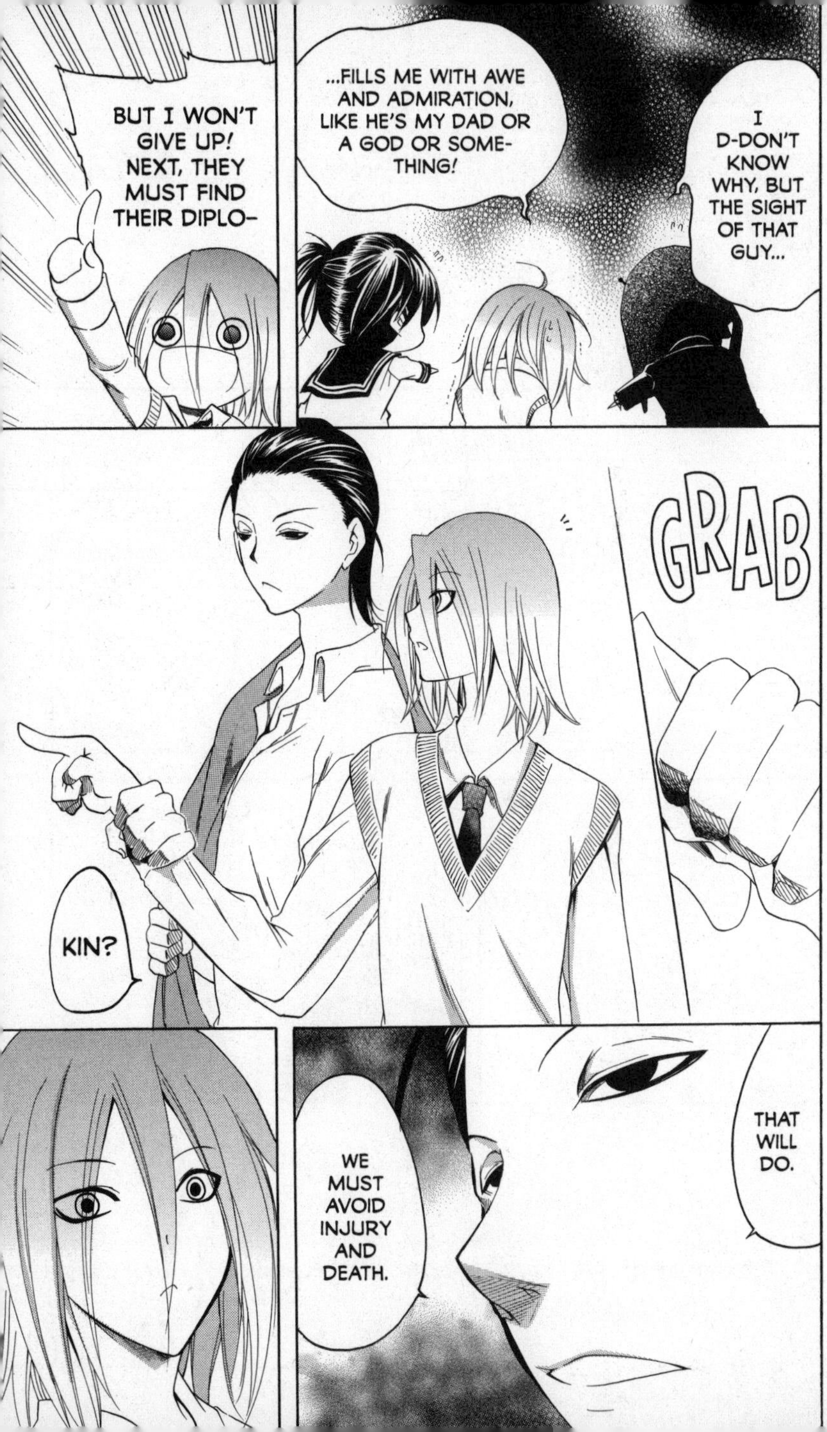
I D-DON'T KNOW WHY, BUT THE SIGHT OF THAT GUY...
...FILLS ME WITH AWE AND ADMIRATION, LIKE HE'S MY DAD OR A GOD OR SOME-THING!
BUT I WON'T GIVE UP! NEXT, THEY MUST FIND THEIR DIPLO-
GRAB
KIN?
THAT WILL DO.
WE MUST AVOID INJURY AND DEATH.

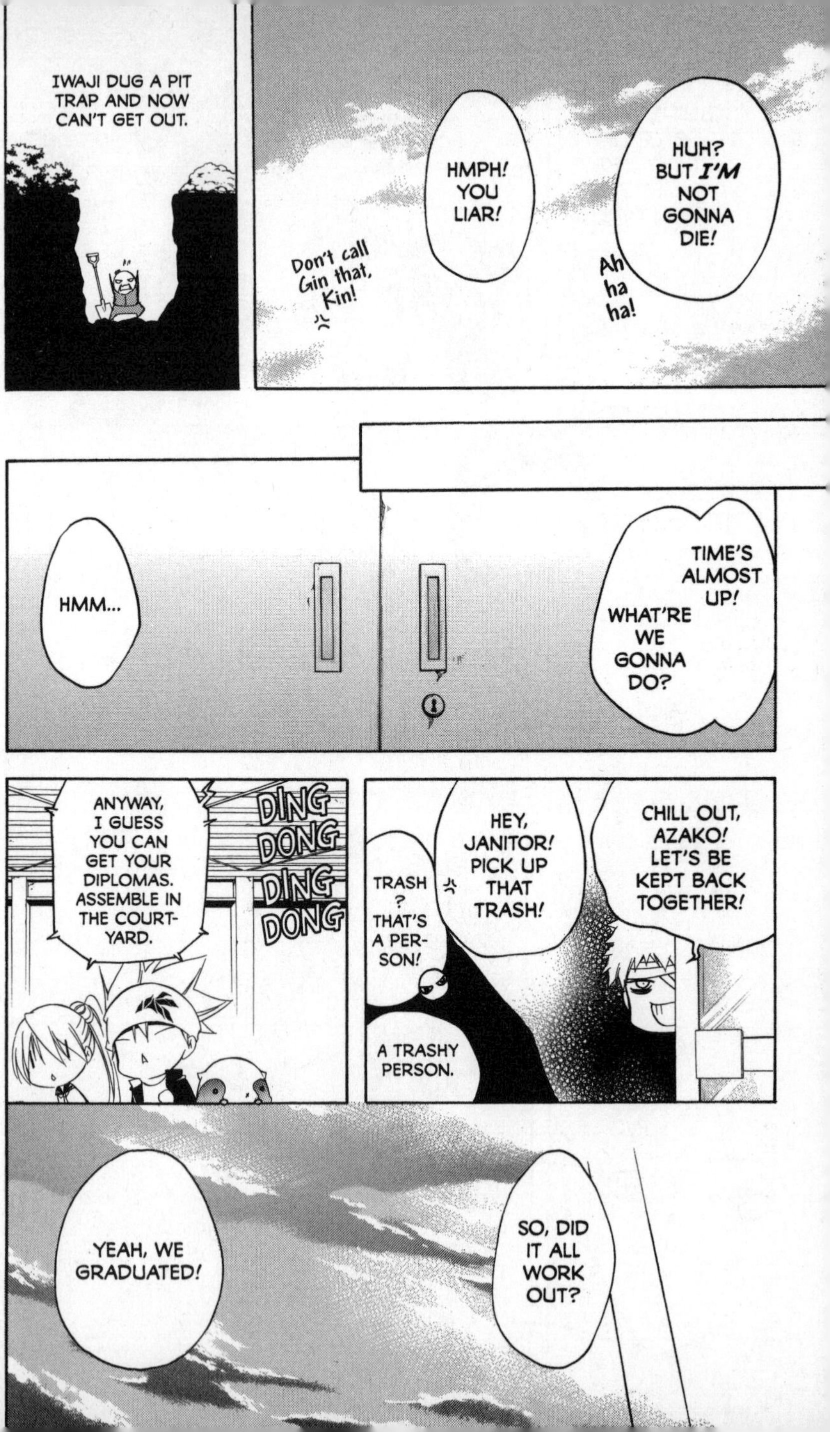
HUH? BUT I'M NOT GONNA DIE!
Ah ha ha!
HMPH! YOU LIAR!
Don't call Gin that, Kin!
IWAJI DUG A PIT TRAP AND NOW CAN'T GET OUT.
TIME'S ALMOST UP!
WHAT'RE WE GONNA DO?
HMM...
CHILL OUT, AZAKO! LET'S BE KEPT BACK TOGETHER!
HEY, JANITOR! PICK UP THAT TRASH!
TRASH? THAT'S A PERSON!
A TRASHY PERSON.
DING DONG DING DONG
ANYWAY, I GUESS YOU CAN GET YOUR DIPLOMAS. ASSEMBLE IN THE COURTYARD.
SO, DID IT ALL WORK OUT?
YEAH, WE GRADUATED!

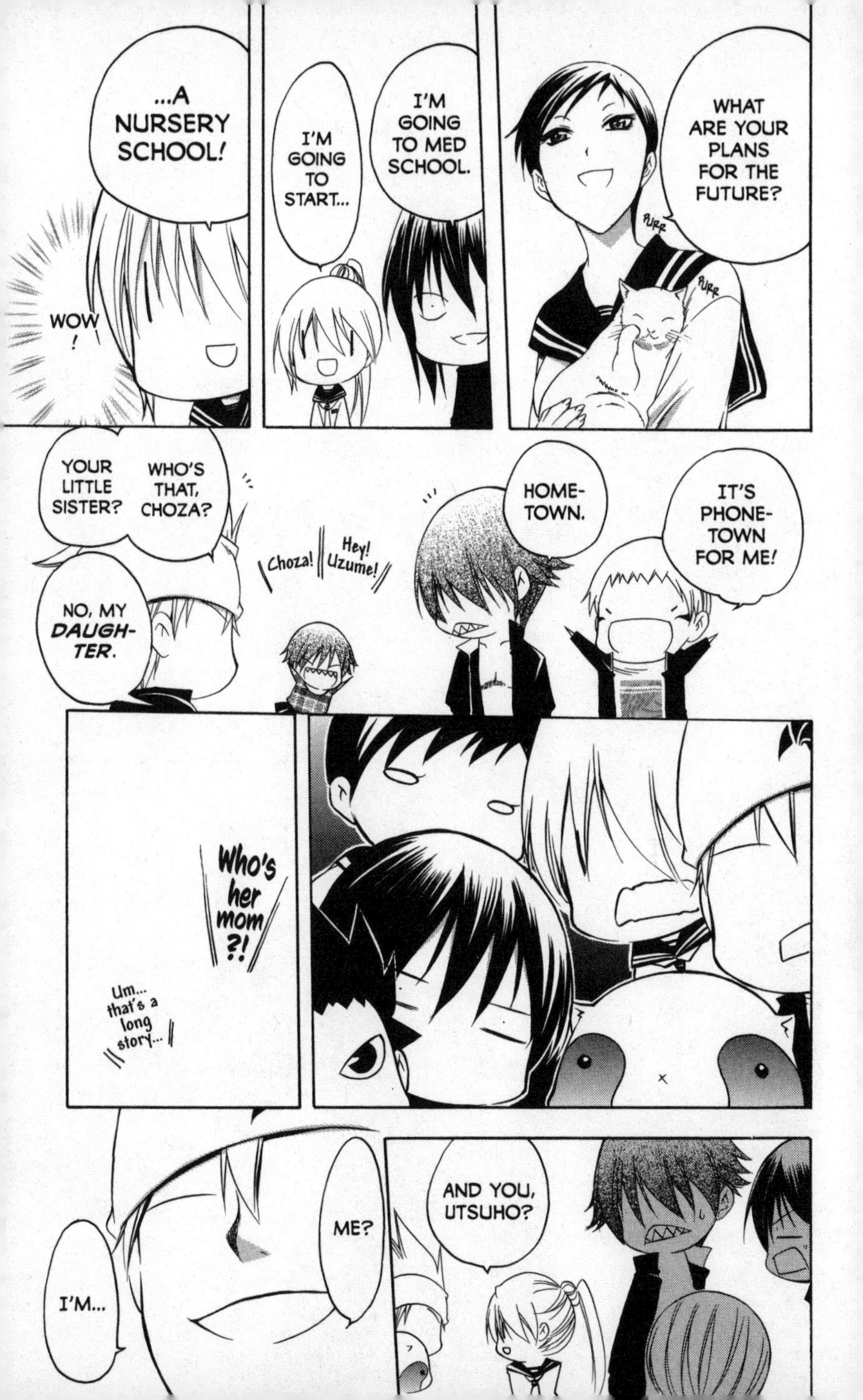
WHAT ARE YOUR PLANS FOR THE FUTURE?
PURR
PURR
I'M GOING TO MED SCHOOL.
I'M GOING TO START...
...A NURSERY SCHOOL!
WOW!
IT'S PHONE-TOWN FOR ME!
HOME-TOWN.
Hey! Uzume!
Choza!
WHO'S THAT, CHOZA?
YOUR LITTLE SISTER?
NO, MY DAUGHTER.
Who's her mom?!
Um... that's a long story...
AND YOU, UTSUHO?
ME?
I'M...

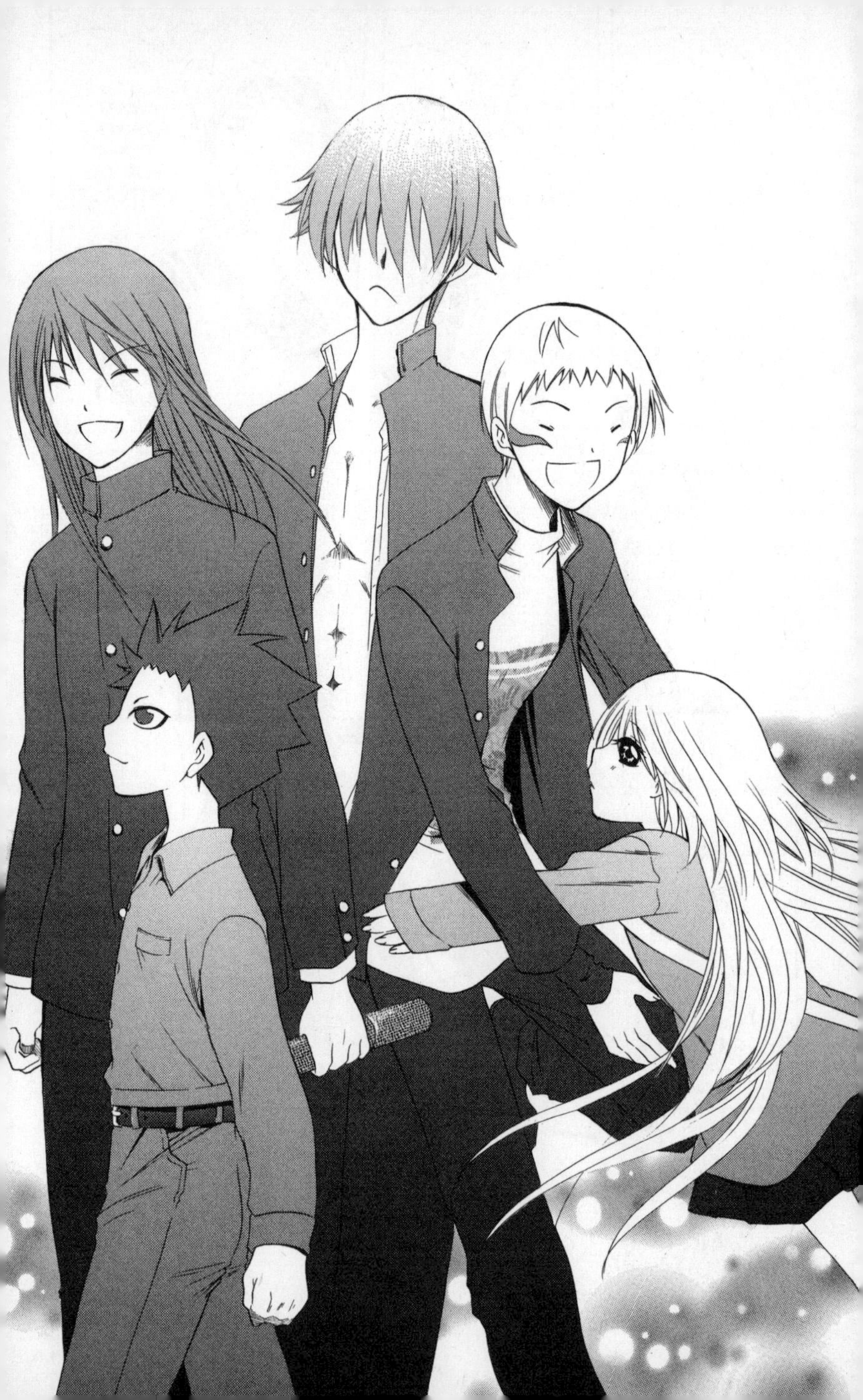

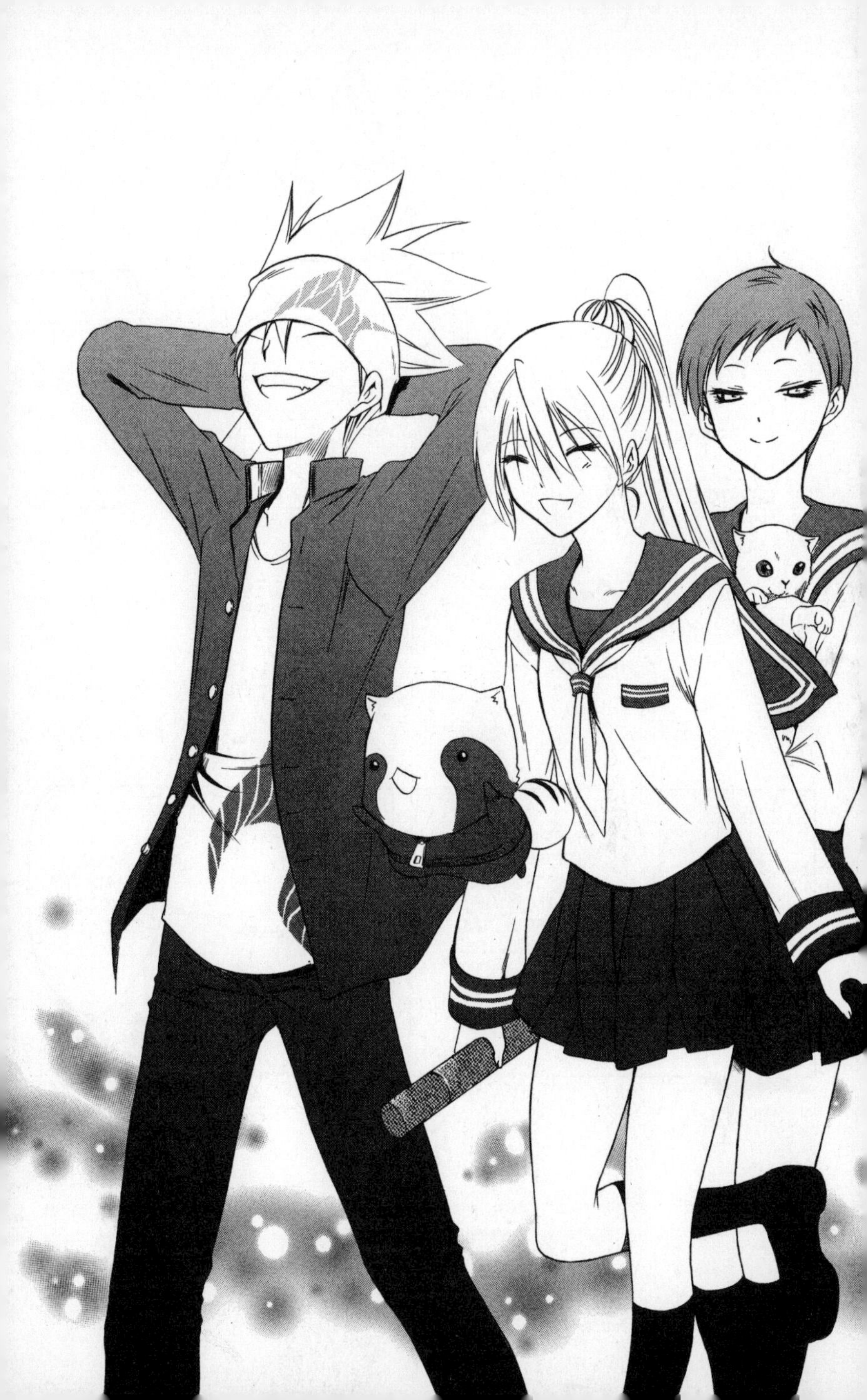

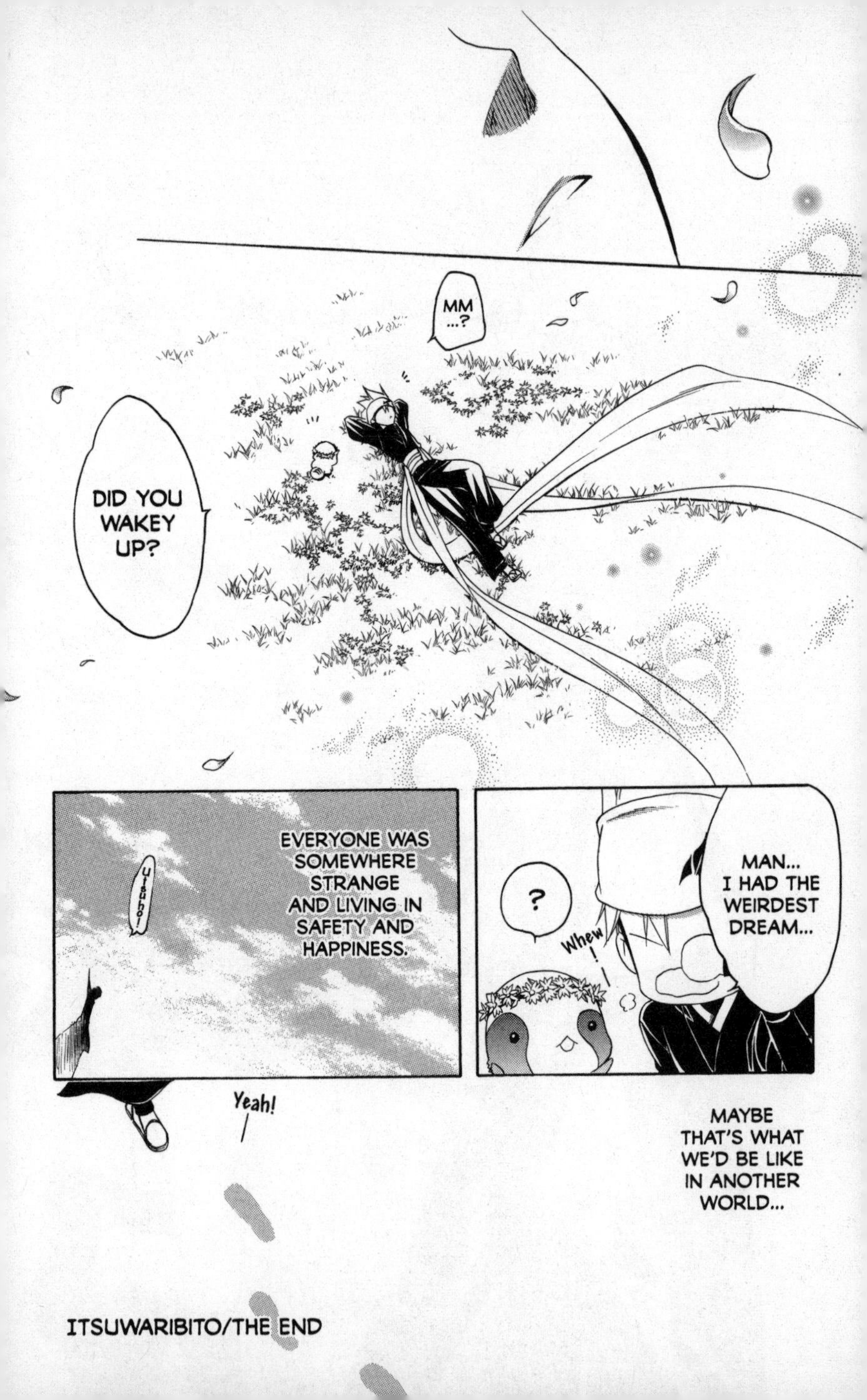
MM ...?
DID YOU WAKEY UP?
MAN... I HAD THE WEIRDEST DREAM...
?
Whew!
EVERYONE WAS SOMEWHERE STRANGE AND LIVING IN SAFETY AND HAPPINESS.
Utsuho!
MAYBE THAT'S WHAT WE'D BE LIKE IN ANOTHER WORLD...
Yeah!
ITSUWARIBITO/THE END

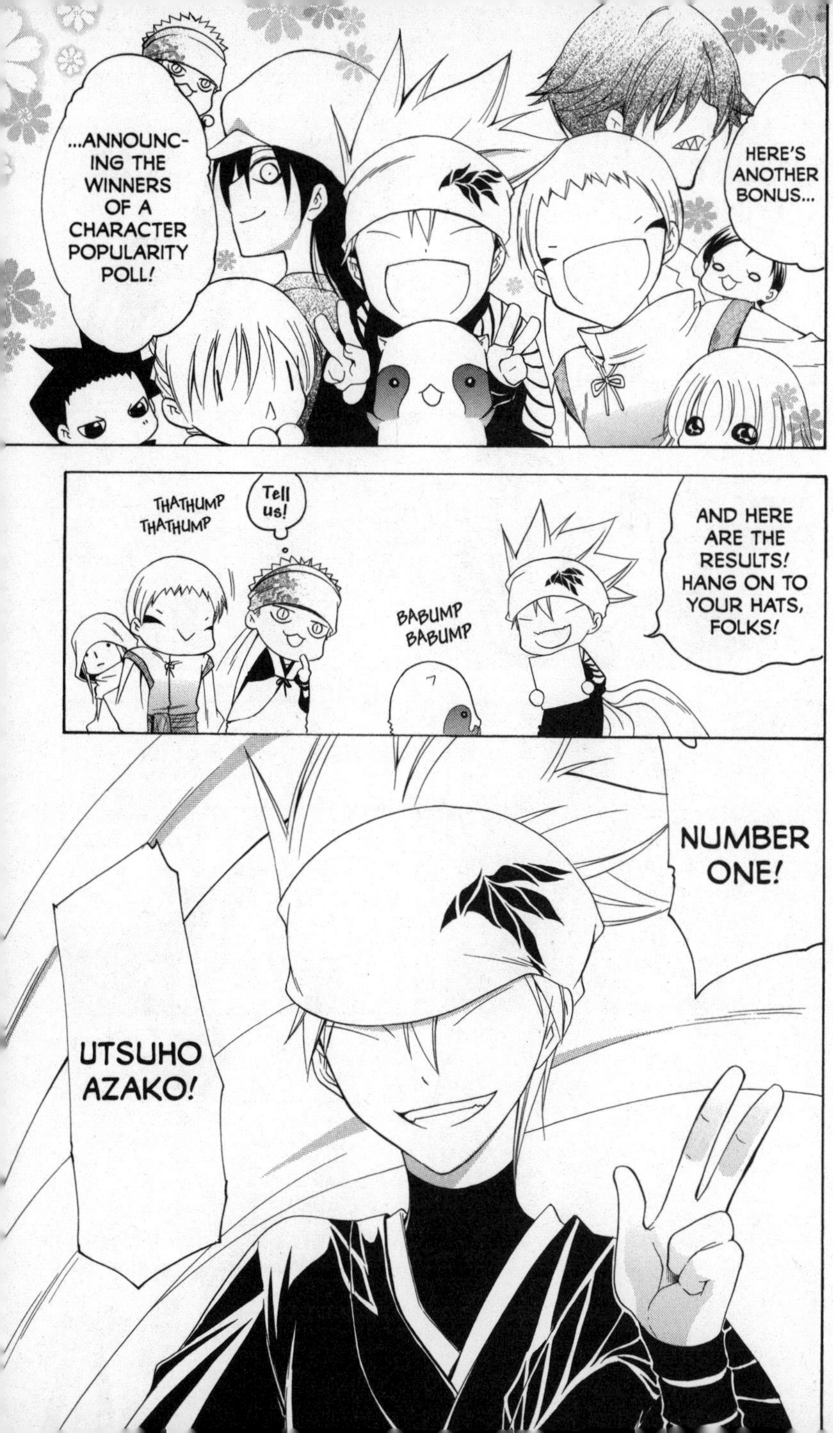
HERE'S ANOTHER BONUS...
...ANNOUNCING THE WINNERS OF A CHARACTER POPULARITY POLL!
AND HERE ARE THE RESULTS! HANG ON TO YOUR HATS, FOLKS!
BABUMP BABUMP
Tell us!
THATHUMP THATHUMP
NUMBER ONE!
UTSUHO AZAKO!

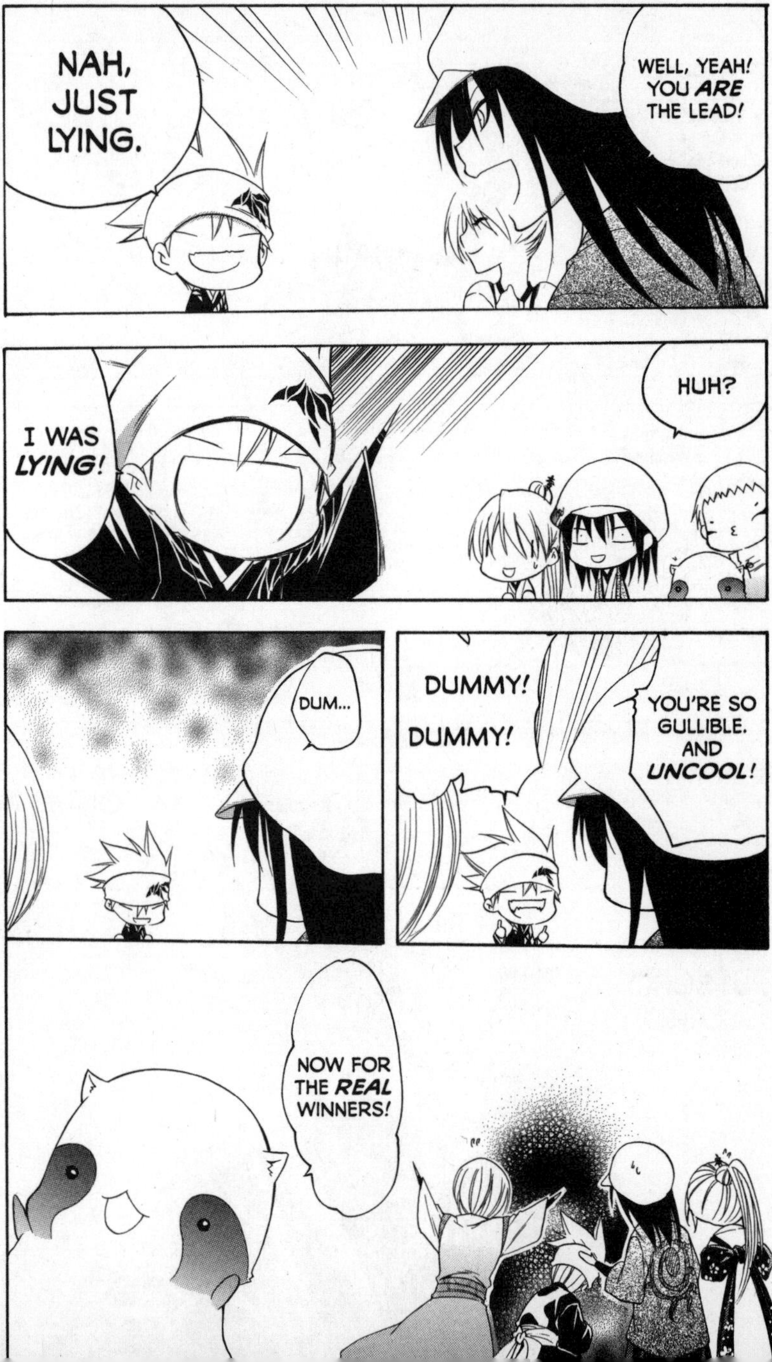
WELL, YEAH! YOU *ARE* THE LEAD!
NAH, JUST LYING.
HUH?
I WAS *LYING*!
YOU'RE SO GULLIBLE. AND *UNCOOL*!
DUMMY!
DUMMY!
DUM...
NOW FOR THE *REAL* WINNERS!

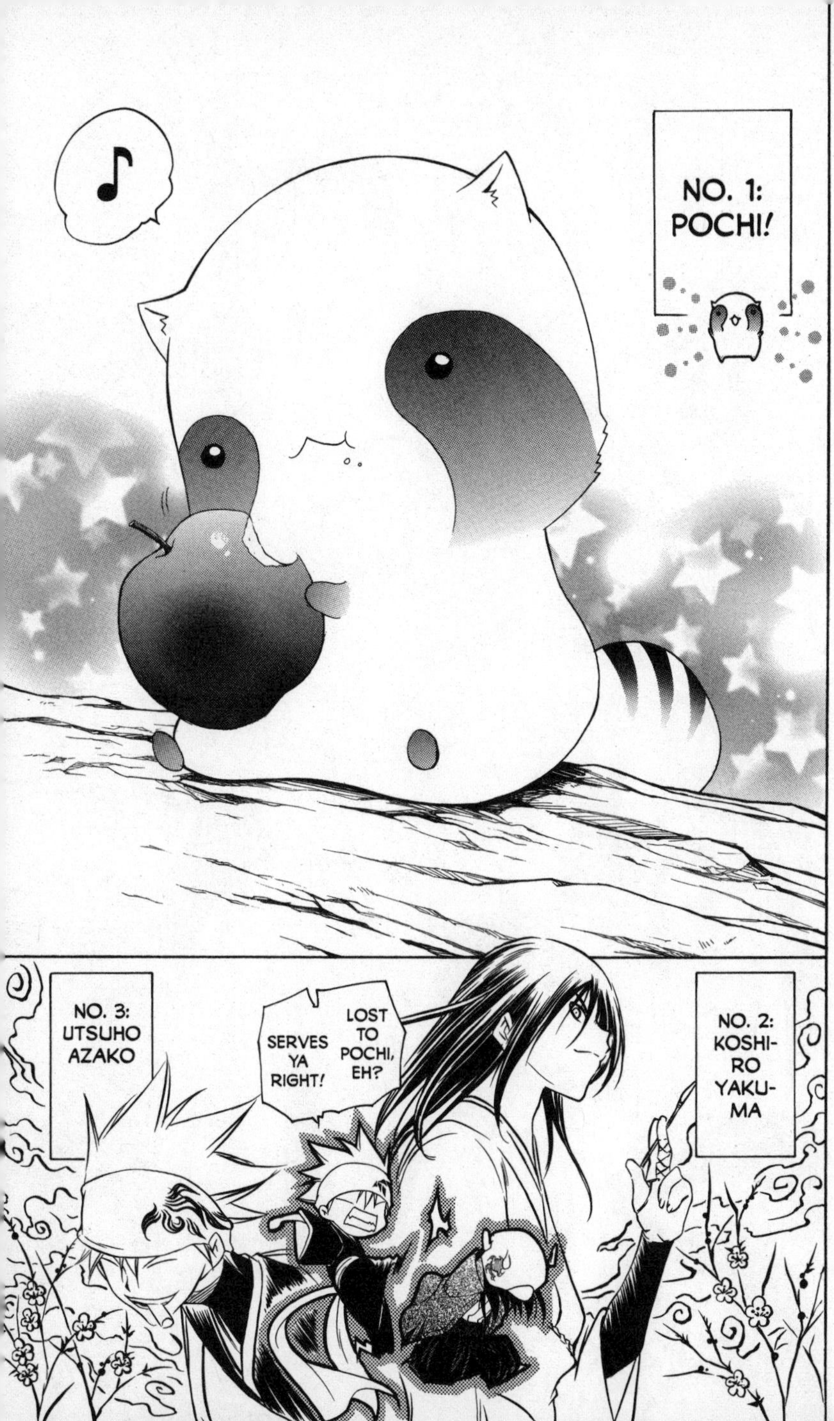
NO. 1: POCHI!
♪
NO. 2: KOSHI-RO YAKU-MA
LOST TO POCHI, EH?
SERVES YA RIGHT!
NO. 3: UTSUHO AZAKO

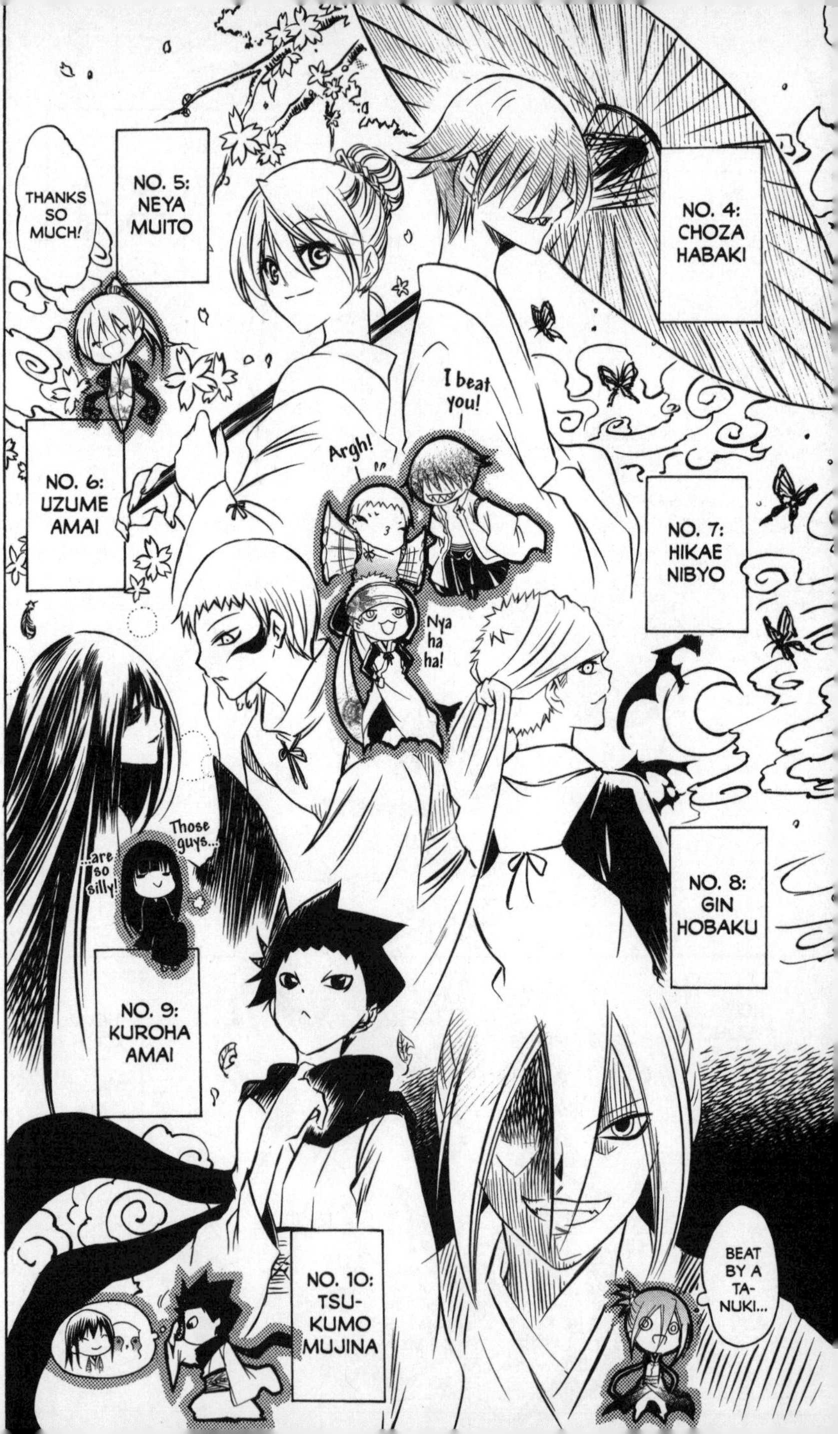
NO. 4: CHOZA HABAKI
NO. 5: NEYA MUITO
THANKS SO MUCH!
I beat you!
Argh!
NO. 6: UZUME AMAI
NO. 7: HIKAE NIBYO
Nya ha ha!
NO. 8: GIN HOBAKU
Those guys...
...are so silly!
NO. 9: KUROHA AMAI
BEAT BY A TA-NUKI...
NO. 10: TSU-KUMO MUJINA

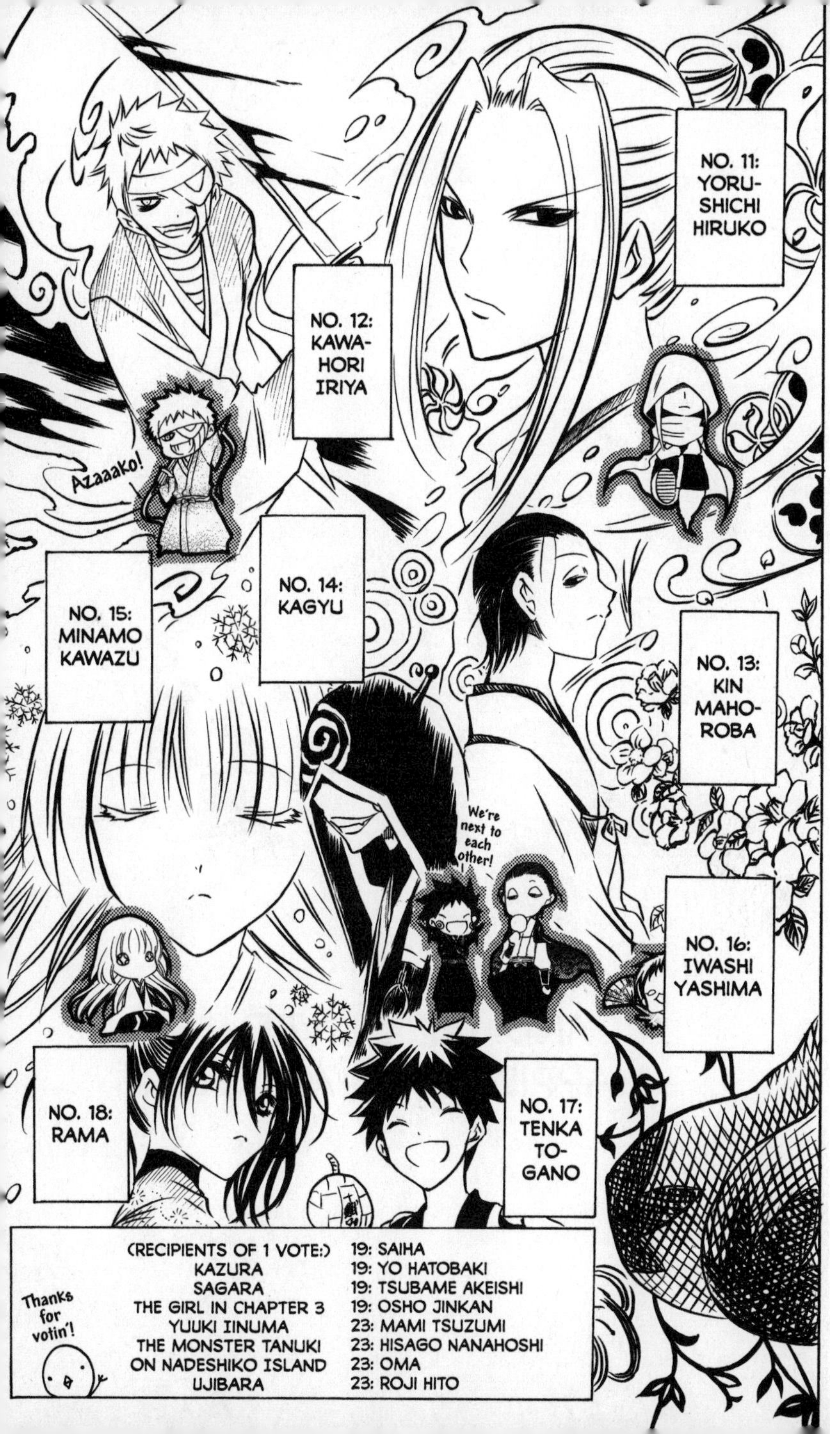
NO. 11: YORU-SHICHI HIRUKO
NO. 12: KAWA-HORI IRIYA
Azaaako!
NO. 13: KIN MAHO-ROBA
NO. 14: KAGYU
NO. 15: MINAMO KAWAZU
We're next to each other!
NO. 16: IWASHI YASHIMA
NO. 17: TENKA TO-GANO
NO. 18: RAMA
(RECIPIENTS OF 1 VOTE:)
KAZURA
SAGARA
THE GIRL IN CHAPTER 3
YUUKI IINUMA
THE MONSTER TANUKI ON NADESHIKO ISLAND
UJIBARA
19: SAIHA
19: YO HATOBAKI
19: TSUBAME AKEISHI
19: OSHO JINKAN
23: MAMI TSUZUMI
23: HISAGO NANAHOSHI
23: OMA
23: ROJI HITO
Thanks for votin'!

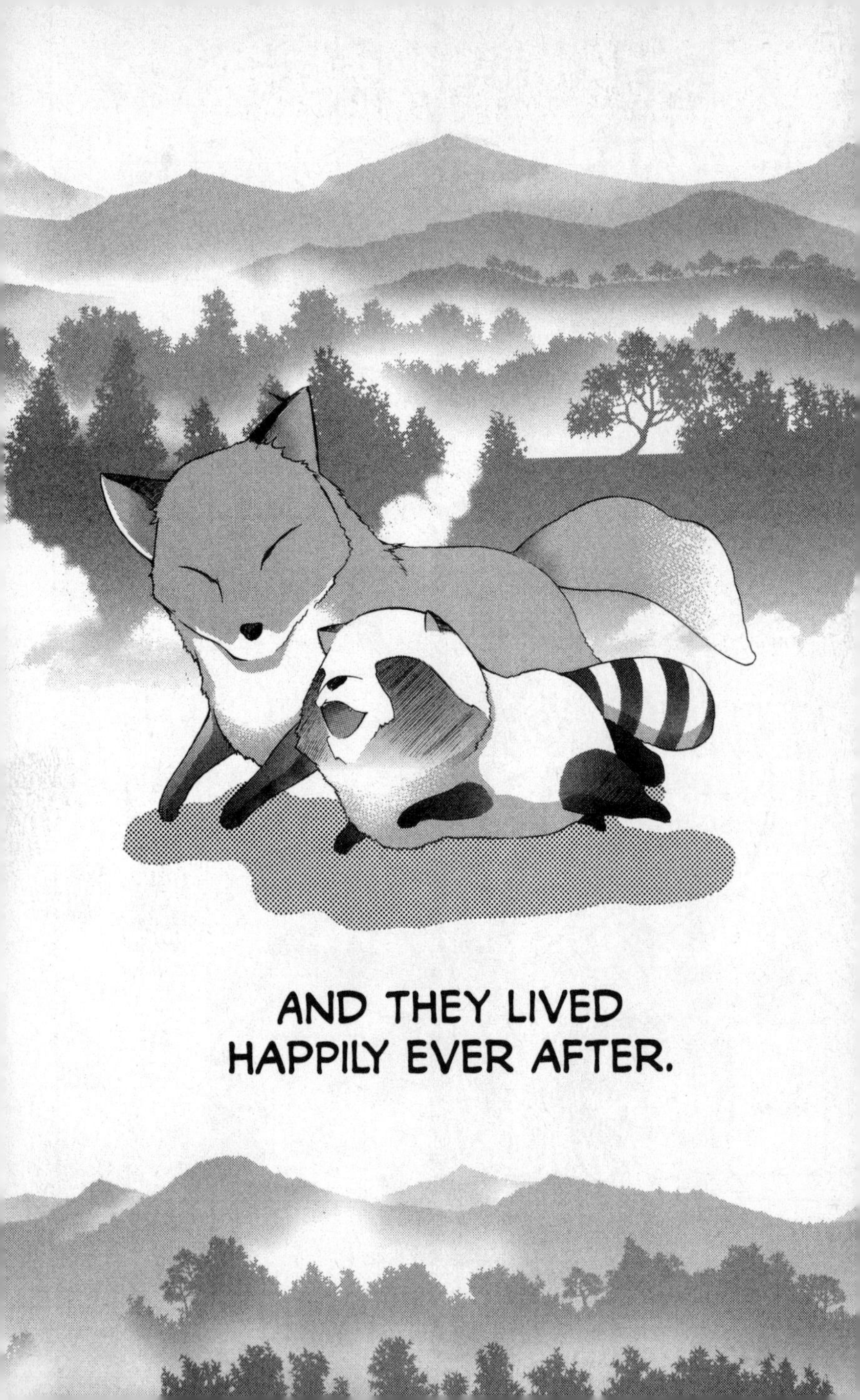
AND THEY LIVED HAPPILY EVER AFTER.